SHAKESPEARE'S HAND

SHAKESPEARE'S HAND

Jonathan Goldberg

University of Minnesota Press

Minneapolis / London

See pages 361–63 for permissions and previous publication information for the essays reprinted in this book.

Published by the University of Minnesota Press
111 Third Avenue South, Suite 290
Minneapolis, MN 55401-2520
http://www.upress.umn.edu

Library of Congress Cataloging-in-Publication Data

Goldberg, Jonathan.
Shakespeare's hand / Jonathan Goldberg.
p. cm.
Includes bibliographical references and index.
ISBN 0-8166-4148-X (acid-free paper) — ISBN 0-8166-4149-8 (pbk. : acid-free paper)
1. Shakespeare, William,—1564–1616—Criticism and interpretation. I. Title.
PR2976 .G578 2002
822.3'3—dc21

2002010186

Printed in the United States of America on acid-free paper

12 11 10 09 08 07 06 05 04 03 10 9 8 7 6 5 4 3 2 1

Contents

Introduction

Shakespeare's Hand gathers work I have written and published, for the most part in journals and collections, since the mid-1980s. While I never intended to write a book on Shakespeare (the closest I ever came to that was in initial plans for *Writing Matter: From the Hands of the English Renaissance*), these essays have a coherence that brings them together in this book. Certainly, the shape of this book does not correspond to any original intention or design. Whatever coherence it has is perhaps fortuitous, perhaps a testimony to concerns that have remained central to my work, although a reader may be more interested in charting changes and shifts that have occurred over the years (and may wish to treat the book as an interesting case study or as more generally symptomatic). Many of these pieces were, in origin, occasional, responses to invitations to contribute to anthologies or special issues of journals or to appear on panels at meetings of professional organizations. In many cases, these occasions were designed to unsettle prevailing orthodoxies; my usual response, in such instances, has involved a desire not only to further such impulses but also to shake up the counterdiscourses as well.

Central to these essays are concerns about textuality that are played out from a number of different angles. At the start, the impetus for these essays was what used to be called "theory"—in this case, premises about writing central to the early work of Jacques Derrida, which was gaining currency in the United States in the 1980s and, minimally, among literary scholars and critics working in the field of early modernity. "Theory," in these terms, never did make much of an impression on Shakespeare studies (Joel Fineman's *Shakespeare's Perjured Eye* in 1986 would be the notable exception to this generalization), which, at this time, came to operate within the orbit of new historicist and feminist studies, which were in the 1980s very much in contention with each other, neither particularly informed by nor responsive to Derridean or Lacanian theory. Christopher Pye's *The Regal Phantasm* (1990) is the counterexample of a study seeking to articulate concerns about history in a high theoretical mode, while the work of Karen Newman (in the chapters on Shakespeare in *Fashioning Femininity*, 1991) would be one strong example of feminist work with historicist and theoretical ambitions surpassing the impasses of much feminist criticism of the 1980s.[1]

My approach to questions of textuality and to the possibility of inflecting this theoretical domain in terms of gender and history was almost from the first positioned in relationship to emerging reconfigurations in bibliographical studies that were calling into question standard procedures in editing, especially in relation to Shakespeare, where the goal was the production of composite texts that aimed at a kind of authenticity. (The title *Shakespeare's Hand* glances askew at this practice and desire.) This field of inquiry has remained vital, although my particular angle of approach to these matters is only intermittently to be found in the work of those most closely associated with textual studies. For from the start (even if not at first explicitly), the desire to mobilize these textual concerns to encompass questions about gender was made in the service of a denaturalizing of gender difference that might open the possibility of reconsidering sexuality from a nonnormative (which is to say, a nonheterosexualizing) position. Although these days it is certainly possible to find bibliographic studies that attend to questions of gender, it is still rare for them to break with such normativizing, despite the fact that much historical work has suggested that the early modern sex/gender system cannot be read in terms of the homo-heterosexual divide that is supposedly the modern truth about sexuality and the gender positions said to follow from these norms. (Eve Kosofsky Sedgwick's *Epistemology of the Closet* shatters such certainties, but it is not a book that could be said to shape the thinking of most Shakespeareans.)[2]

"Textual Properties," although not the essay written earliest, is first in this collection. This is a brief, somewhat polemical piece written in response to editorial work on the multiple texts of *King Lear* and the critical responses to that work collected in *The Division of the Kingdoms,* edited by Gary Taylor and Michael Warren. It gestures programmatically toward many of the concerns developed at greater length in the rest of the essays gathered here. These concerns, to spell them out a bit further, include the relationship between textual characters and the notion of dramatic and human character; the relationship between gender-as-constructed and the debiologizing of (human) character implicit in treating character as a textual production; the relationship between editorial and critical practices as these are affected by the instability of Shakespearean texts; and the historical questions posed by these various instabilities (of text, character, and gender). Uniting the essays, therefore, is a series of interventions posed from the site of theories of textuality that I was once more comfortable than I am now to call "postmodern," a set of inquiries into the conditions of Shakespearean texts, their production, and their critical reception as these are to be reread under the influence of theories of textuality.

My hesitation about "postmodernity" means to register briefly something also implicit in my allusion to "what used to be called 'theory.'" "Postmodernity" now seems to me to be a similarly dated term that no longer registers sites of possibility, openings to alternatives. "Theory" tied to the work of a Derrida or a Jacques Lacan, insofar as it persists, does so largely through a small group of disciples intent on enshrining, as a kind of truth, procedures that seemed to call into question just such a vantage point. (If some of the essays in this volume seem routinized, it is precisely because of the retrospective cast of these developments upon them.) Derridean impulses to break up the text have instead remained rooted in a restricted sense of the text. (This is also true of much of Derrida's own work in recent years, itself influenced in no small measure by the institutional forces that have worked to consolidate and ossify "theory.") Lacanians have become religious. Foucauldians, in their "new" historicizing, became entranced by the repressive hypothesis, precisely the thesis Michel Foucault sought to dismantle. Meanwhile, the demise of "theory"—or, better, the demise of its promise, especially in early modern studies—has prompted moves "after theory," which is also to say, before theory. New historicism, insofar as it is still practiced, is virtually indistinguishable from old historicism; early modern cultural studies divide the world into prefabricated binarisms and think themselves liberatory in so doing. In Shakespeare studies, postmodernity has passed; conservatism has returned.

The essays in Part I of this volume share a number of purposes, and I mean to suggest some connections running through these essays, from the earliest to the latest. Perhaps it is even possible that the early impulses of "theory," however dated, are nonetheless still a set of promissory notes yet to be fulfilled rather than bad checks one could not hope to cash. Many of these essays are polemical, although the target is not always exactly the same. "Textual Properties," for example, takes up Jerome J. McGann's worry that poststructuralist theory (as emblematized in his sense of the Derridean notion of free play) will further a disregard for textual questions in their strict bibliographical sense. Contra McGann, I argue that such critical practices are best suited to the instability of Shakespeare's texts, a rejoinder that some bibliographers—e.g., D. C. Greetham—would now welcome. This essay also briefly engages the relative conservatism of Shakespeare criticism in the face of the two texts of *King Lear* and calls for a critical practice equal to the staggering implications of recent editorial work (a topic to which I return in "The Commodity of Names," about the decision in the Oxford edition to replace "Falstaff" with "Oldcastle"). These worries have been realized in the spate of recent editions of Shakespeare. Some of these include two *Lear*s as a token gesture toward the work done by bibliographic critics, but they otherwise produce composite texts of the most familiar kind. We have yet to have—and probably never will have—texts of Shakespeare capable of conveying the multiplicity and indeterminacy of the objects that go under his name. And even if we did, the canonical effect would almost certainly prevail, especially these days as a return to Shakespeare (after a certain amount of questioning) seems in vogue, and, as Karen Newman has argued, almost any effort in "old studies" seems incapable of registering except as a further instance of work that speaks only to the past.[3]

"Shakespearean Characters," a chapter from *Voice Terminal Echo,* argues for a fully textualized notion of character, relying on circuits of the letter—the actual passage of script and citation in several Shakespeare plays (*The Two Gentlemen of Verona* primarily; *Titus Andronicus, Cymbeline,* and *Hamlet* more briefly) and the sonnets—as the only index to character available in Shakespeare's texts. Although this essay is not overtly polemical, it aims against the kind of naturalizing of character that Shakespeare criticism inherited from A. C. Bradley and that persists even in otherwise sophisticated critics (e.g., those who seek to discern from various texts their effects on readers' understandings of character). Rather than affirming that Shakespeare's characters have psychologies, this essay suggests the pertinence of psychoanalytic insights about the function of the letter in the unconscious (to recall the title of a crucial essay by Lacan). Although this essay is certainly written in a style I would no longer choose, I wanted to include it here not merely for the many connections between it and other essays in this volume but also for the ways it begins to suggest, as it moves among a number of texts by Shakespeare as well as the kinds of texts historicists quarry, that historical materials—indeed, materiality itself—does not merely reside in the supposed assurance that can be provided by way of "facts" or dates.

This is the kind of "sense" that I pursue in "Making Sense," an essay I wanted to call "Stop Making Sense," in which I present arguments for a textual unconscious that exceeds normalizing, psychologizing criticism. It is an answer to Richard Levin's commonsensical view of Shakespeare, a set of arguments he launched against feminist and new historicist work, in an essay that imagines the immediate availability of Shakespeare's texts to twentieth-century readers. For Levin, the transparency of these texts produces the claims that everyone always thinks the same and that there were no unthinkable thoughts in the Renaissance; that is, there is no alterity of other historic periods, other minds, or other texts. This view, entirely rooted in a transhistorical consciousness (even as Levin claims to be speaking for history), ignores the materiality of the letter—whether by that phrase one refers to unconscious processes or to the ways texts impede and make impossible easy transmission. Although, even at the time of my engagement with him, Levin was not a representative of anything except a rearguard action, he had been invited to contribute to various "advanced" journals, perhaps out of some liberal belief in the value of giving time to the opposition, but more probably part and parcel of the increasing conservatism of the profession, a conservatism emblematized in a turn against theory that could be found as easily among "liberal" critics as among those on the Left.

Although my skirmish with Levin is undoubtedly dated and minor,

I think it still valuable for its attempt to show how Levin's common sense tacitly builds upon entirely naturalized notions of gender difference and on the assumption of universal heterosexuality. My brief rejoinder to his work also serves, I hope, to begin to reposition "Shakespearean Inscriptions," an essay that at the time of its publication rankled a number of feminist Shakespeareans. Written from the position of a theoretical problematization of difference, the essay certainly goes too far in effacing the differences of gender as they affected lives in the Renaissance and, more to the point in this context, as they affected the possibilities of Shakespearean representation. In retrospect, the essay seems to me to signal a danger in the ways I understood "theory" at the time. Nonetheless, one point in that essay still seems to me valuable, if overly strident: its engagement with a version of feminism that seeks to preserve, as the truth of gender difference, the differences between men and women that are part and parcel of patriarchal constructions. Shakespeare is, no doubt, much more complicitous with such arrangements than my essay suggests, but this does not lead to the conclusion that some untheorized notion of the "feminine" should be rescued from him. In the mid-1980s, when I wrote the essay, it was difficult to find feminist support for such a position, especially among Shakespeareans. Since the publication of Judith Butler's *Gender Trouble*,[4] that aim of my essay may be more legible, although I readily concede that the essay suffers from an inattention to historical differences that matter. I would also add that the possibility of rethinking gender that I attempted, however problematically (some would say unsuccessfully), in "Shakespearean Inscriptions" had a great deal to do with a subject that occupies me in a number of essays in this volume but that is only made explicit in the 1990s pieces: the question of sexuality. And although current feminist work on Shakespeare no longer clings to essentialized notions of gender (welcome attention to class or status and race has certainly complicated considerations of gender, and essays with these concerns have been regularly featured in *Shakespeare Quarterly* under Gail Kern Paster's editorship), it is not the case, I think, that the position tacitly informing "Shakespearean Inscriptions"—a desire to denaturalize gender as part of a strategy of rethinking sexual arrangements and the "naturalness" of heterosexuality—can be said to be a central goal in much current feminist work on Shakespeare.

To the extent that such goals are now more available, in theory generally and in Shakespeare studies in particular, they are engaged in "Calling Out the Law," a piece I wrote in 1997, initially for a panel at the American Historical Association and ultimately for an anthology on drama and the law (which has been stalled in its publication). I would hope that this essay makes up for the lapses in "Shakespearean Inscriptions," even as it furthers some of its aims. It seems important to add, too, that this essay, like many others in this volume, owes its impetus not merely to professional invitations but also, even more, to the provocations of the classroom. I came to write this piece after having considered its texts and issues in a number of graduate seminars. However, it may surprise readers to know that the germ of several of the essays in this volume, including "Calling Out the Law," were lectures to undergraduates. ("The Anus in *Coriolanus,*" which shocked some members of the Shakespeare Association of America, was the finale for my Shakespeare course one term.) Although I have always been a resistant Shakespearean, the professional lot of someone in my field inevitably involves far too much Shakespeare teaching. Finding ways to denaturalize the most canonical figure in English literature has never been easy or likely to be very successful. (Students, however, are more receptive and inspiring coconspirators on these matters than many professional Shakespeareans are.)

Twelfth Night, the play that is read in this essay, is, not surprisingly, a text that I have often taught as a document in the history of sexuality. Here I ask whether the "law" that mandates heterosexuality is also figured in the apparatus of the law that arrests Antonio in the play, and thus, too, I ask whether the law of genre, demanding a comedic conclusion, necessarily produces heterosexual couples. The essay draws on and seeks to further work done in the history of sexuality by such important historians as Alan Bray and Michael Rocke and by theoreticians (including Butler) and literary critics—especially Valerie Traub, who, in the past decade, has crucially engaged questions of sex and gender in ways that are exemplary. My aims in this essay include an attempt to work against certain normalizing procedures among historians, whose ability to recognize and validate the existence of other than heterosexual persons and behaviors is limited by recourse to various normativities. In this context, I consider the work done by Judith Brown on a so-called lesbian nun, as well as Rudolph Bell's attack on her work. My aim is to try to suggest ways prevailing powers and norms are misunderstood when granted the kind of coherence that leads either to the "discovery" of gays or lesbians in the past or to the insistence that they necessarily could not be made visible. I aim to suggest some of the ways such existence might have been possible—though in terms other than those of modern sexual identity. I conjure up the figure of "sister" (from religious discourse and practice) as one site for female same-sex relations, and of the male friend as its partner. The family reconstituted at the end of *Twelfth Night,* I argue, allows these relations to continue, inside and alongside marriage.

The sentences that end "Calling Out the Law," which gesture toward these reconfigurations, are perhaps the most recognizably "theoretical" in the essay, in style and in substance. "Inside and alongside" says, in an abbreviated and highly abstracted fashion, what I take to be the promise held out in a (non)concept like Derridean *différance:* that no given instance (textual, historical, or embodied) is ever self-identical; that the terms of its intelligibility, as provided by normative institutions, are not exhaustive; and that the work of denaturalizing has as its goal not some epistemological vantage point of the outside but one that seizes on what is already there and available to signify, thanks to the various discursive frames that cross at any moment of intelligibility. The point in such recognitions cannot be merely that of the insurmountable obstacle of differences that fail to coincide or to cohere; nor can it be a kind of sameness that comes from the absolute lack of distinction between differences that arise precisely in their crossings. Something can only become legible from the situated vantage point of an observer. If "theory" makes the seemingly intelligible unintelligible, it is for the sake of displacing intelligibility and with the aim of producing new forms of intelligibility that function not simply as the "opposite" or the "repressed" side of the supposedly intelligible and self-same, but as a "difference" that matters.

The essays in Part II concern three of the so-called major tragedies, *Hamlet, Macbeth,* and *King Lear,* and one not usually accorded such a position, *Coriolanus.* These essays extend issues from Part I in several directions. "Hamlet's Hand" represents the earliest conceptualization of the questions around practices of handwriting that I developed at length in *Writing Matter;* it seeks to relate these material practices to the practice of letter writing in the play. Although the essay thus echoes some of the concerns as well as the terms of analysis of the circuit of the letter that I presented in *Voice Terminal Echo* (which also is concerned with historical practices and conceptualizations of letter writing, for example), it also seeks to develop observations about the relationship between these aspects of textuality in the play and the texts of the play—that is, in terms of variants represented by quarto and Folio versions of the scene of the delivery of Hamlet's letter to the king. This essay thus seeks to find paths among a theoretical agenda about the letter, bibliographical questions, and material ones. The question of materiality, although only intimated in the essay (it is spelled out much further in *Writing Matter*), seems important if only for its theorization—a point that can be found in a number of the essays in this volume and one that has the potential for moving the emphasis away from language per se and toward forms of historical embodiment (including, of course, the embodiment of the text as material object).

Even the first essay on *King Lear,* "Perspectives" (which in its earliest incarnation—not the version printed here—is the oldest of the essays in this volume and, in some respects, its most programmatic in terms of the abstracted goals of textuality as a theoretical object), implies some of these impulses. The essay looks at Edgar's speech describing the (supposed) arrival at Dover Cliff. Since the lines arrive somewhere that the bodies in the text do not, a theoretical line of inquiry is opened around questions of representation and the possibility of referentiality in the text. One concern in this essay is to suggest the stagings of staging that go on in Edgar's lines; these are related not only to divided theatrical practices of Shakespeare's time (the proto-illusionism of masque staging versus the staging of the public theater) but also to major theoretical differences about representation. Subtending the essay's skepticism about the arrival of the letter—about the possibility of referentiality—is the fact that there is no single text of *King Lear.* Rather than dividing the kingdom into two different and coherent texts of the play(s), which is the conservative goal of some critics who welcome multiple texts as simply giving us *more Shakespeare,* this essay's meditation on the limits of representation takes the instability of the texts as its warrant. In a recent (2000) very brief follow-up to this essay on *King Lear,* "Shakespeare Writing Matter Again," written at the invitation of Peter Stallybrass, I stress the function of letters in the play as warrants for a further investigation of a textual materiality. Here I also have occasion to note how one direction of the original essay on *King Lear,* toward the implication of gender in its textualization, has been largely ignored (at least to judge by the fact that versions of that essay in anthologies have always dropped both its theoretical coda and its brief glance toward Imogen in *Cymbeline*). I suggest that the perspective from Dover Cliff houses a gendered plot, a point I make following the enormously provocative work of Christopher Pye in his recent book *The Vanishing*.[5]

The essay on *Macbeth*, "Speculations," takes up a different question about textuality: the question of source (or of intertextuality). In posing questions of the historical relationship among texts (including Raphael Holinshed's *Chronicles* as well as Ben Jonson's *Masque of Queenes*), the essay also broaches some large questions about historicity and ideology and offers some brief formulations about the relationship between history and theory. This essay develops, however briefly, a consideration of the limits of new historicist methodology (including my own practice in *James I and the Politics of Literature*). In suggesting ways the text of *Macbeth* escapes both Shakespeare's hand and our own attempts to pin it down to determinate historic circumstances or to a single ideological effect, the essay also glances at the instabilities of gender in the play as one strong site for these indeterminations.

My gesture toward the bearded witches is left as mere implication, but I hope that other essays in this volume make good on that gesture. Pointing to bearded women as a sign of the kinds of problematics involving even such a supposedly straightforward empirical matter as the question of source means (or so I would like to believe) to overthrow a host of certainties about "source," including the modeling of textual transmission on heterosexual reproduction. In that respect, "Speculations" might be thought to anticipate "The Anus in *Coriolanus*," which, as I note in its opening paragraph, scandalized at least some Shakespeareans when I delivered it at a meeting of the Shakespeare Association of America. (I try assiduously to avoid such events, if only because even the most determined efforts to rethink Shakespeare seem stymied by their immediate incorporation into an institution that enshrines his canonical name and fosters the professional deformation that characterizes all single-author societies, especially this one.) Here "textuality" persists in the obvious sense that the essay insists on hearing something in the name of the hero that can be translated into the erotic politics of the play. As I note, I am not the first to have heard this assonance, and I follow Kenneth Burke's exacting ear, even if not quite where he would have gone with it. In pursuing this course, I take up Stanley Cavell's reluctance to acknowledge what he all but does about the play and, in turn, his reliance on a model of liberal communication that he develops from a feminist psychoanalytic model that had also been influential on my own work in *James I and the Politics of Literature.* I suggest that *Coriolanus* will never be made safe for liberalism; instead, its sexual-political fantasia may represent a radical alternative worth pondering. I'm encouraged to do this in part by the example of Jeffrey Masten (whose work in "queer philology" pursues aims congruent with a number of my own essays), as he is in part by Leo Bersani, whose vision of a nonrelational sociality I seek to make legible in this reading of the anus in this play. For this anal connection is also a productive route, even a reproductive one, while it adverts to an aversiveness in sexual culture—in culture in general, perhaps (work by Daniel Juan Gil provides illumination here).[6]

Part III includes three essays on the second tetralogy, two on *Romeo and Juliet,* and a closing essay on *The Tempest.* These continue to take their impetus from inquiries into textual questions of the bibliographic sort and seek to mobilize them toward the question of sexuality raised in the essay on *Coriolanus.* In "Rebel Letters," concerns about the transmission of the letter are used to theorize the political differences between sovereign power and rebel energies represented in the second tetralogy; these concerns also lead to a scene of letter reading in *1 Henry IV* and, as in several of the earlier essays, to the texts of that letter and to editorial considerations of those texts. The concern about character is taken up in "The Commodity of Names," an inquiry into the decision of one recent edition of Shakespeare—the Oxford edition, which also prints two *King Lears*—to call Falstaff "Oldcastle." Here, questions about what lies in a name and what a character is are engaged in an essay that is as much concerned with editorial questions as it is with Derridean theory.

"Hal's Desire, Shakespeare's Idaho" reworks portions of my *Sodometries* and offers a brief account of the relevance of the history of sexuality to the reading of Shakespeare. Comparing *Henry IV,* Parts 1 and 2, to their reworking in Gus Van Sant's film *My Own Private Idaho,* I look at a scene of transformation and reception that foregrounds the differences and continuities within the history of sexualities. This essay argues that the indeterminacy of the homo-hetero divide as a historical condition subtending Shakespeare's writing must cause a rereading of the plays. Along with this essay, I include an exchange with the editor of the volume for which it was originally written. He poses a number of questions, largely from the vantage point of traditional Shakespeare studies, which allow me to suggest some of the aims of the kind of intervention into Shakespeare studies I aim to make. This set of questions and answers also allows me to suggest the limits of my allegiance to the theoretical models that at first guided my work, for over the years I have grown impatient with the politics of deconstruction, which is itself a politics of a kind of patience that risks maintaining the status quo in the belief that the divisions and differences that make any moment or regime non-self-identical are the resources of futurity. While I agree with that point, I do not agree with the stance of biding one's time that seems to go along with a certain "proper" philosophical attitude, and I have even less tolerance for the notion that some spectral regime may some day herald a future worth waiting for. Methodologically, I still think that deconstructive destabilization is a necessary tool and that differences always exist in a supplementary relationship to each other. But I now also think it important to recognize that historical limits impinge upon theoretical possibility and that these cannot be translated into merely theoretical impasses to be worked through or, even more insidiously, to be seen as indistinguishable sides of an always double-sided coin. In retrospect, it is possible for me to see now what was not evident to me once: that the valuable task of deconstruction has often foundered on its inability to recognize the differences between the kinds of solidifications that one must resist and those that one must desire and further. While I believe that the past is not as monolithic as some historians make it out to be—and that, indeed, the future lies in realizing possibilities that are not merely utopian and that must, therefore, be historically available—it seems crucial to recognize, nonetheless, that the indifference of difference, while a fine theoretical point, will not explain prevailing power differences or give one much leverage in taking up a side or claiming stakes.

In this final group of essays, the prime example is that supposed monument to heterosexuality, *Romeo and Juliet* (a critical supposition that I dispute). The route to the reading of sexual relations in the play is once again textual, a meditation first on the name/word of the rose (the question "What's in a name?" haunts many of these essays and is the opening line of the chapter on the Shakespearean character in my *Voice Terminal Echo*). The essay "'What? in a names that which we call a Rose'" looks at an editorial crux, but it is equally informed by an essay by Derrida that contemplates the fate of names and words and characters in *Romeo and Juliet.* In positing that a notion of "textual desire" is what is enacted in *Romeo and Juliet,* both in the play and by the play's editors and critics, I suggest the openness and continual possibility of repositioning desire. The second essay on the play, "*Romeo and Juliet*'s Opens Rs," was written for *Queering the Renaissance.* (As that book's editor, it gives me pleasure to say that that collection contains essays by a number of critics who continue to produce work pointing the way forward for early modern studies and beyond.) In this essay, the textually indeterminate spot has its "own" (im)proper name: the open Rs. The play on the letter is occasioned, once again, by an editorial crux; its consequence, as I suggest, traverses a route of gender transgression that also violates the supposed proprieties defending the "good" quarto of the play from its "bad" counterpart.

Raising questions about names and words, these essays on *Romeo and Juliet* offer a trajectory from strictly textual questions to the questions of gender and sexuality also to be found in "Under the Covers with Caliban." Here, I locate in the play a crux in gender that has gone unnoticed (the Folio lines describing how Sycorax gave birth to Caliban designate her as "he"), and I seek to articulate it with one that has received considerable attention (whether Ferdinand hails his future father-in-law as "wise" or includes his "wife" at the moment of his betrothal to Miranda). The essay thus seeks to articulate relationships between gay and feminist readings of the play and seeks, too, to historicize them by recourse to the figures of the witch and the sodomite. At the time of writing the essay, editors were beginning to read "wife" in place of "wise," a trend that was reversed in the late 1990s back into the masculinist tradition of reading (as evidenced by the latest Arden edition [1999] of the play as well as the new Pelican edition [1999]). The warrant for this reversal has been largely due to a scholar in residence at the Folger Shakespeare Library who has persuaded editors but has yet to produce publicly a shred of evidence to confirm his belief that the reading "wife" that appears in some texts of the Folio is to be rejected. (He has printed two sentences asserting his expertise on the matter.) In this scholar's eyes, what looks like a crossbar on the "f" is smeared ink, a blot that would allow Miranda to be acknowledged by her future husband. I could go on.

This final essay on *The Tempest* forms a bridge to the project I recently completed: the mobilization of the play in anticolonial struggle by twentieth-century Afro-Caribbean writers (among them Aimé Césaire,

George Lamming, Michelle Cliff, and Sylvia Wynter). Glancing toward this work allows me to note that one signal failure exists in all the essays gathered in this volume: an inattention to questions of race. In the reworking of "Under the Covers" for this next project, I emphasize how the limited political questions raised by the theoretical and bibliographical dilemmas are even further limited by the ways they implicate and exclude Caliban and Sycorax from the various forms of sexual relationship that are endorsed in the play. In this new work, it is clear to me, as it was not in the mid-1980s, that the circuit opened by the letter leads not only to questions of gender and sexuality but also, significantly, to the racialization of difference. These paths are not simply congruent or parallel; they cross in intricate ways too particular to allow me to offer in these closing sentences some handy theoretical formulation for such lability. But it is also possible, and useful, to register bluntly how massively they support each other by simply asking, When is it likely that the United States will elect a president who is black, gay, female, or poor (or even middle class, bisexual, nonwhite, Native American, or just unmarried—although there *once* was an unmarried [and gay?] president, James Buchanan)? Presidential elections are scarcely the place one can hope to look for political transformation, I know. And this is no doubt an odd question to ask in closing this introduction, especially since it is depressing to think that in the present political climate, if such a person were elected, it would be a Colin Powell, or Condaleeza Rice, or a gay critic like Bruce Bawer, yearning for a place at the table. Nonetheless, without unrealistically overestimating the political work that a literary critic can do, I continue to believe that the possibility of imagining with pleasure that the time when the answer to that question will not be "never again" is decreased so long as Shakespeare remains read as an author who supports—and is to be supported for—his (by which I mean, strongly, *our*) normative values.

PART I

Textual Properties

"With the acceptance of 'free play' as both an operation and a standard in hermeneutics, the relation between extrinsic and intrinsic forms of criticism is further loosened; and textual/bibliographical studies, already conceived as 'preliminary operations,' are all but removed from the program of literary studies"; so Jerome McGann writes in "The Monks and the Giants," a recent essay in which he calls for the recognition that textual criticism is neither preliminary nor extrinsic to literary criticism.[1] Invoking the Derridean term "free play," McGann raises a specter of critical irresponsibility—as if deconstruction were a brand of formalism—and he demands, instead, attention to the historicity of texts. I want to confront the specter that McGann raises and to argue, in opposition to his position, that neither the logic of recent textual work nor the recognition of the historicity of texts consequent upon it is inimical to free play. Recent studies of the Shakespearean text, I would argue, support this contention. The division of the kingdoms has undermined, for instance, the notion that there might be a single Shakespearean text behind *King Lear,* and among the consequences of that is the further recognition that a textual criticism based on a search for an irrecoverable urtext has committed itself to an unfounded Platonism. Shakespeare was a reviser of scripts subject to numerous contingencies; there never was *a King Lear.*

My topic here is the critical consequences of such textual recognitions. To counter McGann's critical anxieties, one must recognize that poststructuralism and the new textual criticism coincide, both historically and theoretically. Both have called the criterion of authorial intention into question, thereby detaching the supposed sovereign author from texts open to and constituted by a variety of interventions. As McGann would have us recognize, quite legitimately, all texts are situated and resituated historically. Randall McLeod, one of the most provocative of Shakespeareans, has called for us to "unedit" Shakespeare,[2] but if we accept McGann's position, "unediting" can never come to an end. There never has been, and never can be, an unedited Shakespearean text. Therefore, textual criticism and poststructuralism agree: We have no originals, only copies. The historicity of the text means that there is no text itself; it means that a text cannot be fixed in terms of original or final intentions. At best, Shakespearean practice authorizes the dispersal of authorial intention.

Free play, as McGann uses the term, would seem to mean that, critically speaking, anything goes and that the rigorous demands of textual historicity are thereby avoided. Yet free play could be construed differently. The term places the text beyond authorial control and points to the indeterminacy of the text precisely because it is always being redetermined. Derrida uses the notion of iterability to clarify the point.[3] It is a fundamental truth about texts that they appear to go on meaning even when they are unmoored from their original situations of production. They function even though the author is dead, even though the intended audience is in the grave, even though the theater has moved indoors and women play women's roles. But they do so not because the text is universal and transcendent or because it is inherently saturated with meaning; rather, they do so because it is open to history. Shakespeare's texts have a unique position in the English-speaking world: They were early identified as the embodiment of artistic (and, for the English, national) value. The historical construction of Shakespeare is not a statement about the intrinsic value of the Shakespearean text. It does not even identify a Shakespearean text; Shakespeare may epitomize English literature, yet no two editions of Shakespeare are identical. There is no

Shakespeare—no single Shakespeare, that is—but only a divided kingdom. If that is the case, free play is not irresponsible; rather, it is a critical position more responsive to the radical historicity of the texts that we miscall Shakespeare's but that are and have always been the product of textual and critical interventions.

McGann would have textual criticism be intrinsic to and coincident with interpretive practice. He insists that what was once thought of as merely external—textual trappings—be recognized as internal and that what has been thought of as merely prior be given the true priority that is inescapably bound to all secondarity. In these ways, the historicity that McGann champions coincides with the conditions that Derrida describes for free play. Textual properties are not merely a corrupt outside masking a true internality; rather, the inside is the outside. What McGann calls historicity Derrida would call writing, a structuration of traces without any positivity. Where Derrida would part company with McGann, then, is in the positivism that clings to McGann's use of the term "intrinsic." A rigorous historicism must suspect that the term reinstates itself as a timeless and transcendent value.

The critical consequences of the historico-textual situation that I have been outlining have barely been faced in Shakespeare criticism. Reading the essays in Gary Taylor's and Michael Warren's edited volume *The Division of the Kingdoms,* one can be struck by the combination of textual audacity and critical conservatism. There are two *King Lears,* we are told, but we are also assured that the Quarto derives from Shakespeare's manuscript and that the Folio represents an authoritative revision. The kingdom has been divided, but Shakespeare reigns supreme, author now of two sovereign texts. One suspects that some of the contributors to *The Division of the Kingdoms* are happy to call the Folio *Lear* a better play because they can construe it as more consoling than the Quarto version. Moreover, the two texts seem to offer these critics further opportunities to practice a character criticism that goes back to A. C. Bradley or to argue for formalistic structures in the plays that are equally suspect. To justify the integrity of each *King Lear,* the contributors to *The Division of the Kingdoms* must often invoke the criterion of "the timeless work of art," to quote Gary Taylor.[4]

That there are two *King Lears* is not a fact unique to those plays. Every text of a Shakespeare play bears signs of the historicity—and therefore of the radical instability—of the Shakespearean text. The printed texts of the plays, including both the Quarto and the Folio *Lears,* cannot be assimilated to an authorial intentionality. Not only do editors, prompt-books, scribal copies, and compositors stand between the Shakespearean scripts and the Shakespearean text; Shakespearean scripts themselves intervene. We will never recover Shakespeare, nor "the timeless work of art," because that notion of the author and text are Platonic constructs. We must therefore, as McGann has insisted, make our critical practices coincide with the nature of textual production.

Shakespearean revision, it now appears (thanks, in large part, to Gary Taylor), was thoroughgoing and took place on large and small scales. Lexical substitution, indifferent variants, mark the Shakespearean text: Apparently, no word in the text is sacred. If this is true, all criticism that has based itself on the text, all forms of formalism, all close reading, is given the lie. If the stability of the word is in question, so, too, is the stability of character. McLeod is surely correct, in his contribution to *The Division of the Kingdoms,* in inviting us to view the two Gonerils as differential characters, characters whose differences are relational. But just as surely, the differences between them cannot be reduced, as they are in his hands, to which of them is more likable. Characters who are differentials are posited upon no natural base; Goneril is a person only if we allow "person" the definition that Thomas Hobbes spelled out from its classical roots: "the *disguise,* or *outward appearance* of a man, counterfeited on the Stage."[5] Characters counterfeit being, and their essence is differential; which is to say, there is no essence to a character. The difference between the two Gonerils is like the difference between any two alternative words in the Shakespearean text, or like the difference upon which language is founded in the model that Ferdinand de Saussure offers: "In language, there are only differences," he writes, "differences *without positive terms.*"[6] That in the two *Lears* different characters may speak the same lines and that the same characters (characters with the same proper names) speak different lines, suggest the radical instability of character as a locus of meaning in the Shakespearean text. Nor can we assume that the text of a Shakespearean play will have a determinate structure; how could it, when so much of the text was expendable? The Shakespearean text is a historical phenomenon, produced by ongoing restructurations, revisions, and collaboration; by editorial, scribal, and theatrical interventions; by material, occasional, and accidental conditions. Some texts, like the one we have for *Macbeth,* betray more visibly the truth about these texts: that they may be called Shakespearean, but not simply Shakespeare.

There are, as I have been suggesting, only composite texts, and all our divisions (which I am not arguing against) will never produce the single Shakespeare text. We must, as McLeod has argued, recognize the textual property of the Shakespearean texts. And in doing so, I would add, we must see that the typographical character is one further sign—literally, a reminder of the compositor—that points to the composite nature of every Shakespearean text. As textual properties, Shakespearean texts are produced by a multitude of determinations that exceed a criticism bent on controlling the text or on assigning it determinate meanings or structures. Although all we have to go on are the texts, we must go on knowing that they do not make the Shakespearean text *proper.* No one can own the text. No one can clean it up.

The irrecoverability of the Shakespearean text is our license as well as our limit. Every text of a Shakespeare play exists in relationship to scripts we will never have, to a series of revisions and collaborations that start as soon as there is a Shakespearean text—which is to say, from the start. The title page of the Folio, claiming its authority in "True Originall Copies," echoes the familiar theory of Renaissance composition as an imitative and counterfeit art that also produced Sir Philip Sidney's definition of poetry as "a representing, counterfeiting, or figuring forth," or Ben Jonson's wholly unoriginal dictum that a poet should "convert the substance, or Riches of another *Poet,* to his owne use. To make choise of one excellent man above the rest, and so to follow him, till he grow very *Hee*: or, so like him, as the Copie may be mistaken for the Principall."[7] The rationale of copytext cannot stand if there are only copies and no original. So, too, must fall all types of positivistic criticism.

The destabilizing, de-idealizing criticism that coincides with modern textual criticism must recognize the historicity of textuality and the textuality of historicity. If texts, even lexically identical texts, are never the same because of history, then history, as the principle of difference, cannot be a principle of identity. Derrida's term *"différance"* might therefore be a necessary neologism for the shared terrain of a new historicism and a new textuality. Shakespeare criticism might then situate itself by recognizing that its task is doubly circumscribed: by the irrecoverability of scriptive formations that were always dispersed and unstable and by their remarkings and effacements in the Shakespearean texts that remain, the quartos and (especially) the Folio, whose attempts to monumentalize and stabilize Shakespeare offer instead the counterfeit properties of the Shakespearean text.

I suggest, since it is all that we have, a return to the letter. "Ourselves we do not owe," Olivia testifies after her first interview with Viola (1.5.314).[8] It seems an apt response to a character who functions as a virtual letter carrier between Orsino and his beloved; apt not only because Viola represents the place where desires meet but also because she articulates the very character of desire—as a character. She recognizes a cover for herself in the "fair and outward character" (1.2.51) of the captain with whom she arrives in the play; "Conceal me what I am," she asks

> and be my aid
> For such disguise as haply shall become
> The form of my intent.
>
> (1.2.53–55)

Self-realization is personation, as the rhetorical tradition of Hobbes would remind us; recognition goes no further than masks. "Ourselves we do not owe": Character is construction, a social and textual production. Olivia disowns herself as she is drawn to Viola; anagrammatic mirrors, their names respell and resituate the same characters. Viola, whose borrowed name, Cesario, suggests the sovereignty of desire—or of a script whose free play answers our desire, what we will—is almost undone by her outside, and she is saved when her outside proves capable of duplication. "'That that is, is,'" is the mad tautology that Feste tries out (4.2.15), a positivism denied when characters split, when the position of the subject is constituted in a discourse that cannot be owned, and when the male Viola is renamed Sebastian—or is it Malvolio? Entirely possessed by the letter, Malvolio can only reclaim himself by investing himself in writing; Malvolio ends in possession of Viola's clothing, the garment of a style that is also the sex that exists only as representation. If he is the scapegoat for anxieties about class and social hierarchies, he is also the locus for the unstable social construction of sexuality. "This is my lady's hand: these be her very C's, her U's, and her T's, and thus makes she her great P's" (2.5.87–89). Malvolio takes his cue from a hand that he reads as a social mark; yet it is a counterfeit hand that has made the class mark a disowned mark. The counterfeit hand possesses the upstart steward. He supplies the letters that cut him down to size; "C," "U," "T," (dis)spells an unspeakable word for female genitalia. They are castrating letters that point to a desire unattainable on a stage that can only impersonate sexual difference. The letter offers some more letters to Malvolio—"M," "O," "A," "I"—and he indulges in the fantasy of the proper name. Malvolio's scene of reading glimpses the social and scriptive construction of character, class, and gender; moreover, it *stages* that observation in a text whose radical instability offers, at best, the counterfeit truths that are its textual property. These are the disowned marks of a radical historicity that also could be called free play.

Malvolio's reading lesson, which I take to be instructive beyond the limits of the text of *Twelfth Night,* coincides with an outrageous diagram that appears in Jacques Lacan's "Agency of the Letter in the Unconscious": two doors, seemingly identical, and above them the words "Ladies" and "Gentlemen," destinations of desire, which are, Lacan indicates, fully arbitrary.[9] Nature did not institute "the laws of urinary segregation," which implies, of course, that gender is socially constructed and that the unconscious is no primordial sea but is, rather, historical—or textual, like the ocean from which the character (call it Viola, or the letter "P") emerges.

The scenes of reading and writing, of character formation and deformation, in *Twelfth Night* point us to similar scenes in other Shakespearean texts. Upon these, criticism might begin its historical and textual work. These scenes, I argue, do not allegorize a notion of the text itself. Rather, they point to a textuality that is radically unstable, upon which plots move, characters are (de)formed, language and observation is (improperly) staged. They point, that is, to historical and cultural demarcations, to what passes for essences, desires, knowledge, and the like. An examination of the textual properties of Shakespearean texts, even of textual props like the letters of *Twelfth Night* or *King Lear,* will never produce a proper, selfsame Shakespearean text. But it is the lesson of recent textual criticism that there is no such Shakespearean text.

Shakespearean Characters: The Generation of Silvia

What's in a name? For Silvia, it is her destiny (already written in the *silva* tradition) and her destination (both in *The Two Gentlemen of Verona* and the texts it generates). In a word, her name is a genealogy, and in the play in which she appears, her generation is the generation of the letter—literally and figuratively.[1]

> **Speed.** She woos you by a figure.
> **Valentine.** What figure?
> **Speed.** By a letter, I should say.
> (2.1.136–38)[2]

Silvia moves through a chain of signifiers to arrive (in the final scene of the play) in the place her name determines, the woods. There, only the letter speaks, and the character falls silent. She is, in that final location, impressed by the letter, barred at last from any attempt to own discourse (her scenes with Valentine play out those possibilities), placed within discourse that is not her own. She is what her name betokens.

If Silvia's ultimate silence makes palpable the proposition that the character functions in a discourse of the Other, the argument could also be made on the basis of her speech. Silvia's last words in the play are "O heaven!" (5.4.59), exclaimed when Proteus threatens to rape her. What she says then had been written earlier. "Is she not a heavenly saint?" (2.4.142), Valentine asks, and he is echoed in Proteus's song to Silvia, proclaiming that "heaven such grace did lend her" (4.2.42) and concluding that "she excels each mortal thing" (4.2.51). The heaven that is on Silvia's lips is a final dissemination of the word as it has passed from mouth to mouth. It derives from Proteus's song much as his attempted rape is a translation of the violence of the song of the pastoral swain singing her to perfection, violent since it imagines perfection as termination, an ultimate metamorphosis enforced by the tropes:

> Then to Silvia let us sing,
> That Silvia is excelling.
> She excels each mortal thing
> Upon the dull earth dwelling.
> To her let us garlands bring.
> (4.2.49–53)

Much as do her repeated appearances on the balcony, the song suggests that Silvia's excellence is not earthly. Yet it marks her perfection by offering her "garlands" culled from "the dull earth" she transcends. In the mouth of a singer in the guise of a pastoral swain, the trope has the funereal ring that Florizel hears in *The Winter's Tale* when Perdita wishes to "strew him o'er and o'er" with "garlands" (4.4.129). Moreover, the flower passage suggests that perfection is a replanting within the tropes of a pastoral florilegium. There is no escaping the soil from which she springs; to be no "mortal thing / Upon the dull earth dwelling," she is hymned to heaven, crowned in garlands. The song inserts Silvia within a poetic economy, Ovidian metamorphosis as her end. Poets have always affirmed that they confer immortality, as Sir Philip Sidney, among others, might remind us.[3] Silvia's excellence is textual; her "being," literally, is figurative. No wonder, then, that she ends up in the forest, voiceless.

Proteus's song and its reenactment as attempted rape do not alone provide paths to Silvia's final "O heaven!" That end had already been written elsewhere; Proteus's name directs us to what might be designated the master text that determines character in *The Two Gentlemen of Verona*, Ovid's *Metamorphoses*. Here, for example, are Philomela's last words:

> [S]i silvis clausa tenebor,
> inplebo silvas et conscia saxa movebo;
> audiet haec aether et si deus ullus in illo est!
> (*Metamorphoses* 6:546–48)

> If I am kept shut up in these woods, I will fill the woods with my story and move the very rocks to pity. The air of heaven shall hear it, and, if there is any god in heaven, he shall hear it too.[4]

Philomela is carried from her father's court to forest imprisonment ("in stabula alta trahit, silvis obscura vetustis" [*Metamorphoses* 6:521]). The plot's trajectory suggests Silvia's story. The movement is, like Silvia's, determined by desire—and by a trope. When Tereus first sees Philomela, her beauty—"such as we are wont to hear the naiads described, and dryads when they move about in the deep woods" ("mediis incedere silvis" [*Metamorphoses* 6:453])—inflames him. The trope of desire becomes Philomela's woodland confinement, literally. From it, there is no escape. Raped, Philomela yearns for the voice that would fill the woods with her story. Finally, she achieves that desire; metamorphosed into the nightingale, she can fill the forests with her song. But to move the air of heaven, she must lose her tongue. Silvia's silence, Proteus's failed attempt at rape, and the doubling of Proteus with Valentine effectively displace the tragic Ovidian story to permit a comic resolution. The Ovidian etiology of song in rape and violation is disseminated in Silvia's textual generation.

Proteus's song asks "Who is Silvia?" and answers by positing a more than mortal excellence for her. Yet translated into textual terms, in which excellence means acquiring the status of a word in a text or of a figure in a rhetorical scheme, the difference that marks Silvia is, in fact, a shared condition: "Who is Silvia? What is she, / That all our swains commend her?" (4.2.39–40). The song assumes—as a trope and a disguise—a community of pastoral shepherds. Proteus sings the song (ostensibly) on behalf of Thurio; he sings as a shepherd and for another imagined as a swain; he sings for the other he *is* in song. This situation is, as Edmund Spenser's *Shepheardes Calender* and its Virgilian antecedents show, essential to pastoral refigurations. In the song, and the community it imagines, it is difficult (perhaps impossible) to separate the device and disguise (the tropes) from the (literal) truth of the scene. "[A]ll our swains commend her" also applies, after all, to Silvia's *true* love, Valentine. Alone, in the forest, he pours out his desire in the "unfrequented woods" (5.4.2):

> Here can I sit alone, unseen of any.
> And to the nightingale's complaining notes
> Tune my distresses and record my woes.
>
> . . . .
>
> Repair me with thy presence, Silvia.
> Thou gentle nymph, cherish thy forlorn swain.
> (5.4.4–6; 11–12)

As "forlorn swain," Valentine is like the Virgilian shepherd Corydon imploring the hollow woods to answer his echoing void: "[I]bi haec incondita solus / montibus et silvis studio iactabat inani" (*Eclogue 2*, lines 4–5).[5] Valentine's "complaining notes," however, are Ovidian, articulated by the nightingale, and the "presence" of Silvia that he implores would seem to be carried on a pastoral song. Valentine's words are the nightingale's, and Silvia's "presence" (literally? in his thoughts? in his words?) reverses the metamorphosis of nymph into nightingale. Here, the nightingale's song delivers the maiden. Valentine's words partake of the pastoral community of Proteus's song to Silvia. The "forlorn swain" projects himself into the bird of night and finds "presence" in the Silvia that he names; thus, he is repaired with the echoing return of the name he sends into the void. His identity seems tantamount to his identification—with the nightingale, her song, and the tropes of nymph and swain. In that context, it is worth remarking that Valentine's career also traces the path marked previously in Ovid's tale of Philomela and echoed in Silvia's story; he moves first from his father's house to Silvia's father's court and then to the woods. There, however exiled, he is at home; the outlaws choose him as their leader in part because he has "the tongues" (4.1.33). He can give voice to the woods and speak the language of pastoral precisely because it is the language that speaks him. As "forlorn swain," Valentine arrives at the end of the play where a pastoral trope had placed him at the start. In the first scene of the play, Speed seeks his master, Valentine, and is told by Proteus that he has left to embark for Milan:

> **Speed.** Twenty to one then, he is shipped already,
> And I have played the sheep in losing him.

Proteus. Indeed, a sheep doth very often stray,
if the shepherd be awhile away.
Speed. You conclude that my master is a shepherd then,
and I a sheep?

(1.1.72–77)

Shipped to be a shepherd, Valentine's destiny is the conclusion Speed derives from the punning play of the letter.[6]

Valentine finds himself as a swain not only because of this textualizing determination of his career in a pun. His destiny is also in his name. In seeking a source for the name of the character (it does not appear in any of the sources for the play), Joseph A. Porter has suggested the romance of *Valentine and Orson* as one possibility.[7] There, Orson is a twin brother brought up by a bear and thus incapable of speech. The romance involves the brothers' meeting, Orson's acquisition of language, and Valentine's recognition of his twin in this pastoral alter ego. Porter argues that Valentine's name is regularly one in a pair, as in *The Two Gentlemen of Verona,* and as it is, too, when it appears in *Romeo and Juliet.* There, the name occurs, in the list of guests invited to the Capulet ball, as a ghost brother for Mercutio (1.2.68) and thus as a simulacrum for Romeo, to whom Mercutio gives his generic names: "Romeo! humors! madman! passion! lover!" (2.1.7). Valentine is not merely the swain of pastoral romance; his name means "lover." Appearing *in* a letter, a valentine, one must recall, *is* a letter, a folded slip of paper on which the name of a lover is inscribed. A valentine is also a legal instrument, a sealed letter from the Crown for the apprehension of persons offending against the law. In the forest, Valentine, the outlawed lover, embodies both these letters that name him. He opens his revery by remarking "How use doth breed a habit in a man!" (5.4.1). If the "habit" is his newfound pastoral guise, it is also his *interiority,* what inhabits him. Hence, the nightingale's song leads him to the Silvia "that dost inhabit in my breast" (5.4.7); the letter folded upon the letter, so might the inside and outside of the character be defined. Thus, earlier in the play, when Silvia's father had pulled off Valentine's cloak, he had asked: "What letter is this same? What's here? 'To Silvia'!" (3.1.137). Inwardly and outwardly, Valentine is folded in the letter that names him and his pastoral/amatory career; he, in turn, enfolds the text "To Silvia."

If Silvia and Valentine are these literal figures—characters, that is, who voice the letters in which they are written—it can come as no surprise that their first scene together is played around a letter. Silvia employs Valentine as a secretary to write on her behalf to a "secret, nameless friend" (2.1.96). Valentine delivers the letter to her, and she returns it to him. Valentine responds by assuming he has been rejected, but Speed penetrates the circuit of the letter and realizes that it has reached its destination: "O jest unseen, inscrutable, invisible, / As a nose on a man's face, or a weathercock on a steeple!" (2.1.125–26). He sees without difficulty that the letter is a figure ("she woos you by a figure" [2.1.136]), and he authorizes his reading of the scene by concluding, "All this I speak in print, for in print I found it" (2.1.155). Speed knows their textual play because he knows he is a character set in type. His "consciousness" involves the recognition that what he voices has been written already, and he ends the scene demanding real food (as if that need were not scripted, too) rather than the insubstantial fare that lovers desire.

The circuit of the letter in this scene traces the path of desire. Speed's analysis of Silvia's behavior suggests how fully she is caught within the play she stages:

> For often have you writ to her, and she in modesty,
> Or else for want of idle time, could not again reply;
> Or fearing else some messenger that might her mind discover,
> Herself hath taught her love himself to write unto her lover.
> (2.1.151–54)

He speaks in print, in fourteeners that suggest Silvia's figure is an old story. Barred from her "own" discourse even before she arrives in the position of Philomela imprisoned in the woods, Silvia can only speak to her lover if he speaks for her. Already, she has no voice. The exchange of the letter plays upon the "sympathetic dative"[8] of pastoral discourse that obscures the propriety of voice: "I have writ your letter" (2.1.95), Valentine says, opening the scene with Silvia, but it is precisely what "your" means that is in question:

> **Valentine.** Madam, they are for you.
> **Silvia.** Ay, ay, you writ them, sir, at my request,
> But I will none of them. They are for you—
> (2.1.115–17)

Silvia's manipulation of the letter is a guise of mastery, and Valentine subscribes to it; he is Silvia's "gentle servant" (2.1.99). Yet her speech is entirely confined to the troping of the letter and to the duplicities and divagations possible within the device. Whereas Valentine balks at the task he has been assigned, Silvia attempts to speak within it:

Valentine. So it stead you, I will write—
Please you command—a thousand times as much.
And yet—
Silvia. A pretty period! Well, I guess the sequel—
And yet I will not name it—and yet I care not—
And yet take this again—and yet I thank you,
Meaning henceforth to trouble you no more.
(2.1.104–10)

"And yet" locates both Valentine's desire to escape the circuit of Silvia's dictates and Silvia's attempt to tell her desire within the turns of the trope. He experiences a frustrating and baffling lack in the situation; she points to an excess.

Clearly, as Speed says, the letter is a figure of desire. Yet its circuit is obscure precisely because it is a figure. Reading the letter, Silvia finds it "clerkly done" (2.1.99), and Valentine apologizes, "For, being ignorant to whom it goes, / I writ at random, very doubtfully" (2.1.101–2). Writing at the command of another and to another, Valentine is incapable of seeing himself as the other for whom he writes. The trope that locates him dislocates him, and also bars him from Silvia's designs—from the figure in which she is located, which in turn bars her from speaking any more straightforwardly than signifying her acceptance of the letter by refusing it. "What means your ladyship?" (2.1.112), the baffled servant asks, and Silvia responds by saying both yes (she likes the letter, although she would like it more if it were more passionate) and no (she will not accept the letter): "If it please you, so; if not, why, so" (2.1.121). The letter is "for" Valentine if he can read his name as "the secret, nameless friend" (2.1.96). Only if, that is, auto-affection will allow him to find within himself the valentine that enfolds the letter for Valentine that another (himself as that other), writing for Silvia, has written within.

The return of the letter offers a virtual Lacanian allegory in which letters always reach their destination (sender and receiver are one); yet their arrival (return) goes unrecognized, since the language of desire (language as desire) deforms (metamorphoses, enfolds) those who desire.[9]

Speed. You never saw her since she was deformed.
Valentine. How long hath she been deformed?
Speed. Ever since you loved her.

(2.1.59–61)

Desire is spoken through an Other. In the scene between Valentine and Silvia, that Other has a social dimension that supports the psychoanalytical one. Silvia is barred from discourse because of the limits patriarchy enforces; but she is also barred because the language of love puts her in a position of mastery in which her beloved must be treated as a servant. Silvia is, at once, empowered and disabled by the tropes of tyrannical desire (hers is the illusion of power), doubly disabled because her power is a trope within a discourse she cannot control. Valentine's figurative submission to the discourse that gives him his name is what makes him unable to recognize himself within the discourse to which he submits; he fails to see that his being (literally) is wrapped entirely within the figure: "O jest unseen, inscrutable, invisible, / As a nose on a man's face, or a weathercock on a steeple!" (2.1.125–26). The situation, Speed's lines say, is so clear that it requires a simile to make manifest the entirely figurative being of something so entirely literal. Silvia's power is as visible as a man's nose or a weathercock. And those, of course, are not figures.

It was Speed's play on the letter (ship/sheep) that led us to this scene played around the figure of the letter, a letter "writ at random" (2.1.102) whose contents are never revealed. Speed and Proteus continue to spin out their pastoral troping in the first scene of the play, trying out the possibilities that *that* letter is also random: Is Valentine or Speed a shepherd? Which one is a sheep? Their inconclusive turns come to a halt when Proteus asks, "Gav'st thou my letter to Julia?" (1.1.94). The letter scene between Valentine and Silvia is hardly a unique event in *The Two Gentlemen of Verona;* there is, before it, this letter to Julia.

Speed's answer to Proteus's question folds the pastoral punning into the question of the letter: "Ay, sir. I, a lost mutton, gave your letter to her, a laced mutton, and she, a laced mutton, gave me, a lost mutton, nothing for my labor" (1.1.95–97). "Laced" is generated from "lost" as a variation upon the letter, and Proteus soon reports that he has nothing from this response, which is also Speed's complaint about his reward for "bearing the letter" (1.1.115). "Fold it over and over" (1.1.105), Speed says. Those who bear the letter have nothing more than "a pinfold" (1.1.104) for their production; they are pinned and penned at once. Saying "Ay" (1.1.108) and nodding his head, Speed makes his body and speech produce the impression of the letter that he bears in his deformations; he says, that is, yes and no at once and identifies "himself" ("Ay" = I) thereby as a character set in print. The only way to receive the letter is so to "mistake" it (1.1.104). Running through these dizzying exchanges is an economics of depletion, figured in pastoral and amatory terms: Speed's empty purse and Proteus's unsatisfied desire. Speed's account of how he bears the letter suggests how desire is carried by the letter; the chain of phonemic variation, metaphorical and metonymic displacement, "*insists* on reproducing itself," as Lacan writes.[10] Yet its reproduction only produces the speaker's voice as the bearer of the letter that deforms and reforms speech along the paths of desire. Such letters reach their destination only in these divagations. The verbal play, an impediment to understanding, is, at the same time, the arrival of the letter.

Speed's punning enacts what he has done; he has carried the letter and barred its delivery, since it arrives at nothing but the endless deformation of the letter, chains of signifiers that fail to arrive at signification. The next scene of the play translates this movement, for now the letter to Julia is in Lucetta's hands, Julia's nurse "being in the way" (1.2.39) of its delivery, and receiving it in Julia's name (1.2.40) from "Sir Valentine's page" (1.2.38). The nurse both impedes the letter and delivers it, yet Julia cannot say she wants the letter, for that would be tantamount to the acknowledgment of desire, and maids are not supposed to desire. She returns the letter to Lucetta; the nurse bears the part of the page—exactly. Julia is defeated by her literalism:

> What fool is she, that knows I am a maid,
> And would not force the letter to my view!
> Since maids, in modesty, say "no" to that
> Which they would have the profferer construe "ay."
> (1.2.53–56)

Her desire is the very violence of the letter that is nothing and that produces the voice that says no and yes at once. Lucetta returns, drops the letter, agreeing it is "nothing" (1.2.71), and Julia insists that it may "lie" (1.2.76) where it has fallen. Lucetta answers that it will not lie unless misinterpreted, and Julia unleashes the violence of her desire for the letter by tearing it to shreds, commanding Lucetta to "let the papers lie" (1.2.101). The truth of her desire coincides with the violation of the letter, a palpable tearing of the words that deform speech and that name characters as the lying texts that truly speak them.

Left alone with the mangled letter, Julia reads from it only names:

> Look, here is writ "kind Julia." Unkind Julia!
> As in revenge of thy ingratitude,
> I throw thy name against the bruising stones,
> Trampling contemptuously on thy disdain.
> And here is writ "love-wounded Proteus."
> Poor wounded name!
>
> (1.2.110–15)

Her existence is in the letter; she *is* her name, and she finds herself in the written text upon which she wishes to enact more violence. Collecting each instance of Proteus's name, which love (her love) has wounded, she would "except" her "own name" (1.2.121):

> that some whirlwind bear
> Upon a ragged, fearful-hanging rock,
> And throw it thence into the raging sea!
>
> (1.2.121–23)

Yet, finally, finding Proteus's name coupled with her own, she decides to "fold them one upon another" (1.2.129), commanding them to "kiss, embrace, contend, do what you will" (1.2.130). Julia has found "each letter in the letter" (1.2.120). The letter is allowed to enact desire (kissing and contending at once), for it is desire that makes her and Proteus share the "wounded name" (1.2.115). In *The Two Gentleman of Verona,* desire is textual; Julia's scene with the letter enacts the being of character as letters named in a text.

Not surprisingly, then, when Julia decides to pursue Proteus, she takes as her "habit" (2.7.39) "such weeds / As may beseem some well-reputed page" (2.7.42–43), a costume that involves the illusory power of "a codpiece to stick pins on" (2.7.56), Speed's pinfold. In the lying truth of that textual disguise (at once a *page*[11] and a sylvan *weed*), she overhears

Proteus serenading Silvia and knows that the pastoral singer "plays false" (4.2.58). As his letter-bearer to Silvia, she first offers a letter she was not meant to send (the letter that impresses her as Proteus's love?) and then the one she was commissioned to deliver (4.4.119–21). Silvia receives and tears up the letter, but she agrees to give the picture of herself that Proteus desired. Julia takes it and looks at it as if she were looking in a mirror, finding that a change of wigs would answer "all the difference" in Proteus's love (4.4.188). A simulacrum of herself (in the page's weeds), Julia contemplates another double, the image of Silvia: "Come, shadow, come and take this shadow up, / For 'tis thy rival" (4.4.195–96). Desire, literally, is for a shadow, an image, a figure. The text that deforms, that offers violence, makes the lover into an image. (Recall that Philomela finds voice in the shuttle, the loom on which she weaves her story as an image.)

True lovers easily play false when the discourse of love is a play on the letter that comes to nothing; Julia's textual habit is hard to distinguish from the texts that Proteus pens. So, too, Silvia returns Valentine's letter as her way of accepting it. Julia accepts Proteus's letter by tearing it up; Silvia's refusal is enacted in the same gesture. Returning her picture as a response to the letter, however, is at best a knowing gesture testifying to desire as the deforming, metamorphic multiplication of images. The being of characters is their textuality. Literally figures, they are placed within an image repertoire in which they seem as interchangeable as the letters they convey (the friendship of Valentine and Proteus is, of course, rooted in their alter-ego relationship). For they *are* those letters, and similitude is their being.

Launce glosses this sliding of signifier into signifier, this literal troping:

> I'll show you the manner of it. This shoe is my father. No, this left shoe is my father. No, no, this left shoe is my mother. Nay, that cannot be so neither. Yes, it is so, it is so—it hath the worser sole. This shoe with the hole in it is my mother, and this my father. A vengeance on't! There 'tis. Now, sir, this staff is my sister, for, look you, she is as white as a lily and as small as a wand. This hat is Nan, our maid. I am the dog. No, the dog is himself, and I am the dog—O, the dog is me, and I am myself.
>
> (2.3.13–22)

Launce's identification with the dog whom he loves is his version of the lover's enfolding. The self that emerges from his attempts to literalize himself makes the statement "I am myself" another similitude, displaying the metaphorization inherent in the copula. "I am myself" divides the self, and self-ownership is as problematic here as it was when Valentine and Silvia wrangled over the propriety of the letter; for whom is it? As the play moves to its close, the violence of Proteus's attempted appropriation of Silvia is answered by Valentine's surrender: "All that was mine in Silvia I give thee" (5.4.83). "I know him as myself" (2.4.59), Valentine had affirmed, vouching for Proteus. True love plays false when all truth is trope.

As instruments of the letter, characters are impressed by its false turns.[12] No better demonstration of the point can be seen than in Valentine's wooing lesson for the Duke. Proteus has betrayed Valentine's designs on Silvia to her father, and the Duke attempts to make Valentine betray himself by asking advice on how to win a lady he would marry. Valentine does betray himself (as *true* lover) by offering the cynical instructions of an Ovidian art of love, assuring the Duke that women never mean what they say, and that "[t]hat man that hath a tongue, I say is no man, / If with his tongue he cannot win a woman" (3.1.104–5). As he describes her, the Duke's fictional lady comes to be the very image of his daughter, and Valentine's strategies turn into his plot to abduct her and is manifest in the letter he secretes beneath his cloak. The revelation in this scene is thus a demonstration of the path to/of the letter, a meeting place of lies and truth, fiction and desire. In the scene, the Duke appears to occupy the place of the Other, and what Valentine articulates for him is what he has indited: The text "To Silvia" pursues the thoughts he sends her and his desire to "lodge where senseless they are lying" (3.1.143). Such "lying" is the truth of his being *à la lettre.* Yet the Duke's patriarchal powers are similarly undermined; his fiction delivers an overwhelming desire. At the end of the play, when he relinquishes his hold on Silvia, he does so out of a textual need: "I thus subscribe," he concludes,

> Sir Valentine,
> Thou art a gentleman and well derived;
> Take thou thy Silvia, for thou hast deserved her.
> (5.4.146–48)

The patriarch submits to the power that writes him; the path of the letter (desire) is not mastered by any character, not even the nominal lord in the play. The derivation to which the Duke subscribes is the textual genealogy of character, also discerned when the Duke turns on Valentine to rename him "Phaeton" (3.1.153)—the *truth* of his revolt discovered in Ovid's *Metamorphoses*—for aspiring to his sunlike powers.

The Two Gentlemen of Verona opens with a scene in which Valentine and Proteus quote old saws and "a love-book" (1.1.19), which determines their positions. When Launce describes the woman he loves, he reads a "cate-log of her condition. 'Imprimis: She can fetch and carry'" (3.1.271–72). Launce's letter scene is, in this first item, dogged by the love that accompanies him and by the appetite that intrudes upon the list of sweets. (But ah, Desire still cries, give me some food.) Launce replays the scene between the Duke and Valentine. Opening by refusing to "pluck" out the heart of his mysterious love, he can barely name her: "'tis a woman, but what woman I will not tell myself" (3.1.265–66). In his scene of reading, the letter is an impediment, and yet it carries him as far as he can go, "your old vice still: mistake the word" (3.1.279).

Speed. What news, then, in your paper?
Launce. The black'st news that ever thou heard'st.
Speed. Why, man, how black?
Launce. Why, as black as ink.

(3.1.280–83)

Throughout, as we have seen, exchanges of letters carry and impede the characters: Proteus holds back a letter of Julia's from his father, claiming it comes from Valentine (1.3.55ff.); the exchange in letters there points to Valentine's ultimate offer to put Proteus in his place. Lucetta and Speed (and Julia-as-page) impede and deliver letters; the Duke's unveiling of Valentine puts him in a similar position, to which he finally subscribes. Launce's unseen love is as black as ink; what we see in the play is similarly indited.

When Proteus arrives at the Duke's court, Valentine begs Silvia to treat him as himself. Alone, Proteus discovers himself in Valentine's place:

Even as one heat another heat expels,
Or as one nail by strength drives out another,
So the remembrance of my former love
Is by a newer object quite forgotten.

(2.4.189–92)

These lines describe the making of character as an act of violence and violation; interiority here involves the effacement of memory and its replacement with oblivion. Yet, as we have seen, internality is itself an inscription, a letter "To Silvia." "This weak impress of love is as a figure" (3.2.6), the Duke counsels Thurio. Proteus's interiority has been invaded with a figure too: "'Tis but her picture I have yet beheld, / And that hath dazzled my reason's light" (2.4.206–7). Silvia *is* the picture he has seen. And what she replaces is equally an image: "She is fair, and so is Julia that I love" (2.4.196). "Read over Julia's heart" (5.4.46), Silvia urges Proteus; later in the scene, Julia reveals her "habit" (5.4.105), the "immodest raiment" (5.4.107) that she inhabits, the page as "a disguise of love" (5.4.108). That text enfolds characters and gives them voice. Bearers of the letter, characters by themselves and in relation to others—in relation to the deformation they undergo that makes self-identity itself an otherness, wrapped in similitude—are *impressed* with the letter. Proteus subscribes to what the Duke tells Thurio:

> [M]y love is thawed,
> Which, like a waxen image 'gainst a fire,
> Bears no impression of the thing it was.
> (2.4.197–99)

The love he calls his is/was Julia herself and her image inscribed on the waxen tablet of his memory. "The thing it was," he says, is "like a waxen image." Its *being* is representation, the image of an image. It is within such existence that characters speak. "But to inscribe it [the subject], it is necessary to define it in a circle, what I call the otherness, of the sphere of language. All that is language is lent from this otherness and this is why the subject is always a fading thing that runs under the chain of signifiers."[13] "How like a dream is this I see and hear" (5.4.26): Such is the scene in the forest when the letter comes to its destination and characters are finally inscribed.

What is a letter? Lacan's definition: "By 'letter' I designate that material support that concrete discourse borrows from language,"[14] by which he indicates that actual speech partakes of the unconscious, that the subject does not own language but inhabits it (to be displaced), that speaking is inevitably metaphoric and metonymic, that *being*-in-language always is stamped and inscribed within a *lack*-in-being. What is a letter? Angel Day's *The English Secretorie* (1586), the first English example of a kind of manual that has a history stretching back to antiquity, offers this opening definition: "A Letter therefore is that wherein is expreslye conveied in writing, the intent and meaning of one man, immediately to passe and be directed to another, and for the certaine respects thereof, is termed the messenger and familiar speeche of the absent" (1).[15] The definition is, apparently, anything but Lacanian: Writing transcribes speech; it arrives transparently at its receiver; it conveys meaning and intention. Yet there are some hesitations even in the definition; is the letter *entirely* conveyed, or does "letter" mean only what is conveyed? Is that why in "certaine respects" it is a messenger (because in "certaine respects" it is not—for example, literally)? Is the "one man" who writes everyman, that is, one whose meanings are entirely public? Or is "familiar speech" a sign of privacy? And *who,* exactly, is absent in this exchange: When a letter transcribes intention, does it indite absent meaning? These questions, in fact, engage Day's definition precisely because his manual of form letters for various occasions continually has to face the discrepancies between formula letters and particular instances. "Their diversities are sundry" (2), Day admits. And, when he turns to the writing of love letters, the commonplace definition falls into question:

> And now the last of all these devisions yet unspoken of, is *Amatorie,* whereof because the humors of all sortes, therewith being possessed are so infinite, and so great an uncertaintie, as perchaunce even in the very writing of his letter, the lover him selfe is sometimes scarce certaine of his owne conceipts, the lesse must of necessity be the precepts of the same directions. (232)

Love letters may inscribe thoughts, but the thoughts arise in their writing, and intention and meaning are both infinite and uncertain. Lover's discourse is self-alienated, the inditing of an absent self.

Speed complains to Proteus that he could "perceive nothing at all from her" when he "brought your mind" (1.1.130, 132), his letter. Julia muses, "I would I knew his mind," and Lucetta responds, "Peruse this paper, madam" (1.2.33–34). The paper that *is* the mind is the mind, quite literally; witness Proteus's speech on the violence of his penetration by the image, or Valentine's woodland solicitations of the letter inscribed on his heart. Such letters are like those that appear in dreams: They speak those who speak. Letters, after all, are, literally, characters:

> Counsel, Lucetta; gentle girl, assist me;
> And ev'n in kind love I do conjure thee,
> Who art the table wherein all my thoughts
> Are visibly charactered and engraved,

To lesson me and tell me some good mean
How, with my honor, I may undertake
A journey to my loving Proteus.

(2.7.1–7)

Lucetta *is,* in this formulation, a writing table on which Julia writes. It is her character to be a letter, to bear the letter, and to return what is inscribed as a lesson. Lucetta attempts to impede Julia's desire, reading moral lessons in the journey, but eventually she falls in with her plans to be a page. Julia's "journey to my loving Proteus" takes place in disguise and ends, as all journeys do in *The Two Gentlemen of Verona,* in the forest, the place that tropes the textual *being* of characters, a final turn to the metamorphoses, displacements, and replacements that mark their paths. Throughout, theirs is the voice of the shuttle; they exist as words and images woven in a tapestry like Philomela's. *Silva* names the trope that is their being.

Although the characters of *The Two Gentlemen of Verona* have frequently been accused of being wooden, the argument here is that their "woodenness" (literally) is the most transparent indication of the genealogy of the Shakespearean character.[16] The troping of the *silva* tradition of pastoral and the allusions to Ovid, and particularly to Philomela, that generate the play are not solely its property, however. These materials come together in another Shakespearean text, the contemporary *Titus Andronicus,* a play (as some recent criticism has emphasized)[17] that repeatedly stages its literariness. Marcus, for example, discovers Lavinia, *"her hands cut off, and her tongue cut out, and ravished"* (2.4, stage direction), and he records her textual source:

Fair Philomel, why she but lost her tongue,
And in a tedious sampler sewed her mind:
But, lovely niece, that mean is cut from thee;
A craftier Tereus, cousin, hast thou met,
And he hath cut those pretty fingers off
That could have better sewed than Philomel.

(2.4.38–43)

Although Lavinia appears to be "cut . . . off" from the disseminative sewing of mind into text, the lines that Marcus recites implant her textually; she is a citation. And her body is a text. Her lopped arms are "two branches" (2.4.18), and her severed hands, "aspen leaves" (2.4.45); retrospectively, Marcus provides a genealogy for those hands, imagining them strumming a lute accompanying the orphic song of her now-severed tongue. Lavinia's history is fetched from Ovid's *Metamorphoses.* Insistently, her broken body bears the textual imprint of a violated florilegium. Marcus takes Lavinia off to Titus, to "make thy father blind" (2.4.52). Titus, however, commands that she be seen, made visible as a text: "Look on her" (3.1.110):

> Had I but seen thy picture in this plight,
> It would have madded me: what shall I do
> Now I behold thy lively body so?
> (3.1.103–5)

The answer is: Make her a picture. Titus had been discovered at the opening of the scene writing in dust (1.1.12–13); in the course of the scene, his hand is lopped off ("withered herbs as these / Are meet for plucking up" [3.1.177–78]) and, at the end of the scene, Lavinia exits with her father's dismembered hand in her mouth (3.1.282). Titus had attempted to "understand her signs" (3.1.143). With his hand in her mouth, she has become a speaking picture, and in the next scene he reads her as a "map of woe" (3.2.12) and "an alphabet" (3.2.44), counseling her to put a knife in her mouth in place of her tongue (3.2.16) or his hand. Writing as violence and violation.

Titus closes this scene by proposing to read to Lavinia: "I'll to thy closet and go read with thee / Sad stories chanced in the times of old" (3.2.82–83). A scene of reading follows, offered as a kind of therapy ("beguile thy sorrow" [4.1.35]) and in remembrance of earlier times when Lavinia read "Sweet poetry and Tully's Orator" (4.1.14). There is, however, no escaping in a text if that is where the characters are. Voiceless, Lavinia is what she once read, and in a frenzy, she indicates that there is "some book . . . that she desires to see" (4.1.31). It is, of course, "Ovid's Metamorphosis" (4.1.42), "culled" (4.1.44) from the "library" (4.1.34) transported on stage:

> Soft; so busily she turns the leaves!
> Help her: what would she find? Lavinia, shall I read?
> This is the tragic tale of Philomel

And treats of Tereus' treason and his rape;
And rape, I fear, was root of thine annoy.
(4.1.45–49)

Turning "leaves," taking "root": the silvan text in which Lavinia is found. "Note how she quotes the leaves" (4.1.50). How? Marcus takes a stick in his mouth and writes; Lavinia imitates, inscribing rape (4.1.78). The scene of reading had virtually reenacted the rape[18] (for the character seizes the book that seizes her), and writing is its violent perpetuation. Titus wishes to make Lavinia's text an unchanging monument—

I will go get a leaf of brass,
And with a gad of steel will write these words,
And lay it by: the angry northern wind
Will blow these sands like Sibyl's leaves abroad,
And where's our lesson then?
(4.1.102–6)

—but the answer to his question is that the dissemination of the text cannot be halted. Lavinia's rapists are branded, "deciphered . . . marked with rape" (4.2.8–9), and Titus spends much of the rest of the play madly reading, dispatching texts as missiles, and ultimately reenacting the Ovidian text, serving up Lavinia's rapists in a stew and then murdering his daughter as a further citational act, "a pattern, precedent, and lively warrant / For me" (5.3.44–45). He is enabled to act by the warrant that arrests Lavinia. Life, in these texts, is lived *à la lettre.*

Whatever the scene, it is always textualized.

The forest walks are wide and spacious,
And many unfrequented plots there are,
Fitted by kind for rape and villainy.
(2.1.114–16)

So Aaron describes the place where Lavinia meets Philomela's fate. The "kind" of its "unfrequented plots" names a generic locale, the sylvan source of the punning leaves and branches that the dismembered characters become, replanted thereby in that (in)hospitable soil. This empty ("unfrequented") place is a virtual echo chamber, Virgilian as much as Ovidian. In the scene in which Tamora's sons pursue Lavinia, the queen hunts deer and the woods echo (2.2.6); this, along with an allusion to the meeting of Dido and Aeneas (2.3.22), is one of a number of references to the *Aeneid* in the play. Lavinia's scene of reading recalls a Virgilian scene, too: "I have read that Hecuba of Troy / Ran mad for sorrow" (4.1.20–21):

> See, see!
> Ay, such a place there is where we did hunt
> (O had we never, never hunted there!)
> Patterned by that the poet here describes,
> By nature made for murders and for rapes.
> (4.1.54–58)

The "place" "by nature made" is made by "the poet," whose patterns "patterned" nature. What we are to "see" is that the place where characters are has been written already and that their being is quotation, whether they voice texts or, silently ravished, embody them. Characters in *Titus Andronicus* write who they are. The "plot" that determines their character is that "place" "made for murders and for rapes"—the place of the text. Writing invades being, violating any possibility that characters have their own being or speak in their own voices. The "integrity" of a character, from this perspective, is coincident with how fully it is impressed by the pattern (Lavinia is most *like herself* when she is most like Philomela). The pattern is not a straitjacket, however; "the forest walks are wide and spacious" (2.1.114), and the permutations of *silva* allow—demand—Ovidian metamorphoses. Character is most itself when violated by the texts that determine its instability. The characters of *Titus Andronicus* and *The Two Gentlemen of Verona* seem to inhabit other texts and to take their being from them; Lavinia and Silvia, in particular, are notable instances of the metamorphic possibilities of Philomela.

There is one more citation that should be added to this set: the example of Imogen from *Cymbeline.* It suggests, even more than the forest revery of Valentine, how fully the *internality* of character is a matter of citation; that is, it suggests how much the texts that characters inhabit inhabit them. This late play suggests, too, that the Shakespearean character of the early plays remains at the end.[19]

A few lines into act 2, scene 2 of *Cymbeline,* Imogen, weary of reading, commands her servant to "fold down the leaf where I have left" (2.2.4); close to the end of the scene, Iachimo picks up the book:

> She hath been reading late
> The tale of Tereus. Here the leaf's turned down
> Where Philomel gave up.
>
> (2.2.44–46)

The scene that occurs on stage takes place within the folds of this leaf, a rape that is, at once, a scene of reading and writing. The closing of the book and Imogen's subsequent prayer for protection from "the tempters of the night" (2.2.9) is answered immediately by the opening of the trunk and Iachimo's emergence from it. Imogen is saved from literal ravishment by the insistent figuration of the scene, which, like all figuration, preserves the literal precisely by ravishing it. Iachimo's trunk is a double of the book, and at the end of the scene he returns "to th' trunk again" to "shut the spring of it" (2.2.47); but the trunk is also his body, from which he emerges all eyes (Imogen shuts the book because her "eyes are weak" [2.2.3]); and the trunk is *her* body. He has "picked the lock and ta'en / The treasure of her honor" (2.2.41–42), has gazed on "rubies unparagoned" (2.2.17). The uncanniness of this scene lies in its embodiment of a dream that is both Imogen's and Iachimo's, a dream that realizes what has been written and read. "To write and read / Be henceforth treacherous!" (4.2.316–17), Imogen exclaims, looking at another "trunk" (4.2.353) later in the play.

"The crickets sing" (2.2.11), Iachimo begins, an allusion, perhaps, to the Phaedran fable of the origin of song;[20] he glosses his actions with Ovid's *Fasti* (and the earlier Shakespearean rewritings of it): "Our Tarquin thus / Did softly press the rushes" (2.2.12–13). Iachimo proceeds "to note the chamber" (2.2.24). But the space in which he moves is one of metamorphic textualization. Seeing himself in the guise of the texts he cites, he sees Imogen as Cytherea; the taper she has left burning are her eyes beneath the shut lids (hence, the scene takes place there), and the lids themselves are "windows, white and azure-laced / With blue of heaven's own tinct" (2.2.22–23). The chamber thus is—by metaphorical condensation, metonymic displacement—within Imogen, as she is within it. Iachimo notes,

> there the window; such
> Th'adornment of her bed; the arras, figures,
> Why, such and such.
>
> (2.2.25–27)

These empty "figures" are supplied by the troping turn of the scene; Imogen lies in an Ovidian chamber; these are the pictures Iachimo sees, "the contents o' th' story" (2.2.27) wherever he turns.[21]

"I will write all down" (2.2.24); Iachimo's inscription treats Imogen's body as a text. Like Launce, like the sonneteer or writer of the blazon, he tallies the parts of the body, lips and eyes, "some natural notes about her body" (2.2.28) "t'enrich mine inventory" (2.2.30). The book he writes is a treasure chest, another trunk of jewels, materialized in the bracelet he takes from her wrist, "slippery as the Gordian knot was hard" (2.2.34). Ravishment is displaced in this token that "witness[es] outwardly . . . as the conscience does within" (2.2.35–36). Lying in a simulacrum of death, Imogen's body is given its witness in this part that stands for all, ravished from her to be her. She is made into "a monument" (2.2.32) in this figuration, given the form of textual permanence. Yet her remains are also ravished, dispersed in similitude:

> On her left breast
> A mole cinque-spotted, like the crimson drops
> I' th' bottom of a cowslip.
>
> (2.2.37–39)

There is no way to see what she is without seeing what she is like; it needs an inevitable florilegium, an implicit Ovidian metamorphosis (whose blood became those crimson drops?). "Here's a voucher / Stronger than ever law could make" (2.2.39–40). Iachimo subscribes (and writes) a text whose very materiality lies in figuration and whose strength is the violation of the difference between inside and outside, between body and word. Like Julia, he folds the letter upon the letter.

And it folds upon himself. "Why should I write this down that's riveted, / Screwed to my memory?" (2.2.43–44). Before the trunk snaps shut, before he turns to the turned-down page, the spring of his mind recoils upon itself in a turn of the screw. Attempting to penetrate Imogen (to get beneath her veiled eyelids), he has been penetrated, written, as riveted as Proteus is by the picture of Silvia that hammers out his memory. There is no need for the supplement of a text if one's inner being is a text, if one's outer existence is in a text, if one, that is, has been supplemented by a text that already claims one's existence.

At the end of *Cymbeline,* "the letter of the oracle" (5.5.449) tells all. It gives the "apt construction of thy name" (5.5.443) in a genealogical tree:

> The lofty cedar, royal Cymbeline,
> Personates thee, and thy lopped branches point
> Thy two sons forth.
>
> (5.5.452–54)

"Hang there like fruit, my soul, / Till the tree die!" (5.5.263–64): So Posthumous names his wife and their relationship. The oracle rewrites her name as "the piece of tender air" (5.5.445). Imogen's "soul" is the "air" she ventriloquizes, the text that speaks in her voice, or in the silence in which she is raped and, like Philomela, rewoven in the text. "The dream's here still. Even when I wake it is / Without me, as within me" (4.2.306–7). "Tender air" names her (etymologically) as woman; Cymbeline calls himself "a mother" (5.5.369). All the characters have been ravished by the Otherness of the text, engendered in a *family tree* that names them as the divagations of a textual play no character can own (Cymbeline casts off his fatherhood and patriarchal power; Imogen dwindles into a wife). And, as even the scenes of reading that we have considered might well suggest, this textual dispersal makes the writer (in them and of them) a further locus of inscription. There is no Other of the Other, no securing textual play. The authority of the Shakespearean character may be named Shakespeare only as that name functions within the writing that characters the Shakespearean text.

The Inscription of Character

What's in a name? What is a character? "I will believe thou hast a mind that suits / With this thy fair and outward character," Viola tells the helpful Captain in *Twelfth Night* (1.2.50–51) as she prepares to don her disguise and he agrees to be her mute: "Be you his eunuch, and your mute I'll be" (1.2.62). The Captain's character is written in the plot he tells Viola, and her disguise figures her inscription in it, an embodiment suited to his words, and rendering him mute. Viola ascribes interiority to the Captain on the basis of his character and conceals herself in "such disguise as haply shall become / The form of my intent" (1.2.54–55). What becomes her she may become; the translation of intention into figuration describes character the way Angel Day depicts the lover's letter. "Conceal me what I am" (1.2.53), Viola asks, folding the letter; the reading of mind in the inscribed character is not the penetration of a transparency. Characters have a material opacity; they are not veils to be penetrated but surfaces to be read and reread. These lines between Viola and the captain begin with a reading of character and close with the writing of one; implicit here is what is explicit elsewhere—in *King Lear,* for example, when Edmund reads a letter ascribed to Edgar. "You know the character to be your brother's?" (1.2.61), Gloucester asks. The question locates exactly the position of the Shakespearean character as a locus of inscription.

Such is the Overburian definition, "What a Character Is":

> If I must speake the Schoole-masters language I will confesse that Character comes of this infinitive moode χαρᾶξω which signifieth to ingrave, or make a deepe Impression. And for that cause, a letter (as A. B.) is called a Character.[22]

The definition, etymologically exact, accounts for the imprinting of the Shakespearean character, Proteus's impression, for example, or Lucetta's entablature. The depth of a character is a result of an inscription, what others read on the surface or, even more tellingly, what the Other that commands the deformations of desire has inscribed there. The styling of character is penned with a stylus, engraving on the wax, so that the being of character (Viola's concealed "what I am") is its becoming. Not surprisingly, in that respect, a traveler's manual published in 1633 worries that the "best wits, and purest receptacles of sound knowledge" will return from their travels "corrupted." If mind (wit) is a receptive capacity, the manual continues, then it may "easily admit any obvious impression."[23] The best minds, in this formulation, are those most open to being charactered. "By *reading* we receive what antiquitie hath left us, by writing we deliver what posteritie craves of us"; so Richard Mulcaster describes the genealogy of character in his *First Part of the Elementarie Which Entreateth Chefelie of the Right Writing of Our English Tung* (1582).[24]

When the Overburian definition proceeds to describe character, it also offers an account of "those Elements which we learne first, leaving a strong seale in our memories" (92). The mind is made by receiving letters; characters are charactered, sealed as letters are, folded. Mulcaster's *Elementarie* warns that making a child's character apt for the learning of letters must itself be the inscription of the child, a folding of the letter upon the letter.

> For if the young eies be acquainted at home with unsemelie sights: if the tender ears be more then half trained to uncomlie hearings, if the pliable minde be unwiselie writhen to a disfigured shape, if the hole conceit be unadvisedlie stained with a contrarie dy, how can that countenance be liked on in school, whose contrarie favor is most honored at home? (23)

The deep impression of tender minds, as Mulcaster describes it, is recorded on the face, a "countenance" whose "disfigured shape" may witness the violence of a tainted inscription, "stained with a contrarie dy" in the blackest ink, "writhen," miswritten.

These accounts of the elementary charactering of character could stand as an archeology for the Shakespearean character, protean in metamorphosis, disseminated in disguise, characters who discover themselves or record others as the locus of inscription and impression. This etiology of character never locates a self, or a space of interiority, that has not been inscribed beforehand. As a further example, take the character of "A Childe" in John Earle's *Micro-Cosmographie.* A child, he writes,

> [i]s a Man in a small Letter, yet the best Copie of *Adam* before hee tasted of *Eve,* or the Apple; and hee is happy whose small practice in the World can only write this Character. Hee is natures fresh picture newly drawn in Oyle, which time and much handling, dimmes and defaces. His Soule is yet a white paper unscribed with observations of the world, wherewith at length it becomes a blurr'd Note-booke.[25]

Earle's child has not yet ventured out into the world that the traveler's guide warned against; he has not, like Valentine or Proteus (or Iachimo), been abroad. The blankness of his "unscribed" soul, however, is belied by the initial impression that makes him, at first, a copy—quite literally, a retranscription—of the Edenic Adam. His being is already inscribed, for he "writes[s] this Character" simply by being, and he has been written/painted by nature to be a first image and reflection of the first man. (As much as Silvia, he is a picture.) This diminutive being (this diminution of *being*) is written as "a small Letter." Time will not enlarge this "unscribed" letter so much as it will blur and deface it. Existence-in-time is an erasure of the first impression which is itself a *copy;* existence-in-the-world is a violation, an overwriting produced by "much handling." But that first impression, we must emphasize, was itself both "unscribed" and a "Copie" of what was already written. The child that Earle describes is not born with a proper, self-owned self; rather, the child is delivered as a replica of a story inevitably retraced. That biblical inscription is one with nature's drawing in oils; the child's nature is entirely textual.

What, then, do character writers do when they write characters? Joseph Hall, in his *Characters of Virtues and Vices,* the first English character book, pauses over the question when he considers the Theophrastian text that provides his model as one "drawing out the true lineaments of every virtue and vice, so lively, that who saw the medals, might know the face: which Art they significantly termed Charactery. Their papers were so many tables; their writings, so many speaking pictures, or living images."[26] The "true lineaments" of a character are as much "lively" images as the "speaking pictures" in which they are (re)written as "living images." The "face" of the character of a virtue or vice is (as in Mulcaster's "countenance" or Earle's "picture drawne in Oyle") itself a picture, lineaments already drawn. Hall's "medal" bears with it the image of stamping, engraving, and sealing—the very material translated in Proteus's image forged on his mind or in Iachimo's treasure chest. It is only a short step from the medal to the coin and to the situation of characters as fully exchangeable: the alter egos of Proteus and Valentine, the replacement of Julia with Silvia, or the specular and dreamlike substitutions that occur in the forest in *The Two Gentlemen of Verona* or the closing scene of *Cymbeline.* Such coining of characters is not confined to the stage or to character books. John Donne, writing to Sir Edward Herbert on the day of his ordination, assures him that this metamorphosis has not removed the old stamp of their relationship, but only added a new one:

> Your power and jurisdiction, which is entirely over mee, is somewhat enlarged. For, as if I should put any other stampe upon a peece of your gold the gold were not the lesse yours, so (if there be not too much taken by mee in that comparison) by havinge, by the orders of our churche, receyved a new character, I ame not departed from your title, and possession of mee.[27]

Donne's existence, as he explains it, is like the situation Julia described for Lucetta as the tablet on which she inscribes. He is a coin stamped by the impression of others. Being, in these terms, is similitude, an origin in secondarity shared by Earle's child.

Thus, the Overburian account of character turns to the writing of characters this way: "To square out a Character by our English levell, it is a picture (reall or personall) quaintlie drawne in various collours, all of them heightned by one shadowing" (92). The "shadowing" here is like the duplication of shadows Julia sees when she looks at Silvia's picture and sees herself, or like the relationship between the "lively" "true lineaments" of Hall's virtues and vices, and the drawing of "living images" in a book of characters. It is the shadow of resemblance and representation, the rewriting that characterizes Lavinia in *Titus Andronicus*, for example. The Overburian character is, similarly, a speaking picture in the very image it bears; the language of picture making is also rhetorical (the colors of rhetoric), and the picture that results—"reall or personall"—is, as those philosophical terms suggest, whether universal or particularized, nonetheless identically shadowed; similitude, representation, overcomes difference. Such impressions—of persons or their inscriptions—are *imprese*. Alongside the devices of Shakespearean characters, their habitual disguising, might be placed this remark in the Overburian definition of "What a Character Is": "Character is also taken for an Egiptian Hierogliphicke, for an impresse, or short Embleme; in little comprehending much" (92).

The Overburian definition of character had begun with the phonetic alphabet, the "deepe Impression" of "A. B." To make such a picture speak, the definition proceeds to an originary language—to language as originally written—the "impresse" of hieroglyphic writing, "in little comprehending much," like Earle's child, "a Man in a small Letter." The letters of the alphabet here (as for Derrida) do not transcribe sound; rather, they have the material density of the hieroglyphic wedding of written word and picture, two sides of a coin.[28] A similar impulse to treat the alphabetical character as a hieroglyph can be observed when Mulcaster enthusiastically describes the "many pretie notes" (111) of the vowels; he waxes eloquent over the wonders of "E," over the fact that the letter not only designates more than one sound but can also be mute: "[T]his is to be noted of E, that it either soundeth or is silent." Mulcaster "note[s]" these "pretie notes," and his elementary instruction inscribes a writing that exceeds sound. Writing, even the ABCs, does not, in his account, transcribe sound; sound, rather, comes from writing. Voice is the effect of charactery. The duplicity of these notes is like that of those Julia hears when Proteus sings "To Silvia" ("He plays false, father" [4.2.58]) or like that of the "note" (1.2.81) Lucetta would have Julia return as she attempts to deliver the letter from Proteus: "Let's see your song. *[Takes the letter]*" (1.2.88). The Egyptian Proteus.[29]

Mulcaster lends characters their representational status when he defines them as images; in the history of writing that he offers, letters were found out as the arbitrary indicators of sound: "[W]hereby the peple that used them [i.e., letters] first, agreed with those, that found them first, that such a sound in the voice should be resembled by such a signe to the eie; and that such a signe in the eie should be so returned to the ear, as the aspectable figur of such an audible *sound*" (65). Mulcaster denies any natural relationship between sounds and letters, and the circuit from sound to letter and from letter to sound is carried entirely by figuration. Letters are "aspectable" figures, pictures that inscribe voice on their faces. Similitude is their only truth, and it is rooted not in natural resemblance but in arbitrary agreement. "What likenesse or what affinitie hath the form of anie letter in his own natur, to answer the force or sound in mans voice?" (65), Mulcaster asks, rhetorically. The "resemblance" of letters is not the same as "likenesse" or "affinitie" but, rather, a matter of "agreement." Hence, Mulcaster concludes his account of the adoption of letters with the sealing of an arbitrary agreement: "[W]hereunto theie subscribed their names, and set to their seals the daie and year, when their consent past" (65). Letters ratify letters, and the circuit of the letter has only the assurance of writing to secure it. In Mulcaster's account, letters are "in the way" as much as they are in *The Two Gentlemen of Verona.* There is no passage for articulation except through characters, notes upon notes.

When Mulcaster pauses, toward the end of his treatise, to consider the essence of language, he comes to an extraordinary conclusion: Its essence is change. This is the "secret misterie, or rather quikning spirit in everie spoken tung" (158). The life of language—its being—is generative. There is, he continues, nothing that sound can do to preserve itself, or that reason can do to attempt to align sound to word, or that custom can do to keep the arbitrary agreement of language intact. Despite all these, there is within language what Mulcaster terms its prerogative: "I cannot compare this customarie *prerogative* in speche to anie thing better, then unto those, which devise new garments, and by law ar left to the libertie of devise" (158). The law of language is its liberty to change devices, to shift costumes; the essence of language—change—is determined by the invasion of such exteriority. The "quikning spirit in everie spoken tung" is writing, the garment of style; an endless refiguration of language is written with the stylus, so that what comes to be on the tongue—in the voice as its very essence and spirit—was first on the page. Prerogative, Mulcaster concludes, is a "stirring quintessence the leader to change in a thing that is naturallie changeable . . . a great princesse in proces, and a parent to corruption, but withall intending to rase another *Phenix*" (159). As the term "prerogative" itself suggests, language is an ultimate, political power; as Mulcaster describes it, it is Queen Elizabeth herself, the culture's most potent figure for the Other. The power of language is imagined as its exception from any rule except its own rule of freedom to change. Such change is, at once, generative and degenerative, "a parent to corruption" in the very violence of imposition and change; yet the intention is to raise a phoenix, to be unique, to rise from the ashes of mutability as eternal (becoming and being at once). Yet were language so *ideally* self-identical, it would necessarily be no one's property, and since the "intention" of language has not yet reached its goal (nor will it ever, until there is no more time), its being/becoming generates a self-identity even more devastating in its exclusions, a self-identity that is also difference (the difference we have seen in the similitude of writing) and that rules out an ideal *being* of language. Language remains no one's property and thoroughly arbitrary in its exclusive powers, and these are not secured by an ideality impervious to the (de)generation of writing. All of this is caught in "rase"; transcendence is annihilation in this Derridean anticipation of the Hegelian *Aufhebung*. The *being* of language is its becoming *différance*. Mulcaster's "secret misterie": The alphabet is a hieroglyph. Writing—characters, letters—is the quintessence of language.

What is a character? The Overburian definition concludes: "It is a quicke and softe touch of many strings, all shutting up in one musicall close: It is wits descant on any plaine song" (92). This close is still an opening, a sleight of hand producing song. Note the notes. A character is a picture of a sound, the "image of the voice," as George Sandys terms Echo.[30] A note. *Much Ado about Nothing*. The writing of the Shakespearean character.

> Thy gift, thy tables, are within my brain
> Full charactered with lasting memory,
> Which shall above that idle rank remain

Beyond all date, even to eternity;
Or, at the least, so long as brain and heart
Have faculty by nature to subsist,
Till each to rased oblivion yield his part
Of thee, thy record never can be missed.
That poor retention could not so much hold,
Nor need I tallies thy dear love to score;
Therefore to give them from me was I bold,
To trust those tables that receive thee more.
To keep an adjunct to remember thee
Were to import forgetfulness in me.
(Sonnet 122)

The sonnets provide fertile ground for tracing the Shakespearean character. Sonnet 59, for example, seeks an image in an "antique book, / Since mind at first in character was done" (lines 7–8); the mind is "originally" a locus of inscription. Sonnet 108 opens asking, "What's in the brain that ink may character / Which hath not figured to thee my true spirit?" In these sonnets, as in Sonnet 122, written characters are inscribed "within my brain" and on external tablets. A search of prior (already written) texts or of the memory on which they are inscribed reveals that the beloved is already written in an image repertoire that even makes seeing the beloved an act of transcription. "Mine eye hath played the painter and hath stelled / Thy beauty's form in table of my heart," Sonnet 24 begins; the placing of the beloved in an internal inscription also alludes to the image repertoire provided by Sidney's *Astrophel and Stella.* Writing is painting when the beloved's *being* is representation and the lover's interiority is a scene of inscription.

Sonnet 122 records the multiplicity of textual inscriptions of character by tracing a path of complex and ambiguous exchanges. The first phrase, "thy gift, thy tables" is an introduction to these opacities. Has the beloved given a gift of a writing tablet, as Stephen Booth imagines?[31] Or has the lover provided an image of himself that is written on an internal writing table: the lover's mind? Is "thy gift" something being given by the beloved or being returned to him? And is that something a blank tablet or an inscribed one? And, if inscribed, written by whom? The appositional structure of "thy gift, thy tables" seems capable of supporting readings that move in two directions at once. This is the circuit of the character, the intertextual situation of the lover and the beloved, and their circulation within the exchange structure of the gift. There are no easy answers to the questions of difference (between internal and external tablets, between lover and beloved) raised. "Thy," the very mark of propriety and ownership, slides in these exchanges. The opacity of Sonnet 122 doubles the obscurity of the texts it treats, since the poem serves not merely to represent them but also to be the writing it describes. Sonnet 122 is not, however, transparently the text in the sonnet that the lover has been emboldened "to give" (line 11). That gift, after all, may be a return of another's text, the one that the beloved has given. What further complicates the situation, as Booth suggests, is that although the same tablet may be returned by the lover, it may (or may not) be written on, just as, at first, it may or may not have been inscribed. If, at first, "thy gift" is either as "full charactered" (line 2) as the internal tablets (and thus superfluous) or blank (as opposed to the internal tablets), at the end what is given is capable of "poor retention" (line 9), which may mean that it is marked (but fails to match the beloved) but may also mean that it is not yet scored. And, it must also be added, the return of the gift (whether it is the same or another tablet, a blank one or one written upon) may also be the rejection of the gift, its "poor retention" compared invidiously with "full" charactering. In any event, Sonnet 122 describes a text that calls into question sameness and difference and that doubles the question in the relationship of the poem to the text it describes. The abundance of possible meanings in the poem is a version of its sustaining deficiency, the impoverishment of character-as-mark that it records twice over.

Sonnet 122 appears to depend upon the familiar (i.e., Platonic) contrasts between internal and external writing and to attempt to preserve interiority from the violence of the letter. These are, however, appearances. Interiority is marked from the beginning by the violent intrusion of the letter, as the first two lines of the poem suggest, however they are read. Interiority, described in the opening quatrain as that which *remains* "beyond all date, even to eternity" (line 4), is a monumental inscription of the sort that appears throughout the sonnets to record *them* as what remains: "Not marble nor the gilded monuments / Of princes shall outlive this pow'rful rime" (Sonnet 55, lines 1–2). The inviolability of the mind to the external pressure of the stylus is denied simply by describing the mind as charactered, incised. The "idle rank" (line 3) as easily suggests the host of texts that this celebration (inscribed in the mind) will supplant as it does the idle thoughts that vanish without a trace. It is this throng (the antique books of Sonnet 59) that the lover has perused, seeking his inner state. The preservation of the beloved's image in this "full" text both supplants and renews those already written. "I always write of you" the lover says in Sonnet 76 (line 9), and thereby "keep invention in a noted weed" (line 6). "Of": the sympathetic dative of the transmission of the letter, from/to; the "noted weed": the device, the garment of style that produces the voice in writing. There is nothing to say that does not make "antiquity for aye his page" (Sonnet 108, line 12). Whose page? Who is "I"? The interior/eternal text of Sonnet 122 is a reiteration with a difference of all that has been written already; the mind is a place prepared beforehand to receive the impression of the character of the beloved.

Eternity is retraced and retracted in the second quatrain of Sonnet 122 ("Or, at the least . . ."); the status of memory and texts as what *remain* replaces the eternal monument: temporality, and with it the present/presence of the text/mind (of "nature," in short), as erosion, erasure, forgetfulness. "Rased oblivion" is the apparent end (Hegelian telos) of what remains. That plot, rather than the account leading to full characters and "lasting memory," is substituted as a second thought ("at the least") that would seem to run concurrently with the first thought. Taken together, the first eight lines of the poem might be said to write and unwrite themselves and yet to write all the while, tracing in their movement the reversibility of "thy gift, thy tables." Time enters in line 5, but only to thematize what has come before. The text described, which "never can be missed" and which will one day be entirely effaced, is, at the same time, the movement of this text. Temporality here, as in Earle's character pad, is a layering of inscription that is also a defacement; Sonnet 122 is, in Mulcaster's terms, a quintessential text of prerogative. "Thy record" separates from what it records and seems almost to have in its present what it will not have in its retention. Memory and forgetfulness here are mutually constitutive—a generative corruption—as they are in the forge of Proteus's mind receiving the impression of Silvia's picture. It seems true that both the "record" and the erasure inscribe what "never can be missed."

Hence "that poor retention" (line 9) would appear to refer to *all* inscriptions, whether external or internal, to the tablet presented to or by the lover and to the image of the beloved (the image that he *is* and will, in time, not be, or the image in the mind of the lover). "Poor retention could not so much hold" (line 9), and what is "full charactered" is simultaneously reviewed as a set of incomplete and unnecessary "tallies," markers that score (multiply and cut) and yet do not strike deeply enough to be retained. Hence *they* are given; they are the characters of Sonnet 122. The gift returned is a pad whose space of inscription is at the same time a space of erasure. Whether a pad full of tallies is rejected, or whether filling a pad with tallies is rejected, both possibilities—of the written pad and the blank pad—are apparently the same scene of inscription and erosion. In this textual economy, the pad, blank or charactered, appears to be compared to "those tables" retained and receiving "more" even as the gift is returned (line 12). Yet what renders "those tables" impervious to "poor retention"? If they always "receive thee more" can they be "full charactered"? Booth denies this appositional structure of similitude and suggests that "those tables" are the same as the "tables" of line 1, returned as blanks so that they can be inscribed to "receive thee more." This is a possible reading, certainly; but either way, "more" suggests an excess on the margin of giving and receiving. We have remarked it tracing the return of the letter that Valentine and Silvia enact. The circuit of writing and the circuit of desire reach a destination in Sonnet 122, a destination that does not escape recirculation. Has the gift been returned to incite the beloved's return? Has he received what the lover wrote—to himself? Has he *emptied* himself to receive more? Or is he giving and yet remaining "full charactered"? These questions go around in circles.

And the concluding couplet is a model of such circularity, for it posits an identification of remembering and forgetting: "To keep an adjunct to remember thee / Were to import forgetfulness in me" (lines 13–14). The adjunct is the mark/character, the writing tablet. To retain the adjunct means that the internal tablet is not full, that there is room there for a further inscription. But inscription, so described, is also the erasing of the (internal) tablet. And hence, the refusal of the adjunct *for the sake of* the integrity of the fully inscribed internal writing pad means that it has been written on and is thereby full—it has been written on, however, by the adjunct that it refuses. Moreover, the adjunct of remembrance produces oblivion. And the oblivion it produces would be imported forgetfulness, not the intrinsic emptiness of the tabula rasa that is the locus of the full charactering of the internal writing tablet, the mind. The protestation of integrity in these lines summons up the image of Earle's innocent child with his tabula rasa as yet unwritten on. Yet its emptiness is coincident with fullness, as "rasing" a Phoenix is both destroying and creating a new one. Refusing the supplement of the adjunct, the beloved claims to be fully supplied. No need for the letter if he has the letter already written within. Even if one cannot tell whether this letter (adjunct) is accepted or rejected, received or returned, one can nonetheless say with Lacan that this letter reaches its destination by collapsing sender and receiver, self and other, inside and outside in the play of the signifier, the eroding impressions of supplementary letters.

The scene described in Sonnet 122 cannot fail to recall Sigmund Freud's comparison of the mind to a writing tablet, or Derrida's reading of that text.[32] Seeking an image that would explain the relationships between consciousness (perception) and the unconscious, and the mechanisms (e.g., delay, deferral, repression) that permitted both the retention and effacement of events (or, rather, of the *images* of events perceived or remembered), Freud recalled a child's toy, the "mystic writing pad," composed of a transparent sheet on which one writes and a wax layer beneath, which stores the impression. When the writing surface is lifted, the marks vanish; they are retained, however, on the wax below. These two surfaces represented, for Freud, the systems of consciousness and the unconscious; their contact and separation explained the relationship of memory and forgetting and their coincidence (what is in the memory is no longer conscious; bringing memory to consciousness is also the obliteration of memory). The "depth" of the mind, in this image, is illusory; depth is also a surface marked by repeated incisions. The more the wax is marked, the less easily can the marks be retrieved or deciphered; that is, more memory, more forgetfulness. It is this simultaneity of erasure/obliteration and retention that the Shakespearean character scores; it is also what Derrida remarks: "Traces thus produce the space of their inscription only by acceding to the period of their erasure. From the beginning, in the 'present' of their first impression, they are constituted by the double force of repetition and erasure, legibility and illegibility." The double layering of the mind—of leaf upon leaf—allows for surfaces capable of "poor retention," for a surface that is always ready to receive (and is thus blank) and that transfers the marks to another surface that retains *and effaces* the marks scored—incised multiply—upon it.

Freud's pad is (for Derrida) a reinscription of a Western tradition that goes back to Plato at least. In the *Theaetetus,* for the sake of argument, Socrates invites us to "imagine . . . that our minds contain a block of wax. . . . Let us call it the gift of the Muses' mother, Memory, and say that whenever we wish to remember something we see or hear or conceive in our own minds, we hold this wax under the perceptions or ideas and imprint them on it as we might stamp the impression of a seal-ring" (191d).[33] In "Plato's Pharmacy" or "The Double Session," Derrida's task involves a reading of the Platonic scene of writing within the Freudian reinscription. For Freud's image of the mystic pad aims at a solution of critical questions about the relationship between its surfaces, a solution that does not reinscribe Platonic metaphysics. As Derrida reads Freud's mystic pad, the fold of these surfaces establishes the "present" and "presence" of the mind within the deferral and differentiation of *différance.* The layers are both in contact and separate; to receive the impression of a mark, one must re-mark. "[W]e are written only as we write," Derrida continues. The "we" he means he terms the subject, the I that is a function of (re)inscription: "The 'subject' of writing does not exist if we mean by that some sovereign solitude of the author. The subject of writing is a *system* of relations between strata: the Mystic Pad, the psyche, society, the world."

Derrida extends the mystic pad to the spacing that constitutes the subject in a field of folds: the echoing woods of *silvae* traced on the Shakespearean character. That space, the fold that joins and separates, Lacan marks with a bar, literalizing the algorithmic graph of the linguistic sign relating signifier and signified and, at the same time, separating them: S/s. The subject, for Lacan, "is" on the bar; what linguistics traditionally designates as the "signified" is, for Lacan (and Derrida), another signifier; hence, movement on the bar is a (re)inscription in a chain of signifiers that Lacan's subject (like Derrida's "sovereign . . . author") cannot master. The Other, in Lacan's system, is that "'absolute Master";[34] Derrida understands that designation to imply a metaphysical securing in an absolute lack. Thus, Lacan defines the Other as "the beyond in which the recognition of desire is bound up with the desire for recognition,"[35] a desire that is always frustrated. And he describes "the subjection of the subject to the signifier" as occurring "in the circuit that goes from s(O) to O and back from O to s(O)," where "O" is the Other and "s" the subject. "It is from the Other that the subject receives even the message that he emits."[36] Lacan's metaphysical leanings are perhaps as inevitable as those Derrida admits to in his deconstructive project,[37] however, and it is worth sidestepping the polemics to notice that the Lacanian chain of recirculation can be compared to Derridean reinscription.

On the Shakespearean scene of writing, characters re-mark each other and are themselves re-marked, and their relationships seem to be inscribed within a system that is not their own. The argument of this essay, put simply, is this: From its earliest instances *(Titus Andronicus, The Two Gentlemen of Verona)* to late examples *(Cymbeline),* the inscription of the Shakespearean character throws into question any identification of the *system* with a "sovereign . . . author." Lacan's "absolute Master" has many names; the Other is also the phallus, the *mother's* phallus, the "name of the Father." Derrida, too, finally locates Freud's scene of writing as a primal scene.[38] At the end of *The Two Gentlemen of Verona,* we recall, Silvia's father himself "subscribes"; Cymbeline calls himself a "mother." What would secure these testaments to the writing of the patriarch in a discourse of an Other who would not also be reinscribed? How could the chain end at "Shakespeare"? What's in a name?

No Shakespearean text is more regularly cited to exemplify the supposed interiority of the Shakespearean character than *Hamlet,* while the textual history of the play (the various quarto versions, the length of the folio text) and the thematizing of theatricality within the play are, with equal regularity, taken to show the author's investment within this text. It seems profitable, therefore, to close this essay on the Shakespearean character with a brief review of this central text. Citation, rather than argument, will, at the least, suggest that *Hamlet* has a place within the echoing of *silvae.*

Polonius speaks to Laertes, offering the traveler advice: "[T]hese few precepts in thy memory / Look thou character" (1.3.58–59). Hamlet, as the play opens, is also remembering ("Must I remember?" [1.2.143]) and suiting his being to his show: "[T]hese indeed seem" (1.2.83). His impression is the image within his "mind's eye" (1.2.185). The father who writes within Hamlet then puts in his appearance and offers his traveler's advice. His word is "remember me":

Remember thee?
Ay, thou poor ghost, while memory holds a seat

In this distracted globe. Remember thee?
Yea, from the table of my memory
I'll wipe away all trivial fond records,
All saws of books, all forms, all pressures past
That youth and observation copied there,
And thy commandment all alone shall live
Within the book and volume of my brain,
Unmixed with baser matter. Yes, by heaven!
O most pernicious woman!
O villain, villain, smiling, damned villain.
My tables—meet it is I set it down
That one may smile, and smile, and be a villain.
At least I am sure it may be so in Denmark.
So, uncle, there you are. Now to my word:
It is "Adieu, adieu, remember me."

(1.5.95–111)

Hamlet's memory is a theater, the "distracted globe," and a scene for the inscription of character. Remembering is at the same time erasing "all pressures past." For the memory to be supplemented, it must also be supplanted. The mind is a locus of *copia;* it is a book. There is, in Hamlet's mind, a scene of writing, and it is the one staged with the ghost in this scene of inscription. Hamlet ends this speech by writing what has been scored on his mind: "[M]y tables—meet it is I set it down." Has he taken out a writing tablet? Or is he still writing on his mind? Would there be a difference? What he writes is the ghost's plot, "pernicious woman," "damned villain." The circuit of writing—from internal to (possibly) external writing—passes through the ghost's words and to them. Hamlet's word at the end—"my word"—is a quotation. He voices his father's text.

The scene of impression is not, of course, quite this straightforward; it is a circuit. The text in the center of Hamlet's speech—"pernicious woman," "damned villain"—is a scene of desire as old as the scene in the garden. Hamlet, who is "too much in the sun" (1.2.67), is divided by the doubling of his "own" text and the ghost's. Hamlet's being is the fold in that single cloth, and it is first manifest in his initial utterances, puns on "kin"/"kind" and "son"/"sun" that make his voice articulate the spacing of writing. The scene with the ghost is a reinscription of what is already inscribed, and it is horrific precisely because it fulfills Hamlet's desire: He is commanded to be in his father's place and yet to leave the woman alone. The ghost's words are tantamount to the recognition of the Other that is the very end of desire; the ghost speaks as the name of the father (the father's law is the law of the dead father), himself constrained by a text that he cannot entirely appropriate:

> But that I am forbid
> To tell the secrets of my prison house
> I could a tale unfold.
>
> (1.5.13–15)

Hamlet is not torn between his "own" desire and the paternal command but, rather, divided within the paternal that writes his desire and in which it is written. Hamlet's divided identity—and with it his delays and deferrals, his resistance to the ghostly plot, his inability to act, and his compulsions to repeat—are the result of his *identification* with his father's words. It is identification that splits Hamlet. The depth of his interiority is his foldedness within a text that enfolds him and that cannot be unfolded. "So, uncle, there you are" (1.5.110). Thus Hamlet ends the scene of writing, and his reiteration of his father's word as his own follows that inscription.

Hamlet's response to the ghost is to write, and through much of the play that is his activity. It is a writing that takes place within the ghostly text. "Who calls me villain?" (2.2.557), he asks, ascribing to himself the ghost's word for his uncle. When Hamlet stages the ghost's script of the murder in the garden, he assigns himself the same part: "This is one Lucianus, nephew to the king" (3.2.235), he identifies the villain. The entirely written world of the play makes it a space of endless *copia,* entirely simulacral. "Look here upon this picture, and on this" (3.4.54); Hamlet draws Gertrude's eyes to the pictures of the two brothers, but he cannot make her see the nothing manifest in her closet when the ghost reappears. Hamlet demands that she see difference while he is commanded by spectral identification, the text that has him ask, "How stand I then, / That have a father killed, a mother stained" (4.4.56–57), where "I" stands in the active/passive position of having being in writing. Being divided by nonbeing: Hamlet's great question, entirely apt for those whose "kind" is textual. Hamlet saves his life by writing. Shipped to die, his father provides:

> How was this sealed?
> Why, even in that was heaven ordinant.
> I had my father's signet in my purse,
> . . .
> Folded the writ up in the form of th'other,
> Subscribed it, gave 't th'impression.
>
> (5.2.47–49, 51–52)

Hamlet writes his (father's) name with the signet/signature that impresses him. Sealed in that text, he can say, "Let be" (5.2.212). Let, that is, stop/permit. Finally, he can entirely voice his father's text, speak as a ghost. "I am dead" (5.2.322, 327), he reiterates, the impossible sentence that inscribes voice within the iterability of writing.[39] Like the ghost, Hamlet cannot tell his story, and he passes it on to be told, a text to be reenacted. "The rest is silence" (5.2.347). Hamlet's remains.

Silvia's silence. Textually inscribed. Engraved as a statue. Hermione. Within the father's text. Love and be silent. Cordelia.

> I could a tale unfold
> . . .
> But this eternal blazon must not be.
>
> (1.5.15, 21)

The text spoken in the name of the father.

> Had I but time—as this fell sergeant, Death,
> Is strict in his arrest—O, I could tell you—
> But let it be.
>
> (5.2.325–27)

The text spoken in the name of the son.

Character: inscribed/effaced. Signed, sealed, and delivered. The letter's destination, as what remains. Arrested/permitted—"let it be"—by death. The text spoken in the name of the ghost of the sovereign author.

Making Sense

For some time now, Richard Levin has been the self-appointed protector of old plays from new readings, and "Unthinkable Thoughts in the New Historicizing of English Renaissance Drama" along with a recent essay in *PMLA,*[1] continues the assault. Homogenizing various new historical practitioners and their practices, Levin charges them with a failure to "make sense." "I would have invoked common sense," he continues, "but most of them regard it as another 'humanist' myth" (443). The *Oxford English Dictionary (OED),* however, hardly a repository of Marxist materialism, records the historic specificity of the concept Levin would invoke. For, despite his assertions, it is not the case that people have always had the same ideas, with their vocabularies simply lagging behind. And even words that appear lexically identical change their meanings. For example, "common sense," in Aristotle, and in Elizabethan physiology and psychology, is literally located in a particular part of the mind; the *OED* cites Robert Burton's *Anatomy of Melancholy* as an example: "Inner senses are three in number, so called because they be within the brainpan, as common sense, phantasy, memory." A more general notion of common sense based in this psychobiology survived it, and the term came to have philosophic force in the eighteenth century. It now underlies the ordinary use of the term to mean "good sound practical sense," a usage that is hardly univocal or unproblematic, as might be inferred from William Empson's brilliant discussions of "sense" in *The Structure of Complex Words,* or the argument of Stanley Fish's "Normal Circumstances, Literal Language, Direct Speech Acts, the Ordinary, the Everyday, the Obvious, What Goes without Saying, and Other Special Cases."[2]

Levin's "sense" cannot be separated from the tail end of an empiricist psychophilosophy that is idealistic, too, in its assumption that the mind never changes. His attempt to prove the unthinkable thinkable founders in the thoughtlessness (the common sense) that thinking has always thought the same. Implicitly, in his argument, there could be no history of philosophy; equally implicit is an equation of the mind with consciousness, of the self with the ego. The thinking denied by such assumptions depends upon "common sense," and thus no sooner has Levin denied himself the term than it insists upon itself: "Our common experience" is glossed with a parenthetical definition "(or common sense)" (443). The term remains unexamined and necessarily so (it is the very term for that which does not *need* to be thought about). Experience is treated as a transparency, as something "we" all have and all have the same. "Without those assumptions there could be no history" (443). These assumptions—however "commonsensical"—need to be queried. For while they seem founded in an egalitarian belief (humanist?) that all humans are the same, in fact, they depend upon massive exclusions. Their homogenizing same rules out spheres of difference that the various new historicisms seek to disclose, differences that rupture history or divide the subject. If those are unrecognizable to Levin and make no sense to him, it is because they threaten the grounds upon which he attempts to stand. But the history he invokes is a history of the same, and no history at all. In Levin's commonsensical history, common sense is a shared possession, something "we" all have and always have had. It is community property.

Levin depends upon the evidence of the senses, "the actual responses of the people of the Renaissance" (439), and these are gathered in one accepted mode of making sense: citation of evidence. Evidence, so understood, is simply that which is evident, self-evident, clear proof (in this case, that Renaissance plays produced emotional effects). "Actual responses," however, are written responses, and they must be read, not merely received as sensory data. "Shakespeare's Prologue to *Henry VIII* asks us to think that we see the characters 'as they were living' and to 'let fall a tear' for them," Levin writes and cites (439). We are to weep: A bodily response is assumed or induced; the body is being made to produce tears (Burton's body has an *organ* of common sense). And how is this response secured? By taking the actor for the character, an assumption governed by an "as": "as they were living." "As" opens a distance in the identification between the actor and the character; tears are wept for a "life" that is also seen as *not* alive. More evidence: "A couplet on the title-page of Beaumont and Fletcher's *A King and No King* predicts that readers of the play will 'weep, as if 'twere done indeed'" (439). *As if.* Such locutions appear in almost every cited instance. They reveal emotions produced *not* on the basis of identification (*not* on the basis of sameness) but within a simulative economy—one recognized in the similes.

Not that these writing effects are necessarily real effects; they are not "actual responses" but written ones, and those works aimed at a reading public have already chosen as their audience the literate portion of the populace. Whether they describe or prescribe remains in question. In short, not only are they not "actual responses," but it is by no means easy to decide whether they describe or solicit a response assumed to be common. If they induce or desire common responses, a *sensus communis* is then *produced* as an effect. These representations put themselves in question, admitting the violence of their imputations and their imaginary force, registered in similitudes whose effect is being denied. It is the work of the historicist to attempt to read the margins of difference in the citations, the ideological space opened by an "as if." Thus, as even these few comments might suggest, Levin's evidence supports the arguments he would deny. The audience made (up) in these citations is produced through difference; it is an audience divided by the simulative presentations that "'strike our sense so deep.'" The descriptions register their violence; and as they strike and divide "our sense," they also arise from the visible division between the actor and the part impersonated. "As if the personater were the man personated," Thomas Heywood writes.[3] On stage or off, all persons, then, are personated.

Is "our sense" (their "sense") "our" sense? "If these critics are to be believed, then a Renaissance woman upon waking up in the morning would not realize that she was the same person who went to sleep the night before" (459). This is an example of Levin's other mode of argument: He offers no self-evident (and unread) evidence, simply the evidence of "our" experience. No one is cited here (though the invocation of "the findings of investigators" presumably would not include psychoanalysts, since their "findings" are not empirical facts; clearly, Levin has no use for the unconscious, no notion either of its existence as a historically differentiated phenomenon). This evidence is so evident "we" need nothing more than the citation of our ordinary experience (but why a woman?) and the assurance that only some inept play (for example, one not by Shakespeare) could ever lead us to such aberrant thoughts (but whose thoughts *are* these?), thoughts no doubt caused by taking literature too seriously (plays are only plays, Levin implies; let's be sensible and not confuse them with the real evidence of our senses; let's not assume that representations have any part in the constitution of reality).

Demetrius. These things seem small and undistinguishable,
Like far-off mountains turned into clouds.
Hermia. Methinks I see these things with parted eye,
When everything seems double.
Helena. So methinks;
And I have found Demetrius like a jewel,
Mine own, and not mine own.
Demetrius. Are you sure
That we are awake? It seems to me
That yet we sleep, we dream. Do not you think
The Duke was here, and bid us follow him?
Hermia. Yea, and my father.
Helena. And Hippolyta.
Lysander. And he did bid us follow to the temple.
Demetrius. Why, then, we are awake: let's follow him,
And by the way let us recount our dreams.[4]

A scene of awakening in a play structured around sleeping and waking, a play in which it is a sign of sheer opacity to wake up and believe that one awakens into the same or as the same (witness Lysander's impassioned declarations to Helena, Demetrius's to Hermia, Hermia's serpent dream and its living realization, Titania's monstrous embrace). It is ordinary experience in this scene for mountains to metamorphose into clouds, to see double, to have and not have at once; common sense is constructed before our eyes, on the authority of the Duke and Duchess and the father. What is "by the way" in this scene can never be separated from the common path these characters follow.

What is to be seen here? What John Downes saw in Edward Kynaston's acting of women's parts "so well, especially . . . parts moving compassion and pity, that it has since been disputable . . . whether any woman that succeeded him so sensibly touch'd the audience as he"? (440). Levin sees to it that the woman is the same, morning and night; by the end of the paragraph in which she appears, she is the child secure in its identity. Downes sees a boy beneath the woman's costume, sees that he is "sensibly touch'd" in a gendered relationship of male identification. He can weep best with the woman if the woman is really a man; Kynaston succeeded only by denying the very character he played. The collusive, communal fiction that binds the lovers and secures their identity for themselves in Shakespeare's play denies the dreams (the play) that continue to structure and to fracture their identities; the communal construction of gendered identity cannot be read apart from this structuration.

Cited above are the last lines Hermia and Helena speak in the play, the one to acknowledge her father, the other to name Hippolyta. They have arrived at the end of "their" desires. At the end of the play, the only woman who will speak will be Hippolyta; if she has a "life" after marriage, it is because class privilege can overcome gender difference (in Hippolyta's case, from the start, it is suggested that as an Amazon a *different* sexuality may also be figured, one that would not be made to disappear in marriage, much as Oberon recelebrates his marriage once he has possession of the Indian boy). "Mine own, and not mine own" names a shared condition in the play, but one everywhere inflected differently, riven and recemented through class and gender hierarchies. This multiple condition is transferred to the audience in Puck's final lines, to be ratified by "our" applause.

It is an idealizing fiction to suppose, therefore, that there is such a univocal thing as "a Renaissance woman." For Levin, "a Renaissance woman" is a wife who had better wake up the same as she went to bed, ready to attend to her family and make "plans for the day" (443; shopping, perhaps?). For Downes, the best woman is a boy. And for Shakespeare? The answers multiply, because the boy actors provide one way of putting pressure on the construction of sexuality, because patriarchal fantasies are exposed and reproduced on his stage, because gender difference is also class difference (a further route of understanding between the position of boy actors and women), and because commonsensical distinctions are community constructions which are seen through (in the double sense of the phrase).

But this is not common sense and will not "make sense" to Levin, so it is time to stop. Better to close with the insidious, elementary definitions of common sense that circulate in his writing. Their bedrock is gender.

Common sense: "Babies with vaginas" are girls, are women, are woman. "Obviously they ascertained the sex of a child at birth, just as we do, and assumed like us, that it determined the child's gender throughout life" (442).

Common sense: "People then, like people today, did conceive of sexual enjoyment as gendered" (442)—that is to say, as heterosexual.

They killed homosexuals, just like we would, and thought of women as vaginas, just like we do.

Stop "making sense."

"The first example that I have selected may be idiosyncratic" (434). (But what else would a commonsensical reader expect from someone who writes about sodomy?) Marshal the evidence: They had the word, they had the concept. What concept? The word without a context (do not read the examples, just count them; readings do not count as evidence). Foils are foils are foils. Nothing ever changes. But is Brian Gibbons's hypostasization of characters as dramatic foils (in his New Arden edition of *Romeo and Juliet*)[5] really coincident with the cited usages? Do any of them imagine an inherent, unchanging character whose sole function is to serve as a contrast to the equally stable, unchanging character of some other character? This skirmish over foils brings us back not only to Levin's inability to historicize the subject (as "they prefer to call it" [436–37]); no doubt my review offended him from its very first sentence: "If the function of a standard edition is to present usual assumptions, widely shared information, and conventional interpretations, then Brian Gibbons's New Arden *Romeo and Juliet* admirably fulfills the demands."[6] It offers, in other words, common sense. It upholds literature (another one of those timeless phenomena for Levin, who is incapable of recognizing that what counts as being "for all time" depends upon the historicity of canon formation; of changes in authorial functions and powers; of the place of critics and criticism; of editors; of pedagogic sites—All these affect the institutionalization of literature, and they are by no means in the same place in the Renaissance as they are in now). For Gibbons, *Romeo and Juliet* stands as "the artifice of eternity."[7] Who could object? Just the "idiosyncratic," the Marxists, the women, the theorists—all those people who have no place in the profession, which Levin protects, of those who profess common sense.

From them old plays must be protected. So: no new readings of old plays; no readings at all. There is nothing to read, after all, it is all the same and always has been. Obvious, isn't it? Don't give it a thought.

Shakespearean Inscriptions: The Voicing of Power

> The penis is what men have and women do not; the phallus is the attribute of power which neither men nor women have.
>
> —Jane Gallop, *The Daughter's Seduction*

> Les masles et femelles sont jettez en mesme moule. [Males and females are cast in the same mold.]
>
> —Montaigne, *Sur des vers de Virgile*

I want to open this essay with some guiding presuppositions; these will not be the matter of my argument, although without them I could not make it. I depend upon the work of a number of literary historians who have investigated the nature of genre in Renaissance theory and practice. From them, I derive the principle implicit in Rosalie Colie's title, *The Resources of Kind,*[1] that generic categories in the period are liberating rather than confining and that the identification of specific limitations within any hypothetical generic type does not match the actuality of the uses of the kinds. Pure forms are a Renaissance anomaly; hybrids are the rule. And, to turn to the subject of this essay, when Shakespeare makes use of the kinds of drama, there is, as Stephen Orgel argues, a sense of genre as a matrix of refiguration, of genre allowing for the redistribution of materials; or, as Louise George Clubb demonstrates, a play, like *Hamlet,* is an anthology of generic principles playing prescriptions against each other, an investigation into the limits of genre and an extension beyond those limits.[2] At the end, Hamlet commands Horatio "to tell my story" and to Fortinbras he sends his "dying voice" (5.2.360, 367).[3] Representation continues and multiplies.

I begin by invoking the work of Colie, Orgel, and Clubb, because recently there has arisen a body of criticism that ignores such complexities of genre and that seems intent upon straitjacketing the Shakespearean text into rigidities of form and meaning. Thus, to take an example, Linda Bamber, in *Comic Women, Tragic Men: A Study of Gender and Genre in Shakespeare,*[4] sets out to argue for what her title implies, a division of genre and gender in Shakespeare that allows for little traffic between the kinds and that denies the play and energy that the critics I began with might argue characterize the multiplicity of the Shakespearean text. In such feminist criticism, Shakespeare is seen as inevitably expressing the positions of a patriarchal culture and replicating them in depictions of men who are capable of tragedy and of women who have power only in the less-exacting world of comedy. For Bamber, Shakespeare can only see men from the inside, and his women remain other, incapable of change and often little more than the projections of male fantasy, since it is impossible for a male author to inhabit a woman's mind or body.

My argument is not with feminism, however, but with the particular kinds of blindness that seem implicit in an account like Bamber's. For, surely, the rigidity that she brings to the Shakespearean text is her own; her categories do not correspond to the historical specificity of the Shakespearean text. Bamber employs a strategy analogous to a mode of historical criticism that used to find in Shakespeare support for the so-called Elizabethan world picture and commonplaces about law and order. Yet Shakespeare's inhabitation of the conceptual apparatus of his time is far more problematic than that; replication of one ideological strain is not his position. Again, for a persuasive counterstatement, I cannot possibly do more here than point to Stephen Greenblatt's masterful account of the improvisatory relationship of Shakespeare to his culture.[5] When we add the recognition that the norms of the period (let us return to genre as our example) are themselves always in play, we must acknowledge the falsity of a scheme that rigidly locates the Shakespearean text. Furthermore, it must be emphasized that Bamber assumes a male/female opposition and a notion of character that lacks historical support.[6] In this, she is not so much like the historical critics just mentioned; rather, like many another Shakespearean critic, she has assumed that an informed common sense will lead her to correct perceptions about this most universal of geniuses.

I pause unconscionably long over Bamber's work because it is in danger of being hailed as the forefront of a new approach to Shakespeare. Carolyn Heilbrun, reviewing three feminist readings of Shakespeare that preceded Bamber's, compliments them for revealing "Shakespeare's essential conservatism and phallocentrism"; she continues,

> [T]he facts are clear enough: Shakespeare, who encompassed all the world, was himself a victim of its essential restrictions upon experience for women, even as he recognized the dangers of these feminine restrictions upon men. Shakespeare did not conceal male weakness or villainy, but he did fail to recognize the possibility of female autonomy and growth.[7]

Although I would not for a moment deny that "the world" inevitably represents a limit upon perception and experience, "the world" is nonetheless a larger and more complex item than Heilbrun imagines. And in Shakespeare's time, it excluded most of the conceptual categories (e.g., autonomy and growth) that she projects upon his world from her modern, liberal vantage point. To say, at once, that it is larger and yet more exclusive than Heilbrun imagines is my attempt to register two facts at once: that the categories of the period are not our own, but that our divisions of genre and gender (to return to the theme of this essay) are not Shakespeare's either.

These are large claims, I realize, and to substantiate them properly would take more than an essay. Nonetheless, something can be done here. To think oneself into the multiple forms of Shakespearean experience and beyond the divisions of genre and gender requires a radical readjustment of approach and vocabulary: For instance, it requires one to give up notions of character as selfsame, owned, capable of autonomy and change; to give up, for instance, the notion that biological difference is an a priori fact and to return to Simone de Beauvoir's essential insight in *The Second Sex* that woman is a cultural construct and category, and therefore not the same then as now. The leap I imagine is one that has been attempted by feminists trying to escape the deadlock of either/or and the same, a deadlock usually called masculine logic. For, ironically, feminists like Bamber reimpose the prescriptions they mean to erase by restating the oppressive categories that must be seen through and must be read beyond for a genuine feminist discourse to arise. My argument here is that such a discourse can be made available even in the Shakespearean text if only because it does not (re)inscribe the differences Bamber enunciates.

I propose here to look at the field of men and women talking within the Shakespearean text. My concern is genre, gender, and power. If it is (among other things) the position in language that points to the powers and limits that situate the sexes, then we might ask of Shakespeare the question Roland Barthes asked so often: "Who is speaking?" This question directs us to a number of issues. Who (or what) speaks in the voice that articulates (it)self? Who, especially, speaks when I do? (I have tried to open this essay in the mouths of others to affirm one essential position for us, since we are in discourse invariably.) The radical shiftiness of the "I" may blur the proprietariness of gender, may obscure the differences. In making arguments about the patriarchalism of Shakespeare's culture, critics forget that both boys and girls in the Renaissance wore female clothes in their early years; femininity was thus the undifferentiated sex from which maleness came. On Shakespeare's stage, there were only men; the image of the culture was reversed. Both images—that there is but one sex—are the culture's. Both images—there is not one sex—are the culture's.

Who is in question. Speaking is in question. Do I speak, or does something speak in me, something no smaller than the entire culture with all its multiple capacities? In arguments of the sort I am calling into question, it is said that women in Shakespeare lack the autonomy of a voice and are barred from discourse or limited and placed by male discourse. Cordelia—to whom I shall return toward the end of this essay—might be an example of this. But my point here is that no one—neither men nor women in Shakespeare—has such autonomy or such power. As an immediate complication in the claim that it is only women who lack voice, we might recall Coriolanus, home from the wars, greeting his wife as his "gracious silence" (2.1.192), but we must remember, too, that Coriolanus will not lend his lips to gain the people's voice, and that he seals his doom when, after his mother has spoken for more than fifty uninterrupted lines, *"he holds her by the hand, silent"* (5.3.182), as the eloquent stage direction describes the moment that determines his fate.

Authority in the Shakespearean text is a matter not of having a voice but of voicing. This is the field of history, a stage of power. "Hear him but reason," "Hear him debate," "List his discourse," (1.1.38, 41, 43) begins Canterbury's rapt account in the opening scene of *Henry V,* describing the transformed Prince Hal, now on the throne and securing his power. Power is voicing here, just as in the *Henry IV* plays it is always a matter of representation, the imposition of stories and the insistence on their truth. Canterbury describes the essential shape of a power play around the issue of voice. Henry's is the voicing of a world of discourse passing through him, vocalized powerfully. And if Henry's domain—"the world" of Heilbrun's review—comprises theology, statecraft, martial discourses, and *raison d'état,* his placement in speech also functions to make others voiceless or to point up the inadequacies of their vocalizations. Here, in part, is Canterbury's account:

> Hear him but reason in divinity,
> And, all-admiring, with an inward wish
> You would desire the King were made a prelate;
> Hear him debate of commonwealth affairs,
> You would say it hath been all in all his study;
> List his discourse of war, and you shall hear
> A fearful battle rend'red you in music;
> Turn him to any cause of policy,
> The Gordian knot of it he will unloose,
> Familiar as his garter; that, when he speaks,
> The air, a charter'd libertine, is still,
> And the mute wonder lurketh in men's ears
> To steal his sweet and honey'd sentences.
>
> (1.1.38–50)

As radical as Bottom's wish in *A Midsummer Night's Dream,* that he might play all the parts, is Henry's accomplishment, conquering the territories of discourse as if he perfectly possessed them and not they him. The effect of the voice in Henry is the provocation of desire, the elicitation of wishes and dreams, the inscription of a life story at odds with the facts, a scene of bodily familiarity as ordinary as the choice of clothes;

yet here, clothes make the man. On the other side of this vocalization is silence; the inscrutability of Henry within this discursive field, the still air and mute wonder in which the audience is suspended, the bees of the commonwealth swarming around the honeyed eloquence that the king manufactures. The effect of speech is to release a Henry apt for anyone's thought, and a release and constraint upon thought so that it takes the shape of the air itself, a "charter'd libertine," licensed and constrained, vocalized and silenced at once. Henry's entrance into discourse involves a suppression of another story (his own) and of others' stories, a play upon the air: Voice is breath, atmosphere. It is the field of power. To be in history, Henry must assume this vocalic situation; it is the mirror of the position the monarchs of Shakespeare's time affirmed. Both Elizabeth and James declared that the king was one set upon a stage.[8]

The play of history (and the history play, that mixed genre) provides the discursive field against which I would read comedy and tragedy and the situation of men and women voicing power. In tragedy and comedy, I pursue and am no doubt caught within the traces of a complicity that Gayatri Chakravorty Spivak enunciates as the field of special concern to the critic who is both a deconstructionist and a feminist (if we must use labels). She writes that the aspect of deconstructive practice that interests her most is

> the recognition, within deconstructive practice, of provisional and intractable starting points in any investigative effort; its disclosure of complicities where a will to knowledge would create oppositions; its insistence that in disclosing complicities the critic-as-subject is herself complicit with the object of her critique; its emphasis upon "history" and the ethico-political as the "trace" of that complicity—the proof that we do not inhabit a clearly defined critical space free of such traces; and, finally, the acknowledgement that its own discourse can never be adequate to its example.[9]

First, the task is to examine the law of the patriarch and find within its power the slippages that undermine authority and permit vocalization. My example is Portia; my main concern, her court appearance. My argument, in brief, is that the play fully problematizes the notion of the law and that Portia has a voice *within* the law; not, I argue, that it constricts and denies her, not that she must submit to the father, but that she *becomes* the father precisely because the law is not the father's and is not exclusively a male territory.[10] The law Portia enacts knows no kind; it is the law of genre.[11]

In the fourth act of *The Merchant of Venice,* Portia arrives in the court of law to function in place of the learned Bellario in offering an opinion on the legality of Shylock's proceeding against Antonio. Portia comes "furnished" (4.1.157) with Bellario's opinion and clothed as Balthazar, bearing the name of the servant she dispatched with a letter to the learned lawyer when she sought his advice (in act 3, scene 4). The letter completes its circuit, returning; before Portia appears in the court of law, a letter from Bellario serves as her credentials. In it, Portia is presented not merely as furnished with his opinion but as one whose outer appearance belies an inner state. For, having "turned o'er many books together" (4.1.156–57), Bellario can report that although Portia bears a young body she has an old head: "I beseech you, let his lack of years be no impediment to let him lack a reverend estimation; for I never knew so young a body with so old a head" (4.1.161–64). Portia herself had commented, upon dispatching her letter to Bellario, that a certain "lack" would be furnished in her Venetian appearance, telling Nerissa that she will arrive in the court

> in such a habit
> That they shall think we are accomplished
> With that we lack.
>
> (3.4. 60–62)

The pattern here is clear, apparently. In order to assume the authority of Bellario, Portia must arrive clothed inwardly and outwardly as a man. Her mind has been made mature through perusal of the law books and through having been "furnished" with Bellario's knowledge; her outer form bears testament to this inner state, for the lack she suffers as a female is compensated for in her male accoutrements. Yet Bellario's letter asks for externality to be discounted. The form of the supposed boy is not to serve as an impediment to the receipt of the graver wisdom of his mature mind. So the pattern is not in fact as clear as it seems to be. On the one hand, the words that Portia says upon sending the letter, and the words that the letter contains, echo: lack against lack, habit against furnishing. Yet on the other, although the echoing texts offer a principle of simple repetition, of mere superimposition, the letter as it returns would seem to deny the principle of echo itself. It invites a cleavage between inner and outer equipage. The letter as it returns cleaves the letter itself; in the circuit of the letter something more (and less) than the circulation of the selfsame seems to be in question.

The letter equivocates, offering itself as a credential that cannot stand the credence of the audience who knows that Portia and Bellario have communicated solely by letter and that the conference reported in the letter is as much a fabrication as the name Portia has taken or the disguise she wears. Even when Portia imagined the power she would have in disguise, it was to tell "quaint lies" (3.4.69) about the power of men (her power as a man), to slay women by denying them love, to offer repentance when it is too late. In short, she says,

> I have within my mind
> A thousand raw tricks of these bragging Jacks,
> Which I will practise.
>
> (3.4.76–78)

In the certifying letter, however, her mind is furnished with the tricks of the law, and they become her practice. Nerissa's response to Portia's project—which she calls a device—is instructive: "Why, shall we turn to men?" (3.4.78) she asks, and Portia hears the equivocation in her words: shall we become men? shall we lend ourselves to male purposes? "Fie, what a question's that, / If thou wert near a lewd interpreter!" (3.4.79–80). Is the assumption of male power the submission to male domination? Does the accomplishment of the lack only serve to reinforce it? What is the circuit from the letter to the ring?

The "turn" that Portia takes calls into question the differences upon which the play rests, male and female, Jew and Christian, letter and spirit, for the lewdness of the play that she initiates—sending the letter and donning the disguise (the device)—rests upon equivocations within the letter, differences within the selfsame. Portia's "whole device" (3.4.81) involves filling a place—the place of Bellario, the place of the law—through an act of replacement that calls into question the possibility of duplication (the repeatability and selfsameness upon which the law rests). Portia "comes . . . to fill up your Grace's request in my stead" (4.1.159–61). She appears as the equivocation of an *instead,* furnished with a voice that carries the letter and the body as the meeting point of within and without. The lies she will speak, the lewdness of her play, are carried on an equivocal vocal reed. She tells Nerissa that she will

> wear my dagger with the braver grace,
> And speak between the change of man and boy
> With a reed voice, and turn two mincing steps
> Into a manly stride.
>
> (3.4.65–68)

The lack is supplied doubly, with a dagger and a voice, a reed. The reed is the instrument that conveys the turn, the change, a state between inside and outside, man and boy (the undifferentiated), man and mincer. To be the reed is to be the poet's instrument. Pan and Syrinx. "Shall we turn to men?" (3.4.78). "We turned o'er many books together" (4.1.156–57). The circuit of the letter.

Portia begins the play bound by the law, deprived of her will because of her father's will inscribed in the living force of his dead letter, locked in a leaden casket. "So is the will of a living daughter curb'd by the will of a dead father" (1.2.25–26). The equivocal form she assumes in act 4 conveys the law of the father. Although she is (within the father's will) inert and inexpressive, a dead letter to be penetrated, she is also the meaning of the letter, the life which can be released. "Who chooses his meaning chooses you," Nerissa comments (1.3.33–34); Bassanio views the leaden casket and comments, "Thy paleness moves me more than eloquence" (3.2.106). Silent Portia is sacrificed for her father's word; Bassanio chooses, and words—in "excess"—are released, the "shadow" within the casket "confirm'd, sign'd, ratified" by Portia (3.2.112, 128, 149). The former contract is apparently reinscribed, the rings the tokens, when Portia submits to Bassanio as to "her lord, her governor, her king" (3.2.167); but Bassanio reports that he is as speechless now as Portia, and similarly awed, like a subject hearing "some oration fairly spoke / By a beloved prince" (3.2.180–81). The experience is so excessive that it surpasses the differences upon which meaning rests:

> Every something, being blent together
> Turns to a wild of nothing, save of joy
> Express'd and not express'd.
>
> (3.2.183–85)

These turns, relays of power, express the circuit of the letter, the equivocations of voice articulated "between the change," "Express'd and not express'd." In the blending together in which the law (the contract, the bond) is ratified, the signature—the kiss—renders difference problematic.

In the court of law, Portia replays her contract with Bassanio, that marriage of her father's will and her own; she replays it with another father deprived of his daughter and his ducats (see act 2, scene 8), crying for justice to repair what he lacks, to exact his loss upon another, to make the word flesh ("my own flesh and blood to rebel" [3.1.37], Shylock laments when Jessica has fled). It is a grim scene, and it should not be sentimentalized. Shylock may have a legitimate complaint against the society that has treated him like a scapegoat and carried off his daughter in a masquerade not unlike the one Portia plays with him in this scene, but that does not excuse his murderousness. Portia explicates mercy but offers justice; justice is what Shylock desires. There is no going outside the law, for its excess lies within, in the return of the letter, in the closing of the circuit: "A Daniel come to judgment! yea, a Daniel!"; "A second Daniel! a Daniel, Jew!" (4.1.223, 333). Nothing is the same the second time.

The travesty of the law, the transvestitism of the law, is *already inscribed* in the father's will, in the circuit of the letter, in the return in which doubling discovers the difference *already* within the same. Two wills are satisfied at once. "There is no power in Venice / Can alter a decree established" (4.1.218–19), the Duke declares; "There is no power in the tongue of man / To alter me," Shylock swears (4.1.241–42). The power is in "the very words" (4.1.254). "A Daniel, still say I, a second Daniel! / I thank, thee, Jew, for teaching me that word" (4.1.340–41). Within the word Portia pauses, to find "something else" (4.1.305): "This bond doth give thee here no jot of blood; / The words expressly are 'a pound of flesh'" (4.1.306–7). The limit represents an exclusion, releases a superfluity: No more or less means nothing at all. This was Portia's condition under the law, the "good sentences, and well pronounc'd" (1.2.11) that Nerissa read in her state, bound to a father's will and deprived her own. Portia comes to ratify the law and to reveal its bankruptcy in the very superfluity of her "sentence" (4.1.304). The word cuts two ways, and she is the lewd interpreter of the turn upon itself that the letter represents: "The Jew shall have all justice. Soft, no haste. / He shall have nothing but the penalty" (4.1.321–22). Having all, he has nothing, Bassanio's condition when Portia submitted entirely to his dominion, putting herself in bonds with him, ringing him 'round. Her signature was the kiss. And Shylock's? All but ratified, he vocalizes his "content" (4.1.394), that will-less middle ground that is no place (no more, no less). His final word promises the signature that will deliver him, signed, sealed, and bound—and forever silent:

> I pray you give me leave to go from hence.
> I am not well. Send the deed after me,
> And I will sign it.
>
> (4.1.395–97)

The circuit of the letter, completing one loop (the rings lie ahead), turns upon itself: "Your Grace shall understand that at the receipt of your letter I am very sick" (4.1.150–51), so Bellario/Portia begins; then, the letter can become the ring, the circular bond returning upon itself, making two wills one, binding father and daughter, male and female, inner and outer: turning to men. "Pardon me, Bassanio; / For, by this ring, the doctor lay with me" (5.1.258–59)—a lewd interpretation of the letter.

Or, to put it more succinctly, listen to the lesson Theseus preaches to Hermia in the opening scene of *A Midsummer Night's Dream:*

> To you your father should be as a god,
> One that compos'd your beauties, yea, and one
> To whom you are but as a form in wax
> By him imprinted, and within his power
> To leave the figure or disfigure it.
>
> (1.1.47–51)

At the end of the play, Theseus overrules Egeus, imposes his will, inscribing both father and daughter within his power and law, and Hermia responds, "Methinks I see these things with parted eye, / When every thing seems double" (4.1.193–94). A moment later she agrees to follow the Duke: "Yea," she says, "and my father" (4.1.199). It is her last word. Figured and disfigured, she is doubly stamped by the authorizing powers: testaments to the inscription of the letter, the circuit of desire turning back upon itself, encompassing *both* father and daughter, male and female, within its course.

Portia's career in *The Merchant of Venice* takes place between the will of her father and Shylock's suspended signature, the imprimatur that would authorize her position. His voice is silenced. The voice that Portia assumes, however, is not a man's voice, nor does she merely affirm the coincidence of her will with her father's or the coincidence of the legalism she displays with Shylock's demand that only the letter of the law be observed. Portia's equivocal place in the text, her voice "between," her ratification, plays on the "turns" taken by the circuit of the text. Through the letter she passes. Rather than reading her career as her inscription in the patriarchal order, let us read it otherwise. It is not that she has found some realm of feminine discourse. Rather, she moves through the text, affirming the meeting of, and the suspension of, difference. Almost as Luce Irigaray would have it, Portia's voice plays on the unconscious of the text, reveals what is repressed when the law acts as if it were univocal, when the father acts as if his impress would turn the blank page of the daughter into his character. The return of the letter doubles back upon itself, revealing the duplicity in the text, revealing, in Irigaray's terms, the sex that is not one:

> In her statements . . . woman retouches herself constantly. . . . One must listen to her differently in order to hear an *"other meaning" which is constantly in the process of weaving itself, at the same time ceaselessly embracing words and yet casting them off to avoid becoming fixed, immobilized.* For when "she" says something, it is already no longer identical to anything.[12]

Such is the circuit of the letter.

Such, too, is the law of genre, if I may borrow Jacques Derrida's title[13] and recapitulate his argument merely through the act of (re)citation. Derrida argues that although the law of genre insists on demarcation and difference, genre is self-invaginated, cast, as Montaigne would have it, in the same mold. The very law that establishes genre—the will, contract, and rings in *The Merchant of Venice,* for example—is no law outside textual play; rather, it is implicated in the play: Portia in her father's place; Portia as the law. Genre represents an arbitrary limit upon the generativity of language; it provides the end that otherwise would not be reached.

If we have seen that Portia's acquisition of voice and Shylock's silencing cannot merely be described as the ratification of the patriarchal order, we can best explore the question of the loss of voice—as the fate of both men and women—and the coincidence of this loss with the law of genre, in the final moments of *Measure for Measure,* a play, as I take it, intent upon representing itself (as the figure of the Duke suggests)—as representation.[14] The drama of substitution and replacement that I have argued exists in *The Merchant of Venice* hardly needs to be argued for in the later play. From the initial replacement of the Duke with his deputy, Angelo, to the plot to substitute Mariana for Isabella, the question of replacement is in the foreground, in the disposition of character and in the arguments they make. For what the Duke plots for Isabella is also her argument with Angelo: that he should put himself in another's place and think of Claudio's crime as his own. The Duke's substitution plot satisfies Isabella's argument.

Generation by substitution is the representational law of the play, its mode of government, a literalization and corporealization of the drama of representation. No one is above this law in the play. The Duke, who appears to initiate the chain of substitutions and to call it to a halt, has to endure Lucio's representations of him to the very end of the play, in part because he has engendered himself as a substitute in the guise of Friar Lodowick. Although the Duke may appear to be in control of or outside the situation of the play (he may appear, that is, as the dramatist within the play), there is no outside of representation, and the play suggests this, too, by seeming to include King James in its designs. Within the play, resistance to representation is to be found not only in the Duke's protestations but also as the essence of the role of Barnardine. As the Duke attempts—not all that successfully—to juggle heads and find a substitute for the condemned Claudio, he lights upon Barnardine, named in a letter Angelo has sent to the prison (4.2.119ff.). Barnardine's name, so casually introduced as a counterpart to Claudio's, is picked up by the Duke; the convict's history is told—a life spent in prison, more often drunk than sober, more often asleep than awake. Barnardine would seem to live solely to die; yet when he is brought forth in the following scene, he will have none of the Duke's scheme or Angelo's; as far as he is concerned, their letters are no warrant, and, refusing to consent to die, he returns to his straw and drink.

Yet, this is *represented* resistance. Barnardine's refusal to be Claudio's substitute only further identifies him with Claudio, for Claudio does not die. Yet he almost does, and the generation of Claudio through the last acts of *Measure for Measure* is through such substitutes as Barnardine. The Duke's abandonment of Claudio to death—"Be absolute for death"

(3.1.5) is his counterpart to Isabella's more violent repudiation of her brother—is itself abandoned. From his images of life as death, inanition, decay—at best sleep—Barnardine emerges as the corporealization of those words, "a man that apprehends death no more dreadfully but as a drunken sleep" (4.2.149–50). If life and death are as indifferent and as much alike as the Duke's speech argues, Barnardine takes him (as it were) at his word. He refuses to die. And the Duke, in a rage like Isabella's at Claudio, sputters, "Unfit to live, or die" (4.3.68), naming thereby the equivocal space of representation filled by Barnardine.

Not by him alone; from such equivocations, the end of the play is reached. Claudio, although saved, is silenced; after act 3, scene 1, he barely says another word, existing through his substitutes (Barnardine, the head of Ragozine the pirate) and through the substitutive plots of the Duke and Isabella. He is placed by the plot and replaced by it; the law of the play determines and limits his position. This explains the curious nature of Claudio's final appearance. Unlike Shylock, who disappears to be replaced and whose signature hovers over the play's end, Claudio's body needs to be displayed as the sign that justifies the substitutive play of the last acts of *Measure for Measure.* Yet within the economy of the play's conclusion, Claudio has been reduced to a cipher, and there is no need for the character to speak; there is barely the need for him to be recognized. Thus, no one says a word to him at his final appearance, nor does he speak. The provost "unmuffles" him, identifying him as

> another prisoner that I sav'd,
> Who should have died when Claudio lost his head;
> As like almost to Claudio as himself.
>
> (5.1.491–93)

Claudio appears in the company of Barnardine and in a nomination in which selfsameness is affirmed as an otherness; selfsameness is only as proximate as the likeness of one self to oneself. At the end of the play, this is also Isabella's position, silenced, too, as the Duke enacts a justice that might better be called his voicing of the power of a text in which he, too, is inscribed. For, as much in the compulsion of genre as anyone, the Duke turns to Isabella—silent from the moment her represented brother stands before her—to invite her into a proper finale. His words echo against the provost's problematic identification of Claudio:

If he be like your brother, for his sake
Is he pardon'd; and for your lovely sake—
Give me your hand, and say you will be mine—
He is my brother too. But fitter time for that.
(5.1.495–98)

Isabella is asked into a family of similitudes, the moving principle of replacement and representation in which she finds her end, like unto like, "his sake," "your . . . sake." The Duke asks for the hand that would ratify, the voice that would assent. Some lines later, he reiterates his proposal; repetition is the other side of the silence of Isabella and Claudio.

To remind us of the coincidence of the law of representation with the justice that the Duke enacts in the final scene—giving measure for measure in reductive and silencing replacements—we need only notice Lucio's last words in the play. Condemned—like Angelo and like the Duke—to marry the woman he has wronged, he utters a final protest: "Marrying a punk, my lord, is pressing to death, whipping, and hanging" (5.1.528–29). Lucio treats his marriage as a punishment, and with "pressing to death" he summons up the grisly fate of one who, rather than admit his guilt or plead his innocence, suffered *peine forte et dure,* "being crushed slowly to death by weights on top of his body,"[15] the sole right of silence granted those who refused to accept the constructions of others and wished to preserve their own—their property, if not their lives (Shylock's case inverted).

Thus far, I have taken my examples from comedy. But the situation I am describing applies in tragedy too. Deprivation of voice does not signal the marginalization of women. Let us, for example, consider the silencing of Portia in *Julius Caesar.* In act 4, Brutus reports her death to Cassius, "No man bears sorrow better. Portia is dead" (4.3.147), and proceeds to describe it in response to Cassius's question, "[U]pon what sickness?":

Impatient of my absence,
And grief that young Octavius with Mark Antony
Have made themselves so strong,—for with her death
That tidings came,—with this she fell distract,
And, her attendants absent, swallow'd fire.
(4.3.152–56)

Brutus's lines embed Portia's death in political action: His repeated preposition is *with;* the alliance of Antony with Caesar arrives in the letter bearing the news of Portia's death. Their proximity in report makes for Brutus's causal linking. It is "with this" alliance that Portia "fell distract"; her lord's "absence" doubled with "her attendants absent" led to self-slaughter. Portia suffocates herself, denying herself life and breath by swallowing fire. The mouth incapable of speaking now swallows its own silence.

Portia's suicide is a political act. In a play in which wounds speak, Portia's death reverses the flow of power that streams from Caesar's corpse. Antony articulates the connection of voice and power that marks the death of Portia—and ultimately of Brutus, too:

> Over thy wounds now do I prophesy,
> Which, like dumb mouths, do ope their ruby lips
> To beg the voice and utterance of my tongue:
> . . . .
> And Caesar's spirit, ranging for revenge,
> With Ate by his side come hot from hell,
> Shall in these confines with a monarch's voice
> Cry "Havoc," and let slip the dogs of war,
> That this foul deed shall smell above the earth
> With carrion men, groaning for burial.
>
> (3.1.259–61, 270–75)

The silencing of Portia shows her place in Antony's text, a script that the play unabashedly calls the sphere of power, politics, and history.

Yet Portia's silence is not the result of her exclusion from the world where men destroy themselves and each other. Rather, it marks her participation. Brutus, reading her death in the letter that marks his own fate, is not merely projecting or unconsciously amalgamating her death with his own. The division (from herself, her husband, her servants) and the multiplication (Octavius with Antony, "with her death . . . with this") point to the constitutive alienation of her participation in the plot—literally. Early in the play, Portia has a voice, demanding from Brutus that he acknowledge the equality of their partnership by revealing to her the distraction that so palpably divides him from himself. She recounts her repeated questionings, her urgings, her insistence, her voice—and Brutus's refusal to speak. "It will not let you eat, nor talk, nor sleep" (2.1.252), she concludes, and were what is consuming him to surface, Brutus would be effaced, unknowable. It is with this "it" that Portia begs acquaintance (2.1.256). Brutus at first insists that it is a sickness—though, if it is, it is the sickness that kills Portia—but Portia discounts this reading, driving toward "some sick offense within your mind" (2.1.268). Portia would be *with* Brutus, and within him. She takes literally their incorporation (2.1.273) and asks Brutus to take the mantle off, to unmuffle himself, to speak out. For, she assures him, once she has received the words, she will not reveal them. The power lies in that promise, just as it is intimated in the thigh wound to which she points as a sign of her constancy. Yet this is not merely a scene of wifely submission, for it is how she becomes again her husband's equal. Portia kneels, but Brutus will not have her on her knees; Portia complains of being exiled to "the suburbs" of his heart (2.1.285), and Brutus affirms her right to occupy the secret, to penetrate the mask, to break the silence, to participate in what is within. He offers her the "ruddy drops" of his heart (2.1.289), promising an off-stage revelation that has occurred when Portia next is seen on stage. Here is the promise:

> Thy bosom shall partake
> The secrets of my heart.
> All my engagements I will construe to thee,
> All the charactery of my sad brows.
> (2.1.305–8)

The revelation of the plot is like the dagger offered to her thigh or the one that will plunge into Brutus's breast. Portia has insisted that Brutus read to her what lies within the text that is his body, what lies charactered on his forehead. The opening of the body, the revelation of the equivocal life-in-death of the text, will place Portia within the economy that leads to her silencing.

After this scene, Portia can only speak with two voices. Tormented, self-divided, she sends word to her husband that she is merry when she is anything but; desirous of imparting the disease that now eats at her, she cannot speak. Swallowing fire is the counterpart to the voice that has been divided against itself, condemned to the equivocations in which selfsameness is lost forever. One with Brutus, she is two. And the testimony of this not only inheres in the suicide that she becomes—that assault on her throat, the suffocation of her breath and spirit in token of the raging, burning spirit of Caesar—but it also lies in Brutus's response to her death. For, as we know, there are two responses to it. One we have seen, with its poised marks of alienation and participation, of absence and presence cohering in the destructivity of the plot, in the effacing of his character, razing the tablet. But then, as if to mark further that erasure, Brutus responds again. "Had you your letters from your wife, my lord?" Messala asks (4.3.181), just after Brutus and Cassius have re-cemented their friendship, grieving over Portia. Brutus denies the letter, denies all knowledge, coaxing Messala to reveal the brutal truth: "[S]he is dead" (4.3.189). "Why, farewell, Portia," Brutus responds. In a politic suppression, a bid for power, Brutus almost swallows fire himself, dividing himself from himself in this answer. Both he and his dead wife bear a single character, share a voice of power and alienation that divides the self from the self, that marries the self to its otherness.

The generation of character from text, the effacement of voice, or the submission of voice (silence *or* speech) to serve the generic design that limits text—it is upon these connections that the argument of this essay rests. Portia returns to Belmont, completing the circuit of her career, carrier of the letter, enacting its course. When Bassanio first mentions her as the "lady richly left" (1.1.161), she is rightly named:

> Sometimes from her eyes
> I did receive fair speechless messages.
> Her name is Portia, nothing undervalu'd
> To Cato's daughter, Brutus' Portia.
> (1.1.163–66)

She and Portia in *Julius Caesar* are counterexamples, their careers inverse and complementary mirrors of the condition of having a voice. At the end, when Portia returns, she is heard first as a voice: "That is the voice, / Or I am much deceiv'd, of Portia" (5.1.110–11).

Entrance into voice, then, although it may mean arrival on the scene of power, always bears its equivocations. When speech occurs, when the voice sounds, there is always another in the voice, an otherness that accompanies the utterer. In the examples we have considered thus far, that voice may be called the text, if by text we mean not something that is selfsame on the page, not the inertness of an implacable letter, but rather those slippages and multiplications that determine and fix only to unmoor again, making all places provisional, all sites relational, all identity a matter of differences scarcely perceivable because forever changing. The situation of being in the text is one that governs men and women in Shakespeare; becoming voiceless, effacement, is the end of all characters traced on his mystic writing pad. Acquiring voice, characters sustain the play and are caught within the play. It is not necessarily a sign of power to have a voice, nor is it necessarily a sign of subjection to lose it. The economy of the text, generic disposition, determines the distribution of parts and provides the arbitrary limit on texts that would never end otherwise (as the characters at ends of plays so often suggest, directing us beyond the end with promises of revelations or recoveries not evident on a stage filled with corpses or married couples). True, the Renaissance has more than its share of the fear of giving women power or of allowing them to have a voice, but that is not invariably the situation within the plays, and when it is, the fear is not limited to one sex.[16] No one escapes bearing the trace of an otherness that shows the equivocation of the letter. Or, as Jacques Lacan would say (for he has been behind this text throughout and perhaps should be named now, allowed the flourish of his signature), when I speak, it is always from and to an Other; my voice passes through and attempts to return to that unacknowledged, unreachable goal. The entrance into the symbolic stage—the entrance into language—is marked by the alienation of voice that raises Barthes's question: "Who is speaking?"

That question pervades *Othello;* all relationships in that play are carried on the voice, and the play represents a struggle to discover if anyone can be said to have or own a voice.[17] At the end, paradoxically, the answer to this question finds power in inarticulation. The perils of speech are marked from the start, in Othello's "witchcraft," when he seduces Desdemona by rehearsing "the story of my life" (1.3.129). It is because she displays "a greedy ear" to "devour up my discourse" (1.3.149–50) that Othello reads in her rapt and silent attention a desire to hear his words and to take them in. Desdemona's desire is for his voice. This becomes a fear, but even as he first reports it, Desdemona's desire is itself accompanied by a resistance: "She wish'd she had not heard it; yet she wish'd / That Heaven had made her such a man" (1.3.162–63)—wished she were a man, wished such a man had been made *for* her. Othello's story overcomes Desdemona's resistance; retelling it to the Venetians, he overcomes theirs to his marriage to her. When Desdemona appears before them, her voice is heroic; she requires from the senators a "prosperous ear," asking them to give "voice" to her desires; Othello reiterates her words: "Let her have your voice" (1.3.245, 246, 261).

And Iago is nothing if not a voice; his device is to "abuse Othello's ear" (1.3.401); a full range of mimicry and the assumption of voices is his province. "I'll pour this pestilence into his ear" (2.3.362), Iago affirms, yet the situation is more complex than that, for it repeats the wooing and commingling of Othello and Desdemona. The voice that he offers Othello is so much a version of his own, so complete an echo, that Othello loses all ability to identify himself or his wife.

> What dost thou think?
> Think, my lord?
> Think, my lord? By heaven, he echoes me.
> (3.3.105–6)

Iago stages his silence as more significant than his speech; Othello draws from him those words that he desires and wishes not to hear. The scene recasts the wooing of Desdemona; here, too, a reading of hints delivers the voice of an ambivalent desire. To want another's story is to want a part in it. To recognize one's desire in another's story is to affirm that one's desire is not one's own but for and of another. In *Othello,* everyone is caught within the desire that catches Othello; even Cassio was his go-between, carrying words to Desdemona. Iago can imagine that his wife has done in bed what Cassio has done in words; there is, perhaps, no difference.

In *Othello,* speech and desire are the same thing, and the murder of Desdemona, denying her breath and speech, is a sexual assault; mouth and throat are the visible zones of sexuality in the play. "Will you think so? Think so, Iago: What, / To kiss in private? An unauthoriz'd kiss" (4.1.1–2). Two voices are as one, echoing; conversation in the middle is sustained on a vocality that goes beyond the utterer; the unauthorized kiss is the counterpart of speech without author, speech against authority, breaking down the resistances of desire, the structures of law and order. To speak, to kiss, to die: their conjunction provokes stifling, assails the voice because the voice is itself an assault. To launch speech but not to be *in* speech, to sustain silence in speech, would be, in this play, the nature of genuine power. It is manifest at the end.

Desdemona dies, kissed and stifled; dead, she speaks nonetheless, identifying "Nobody" with "I myself" (5.2.124). Emilia bursts forth despite Iago's attempt to "charm" her tongue: "I will not charm my tongue; I am bound to speak" (5.2.184), bound as in an Elizabethan court of law, where witnesses had no right to silence, even if speaking was self-incriminating.[18] Emilia pays for speech with her life. And Iago—an agent provocateur throughout so much of the play, ventriloquizer of the voices of others and supplier of an excess to his own voice so that we can never be sure we have him—at the end, embraces silence: "Demand me nothing; what you know, you know. / From this time forth I never will speak word" (5.2.303–4). The assertion of inscrutability, the refusal to be accountable or to recount, represents a seizure, a taking hold through the voice, of the situation at which others arrive at the ends of plays, rendered silent by the plot, mastered by an otherness, stifled, self-mastered. All these solutions are appropriated by Iago's final assertion, in which the condition of character at the end of the play becomes something he takes control over by relinquishing—by withholding—his voice.

The god of eloquence—Hermes—has his finger on his lips.[19]

What we cannot hear may be a sign of depletion or of a reserve that is impenetrable. Full speech always carries with it, as its other side, an emptiness; recall Henry V: not only does he render others silent, but the very mastery of discourse that he displays leaves obscure who he is, where he is in his discourse. Voice masters and dissolves the limits of the self; character is a function of voice. The silence of Iago is his power. It is Cordelia's power, too, as is suggested at the end of *King Lear,* when Lear looks to Cordelia's lips as if from them words and breath yet might come. Cordelia begins the play wedded to silence, and she ends there, implacable. Her claims to an interiority and an integrity are as potent as Iago's slippages, his maintenance of a fort of silence about a self that exists only by not being articulated, his refusal to breach definitively the inside and outside through an owned vocalization. Cordelia refuses to enter the sphere of speech because to speak is always a kind of betrayal, a violation of interiority, an emptying of value that exists when it stays inside. She refuses her father's plot of exchanges. The structure here is not unlike the opening of *Othello* or of *The Merchant of Venice.* Here, too, the articulation of love is the problematic zone.[20] Cordelia's power in the play lies in her refusal of construction, in the demand that her silence represents, a resistance to the end of the megalomaniac acquisitiveness marked in Lear's attempt to appropriate everything, even her death. Her silence resists his speech, making his initial rages appear to be childish tantrums. His final negations are more finely tuned to her silence, a submission at last to the limits of utterance, a facing of the unutterable disowning displayed by a universe seemingly without respect for human values and constructions. The shriveled sphere of human survival lies in the divestment that Edgar represents; what remains is not a man's sphere necessarily but the impulse to stage power, to save voice—or the illusion of one's own voice—perhaps by withholding, perhaps by disowned expenditure. Cleopatra lurks in the wings.

"The rest," as Hamlet says, "is silence" (5.2.369). This is the universal fate. But, as Hamlet adds, those who survive do so to tell the story again. Representation is the only truth, one that in fact has no end despite the arbitrariness of the ending of any particular performance. This, too, is the point about the epilogue of *The Tempest,* the extension of the play into the hands of the audience, attributing to us the breath and life necessary to send Prospero to Naples, his sails filled with the air we can move, by our applause or prayers or hisses. This turn to the audience represents Prospero's last attempt to appropriate responses, a desire shown up throughout the play—in act 4, for instance, when Prospero commands silence before the performance of the masque, only to be interrupted by Ferdinand (at 4.1.118) and distracted from the play that goes on while Ceres and Juno whisper behind his back. Unheard vocalization is the manifestation of their life, a sign of the limits of authority and authorship, of a slippage in control, as is readily apparent at the end of *The Tempest,* when Antonio, seemingly chastened, stonily silent, says just enough to make it clear that the experience of Prospero's play has meant nothing to him. So much for the power men have over others, the power fathers have to shape the world to their desires, so much even for the playwright's fantasy that he can claim the words in his text as his own. There are laws beyond that law too.

One last case: In the final act of *A Midsummer Night's Dream,* Hermia and Helena, vocal throughout the play, are silent. They say nothing after their marriages (reported in act 4, scene 2). After the forest, they return to Athens as bodies, married, barred from discourse. The text marks, but does not necessarily condone, their place in patriarchal culture. And in the last act, Hippolyta, also married, is hardly silent, and the fullness, range, complexity, and diversity of her vocality must be read in counterpoint to the silence of Hermia and Helena. Both these are images of women. And for the men? Hippolyta urges Theseus not to hear the play, and he responds that he must hear it, claiming noblesse oblige, his capacity to make something out of nothing. The ironies are deep, for, of course, the men comment upon the play without a trace of self-recognition (and Hermia and Helena's may be a knowing silence). But here is a final irony: This play, performed before Queen Elizabeth, pays homage to her voice, too. Theseus's claim, however ironic when taken to refer to him, is perfectly straight elsewhere—we need simply recall how often Elizabeth interrupted performances put on before her, how graciously she supplied whatever the performers lacked.[21]

In her coronation procession through the streets of London, Elizabeth paused repeatedly before the various shows staged for her benefit. She paused and spoke, demanded silence so that the actors could be heard, answered them, delivered speeches of her own with all the spontaneity of a good actor. This is one way of staging power in the voice, one way that monarchs on the throne are like those on stage. Here is the other: James repeated Elizabeth's performance, trod the same streets, stopped at the same scaffolds, attended to their plays. And he never said a word. Power lay in the withholding of utterance, the staging of the self as a spectacle unfathomable because inaccessible.[22]

But is Elizabeth in her voice? James in his silence? Their performances are invitations to decipherment, parts of the design that placed them on those prescribed streets, following those routes. The theatricalization of power is not confined to theaters; rather, it extends into the streets. Perhaps—just perhaps—the reason we cannot find Shakespeare reflecting his culture's supposed patriarchalism and sexism[23] is that the culture represented on stage *is* the culture offstage. Saying that does not mean denying the real, material, legal, social, and educational differences between men and women in Shakespeare's time. Thus, no woman, as Roman law declared, could actually have the power invested in a lawyer's voice; as Constance Jordan has pointed out to me, having a voice—as a legal right—must be distinguished from voicing. Portia's performance, in that regard, is a fantasy that blurs the distinction. But the point is that the fantasy is *also* part of the culture. It is inconceivable that Shakespeare was the only person to have it; his words found a responsive audience. Numerous antifeminine tracts deplored women's voices; unauthorized, they were nonetheless clearly powerful enough to be heard. Elizabeth's rule (and Mary's before her), especially in her insistence both on her femininity *and* on her male sovereignty (she called herself a prince), represents a serious complication in the alignment of power with sexual difference. Her verbal skills (or James's silences) *realize* aspects of the culture that challenge modern readings of patriarchy as a simple dualistic hierarchy of the sexes operating with an all-embracing, hegemonic power. Power entails a disturbing heterogeneity, owned by no one voice—a voicing, as Irigaray might say, that is not one.

Calling Out the Law

The category of sodomy, as historians of sexuality know well, is exceedingly complicated; "utterly confused," as Michel Foucault claimed, it can appear in any number of discursive situations, an ideological weapon that names without precision a range of disparate acts supposedly charged with world-shattering powers.[1] When deployed in the arsenal of the church or state, it fastens on bodies that represent threats to social stability, heretics denounced for challenging the centralizing powers of churches new or old, persons of different races and religions for standing in the way of world conquest or state consolidation. The sodomite is the enemy within or the inhabitant of territories to be conquered abroad. It is most often the law that fastens on the body of the sodomite, and most often its embrace is annihilative.[2] The strictures of sodomy represent the will to make disappear, an absolute repression, and were responsible in the early modern period for the deaths of countless Moors in Spain and natives in the New World. The one site where the juridical apparatus of sodomy seems most lax has to do with the bodies of women. Only a handful of cases can be found—the work that sodomy did for males, witchcraft did for women—and from this lapse in the working of the law has followed the widespread assumption that in the early modern period, female sexuality was not recognized, an assumption that repeats the belief of the sovereign after whom prudery is named, that women do not have sex with each other.

There is enough work by now to counter this belief, to demonstrate that the phenomenon of sex between women was known, and to argue that even the occasional instances of the deployment of sodomy laws against women shows this, no matter how confused their application, no matter how difficult to generalize from the cases in which different acts count as what will be called sodomy, although what it shows beyond that will necessarily remain in question.[3] The visibility of the female sodomite is so often tied to her masquerading as a man to leave in question whether the challenge to gender hierarchies that calls out the law tells us anything about sexuality per se. Indeed, it raises the question whether there is such a thing as sexuality in itself. If so, a cautionary warning must be sounded to the assumption that those bodies apprehended by the law are fully legible within the domain in which sodomy functions for us: as a designator of sex acts unmoored from the situations that once called it forth and now, within the law as presently deployed, attached most often to the bodies of gay men.

In this framework, I would like to return to what, on the surface, was a most unpromising debate, staged in the late 1980s in the pages of *Renaissance Quarterly*, over Judith Brown's *Immodest Acts: The Life of a Lesbian Nun in Renaissance Italy*, a critique offered by Rudolph Bell, and Brown's response to it.[4] While motivated by the historians' shared sense that the documents about Benedetta Carlini are, in Bell's words, "virtually unique for what they may tell us about lesbian sexuality" and "merit very close examination" (487), Bell's attempts to prove Brown less than competent at interpreting the archival evidence—mistaking dating, identification of participants, and the like—warrant Brown's exasperated conclusion that Bell fails to raise any "important new issues . . . about sexual identities, sexual relations, and sexual perceptions in early modern Europe" (505).

To go further, Bell's critique represents a will to make disappear. Taking Brown to task for deploying the anachronistic term "lesbian" to describe Benedetta Carlini's sexual relations with her companion Bartolomea Crivelli—a caveat already operative in Brown's work, which regards the term merely as a convenience—the thrust of Bell's critique is that

Brown misrepresents the investigation in which the sexual behavior was discovered. Brown's narrative organizes this inquiry into two stages, the second of which issued in the climactic revelation that the two nuns had sexual relations. For her, this brings the inquest to a close, just as it provides the final frame for the historian's understanding of Benedetta and occasions the deployment of the term "lesbian" as the way in which we can understand her. For Bell, there was but one inquiry, and it had no final payoff. "Brown proceeds to create an inquisitorial scene, with the investigators first establishing exactly what had happened, then pressing for details on how long and how often the lovemaking had gone on, and then trying to determine Bartolomea's cooperation in the affair," Bell writes, continuing, "with due respect for the historian's right to tell a good story," he "can see nothing in Brown's translation of the one page on which all this is based, or in the document itself, that supports her scenario" (497).

Bell presumably has in mind a passage like this, in *Immodest Acts,* in which Brown imagines the effect of Bartolomea's testimony on the investigators:

> Unlike Bartolomea, the ecclesiastical officials who heard her testimony did not believe that the relationship between the nuns was sinless. But the question was, what sins had they committed? To determine this they had to establish as precisely as possible what the two nuns did with each other. It was clear from Bartolomea's testimony that no "material instruments" were involved in the relationship. But the officials found out that they engaged in other practices, which according to some jurists were equally offensive. (120)

That is to say: Brown's ventriloquization of the investigators' thought processes tests Bartolomea's description of sex acts performed—mutual masturbation, cunnilingus, and genital rubbing leading to orgasm—against classic juridical definitions of sodomy; while the use of a dildo, absent in this case, would be clinching evidence, Brown nonetheless concludes that the activity "could be interpreted as the classic form of female sodomy" (120). To bring her story to a dramatic finale, that is, to convincingly present the nuns as engaged in lesbian sex, a conviction is necessary. Brown calls out the law.

Bell, on the other hand, does not; for him the nuns engaged in fairly minimal, not world-destroying, sexual behavior, acts easily covered by the two years' penance required by Saint Charles Borromeo, for instance, for fornication between women. Unlike Brown, he thinks the case was utterly unexplosive, and he is struck by "how lightly the visiting friars treated the entire matter" (497), arguing that "the clergy ultimately had no lack of imagination or conceptual framework for describing love between women" (498). The investigators "were in no sense behaving as proto gay rights activists" (496), Bell writes. This strange sentence perhaps delivers the point of the dispute: Brown's gay-affirmative discovery of lesbianism runs parallel to the supposed desire of the investigators to annihilate the female sodomite. A juridical apparatus is involved in either case. In Bell's refusal of a gay-affirmative reading of the story, if the law was not called out, then there was nothing to find. Brown deploys the anachronistic term "lesbian" to designate, from the vantage point of modern knowledge, what Benedetta did not know about herself. Bell rules the term out of order: Benedetta and Bartolomea were not lesbians; there was a vocabulary for what they did, and it did not amount to anything much. Two years' penance: Nothing could be more ordinary than this behavior, nothing less significant. To signify, apparently, is to operate within the apparatus of the law: This is the belief that Brown and Bell share. Brown produces lesbians by her investigation; Bell produces random sex acts that the law does not bother to notice and that the historian ought not to notice either.

"I know what you are saying better than you"; in other words, "[m]y knowledge can position itself in the place whence you speak"; these are sentences in which Michel de Certeau ventriloquizes the position of the exorcist or the doctor confronting the spectacle of the possessed woman; they are also prototypically the sentences of the historian translating the past into terms of modern understanding.[5] Brown's deployment of "lesbian" as the final truth about the condition of Benedetta Carlini is of a piece with these protocols of knowledge. I invoke de Certeau here as much for the acuity of his description of the historiographical operation as for his willingness to attempt to recapture the position from which the possessed woman speaks. For Benedetta also was a possessed woman. Her testimony records visions often assaultive in their demands—that she bare her body, for instance, before a host of figures invading her bedchamber. Her visions hurled her into spheres of visibility that she knew to shun—as in the public celebration of her mystic marriage, over which she presided and preached. Or, rather, to follow de Certeau, the life story that Benedetta produced for the investigators represents an act of translation, turning her mystical experiences into the spheres of their discursivity, "entering into the network of symbolization that a culture offers her" (262). Finally, under the pressure of her investigators' inquiry, she admitted that her visions were demonic, and the visions ceased. Finally, the other nuns, who had witnessed her mystic marriage to Jesus and had sat enraptured listening to her preach in church for three hours, reveal that she had inflicted on herself wounds to make her stigmata bleed and had painted on her finger the ring that she had been given at her marriage. Retrospectively, they claim always to have known what they now know: that she was a fraud. She accepts herself as fraudulent. The historian appears to agree; this is the truth about Benedetta. Through the working of apparatuses of knowledge and power—for the investigators may not be the law, but a papal nuncio is involved, and male authorities are examining this peripheral and newly founded establishment of nuns seeking church recognition—a charismatic leader is sacrificed and the Theatine nuns find their proper place in the church. As de Certeau suggests, while the scene of the exorcist and the possessed woman is one of struggle, this scene is one of consolidation; the nuns and the churchmen band together to form a community from which Benedetta needs to be isolated and removed.

For her speech is not theirs, and this is what her condition reveals. When she speaks, a man's voice is heard; indeed, when this voice speaks through her, she appears to be an adolescent boy. She inhabits another reality, one in which she does not speak but is spoken. She is not a subject in the grammatical sense. She cannot inhabit the position of "I"; it is already inhabited by the voices that possess her. As a subject, she is subjected to the ecstatic pressures that locate her elsewhere. This is seen not only in the mystic marriage but in the more intimate scene, witnessed only by Bartolomea, in which Benedetta exchanged her heart with Jesus. Another scene of violence: The heart is ripped out, for three days she has none, and then a massive heart is forced into a small space. In *Immodest Acts,* Brown cites the records as Bartolomea testifies to how she felt the wound and the bulge:

> [S]he had me put my hand on her heart because she seemed to feel less pain that way. And while I had my hand there it felt as if a dagger were hitting it, so strong was it. . . . And when she [Bartolomea] touched her

> heart she never heard her say anything else, except when Jesus took out her heart. I went to her and I put my hand on the side of her heart. I seemed to feel a hole. (152)
>
> And when He put it [the heart] inside her I began to see that the flesh rose up and she moved slowly, slowly with these rays in front; and all the ribs, which I could see, were lifted up. And when it arrived at the place where the heart belongs, it stopped. . . . I touched it and it felt so large and so hot my hand could not stand it. (154–55)

Benedetta is a subject only by being subjected to a violence that she does not will.

And Bartolomea? When she confessed their sex acts—a confession that Benedetta never made, since, presumably, she was never aware of these acts—she reported it also as a violation, acts of force in which Benedetta thrust her body upon hers, forced her hand into her genitals, pressed her lips to her vagina, speaking, all the while, in the voice of one of her guardian angels, Splenditello, promising love for ever, promising sainthood, assuring Bartolomea that no sin was involved (162–63). As Brown delivers these "immodest acts" in the climactic final pages of her narrative, she ventures multiple explanations of what happened between Bartolomea and Benedetta. On one page, Bartolomea "could well have been the helpless victim of sexual coercion" (124); on the next, it is the desire "to be loved, to be wanted, to be caressed and kissed" that "surely bound Bartolomea to Benedetta" (125); so too, Brown opines, Benedetta "sought . . . more than sexual gratification. She wanted love in every sense" (125). The two nuns seem very modern in their psychologies, as Brown imagines them; and in wanting more than sex, a core of personhood, of identity, seems to follow from the sex acts. This makes the sex comprehensible, but as de Certeau has pointed out in his examinations of mystic speech, the mystical experience is precisely that of a violation of borders, of identity; a love experience so extreme that the beloved is lost in the other.[6] This, I would venture to say, was Benedetta's experience of her visionary raptures; into this rapture Bartolomea entered. "I didn't want to leave and indeed I couldn't leave, feeling as if I were being held" (154); so Bartolomea states, describing her compulsion to witness and participate in the scene of the exchange of hearts. "Hold me because he wants to put the ring on me, but I don't want to do it no matter what" (155); this is what Benedetta says, resisting a forced marriage, declaring her desire to marry Jesus. "Give yourself to me with all your heart and soul and then let me do as I wish" (163); this is what Benedetta/Splenditello says to Bartolomea.

Bartolomea puts her hand on Benedetta's side; she feels the heart heaving, "and I would work so hard that I would sweat" (152), she reports, describing how she clung to Benedetta's body as it was transported elsewhere. When the investigation draws to a close and the visionary experiences are declared demonic possession, Bartolomea tells another story. Now she is not putting her hand on Benedetta's heart, not feeling the gaping aperture there, not entering into the abyss of the loss of identity; rather, she is forced to put her fingers in Benedetta's genitals, forced to submit to unwanted caresses. Through the regime of the investigators' questions, Bartolomea learns how to turn mystical experience into forbidden sex, learns a juridical code to reclassify her activities. To couch this as pedagogy is to recall another scene of instruction, Bartolomea learning to read and write: "This angel Splenditello through the mouth and hands of Benedetta, taught her companion to read and write, making her be near her on her knees and kissing her and putting her hands on her breasts. . . . and Benedetta's two other angels listened to the lesson and saw the writing" (163). This scene of writing will be replaced by the scribal scene of investigation, the demand to produce a new form of speech in which religious ecstasy will be fraud, in which sexual ecstasy and communion will be rewritten as shameful and immodest acts. The scribe's hand, we know, trembles; Bell and Brown scrutinize the page of the transcript describing these immodest acts and its uncharacteristic blots. Who trembles? For Bell, it is Bartolomea, betraying her lover, and the scribe records her lapse; for Brown, it is the scribe himself, not able to believe what he is hearing. The trembling of the hand, I think, cannot be so located; it is not to be ascribed to the failed agency of either of these individuals, for they are complicit in the story being recorded. The trembling is the moment of a transcription from one language to another; it is the turning of the call for ecstasy into the languages that will judge it, condemn it, and classify it, producing a lesbian or a sodomite.

Produce from what? What is the condition, the status of these acts, mystical/sexual, before the intervention of the investigators, juridical or quasi-juridical in their inquiry? There is no easy answer to this; indeed, in this respect, Bell is of use here when we note what is said prefacing Bartolomea's testimony, now that she is no longer Benedetta's companion:

"[S]he sleeps next to the superior, Felice; and last year next to Benedetta" (151). She has been passed from one abbess to another. Presumably only the abbess is given a companion, whose tasks involve intimate bodily attendance, such as undressing the abbess, for instance, or sharing her bed; she exists to tend to the body of the abbess, who presumably has more important matters—of the spirit, but also of administration—on her mind. Bartolomea has been placed where she can serve. When does that which goes without saying become that which must not be said? How do these quiet complicities, these violent denials, map onto mystical/sexual experiences? These are the questions that remain for the historian of sexuality, questions lost in modern translations. They caution wariness of the juridical protocols that either produce identity or deny it. The sexuality we seek in this case of a lesbian nun may be in a place we cannot recognize, in bodily experiences we no longer have or for which we have no name, in regions unavailable to the law.

And if so, the question remains: Are these experiences therefore unavailable to the historian? If, as de Certeau claims, the effect of translation involves "what is unspeakable and what can be signified," then "something else" must be brought to the "side of signification."[7] In a parallel consideration, Jacques Rancière has commented in *The Names of History* on the use of heresy for historians (he has in mind particularly those of the Annales school, including Fernand Braudel and Emmanuel Le Roy Ladurie, but literary historians will immediately add Stephen Greenblatt to this list).[8] Commenting on the procedures in which the historian returns heresy to its roots (in the land—a tactic also offered by Brown as she contrasts Benedetta's agrarian and mountain backgrounds with the urban sphere in which she arrived), Rancière argues a chilling parallel: "The inquisitor suppresses history by eradicating it: he marks it, he locks it up, he kills it. The historian, on the contrary, suppresses it by giving it roots. He removes it, as it were retrospectively, from the inquisitorial condemnation by giving it the color of the earth and the stones, by rendering it indiscernible from its place" (73). Opposing this operation, Rancière gestures instead to a heretical history: both to a history of heresy that continues to hold out a promise for the future as well as to a history heretical in its operation, in its refusal to consign history to the act of signification. For him, this is "the heresy that is inherent in democratic and social historicity" (93), a modern errancy that Rancière attaches to the figure of the worker, although this is the wrong way to put it. For both the individual and social bodies that Rancière designates refuse such borders of determination: They cannot be given such names. Rather, "they are the singular names, falsely proper and falsely common, of a being-together without place or body—of a being-together that is a being-between: between several places and several identities, several modes of localization and identification" (94).[9]

Rancière's gesture toward a heteronymy (not mere pluralism) and to betweenness means, I think, to capture the possibilities that still inhere in history; rather than freeze history into a determinate narrative, tethered wherever it may be, it opens history and leaves history open. And to return to the more immediate concerns of this essay: What Rancière suggests could find a parallel even in the graphic form of the title of an essay by Valerie Traub, "The (In)Significance of 'Lesbian' Desire."[10] Placing "in" in parentheses, Traub suggests the intimate relationship between the significant and the insignificant and gestures summarily to the difficulty of moving the insignificant into the domain of signification. Her subject, "lesbian" desire ("lesbian" in scare quotes), is immediately desituated between the modern identity category and the earlier sets of behaviors, social relationships, and possibilities of representation that Traub explores. Traub is explicit in her uneasiness with theology and the law, especially the latter, as the privileged discourse in which sodomy—and by extension, sexuality—has been located in early modernity; the "legal category of sodomy has functioned implicitly as a regulatory mechanism," she writes, "preempting all possibility of analysis precisely because the discourse of law has stood as arbiter of social fact: if no Englishwoman was brought to trial under the sodomy statute, ipso facto no women practiced such behaviors" (64). Traub's statement pursues to its illogical conclusion what follows if one takes the law as the only mechanism for identifying sexual behavior, and it thus handily explains how Brown can make Benedetta signify as lesbian and how Bell can deny significance to the sex acts of the nuns. Multiplying the discursive sites and possibilities for locating sex between women, Traub places on the side of signification a range of figures, all characterized by a logic of supplementarity: the French female sodomite with her strap-on; the tribade with an enlarged clitoris, who appears in gynecological treatments; the transvestite, especially in theatrical disguise. By allying these figures to the Derridean supplement, Traub moors them to a signifying system of gender difference that is at the same time unmoored;

these supplementary figures both imitate and also reoccupy territory that the law denies them. But the privileged site for Traub in this essay is the virtually invisible coupling of woman with woman: those whom the law does not discover, a group that Traub refers to, courting a different anachronism, as "femmes"; women who are not marked by the use of dildos or enlarged clitorises; women, that is, who are not thought to simulate male-female sex in their sex acts. These are the insignificant lesbians whose significance Traub seeks to make visible, and their sphere of operation—in dramatic texts—is seemingly placed outside the law, beyond even the logic of the supplement.

These gestures—on the one hand, to trouble the selfsameness of the law; on the other, to locate a domain untouched by the law—resonate with the possibilities in de Certeau and Rancière and go beyond these historians precisely in imagining sexuality as a site for new futures and new social organizations. Traub's reading reverses what happens in the plays she examines; there, the enunciation of a woman's desire for another woman only takes place within the bracket of heterosexual coupling; "symmetrical, 'feminine' homoerotic desire was granted signification only *after* it was rendered insignificant" (72). Rather than countenacing this erasure, Traub sees it also as a productive moment. But productive of what? This is a question Traub herself raises. If it is only by (supposed) usurpation of male gender that female-female eroticism enters into (and potentially disrupts) the signifying system, then what are the terms for conjuring the femme into existence? Traub answers, "I find it inconceivable that within the vast array of erotic choices reported by early modern culture, 'feminine' bodies did not meet, touch, and pleasure one another," that "in light of the fact that gynecological texts encouraged men to arouse their wives by caressing their breasts and genitals, it seems implausible that women's pleasure was exclusively centered on penetration" (79), the latter the model assumed for the female sodomite.

There are some troubling suppositions here. For one thing, Traub wants to preserve, as feminine, erotic experience untouched by phallic penetration, yet she grounds feminine experience on the model of the precopulative behavior recommended to husbands. Although "feminine" is in scare quotes, Traub here seems closer to Brown's regulatory deployment of "lesbian" than she might imagine.[11] For Brown, the limit to Benedetta's self-understanding lay in the "male identity [that] . . . allowed her to have sexual and emotional relations that she could not conceive between women"; only disguised as Splenditello could she express her "preference for a sexual relationship with another woman" (127). Brown calls Benedetta a lesbian because she sees through this disguise, as well as her religious fraud, to her gendered, sexual truth. Traub similarly identifies the femme and the caresses that women prefer to the disguises of masculinity and phallic penetration. The femme resecures the law of gender, lesbian desire untouched by the masculine. But can this be the case if, as Traub argues, the unnoticed and now signifying femme was simultaneously possible and invisible thanks to her presumed availablility for marriage and the task of reproduction? While Traub certainly knows that marriage need not terminate the possibility for women to have sex with each other, comedy, she claims, does close off that possibility. In drama, at least, there is, it seems, no way outside of the law. The law of gender is also the law of genre. Its name is "marriage." This is an argument to which I will return at the close of this essay.

Traub's formulation echoes a dilemma that structures the discussion of "gender trouble" offered by Judith Butler, a theorist upon whom Traub explicitly depends. For if the tribade visibly disrupts gender, the seeming conformity of the femme locates gender trouble inside of the norm of femininity. Thus, while the female sodomite calls out the law, "absence of outcry" (in Traub's phrase [78]), surrounds the femme. In this respect, it could be argued that the femme troubles the very distinction between the law and that which is illegal, troubles the distinction between what is inside and what is outside the law.

Butler's *Gender Trouble* is often misconceived as a celebration of ludic performativity.[12] However, it too finds the law inescapable. Butler acknowledges that "there is no reason to assume that the law . . . is impervious to historical variability and possibility" (66); this leads her to precisely the right questions, doubting whether the law is all-determining, pondering that "'the' law may not even be singular" (67). Nonetheless, her arguments in "Subversive Bodily Acts," the third chapter, which leads to the articulation of a politics of the performative, invariably mobilize the very category she has questioned. She calls on the law to dismantle arguments by Julia Kristeva, Foucault, Monique Wittig, and others. Relentlessly, she shows how their positing of regimes before or outside the law are ruses produced by the law. Kristeva's originary semiotic and maternal, for instance, is relocated by Butler as regulated by a paternal law that makes itself invisible in this affective state supposedly before the law—a state of nature, Butler acutely argues, necessary precisely to locate women in terms of the maternal task they perform within the law. (This parallels Traub's relocation of the femme in the normative position of the reproductive woman, available therefore to the apparatus of marriage determined by the law.) So, too, Butler argues that the hermaphrodite Herculine Barbin, in whom Foucault finds an example of a body that refuses the juridical categories of gender, is 'outside' the law only as "the law maintains this 'outside' within itself" (106). These are compelling arguments, to be sure, not least for suggesting that regimes of possibility already occupy signifying systems; gender trouble and nonheteronormative forms of behavior are located within a social order whose parameters are significantly widened. The price paid for this argument, however, is that the law, however less monolithic it may be, is also resecured. Butler writes, concluding her argument with Kristeva, "If subversion is possible, it will be subversion from within the terms of the law, through the possibilities that emerge when the law turns against itself and spawns unexpected permutations of itself" (93).

Butler's question must be asked again, what is this law in the singular? Certainly, for the inquiry at hand, sodomy laws in the early modern period are noteworthy for a lack of uniformity. In their variability, they are a textbook example supporting Foucault's critique of the repressive hypothesis, that is, the notion that it is only what the law allows or disallows that makes visible what a culture will recognize as licit/illicit sexuality. The very variability and incommensurability of the law as it fastened on gendered and differently raced bodies in early modern Europe points not to the ability of the law to allow to appear or attempt to deny some preexistent sexuality, but only to its productive ability to name certain bodies as sodomitical. Licit/illicit may hardly describe the parameters of sexuality.[13] This point subtends Alan Bray's *Homosexuality in Renaissance England,* a book wary of using the law as a privileged site for the production of knowledge and of importing modern identity categories to the Renaissance. Nonetheless, on Bray's account, the emergence into visibility of the sodomite is always tied to a juridical apparatus: For Bray, the sodomite appears when the law calls him out. Moreover, while there are no homosexuals in Bray's book, their very invisibility, as Elizabeth Pittenger has argued, is figured through the model of the (modern) closet. Bray's discovery of sexuality takes the form of an outing of a latent truth hidden beneath a vocabulary that does not know how, or fears, to name itself properly.[14]

This problem in signification parallels Traub's, and it emerges from the historical situation Bray locates so brilliantly, a fundamental dehiscence between the image of the world-shattering sodomite and the paucity of legal cases in England; between the *social* disruption that attaches to those condemned and their sexuality. Indeed, for Bray, "sodomy" does not necessarily signify a sexual activity. Thus, the question of finding "homosexuality" in Renaissance England must depart from the law. Bray locates sexual activity in the hierarchized world of normal social structures, in the disproportionate power relations between masters and servants, teachers and pupils, and the like, thereby situating the potential outlaw within the constitutive structures of Elizabethan society. The relationship between sodomy and such sexuality must be occluded, since it is constitutive of normative hierarchies, a nonrelationship insofar as "homosexuality" remains a secret both to the society that has only the word "sodomy" for same-sex sex and to the individual who cannot afford to recognize his ordinary sexual behavior as world-shattering.[15] In a subsequent essay on sodomy and friendship, Bray demonstrates the virtual impossibility of distinguishing between a cultural ideal and a form of utter stigmatization, seeing in friendship (the male equivalent to the femme-femme configuration in Traub's account) a discursive and social form that prescribes precisely those intimate behaviors that the law proscribes.[16] The difference between friend and sodomite is contextual rather than absolute.

The kinds of epistemological spaces opened in Bray's work could be mapped more widely in early modern Europe by recognizing that the model of the sovereign repressive law was not, in fact, the only model to operate in the identification of sodomites, as has hitherto been assumed. It is in this respect that Michael Rocke's *Forbidden Friendships* is especially revealing. Rocke's work details the working of the Office of the Night, a special quasi-juridical magistracy composed of selected citizens devoted to the apprehension of sodomites in quattrocento Florence. While the rhetoric of the law in this period insisted on sodomy in the usual terms, as an "abominable vice" and as condemned in the scripture as "the most evil sin" (143), the provisions of the law under which the Night operated were bent less on eliminating sodomites than on identifying them: Its punishments were fines rather than the stake, and it usually failed to punish anyone under the age of eighteen or anyone who condemned himself to the officials.

The Night functioned in tandem with a more regularly constituted legal body, the Eight, which handled cases of the kind one might usually associate with the heinous crime of sodomy: violent assaults, desecrations of sacred sites, acts involving other crimes or committed by non-Christians; it was left to the Night to punish what Rocke considers to be more consensual as well as more "mundane sexual activity" (67). Thus, these two offices covered and apparently recognized both sides of the divide that Bray identifies as occluded in England. Indeed, from the staggering numbers of cases brought to the attention of the Night—almost 17,000—Rocke argues that no distinction can be drawn between sodomite and the larger male culture, that sex between men operated "within a framework of cultural premises about masculinity, status, honor, and shame" (88), that it "embodied and expressed social division and rank" (112) coextensive with the dense networks of locale, work, friendship, clientage, and patronage of Florentine society. Rocke's evidence supports the claim Bray makes in his essay on sodomy and friendship and in fact goes further in locating male-male behavior within gendered norms as "an integral facet of male homosocial culture" (191). Indeed, demonstrating that such recognition was available in Florence (unlike in England), Rocke cites a letter by Niccolo Machiavelli to his friend Francesco Vettori assuring him that so long as a person appears upright in his daily life, his nighttime behavior will not be subject to reproach: "Rather than being called a bugger or a whoremonger, one says he is a man of broad interests, easygoing, and a good fellow" (147).[17]

Thus, whereas Bray poses questions of (non)signification that can also be seen in Traub's work, Rocke maps known terrains, the "norms and conventions of sexual behavior" (9) revealed in the working of the Night. Like Bray, Rocke finds sodomy expressed through hierarchical structures, especially age differences; these dictated positions to be taken in sex acts over the course of adolescence and young manhood as well as the direction of the flow of gifts and favors. Like Bray, he assumes that a culture that delayed marriage for males accounts for the proliferation of same-sex behavior (in Florence, marriage occurred even a bit later than in England, and "youth," Rocke argues, defined men into their thirties). Because for Rocke there is no epistemological aporia as there is for Bray, he does not venture much of an explanation why an apparatus was mobilized against such supposedly normative behaviors. To cover the distance between the rhetoric of excoriation and the ordinariness of a practice that, he claims, involved at least half the male population of Florence, Rocke regards the Night as a socially regulatory body that "probably did not really intend to 'eradicate' the 'vice' . . . but to confine it within tolerable limits" (84), a hypothesis reiterated as a conclusion: "[T]he Night Officers were probably never seriously intended to root out sodomy completely, but rather to contain it within acceptable bounds" (226). The Night, that is, did not mean and never were meant to uphold the letter of the law.

Since they did condemn some three thousand men, Rocke determines the biases in the operation of the Night. Not surprisingly, it was usually poorer men, rather than the rich, who were fined; bachelors rather than married men; "inveterate" rather than casual sodomites. Even this social regulation was recognized; one text Rocke cites makes the point quite graphically: "The great impose penalties on those who fuck in the ass for no other reason than this: since it's their profession, they don't want ruffians to use it" (136).

Just as the Night contained sodomy within the limits of the tolerable, Rocke seeks to "restore" same-sex behavior "to its legitimate place as an integral part of the society and culture of late medieval and Renaissance Florence" (5), to, he reiterates, its "proper" place (16). It is here that we encounter again the problem of historical significance that Rancière enunciates. Indeed, in furthering his claim that the Night discovered social normativities, Rocke ventures the possibility that same-sex couples occasionally married, that accusations referring to boys kept as wives may reflect a real practice. Just as Rocke reads through the vitriolic antisodomy rhetoric of the time (especially evident in the sermons of Bernardino da Siena) to find in it a "reflected . . . social reality" (40)—precisely *Rocke's* demography—so, too, metaphors of marriage, Rocke opines, may refer "to something more tangible" (171). Although Rocke recognizes that power differences and violence characterized relations between men and boys and that calling a boy a woman was not exactly praise, he revalues that terminology as indicative of relationships characterized by affection, companionship, and love (167), concluding that while "this society could hardly have sanctioned same-sex 'marriages,' . . . their existence was evidently acknowledged and to some extent tolerated, as the generally lax control of sodomy implies" (172). It is perfectly comprehensible why Rocke might like to believe this: It gives Florentine gays a place at the table. What it fails to explain is the relationship between supposed toleration and the patterns of persecution.

Nagging questions therefore remain, even if one grants the likelihood of widespread same-sex activity, questions that may not easily be answered by the archives or through the method at work in Rocke's restorative project. Since accusations remained anonymous and were solicited by reward, the motives behind them remain obscure. While Rocke, like Bray, shows that political exigencies (usually involving transfers of power) triggered especially numerous convictions, the meaning of these statistics remains in question: How was sodomy a political crime, an instance of lèse-majesté, as the law passed at the beginning of the Night's operations affirmed?[18] If homosexual behavior was part of the homosocial, what irritation beyond "normative" masculinity remained? Can the sodomite simply be subsumed into a normative gendered position? Might relations to boys have threatened rather than resembled marriage? Finally—and this is the crucial question, I think—what made accusation as normative as the activity itself?

One theoretical answer might lie in remarking that the law Rocke deals with does not function on the sovereign model; rather, it works as what Foucault would call a disciplinary regime, a policing function. It created the archive that allows Rocke to argue that sodomy was contained within social normativity, effectively managing recidivists or the unruly classes, assuring "proper" masculinity. This is what the archive reveals, what it produced through its mechanisms of accusation, self-confession, threats of torture, and promises to boys of immunity. Indeed, the Night's treatment of boys parallels the behavior of sodomites and perhaps suggests one way the apparatus may have incited sodomy. What Rocke reads as evidence of social norms may instead be an archive inventing them; those whom the Night failed to punish may serve to create a regulatory fiction that Rocke embraces as social reality. Rocke's sense of the norm conveyed by the records has mainly to do with the strict observation of age difference as a control on the stages and positions taken. What, then, is to be made of the fact that a tract advocating pederasty takes to task those men who pursue other adults as "rebels of love, men of brutish and corrupted sense" (95)? Does this not suggest that such men existed, even if the records do not show this? What, indeed, is to be made of a remark that Rocke terms "intriguing" offered in one denunciation of an older "passive" partner that explains the rarity of cases this way: "Everyone likes to fuck the older ones, because they wont tell" (102). This further suggests that the records of the Night may conceal as much as they reveal to produce their picture of sodomy contained within the bounds of acceptability.

Rocke tends to (mis)recognize the Night as a relatively lenient apparatus. While the rarity of the death penalty might justify such a characterization, this was also the case with the Eight; the crucial difference in the punishments meted out lay in the amount of public humiliation the Eight inflicted. But this once again means that there was a gap between what many did, what was known, and what could be said. It also means that the Night (and Rocke's reading of their behavior) made acceptable a level of intrusiveness and surveillance that is one of the ruses of the extralegal domains of government. It fostered accusations upon which it acted in ways that Rocke labels lax and inconsistent. Yet this inconsistency is the effect of the statistics that Rocke extrapolates on the basis of the categories of age, marital status, or social status that his archive (along with a contemporary census) makes available to him. Rocke likes statistics and bar graphs: These are tools of normativization.[19] What appears to be laxness and inconsistency beyond the operation of gross bias is unavailable to the historian who confines himself to what the archive provides, but this does not mean that explanations were unavailable. It may mean that they lie elsewhere, that there are levels of occlusion that disappear in the perfect symmetry and homeostasis that Rocke reads between the norms produced by the archive and his reading out from it to a social normativity into which homosexuality somehow disappears and yet remains policed and punished.

The apparatus that Rocke explores offers a model of government quite different from one based in the sovereignty of the law. It anticipates a host of recognizable apparatuses of modernity and suggests that even in the early modern period—which, according to the Foucault of *Discipline and Punish,* is the time of the law—the model of "the law" and "the symbolic" needs to be multiplied in the direction of "governmentality" rather than couched in the singular.[20] The effect of this would be to deprivilege the law and the sovereign; it might afford latitude for cultural and sexual forms of expression and behavior that are not caught in the double bind of the law or the diacritical difference of signification. These are not quite affordances provided by Rocke's study, which effectively folds the sodomite back into social normativity (yet Rocke's conclusion that the Night was abolished as a public embarrassment suggests that it revealed something that was meant to remain invisible, a norm that also disrupts). If sodomites were everywhere, this may not have been a messsage the government wished to sponsor even at a time when the supposed discreteness of sexual identity was not an operative concept. The temptation to legislate a "proper" definition of the sexual subject—which, as we have seen in the cases of Traub and of Rocke, reinscribes a gender normativity—remains even in work that seeks to distance itself from the apparatus of the stigmatizing and revealing hand of the law that supposedly performs the double motion of allowing or disallowing the sexual subject to occupy the historical stage.

And what of "the stage" itself? To ask this question is to gesture toward those domains of cultural production that Bray handles warily, Rocke even more so. It is also to return us to Traub's claim that only a momentary lapse allows for the appearence of the femme-femme couple in early modern English drama, that ultimately dramatic necessity is tied to heteronormativity, one law regulating marriage onstage and off. Rather than one of the texts that Traub examines in the essay discussed earlier, I wish to consider *Twelfth Night* (a text about which she also has written) because it offers an instance when the law appears on stage.[21] Although the immediate occasion for the police to arrive involves a male character—indeed, a character who is almost unique in Shakespeare for the fervor of his declarations of love for another man and for having no female partner[22]—the arrest of Antonio in act 3, scene 4 also coincides with the movement in the play to bring to an end Viola's assumption of male drag, to eliminate all improper suitors for Olivia, making way for the arrival of Sebastian, Antonio's lover, as Olivia's husband; the arrest of Antonio arrests the plot—it now begins to unravel—and precipitates the move toward proper heterosexual coupling that comedies seem to offer as their close. What needs to be asked is whether the law that apprehends Antonio is also the law that dictates that the social order can only maintain and reproduce itself through exclusively heterosexual marriage relations, that is, whether we witness here, in effect, the eruption of the law to eradicate the sodomite and to make way for the licit.

Why is Illyria dangerous to Antonio? At first, declaring he will follow Sebastian to Orsino's court, the "danger" (2.1.47) lies with "enemies in

Orsino's court" (2.1.44); neither Antonio's crime nor his danger is specified.[23] Only the fact that he adores Sebastian suggests its extremity and the degree of self-sacrifice involved in Antonio's pursuit: "But come what may, I do adore thee so, / That danger shall seem sport, and I will go" (2.1.46–47). When, driven by "desire / More sharp than filed steel" (3.3.4–5), Antonio joins Sebastian in Illyria, he explains his "danger" (3.3.25) by offering a narrative about "a sea-fight 'gainst the Count his galleys" (3.3.26) which, he insists, in answer to Sebastian's worried question, was not a matter of blood but money: He alone refused to return the booty taken at that occasion, "for which, if I be lapsed in this place, / I shall pay dear" (3.3.36–37). Sebastian's worry is not quite answered, since the dear price seems almost certainly to be Antonio's life, not his money; while the offense may not have been of a "bloody nature" (3.3.30), the payment would seem to be. And indeed, without specifying what the offense was, Antonio alludes to a "bloody argument" (3.3.32) that might well have led to the bloody offense he claims not to have committed. Finally, brought before Orsino, charges are made: that Antonio is a thief and a pirate, charges that Antonio as insistently denies:

> Antonio never yet was thief, or pirate,
> Though I confess, on base and ground enough,
> Orsino's enemy.
>
> (5.1.72–74)

Something is being admitted—confessed—here, although the "base and ground" seems as incapable of specification as the "bloody argument" to which Antonio had alluded earlier.

Or perhaps not: In addition to the charge of piracy, the police officer alleges that Antonio boarded a ship when Orsino's "young nephew Titus lost his leg" (5.1.61). This gratuitous detail may retrospectively explain Antonio's earlier insistence that *he* committed no bloody offense although there was some question of blood in his enmity. And while his later denial of piracy and theft may mean to insist on the legitimacy of his sea fight, what remains unsaid is the "base and ground" for enmity—and its relationship to Orsino's wounded nephew, who seems to be produced out of nowhere for the one line in which he appears. Orsino, that is, does not charge Antonio with the crime against Titus; even the officer seems only to be offering circumstantial evidence: Antonio was there when Titus lost his leg.

The possibility of defining Antonio's crime seems to evaporate even as it draws nearer and nearer to the body of Orsino: Antonio goes from having enemies at court to being implicated in the wound to the duke's nephew. What begins and remains for Antonio as a legitimately founded controversy is nonetheless a matter of singularity, retrospectively illegitimate from the moment when everyone but Antonio agrees to pay the price. In this refusal, Antonio thus seems to be an enemy of the state—his own as well as Orsino's. Indeed, given his parallel in the plot with the sea captain who rescues Viola on the coast of Illyria, Antonio's own state may well be Illyria too, and the shipboard fight could represent Antonio's place in a faction opposed to those closer to Orsino.[24] The wounding of Titus may figure in this context; the officer does not specify when Titus lost his leg, whether it was before or after Antonio "took" (5.1.59) Orsino's treasure. He mentions the wound second, and in a sightly more emphatic past tense than "took"; Antonio "did . . . board" the ship on which Titus lost his leg. This may locate that event further in the past, as an older ground of contention between Antonio and Orsino. At any rate, this additional, unanswered quasi-charge against Antonio has undoubted symbolic resonance. Suddenly Orsino has a "young nephew" (5.1.61), and, just as unexpectedly, this possible heir to the unmarried Duke has a wound that displaces but nonetheless suggests castration.[25] One-legged Titus—Orsino's legatee, if he is that—may be the leg that Orsino stands on for succession; in which case, his legacy and legitimacy are in doubt. The wound to the state involved in the refusal of trade is repeated on the body of the boy, and Antonio's crime may be a capital one, may be lèse-majesté.

> Antonio never yet was thief, or pirate,
> Though I confess, on base and ground enough,
> Orsino's enemy. A witchcraft drew me hither:
> That most ingrateful boy there by your side . . .
>
> (5.1.72–75)

Just as the mention of Titus seems unmotivated, out of place, gratuitous, the sequence of Antonio's lines, even as they answer Orsino's questions about what motivated him to put himself in danger, arrive at a virtual non sequitur. The confession of ground leads to another boy, the ingrate in Orsino's company, at his side, the boy who refused to give Antonio back his purse, refused just the kind of monetary exchange that Antonio claimed for himself. In naming this "base and ground," Orsino and Antonio are positioned as rivals for the love of the same boy. Retrospectively that is the reason for their ancient enmity; Laurie Osborne puts the point bluntly: "Orsino's and Antonio's initial argument originated over the body of a (castrated) young man; in the final scene, their quarrel resurfaces, this time explicitly as rivalry over another youth who lacks something of a man." As she notes as well, even the dispute about tribute is reenacted by the "ungrateful boy."[26]

In these ways, Antonio's crime against the state moves into the orbit of the unmentionable and capital crime; the word "sodomy" is never uttered, but that something palpably remains unsaid as explanations are offered for the enmity furthers this supposition. If so, it would seem to be dispelled when the boy is doubled with the appearance of Sebastian:

Sebastian. O Antonio! O my dear Antonio,
How have the hours rack'd and tortur'd me,
Since I have lost thee!
Antonio. Sebastian are you?
Sebastian. Fear'st thou that, Antonio?
Antonio. How have you made division of yourself?
(5.1.216–20)

These are the only words exchanged between Sebastian and Antonio in the final act of the play, and while they restore Antonio as Sebastian's "dear Antonio" and render assurances that he is no ungrateful boy, as had been feared, the Sebastian who appears now also is married to Olivia. The economies that had bound the two men—the risk of life and purse that had been ventured against the earlier refusals of normal trade and succession—are resituated. It would seem as if the threat represented by Antonio has been folded into the relocation of Sebastian as married man. Indeed, in this context, it is worth noting Orsino's response to Sebastian's lines about nature's bias (5.1.258), about his status as both man and maid—lines that have exercised recent critics attempting to adjudicate the relationship between his attachment to Antonio and his marriage, to measure Olivia's attractions to Viola, now revealed as female in gender—"Be not amaz'd," Orsino counsels, "right noble is his blood" (5.1.262).[27] When we recall the prevarications around "blood" in Antonio's explanation to Sebastian about his crime, when we add that the wound to Titus may be understood as directed at Orsino's blood (at his lineage), it would appear that, for Orsino, the crucial question raised by the question of nature and of gender has been answered by the assurance of blood status. The worry seems to have been not about inappropriately gendered objects but about the failure of the aristocratic line that might have followed from marriage between a duke or a countess and a lowborn maid or man. That would seem to be the issue resolved, sorted out in the division of Viola/Sebastian: not merely heterosexual resolution, then, but the preservation of the aristocracy from lower-class incursion.

The duke's assurances about Sebastian's lineage would be news to everyone on stage except Antonio, to whom Sebastian confided this information at the moment he supplied him with his proper name (2.1.16–17). Thus, while Orsino dispels the worry that people might wind up married to those lower in rank (an assurance that does not dispose of the fact that both he and Olivia fell in love with their servants, or that Toby has married Maria, the servant who can simulate Olivia's hand), Antonio's union with Sebastian has not operated under this misapprehension. Rather, the opposite: Antonio loves a man above him in station but diminished in wealth and position. Sebastian is Antonio's upper-class rent boy; the feared betrayal of Sebastian is manifest at the moment when the boy refuses to return Antonio's purse. Thus, the economic relationship between Sebastian and Antonio, a seaman who has enemies at court and who may have been involved in wounding the duke's nephew, overturns status relationships. It reveals what Orsino's assurance meant to cover, the insecurity and possible dependence of the aristocracy on resources they do not control. If Antonio appears as a sodomite in this context—if the crime of sodomy aimed at the body of the ruler is also the "crime" of reversing class and status—the sodomite anticipates and instantiates the social transformation in which capital rather than inherited status determines power.[28]

At the close of *Twelfth Night,* when Sebastian recovers his name and place, as well as Olivia's fortune, Antonio may be a welcome friend and not a threat, inside not outside the social order. This is not to suggest, however, that there is no outside. Antonio's arrest, as I remarked earlier, brings to a halt the multiple false suitors at Olivia's door: Cesario/Viola will be replaced by Sebastian, Sir Andrew will give up his suit (he has already sacrificed his wealth to Toby and his horse to Cesario), and Malvolio, who appears cross-gartered in the same scene in which Antonio is arrested, will next appear in prison—that is, the very place where we presume Antonio has also been taken after his arrest. Malvolio returns at the end of the play. Although he has, in prison, undergone a virtual exorcism to cure him of *his* version of "witchcraft," he refuses to be reintegrated into the restored social order, which in reaffirming the aristocracy can find no place for someone who dreamed of being Count Malvolio and playing with his . . . rich jewel. Orsino's assurance about Sebastian and Viola's rank, which implicates Antonio in the threat of social upheaval, of the infiltration of the aristocracy by base blood, aligns Antonio with Malvolio. Moreover, as his name graphically suggests—"Mal-volio"—he is a male Viola. A rival for the hand of Olivia, he is also positioned as a false Sebastian, both as Viola and as the betraying boy misapprehended by Antonio. With the expulsion of Malvolio, all threats seem to have been contained, including the specter of a male-male couple and economies that refuse the exchanges of heteronormative, aristocratic society.

And yet with all these movements to secure closure, Malvolio is outside; the threat has not been contained, and the social order remains incomplete. The hole is suggested by the silence of Antonio. Assured by Sebastian of his love, he speaks as Sebastian's marriage is revealed, a marriage that is also coincident with a racked and tortured Sebastian, fearing the loss of Antonio, a displacement of death and imprisonment from Antonio to Sebastian. Antonio's inclusion is bought at a price, one sign of which, as Osborne has shown, is a hundred-year-long stage tradition (from the late eighteenth to the late nineteenth centuries) in which Orsino explicitly pardoned Antonio.[29] Malvolio's raging exit line takes the place of this silence, puncturing closure, moreover, since someone *in his power* yet remains under arrest: the sea captain, Antonio's double, who has Viola's female attire. Orsino ends the play holding his future wife at arm's length, waiting for something that will never come: precisely the legitimacy he hailed in naming Sebastian as an aristocrat, resolving the questions of gender and the bias of nature in terms of the maintenance of lineage. Viola remains a boy until then. The relationship of male-male to male-female coupling remains in question rather than resolved, displaced from Antonio-Sebastian to Orsino-Cesario. Female-female coupling also is in question in the marriage of Olivia and Sebastian, and not simply in Sebastian's prevarication on "maid," which beyond assuring his virginity may also suggest his continuing dependence upon Antonio. For Viola in male drag is also a visible tribade.[30] "A sister! you are she" (5.1.325). This is the acceptable form in which Olivia embraces Viola, a parallel to the restoration of Antonio to married Sebastian, paralleled, too, when Olivia invites Orsino to think of her as a sister (5.1.316), which he does (5.1.383). It is as if the initial problem in the play—Olivia's love for a dead brother, Viola and Sebastian's belief that the other is dead—has been solved through a substitute sibling; the normative institution of marriage, with all its regulations of proper coupling, is brought into proximity to incest; the attempts of the aristocracy to preserve its blood is implicated in the prime violation of the law. "Sister" contains within the family, moreover, the cross-dressed woman left onstage, a problem unresolved as long as the sea captain remains in jail—which he always will in this play. "Sister"—the address of one woman to another, the making proper of their erotic feeling as family feeling—the word is spoken by a "femme" to a "tribade."

What are the conclusions to be drawn? Perhaps simply this: that in considering the relations of Viola and Olivia—or of Benedetta and Bartolomea, for that matter—the working of the law, the categories of the licit and the illicit, are inadequate analytic tools that give us only limited purchase on historical realities or representational regimes. "Sister," in the final moments of *Twelfth Night,* provides a term for continuing relationships, a familiar locution that also is defamiliarized. And not just by recalling that the family is the locus and productive site of desires supposedly inimical to it: "Sister" is also the usual term one nun calls another, and it thereby suggests one way that family terms have unfamiliar resources, pointing again to how unstable the boundary might be between the licit and the illicit. Indeed, more than that, the use of "sister" enacts a displacement of such a binarism by a term that only seems to participate in it, and this precisely because "sister" can name blood relations or relations of affinity created by marital ties or affinities necessarily outside marriage; "sister" names at once the forbidden object of incestuous desire, the displaced object of desire, and the displacement of desire itself.

PART II

Hamlet's Hand

In his 1942–43 lectures on Parmenides, Martin Heidegger inveighs against the typewriter: "typewriting . . . hides handwriting," he writes, "and, thereby, character" [die Maschinenschrift . . . die Handschrift und damit den Charakter verbirgt].[1] As Heidegger's usage reminds us, character is, precisely, a scriptive formation; individuals are delivered in their hands and authenticated by their signatures. Historians of literacy depend upon these marks.[2] For many of them, as for Heidegger, the evidence of the individual hand implies a metaphysical investment; it is explicit when Heidegger posits as essentially human the possession of language—and the possession of the hand. As he puts it in *What is Called Thinking?*: "only a being who can speak, that is, think, can have hands."[3]

I begin with a modern instance in the history of Western philosophy, which Jacques Derrida has summarized as logocentrism, although I might as easily have invoked ancient or Renaissance examples; Gregory of Nyssa, for instance, writes that "it was above all for language that nature added hands to our bodies." He continues, "Hands are the characteristic of rational nature," since "it is, in effect, one of the marks of the presence of reason to express itself through letters."[4] Or I might have cited the Spanish writing master Andres Brun, writing in 1583: "Plato says that the difference which divides us humans from the animals is that we have the power of speech and they do not. I, however, say that the difference is that we know how to *write* but they do not."[5]

(Human) Being is in the hand. Yet Heidegger also proclaims Socrates "the purest thinker of the West. . . . He wrote nothing";[6] the mind does not need a hand. And Gregory of Nyssa would subordinate the hand to speech, even though he equates rationality with the hand. The Spanish writing master out-Platos Plato by installing writing in place of speech as the sign of a transcendental difference. In these instances, the metaphysical hand barely maintains an essential humanity, nor does it easily uphold transcendental Being. Pretending to an instrumental transparency, these formulations about the hand point instead to a recalcitrance; they point, in a word, to writing as the founding instance of that which causes the metaphysical foundations to founder.

Heidegger inveighs against the machine and also, like Andres Brun, against the animal. "No animal has a hand," he writes.[7] But what if the hand, and with it materiality, and with it the individual, had no foundation but the characteristic mark, a mark no hand could own? In Friedrich Engels's fragmentary and exploratory essay "The Part Played by Labour in the Transition from Ape to Man,"[8] where, according to Elaine Scarry, Engels accurately speculates "that the crucial location of the transition from ape to man had been in the hand, the organ of making, rather than in the skull, the attendant of the organ of thinking."[9] "No simian hand has ever fashioned even the crudest of stone knives," Engels writes, and it is only when the hand makes that the hand becomes human. The human hand "is not only the organ of labour, *it is also the product of labour,*" he emphasizes (81). The hand is made by what it makes. It is, it has being, precisely as an artifact. The hand that extends into matter through the instrument is itself materialized, the founding instance of a being-in-the-hand stripped of its metaphysical dimension, an instance that finds its echo—or so I intend to argue—in a Shakespearean moment like this one in *Hamlet:* Claudius receives a letter from Hamlet: "Know you the hand?" Laertes asks; "'Tis Hamlet's character," the king replies (4.7.50).[10] The play offers an *equation* of hand and character, but it is not the same as Heidegger's equation. Nor is the equation the same in *King Lear* when Edmund reads a letter ascribed to Edgar: "You know the character to be your brother's?" (1.2.61); nor, again, when Malvolio (mis)recognizes Olivia's "sweet Roman hand" (*Twelfth Night,* 3.4.26). In these instances, the characteristic hand has been charactered, made by what has been made. In these instances, the hand, materialized as writing, is emphatically a social hand, the disowned mark of material production.

Sentience, as Scarry says, is "itself an artifact" (255) when the hand is extended into the materials it makes, and it gains from those materials the ability to participate in the world of things made. For Scarry, "the socialization of sentience"—the ability of our language and our objects, indeed, of our language as an object—to be shared is what characterizes human beings. But sharing (or communicating) may sentimentalize the notion of labor that Scarry takes from Engels. For Engels, the liberation of the voice that follows upon the liberation of the hand is a fact of labor. "Men in the making arrived at the point where *they had something to say* to one another" (83), he writes; language thus arose from labor as an artifact, not as something owned but as something made. Only in some Edenic fantasy of origins would such sociability produce the transparency of nature or of human nature. Or, as Engels says, profoundly, only at some later stage in the history of man would the ability to communicate be taken as a sign of the superiority of our minds rather than of our hands. He writes, "All merit for the swift advance of civilisation was ascribed to the mind, to the development and activity of the brain. . . . And so there arose in the course of time that idealistic outlook on the world" (87). The being that locates the Shakespearean character would seem, however, to reside in a hand whose sociability is not Edenic. Yet the Shakespearean hand also appears not to have forgotten its materiality.

Derrida might situate for us the materiality and sociality of the Shakespearean hand and the Shakespearean character. His programmatic statement in *Of Grammatology* generalizes the labor of the hand as the site of a cultural graphology invested in graphic substances and instruments, an informing materiality transformed not only by the hand but by idealization. As opposed to the idealistic tradition, which Derrida summarizes as logocentrism, he recognizes that "access to the written signs assures the sacred power of keeping existence operative within the trace;"[11] he insists on the ideological force of the scriptive order. Neither Engels's vision of a moment when man emerges as a social being (a moment, by the way, that is virtually Edenic, despite Engels's materialism) nor Scarry's hopes for human communication can withstand Derrida's analysis of the alliance of power and writing.

If we are to explore the cultural graphology that locates the Shakespearean character, it must be emphasized that Hamlet's fair hand, *his* character, is a recognizable princely mark.[12] Elizabeth I, for example, had been taught a fine italic hand by Roger Ascham, as her brother before her had been; indeed, Ascham found that of the queen's accomplishments, it was "most praiseworthy of all"; as he writes in *The Schoolmaster,* "[W]ithin the walls of her privy chamber she hath obtained that excellency of learning, to understand, speak, and write, both wittily with head and fair with hand, as scarce one or two rare wits in both the universities have in many years reached unto."[13] Jean de Beau Chesne, author of the first writing book published in England, tutored Princess Elizabeth (daughter of James VI and I), writing out copies for her practice; in the dedicatory poem to a set of copytexts that survives in Beau Chesne's hand,[14] the royal writing master offers himself and his pen, as if he were produced by his own labor: the princess is asked to receive with "a good eye" both the work and the worker. But if he is in the hand that she is to regard, so, too, is she. The dedicatory poem reminds his royal reader that the names of princes cannot be read, would not survive, without the pen.

Prince Henry, Elizabeth's brother and the heir apparent, had his writing masters too, Peter Bales and John Davies of Hereford; and Martin Billingsley, author of *The Pens Excellencie; or, The Secretaries Delight* (1618), taught the future Charles I. "And what should I say of the Excellency of this Art?" Billingsley asks. "Is it not one of the hands by which not only this, but al other common-wealths are vpholden? The key which opens passage to the descrying and finding out of innumerable treasures? The handmaid to memory? The Register and Recorder of all Arts? And the very mouth whereby a man familiarly conferreth with his friend, though the distance of thousands of miles be betwixt them?" (fols. C2v–C3r). Billingsley's hand undergoes the idealization of material investiture; the hand that writes is metamorphosed into the hand that upholds all commonwealths. The force of the metaphor serves, for a moment, to obscure the very literality of the statement (there is no power placed in the hands of illiterates), just as the generality of the statement—all commonwealths, not just England, are upheld by the hand that writes—allows for specific social configurations to be ignored.

They emerge, however, in the metaphors that describe writing as a key to treasures or as the handmaid to memory, invoking thereby a technical hierarchy inflected with class and sexual arrangements. The supporting hand becomes a subordinate hand, an outside providing the means of access to a more highly valued interiority, a treasury that is one with the mind. Yet the ambiguity of this instrument—support and upholder, (male) key and (female) maid—arises precisely from the ideological and idealizing argument. These insides are produced by the outside; writing, which registers and records, inscribes sociality within its domain.

What emerges at the end of this passage is the mouth that the pen produces, "the very mouth whereby a man familiarly conferreth with his friend." The true mouth is this artifice. As Engels suggests, language is the product of what the hand makes; and, as Derrida suggests, it is precisely that material fact that language obscures. The sociality that arises in Billingsley's account, even the private domain, is made by the hand. Ascham, we might recall, had found it remarkable that the queen could make her bedchamber into an alternative university. But Billingsley's celebration of the pen's excellency might illuminate how ordinary sociability, privacy, and public communication are ideological constructs. Writing locates the schoolhouse within the world; thus Ascham speaks of his book as "a New Year's gift" (9)—it is part of a social system and it reinforces that system—and, in the next sentence, he refers to his book as "my poor schoolhouse," a metaphor that expands over the following pages. The book can enter any bedchamber; the schoolhouse can be erected anywhere. Thus, John Hart, the Elizabethan spelling reformer, promoted his new orthography in a fantasy in which his new letters could be seen everywhere "drawen on the walles, pillers, and postes of churches, tounes and houses";[15] but he is quick to assure his readers that such legibility will not disrupt the social order; eyes that can read leave the hands free: "[T]heir handes may be otherwyse well occupied, in woorking for their liuing" (A6r). And if their work is writing, the hand is inserted into social practice. For writing, like reading, occurs within the privatized social space that characters engender and that engenders character.

Ascham's New Year's gift of the book as schoolhouse, or Hart's inscribed landscape, suggests that royal inscription offers a model for literacy and its extension, for as François Furet and Jacques Ozouf conclude in their study of reading and writing in France, writing as a private and silent mark engenders "the individual," but it is, as they add, "the individual in his social context."[16] Subjectivity is opened up at precisely the cost of subscription to the society that only puts the instrument of rule—the pen—into the hand of citizens it has already ruled. Hence, it is no accident that the largest cache of documents available to historians of literacy in the early modern period includes loyalty oaths, court affidavits, and marriage licenses: explicit signs, that is, that those who write subscribe to the laws, that the private realm is placed under the scrutiny of church and state and produced by it. Hence, the title page of the 1602 printing of the first English copybook (published initially in 1570)—written by Jean de Beau Chesne, the future royal tutor, and John Baildon—depicts two angels writing; above them, guaranteeing their marks beyond the transcendental warrant of that image, are two allegorical figures, Piety and Justice; Piety, the figure in the upper-left-hand corner, displays the royal coat of arms (Figure 1).

"Who builds stronger than a mason, a shipwright, or a carpenter?" (*Hamlet,* 5.1.47–48). The Clown insists on his riddle, and while a literary (or

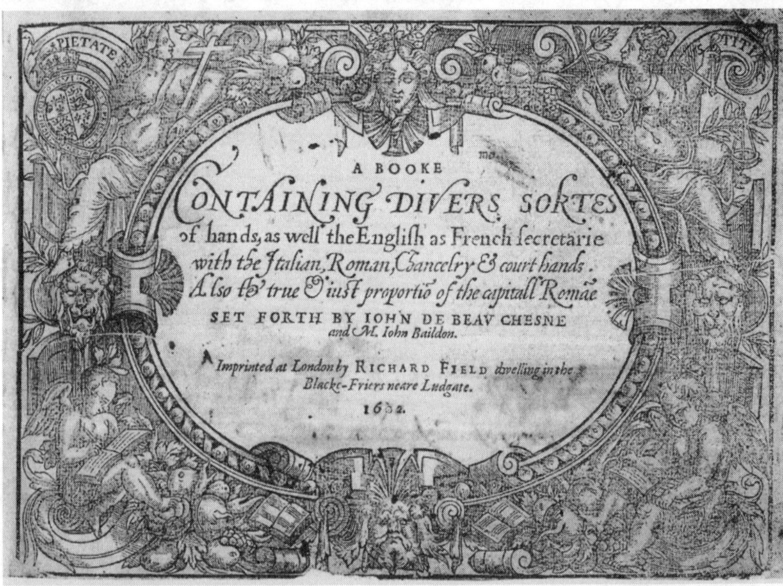
PIETATE

A BOOKE
CONTAINING DIVERS SORTES
of hands, as well the English as French secretarie
with the Italian, Roman, Chancelry & court hands.
Also the true & iust proportio of the capitall Romae
SET FORTH BY IOHN DE BEAV CHESNE
and M. Iohn Baildon.
Imprinted at London by RICHARD FIELD dwelling in the
Black-Friers neare Ludgate.
1602.

Figure 1. *A Booke Containing Divers Sortes of Hands . . . ,* title page. Jean de Beau Chesne and John Baildon (London, 1602). Photograph courtesy of the Bodleian Library, Oxford, from Douce B 675.

literate) audience might think that the answer to the riddle is "a writer," the Clown has a material answer: "Say 'a grave-maker'" (5.1.55).

Hamlet offers numerous instances of the literal embodiment of character, the socially scriptive formation that produces Hamlet's letter as the mark of character.[17] Hamlet, burdened by memory, encounters a ghost, stages a play, both haunted by the memory of earlier scripts; and although the highly theatrical Senecan Ghost speaks only to him, Hamlet receives the Ghost's *words* as a scriptive command, one that re-marks his haunted memory as a locus of inscription, erasure, and reinscription:

> Remember thee?
> Yea, from the table of my memory
> I'll wipe away all trivial fond records,
> All saws of books, all forms, all pressures past
> That youth and observation copied there,
> And thy commandment all alone shall live
> Within the book and volume of my brain,
> Unmixed with baser matter.
>
> (1.5.97–104)

In these lines, subjectivity is a scene of writing. Hamlet proceeds to write in his copybook what is inscribed in his brain, initiating a career continually invested in scriptive gestures. His instructions to the actors repeat the Ghost's commands; they are to hold "the mirror up to nature," to produce an "image" that will give "the very age and body of the time his form and pressure" (3.2.20–23). The actor's body—Hamlet's body—thus stands as a letter, "form and pressure," here echoing the ghostly copybook command: the body as the locus of inscription, to be read rather than heard; acting as dumb show, inscrutable as the silent letter that assures privacy. Hamlet has no sooner written and had produced a script for the play within the play (scripting the oral world of theatrical performance) than the Ghost returns, now seen only by Hamlet; the Ghost has entered the performance of Hamlet's scriptive world. Yet from the start, the Ghost exists within a scriptive order, and not merely that of the Senecan tragedy in which his lines are written. For when Horatio offers to vouch for the Ghost, he tells Hamlet, "I knew your father. / These hands are not more like" (1.2.211–12). The identity of the Ghost is confirmed by the identity of the hand. This is not surprising; the Ghost exists only within similitude, appearing "in the same figure like the king that's dead," "Most like," "Mark it, Horatio" (1.1.41, 44, 43). And Horatio marks it by likening the likeness to the hand that marks.

Not surprisingly, then, when Hamlet returns to Denmark, he arrives in letters, first to Horatio (in act 4, scene 6) and then to Claudius:

> **Laertes.** Know you the hand?
> **King.** Tis Hamlet's character. "Naked"!
> And in a postscript here, he says "alone."
> Can you devise me?
>
> (4.7.50–52)

That letter presents Hamlet as mere body, unclothed with social trappings, solitary; Hamlet as the private individual produced by script; the naked, solitary body is a character, a scriptive formation that Claudius literally finds baffling and opaque. "What should this mean? . . . Is it some abuse, and no such thing? . . . Can you devise me?" (4.7.48–50, 52). A letter the messenger says he has from someone named Claudio (4.7.40), and to which Laertes answers, "I am lost in it, my lord" (4.7.53). "I beg leave to see your kingly eyes," the letter says (4.7.44–45); but in this letter scene, seeing is reading, and being does not go beyond the letter, beyond copies observed, a circuit from Claudio to Claudius where all characters are lost in the letter;[18] as Hamlet was from the first, in his "inky cloak" (1.2.77), like Rosaline in *Love's Labor's Lost,* "Beauteous as ink . . . / Fair as a text B in a copy-book" (5.2.41–42).

Or as fair as the text A in Beau Chesne and Baildon's copybook (Figure 2), where the letter has flourished not only to produce natural growths sprouting from its swirls but even to serve as the support for a figure to its right blowing a horn. The letter produces the person who speaks at a distance: The embodied character is a scriptive formation; the mouth here, as in Billingsley's treatise, is produced by the letter. The speaking subject, as Engels suggested, is the product of the labor of the hand. "All men are by nature equal," the copytext reads, "made all by one workman of like myre, & howesoever we deceave our selves as dere unto God is the poorest begger, as the moste pompous Prince liuing in the worlde"; the text (ascribed to Plato) resounds in Hamlet's naked arrival, clothed in the letter whose circuit baffles and nonetheless produces the king within a sphere of nomination and visibility, "devised" *à la lettre,* in the letter, literally.

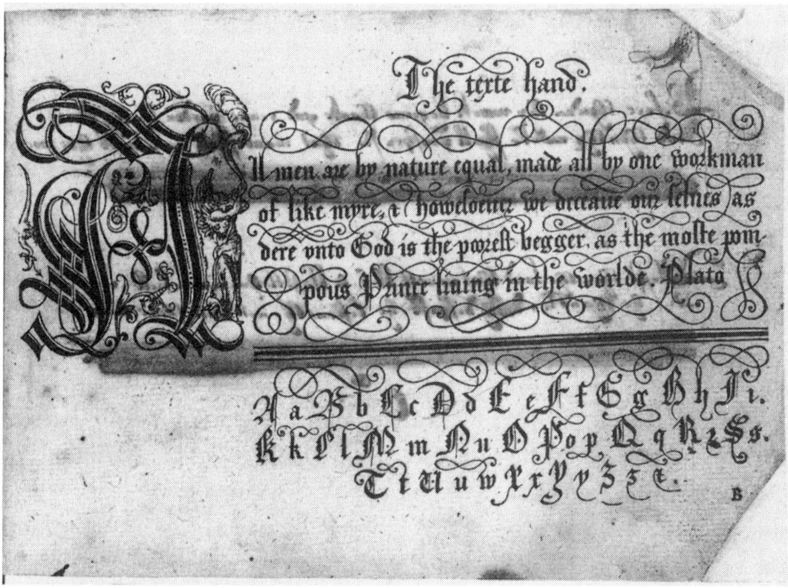

Figure 2. *A Booke Containing Divers Sortes of Hands . . .*, sig. B1r. Photograph courtesy of the Bodleian Library, Oxford, from Douce B 675.

In the copybook Beau Chesne prepared for Princess Elizabeth, he offered a French version of the same text that appears in his printed copybook. "We are all born naked and neither nature nor God has any regard to greatness," he writes; the grave is everyone's destination. In the margin of the copybook, another hand (perhaps the hand of Princess Elizabeth) has written, "Dieu, non; il n'a point" [God, no; he has none], the fierce negations of the letter that Hamlet also inscribes and in which he has been written.

And not him alone; consider Laertes. Polonius prepares Laertes for his departure in the terms that the Ghost uses two scenes later with Hamlet, the language of the copybook: "And these few precepts in thy memory / Look thou character" (1.3.58–59). Here, too, the mind is imagined as a writing tablet, and Laertes' character is generated as the locus of commonplaces, a repository for the moral saws that Polonius utters, culminating in, "This above all, to thine own self be true" (1.3.78). Laertes' "own self" is the superficies of Polonius's sentantiae, and the interiority of the character might be no more than the depth of the incision of characters in stone or wax.

Laertes is charactered within a pedagogical and ideological apparatus. "Writing must needes be," David Browne explains in *The New Invention, Intituled Calligraphia,* "or else there could be litle Civile order."[19] Even royal hands subscribed to this belief. James I, who wrote an exceedingly legible version of an italic hand, pauses in a 1603 letter to Prince Henry to praise Henry's handwriting and to hope that the prince will come to "endite" as well as he writes. "Not that I commend not a fair handwriting," James writes, but he urges the prince to write a letter that is wholly his, "as well matter as form, as well formed by your mind as drawn by your fingers."[20] Yet as the language of the letter suggests, what is formed by the mind is also formed by the fingers, and the matter of the mind may be in the hand. And indeed, like Polonius or the Ghost, James insists that the mind of the prince should be furnished with writing: "For ye may remember that in my book to you, I warn you to be wary with that kind of wit that may fly out at the end of your fingers" (219). For the prince to "endite" as well as he writes, he needs not only the training of his hand that Bales or Davies furnished but also his father's text, the *Basilikon Doron* that James wrote as a letter—and a last will and testament—to Prince Henry, ghostly marks that survive the king who predeceases himself to produce them. To reinforce the point, James's letter concludes with quotations (in Latin) from the Bible and Virgil, exemplary precepts culled from authoritative texts. This prince will be most himself when he is most fully inscribed, when his "being" is entirely the product of his hand—a hand, of course, produced entirely by writing.

The civil order of inscription, implicit in James's letters to his son, is perhaps more explicit in a text like John Brinsley's *Ludus Literarius* (1612), a pedagogical treatise dedicated to Prince Henry and Prince Charles, "the flourishing branches . . . of that happy spreading Cedar," the king.[21] Brinsley's metaphor implicates Shakespeare as well, since his words echo the lines the Soothsayer speaks at the end of *Cymbeline,* explicating (after some delay and deferral) the text that Posthumus had found inscribed on a tablet attached to his breast by Jupiter:

> The lofty cedar, royal Cymbeline,
> Personates thee, and thy lopped branches point
> Thy two sons forth.
>
> (5.5.452–54)

Posthumus claims that his book—or is it more properly Jupiter's?—is a "rare one"; its value derives not merely from its regal donor but from its transparency. No "garment / Nobler than that it covers" (5.4.134–35), it is (or so he hopes) "As good as promise" (5.4.137). Yet what this text promises and delivers in the protracted rereading and revelation of the Soothsayer is itself inscribed within pedagogic and ideological practices; in the Soothsayer's explication of Jupiter's text, nature is mystified so that it is nothing less than a royal emblem book, while Posthumus's hopeful reading leads toward the possibility that makes the external text nothing short of a transparent revelation of his own interiority (but an interiority, we might recall, that had been figured a moment before in a dream in which Jupiter appeared). In such a moment, the historicity of the unconscious is staged. That the "person" is an artifice is suggested, moreover, in the Soothsayer's explication; the text he reads figures personation, and the Soothsayer's truth—which I take to be the truth of the Shakespearean character—is that persons exist within the realm of the personated.

These Shakespearean echoes have a place in Brinsley's treatise, which describes a typical educational scheme that begins in reading and ends in writing. Brinsley hopes that students will enter the grammar school already able "to reade English: as namely that they could reade the new Testament perfectly" (13). The work of the primers is to ensure religious conformity; English is the same thing as the text of the New Testament. Such elementary texts as the psalms or *The Schoole of Vertue* or *The Schoole of Good Manners* should be reread, Brinsley urges: "For, the second reading of any booke dooth much incourage children, because it seemeth to bee so easie then; and also it doth imprint it the more" (17). The discipline of the hand—copying—begins in repetitive reading; what is *made* easy and natural is an imprinting of "precepts of ciuilitie" (18). Brinsley's schoolchildren are impressed with the letter, given an interiority that corresponds with the external print by creating that interiority as the depth of inscription. The discipline of writing involves "good copies, continual eying them wel, a delight in writing" (39), a delight Brinsley produces by seizing the hand at one in the afternoon when it is "warmest and nimblest" (32). His copytexts, like those of most copybooks, are the same kind of moral saws that Polonius utters—for if he would make his son a text, it is the one he himself is. (The Ghost, of course, would write a revenge tragedy, and the copia of *Hamlet,* however much it exceeds that model, does not offer a theory of composition other than imitation.)

It is precisely because there is no notion of human character save as a locus of inscription that the literal act of copying can be an ideological practice. Renaissance writing masters, intent upon having their pupils replicate as perfectly and as exactly as possible the hands they taught, promoted neither a notion of the individual hand nor the idea that the hand is a means for self-expression. Copybooks do not simply offer copytexts; they provide hands, numerous varieties of hands and the texts suitable to them: text hand; documents in special court hands (Chancery, Common Pleas, King's Bench, or Exchequer hands, for instance); Latin (as well as Italian, French, and English) texts in italic script or Roman majuscules; business forms in various secretary hands (true secretary, engrossing secretary, bastard secretary, small bastard). In a typical copybook, biblical citations account for about half the texts, and these can be written in virtually any hand. Their disciplinary force runs through all hands. Other texts, with their special uses and special pencuts and penholds, reinforce the fact that the hand that writes is inserted within the practices of inscription and is made to conform to them. The individual produced by writing is not an individualized subject but one conforming to the characters inscribed: the letters and ultimately the words of the copytexts. Writing well is a social sign, a sign of socialization. The written mark is a class marker. And the human hand—the *material* hand, the individual hand—is the hand produced by the copybook and the practice it maintains through reinscription. No wonder, then, if Polonius's directions to Laertes appear to clothe him in inauthenticity; the "being" of character is nothing but these marks. The hand moves in language, and its movement retraces the "being" of the individual inscribed within social practice.

Consider the illustration that appears in Beau Chesne and Baildon's *Booke Containing Divers Sortes of Hands* (Figure 3). The hands in the book are not only the varieties of handwriting that a skilled hand can perform; the book illustrates the hand itself, the hands produced by these hands. "How you ought to hold your Penne," the picture is labeled. In the absolute world of these injunctions, the possible positions are either "good" or "naught." Perhaps what is as striking as the production of the hand within that moral framework is the literal frame in which the hand is depicted. These are hands that seem to have been

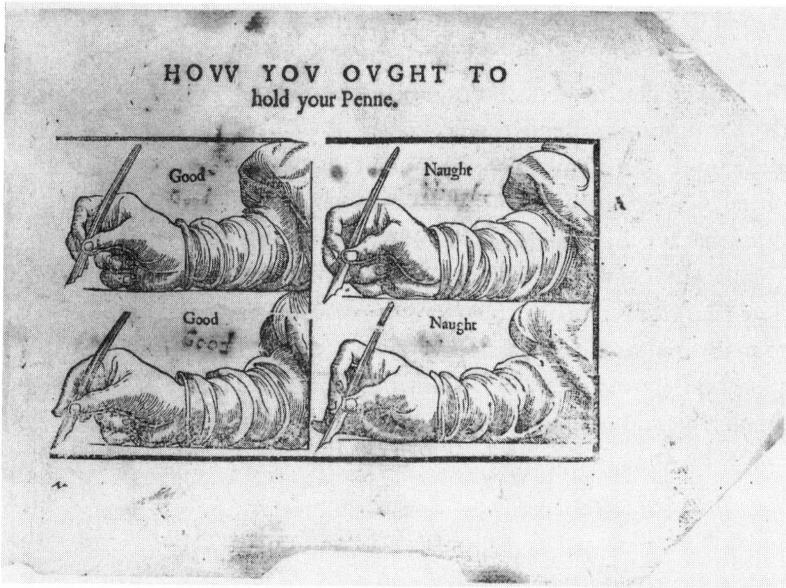

Figure 3. *A Booke Containing Divers Sortes of Hands . . .*, sig. B1r. Photograph courtesy of the Bodleian Library, Oxford, from Douce B 675.

detached from bodies, severed arms ruled by the pictorial frame. And such illustrations are commonplace; in fact, no writing-book of the period ever illustrates a penhold by picturing a hand attached to a body. It is as if such detachment were necessary for the socialization of the hand or for the placement of the hand within a social network: "[T]hy lopped branches point / Thy two sons forth" (*Cymbeline*, 5.5.453–54). The texts that appoint hands point to hands that are made by such texts, hands writing that are the products of the labor of the hand.

A picture like the one in Beau Chesne and Baildon illustrates the material circuit from a hand writing to handwriting, a production of value—good or naught—and an implicit idealization and dematerialization of the hand inserted within the practice of writing. For the hand appears to be produced by or regulated by the frame; the body has been detached from the hand, and the material production of letters has been moralized; spiritualized; placed, in short, within a regime of value that appears to take its source from some transcendent realm. "Good" and "naught" are judgments as absolute as the one God registered creating the world; the hands here uphold those values. Or, to make my point more radically, the hands here produce these values and are produced within a system of writing. "Only by labour," Engels writes, "has the human hand attained the high degree of perfection that has enabled it to conjure into being the paintings of a Raphael, the statues of a Thorwaldsen, the music of a Paganini" (81–82)—or, we might add, the writing of a Shakespeare or of the Shakespearean character. And only by forgetting the labor of production have these hands been granted transcendent status.

The frame in Beau Chesne's copybook is disciplinary, and we might note that the picture of the hands is preceded by a page of rules: how to make ink, how to hold a pen, how to sit, how to write fair. These are rules that appear to be directed at the making of materials and instruments, ink and quill, but that also produce the body and the hand.

> To write very fair . . .
> . . . false writing eschew:
> Neatly and cleanly your hand for to frame.
> (A2v)

The hand is inserted—framed—within a set of practices that regulate the body and its movements, a set of regulations at once moral and aesthetic. These are rules to write "comely" and "seemly"; a realm of values—aesthetic judgments that are also social discriminations—produced by a hand that has already subscribed to the frame in which the hand is placed.

For the value of these illustrations is the value *of* illustration, the regimen of copying that regulates the hand.[22] Thus in *The Writing Schoolmaster* (1590), Peter Bales, the tutor of Prince Henry, versifies his precepts about letter formation:

> First haue an eye unto your coppie set:
> And marke it well, how everie stroake is fet:
> Then as before, goe softly with your hand,
> When in your minde the shape thereof is scand.[23]

"Look here upon this picture, and on this, / The counterfeit presentment of two brothers" (*Hamlet,* 3.4.54–55). Hamlet draws Gertrude's eye to two pictures like those of the hands that are good and naught in Beau Chesne. Gertrude responds,

Thou turn'st mine eyes into my very soul,
And there I see such black and grained spots
As will not leave their tinct.

(3.4.90–92)

Viewing the simulacra—these counterfeit productions—she is moved to discover an interiority that participates in what has been seen. In her closet, Gertrude enters the private space that writing affords. The eye trained within the counterfeits of the copybook discovers momentarily an interiority, a mind shaped by the hand. "Mind, hand, and eye, must all together goe" (Rlr), Bales insists. The regimen there, as much as when Hamlet offers the images of two kings, insists as much on the social production of the body, sight, and mind (exteriority and interiority) as on the domain of the hand.

Thus, to take another example, consider the hands that illustrate Gerardus Mercator's *Literarum Latinarum* (1540) (Figure 4), the first book demonstrating the italic hand to be published in the Netherlands.[24] Here the arms are even more visibly detached from bodies, and here they are also more visibly inserted within an order of writing. "Bona gubernatio" and "Mala gubernatio" are the accompanying labels pointing out the hands: The italic handwriting illustrates what the well-governed hand should produce. And the labels beside the fingers and arm indicate good and bad penhold, fingers well and badly arranged. The vocabulary of such judgments, "bona comprehensio calami," "bene succedetes digiti," is drawn, as we might expect by now, from handwriting. The hand that holds also comprehends; the well-arranged fingers produce the letters in a line. In Mercator's illustration, in short, the ordered hand is a well-governed one; handwriting produces and is produced by social practices and regulations. And the social sphere is conceived of through the practice of writing. Here, too, the frame of writing would seem to also be the locus of moral and aesthetic judgment, while "comprehensio" might suggest that the mind arises from the hand.

What the hand produces is suggested even further by the elegant illustration to the 1574 *Lo scrittor utile* of Guilantonio Hercolani (Figure 5),[25] a copybook that had initially appeared in Bologna in 1571 (as *Essemplare utile di tutte le sorti di lettere*) and that was the first copybook to use copper-plate engravings rather than woodcuts. These hands, writing on

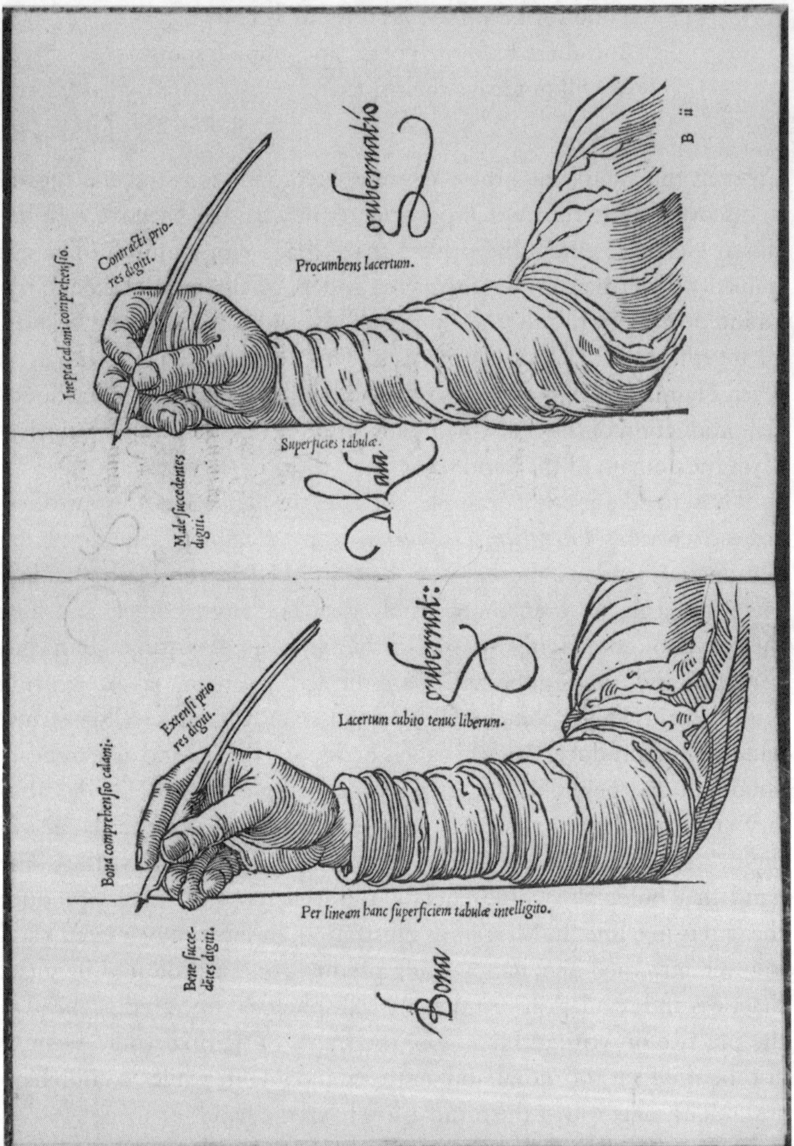

Figure 4. *Literarum Latinarum,* fols. B1v and B2r. Gerardus Mercator (Netherlands, 1540). Photograph provided by the Library of Congress, Washington, D.C., from the Rosenwald Collection.

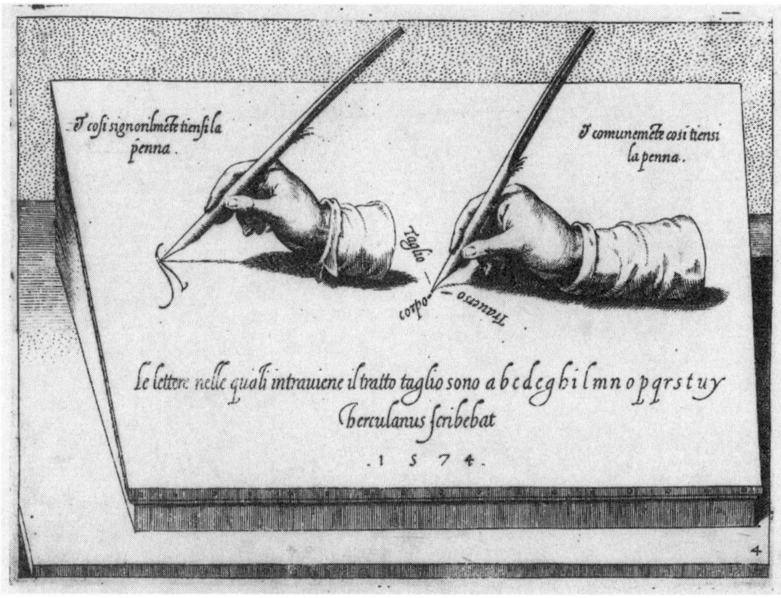

Figure 5. *Lo Scrittor Utile,* fol. 4. Giuliantonio Hercolani (Bologna, 1574). Photograph courtesy of the Newberry Library, Chicago, Illinois.

a desk, are the most eerily disembodied members. Here, they demonstrate the basic strokes that form letters; these are named in the middle of the illustration: "traverso," "taglio," "corpo." The strokes that produce letters suggest embodiment; letters have tails ("taglio") and bodies ("corpo") even when the hands that produce them seem to be disembodied, lopped off to be produced by the hands writing. Characters are embodied letters, we might then observe: The human body is a scriptive formation. Here, as in the illustration in Beau Chesne and Baildon's book, two hands are depicted writing properly. The point of this is spelled out in Hercolani's labels: one hand demonstrates the penhold appropriate for a lordly writer ("e cosi signorilmete tiensi la penna"); the other is fit for more ordinary hands ("e comunemete cosi tiensi la penna"). Lettering is a social practice that maintains the social structure; the hand is not merely natural—as disembodiment would suggest. But it is, or so the copybook seems to affirm, naturally social. Hands and bodies, materiality itself, are social productions.

One final example: If we look at the frontispiece to Richard Gethinge's 1619 *Calligraphotechnia* (Figure 6),[26] we find a portrait of the writing

Figure 6. *Calligraphotechnia,* fol. 2v. Richard Gethinge (London, 1619). Photograph courtesy of the British Library, London.

master, his pens circled with a crown, his art transcendent, and, to make the same point, his hand, detached, culminating in swags of cloth whose knot perhaps replicates the swirling handwriting that demonstrates absolute control over a pen that has scarcely been lifted from the paper and that writes itself in these inscriptions: "Quill" and "plume" are the words inscribed in the swirls above and below the hand. Portrait, hand, writing; each suggests the production of the writer within a set of reinforcing frames. Gethinge's book adds further witness that such regulation and production of human character is a social and not a natural phenomenon. The title page facing this frontispiece produces one additional piece of evidence: the fact that the sign that hung over Gethinge's place of business depicted a hand.

At the end of the play, Hamlet, with all the urgency of the Ghost, asks Horatio if he remembers: "You do remember all the circumstance?" "Remember it, my lord!" (5.2.2–3), Horatio replies; and then, like Prospero with Ariel, Hamlet proceeds to recount what has been remembered. Handing the king's commission over to Horatio (5.2.26), Hamlet proceeds to the story of the substitution of letters already enacted before our eyes:[27]

Being thus benetted round with villainies,
Or I could make a prologue to my brains,
They had begun the play. I sat me down,
Devised a new commission, wrote it fair.
I once did hold it, as our statists do,
A baseness to write fair, and labored much
How to forget that learning, but, sir, now
It did me yeoman's service. Wilt thou know
Th' effect of what I wrote?

(5.2.29–37)

The text is already within his head, a play in progress to which he subscribes, literally: He descends to the base matter, the materiality of the letter, a social descent to the yeoman's secretarial skill, manual labor that nonetheless produces the royal word; not only are literate skills suborned, but Hamlet also has to hand the royal seal (the proprietary mark of oral culture) to falsify and ratify the document. His father's seal: Hamlet has turned the Ghost's words into the script that he has written.

Horatio. How was this sealed?
Hamlet. Why, even in that was heaven ordinant.
I had my father's signet in my purse,
Which was the model of that Danish seal,
Folded the writ up in the form of th' other,
Subscribed it, gave't th' impression, placed it safely,
The changeling never known.

(5.2.47–53)

In the ninth dialogue of his *Linguae Latinae Exercitatio* (1538), Juan Vives presents the laments of a writing master; the nobility, he claims, "think it fine and proper . . . not to know how to shape their letters properly. You would think that it was a lot of chickens scratching about; unless you know beforehand who the writer was, you'd never guess. . . . We see them signing letters composed by their secretaries with totally illegible signatures; nor would you know who sent the letter unless you were told by the bearer or you recognised your correspondent's seal."[28] The master offers legibility as the path to true nobility. It is not mistaken advice; Francesco Guicciardini, for instance, reports in his *Ricordi* that as a young man he, too, scorned the skill of writing fair, but he then came to recognize that such ability opened the way to royal service.[29] Legibility offers social legitimation; but it does not authenticate an individual. "None but best hands may alwayes best please" (A2v), a verse in Beau Chesne and Baildon's copybook enjoins.

We might add a cautionary tale to such social production of the hand. Among royal secretaries, Pierre Hamon's productions are rare commodities. In the dedication to Charles IX that prefaces his 1566 writing-book, Hamon extols the pen as the giver of all graces, the pen, he writes, lent to him so that he might serve his monarch. Yet Hamon became his task all too well; so skilled was his hand that his signature could not be distinguished from the king's, and he is reported to have paid with his life for his perfect counterfeit art. It is difficult to know if the story is to be credited, however; it may well be a modern story that registers our discomfort with the social production of the hand. There are, after all, records of royal injunctions from the fifteenth and sixteenth centuries commanding secretaries to imitate the royal signature.[30] "O, 'tis most sweet / When in one line two crafts directly meet" (*Hamlet,* 3.4.210–11); so Hamlet responds to the fact that "there's letters sealed" (3.4.203) before he proceeds to his subornation of the seal and the hand. Hamlet achieves the secretarial perfection of sheer instrumentality, royal power.

Hamlet's hand is inserted within social practices; the mark of "character" becomes a characteristic mark (that is, a mark of class and social standing); it becomes the hand of power precisely because the hand is not individualized; the fair hand is legible, but its very legibility means that it cannot be owned as a mark of individuality. It represents transcendent authority and appears to be decorporealized, moving in language but not through an individual's body. The hand replaces the seal as a mark of property and ownership. But the seal, the mark preferred by cultures that conduct their business orally, was, as Michael Clanchy has argued, a prototype for the disowned mark, since it could be used by anyone; for Clanchy, movable type takes its cue from the seal.[31] And the handwritten signature, suspected from the first as able to be forged, is no more secure a mark of ownership or of propriety. Hamlet's skilled hand ensures the force of the document he inscribes, but it does not reveal the writer. The document written fair has the anonymity and inevitability of social practice. Hamlet writes a royal commission. Suborning his father's seal, making himself the image of Claudius, Hamlet achieves, momentarily, the form of power within the scriptive world that replaces (that has always already replaced) the oral in the course of the play. Claudius, recall, murders the old king by pouring poison in his ear. Hamlet dies by the hand: the poisoned tip of a sword. In the very scene in which Laertes witnesses the letter that Hamlet sends to Claudius, Claudius bears witness to Laertes' hand by recalling the praise of the master swordsman Lamord. Margaret Ferguson has reminded us that the name is a pun on the order of death—and language—in which Hamlet moves to be incorpsed. Hamlet moves to occupy "the place of the king as the play defines it," Ferguson writes, with some disapproval, "a *role* associated . . . with the power to kill."[32] That role, Hamlet's embodiment, we would add, rehearses the scriptive order; it also might be attached to the "desp'rate hand" (5.1.207) of Ophelia that took her own life, grasping "dead men's fingers" (4.7.170).

Vives's writing master turns to the lads, having impressed upon them their need to write fair. "Did you come here properly armed for your task?" he asks, and the young man first takes him literally and needs to be disabused: "Come now! I'm not talking about the bloodthirsty arms of the soldier but those of the writer, which we need now. Have you your pen-case and quills?"[33] The violence of the letter: "I will speak daggers to her, but use none," Hamlet says, as he proceeds to his mother's closet (3.2.381). "These words like daggers enter in mine ears" (3.4.96), she testifies. The hand, as Claudius remarks, is "instrumental to the mouth" (1.2.48), an instrumentality that produces the mouth as well as the hand within the scriptive order. Claudius sends dispatches throughout the play; and Hamlet writes the dead character, folding Rosencrantz and Guildenstern, Claudius and Laertes in his path. This is the writer's path: For "many wearing rapiers are afraid of goosequills" (2.2.336). The pen, mightier than the sword, is a mortal instrument: "The treacherous instrument is in thy hand" (5.2.305).

For the pen produces the character, the letter, and the person, and the etymology of "character" reveals the violence of this engendering. In Greek, "to character" means to brand or sharpen, and a character is as much the instrument that engraves or brands as what is engraved or branded. Hamlet's place in the scriptive order, in the economy of death, is marked in his final utterances. Twice he says the impossible sentence upon which, as Derrida insists, writing rests. Hamlet says twice, "I am dead" (5.2.322, 327).[34]

Hamlet's character is—literally—the character. And so we might turn to the letter (in the second quarto and Folio texts of the play) that marks Hamlet's return to Denmark and the mark that authenticates the character *as character.* How is the letter to Horatio signed? In the second quarto (1604–5), the final line of the letter is printed in italics. It reads: *"So that thou knowest thine Hamlet"* (L3r). In the Folio (1623), the letter closes with *"He that thou knowest thine"* in italics and with the name "Hamlet" printed in Roman (through line number 3001). Thus, in the quarto text, Hamlet's signature forms part of the closing line of the letter—the *only* line of the letter printed in italic type (Figure 7). The italic signature, *Hamlet,* is not produced simply as part of the line,

Hor. Let them come in.
I doe not know from what part of the world
I ſhould be greeted. If not from Lord *hamlet.* *Enter Saylers.*

Say. God bleſſe you ſir.

Hora. Let him bleſſe thee to.

Say. A ſhall ſir and pleaſe him, there's a Letter for you ſir, it came frõ th'Embaſſador that was bound for *England,* if your name be *Horatio,* as I am let to know it is.

Hor. *Horatio,* when thou ſhalt haue ouer-lookt this, giue theſe fellowes ſome meanes to the King, they haue Letters for him: Ere wee were two daies old at Sea, a Pyrat of very warlike appointment gaue vs chaſe, finding our ſelues too ſlow of ſaile, wee put on a compelled valour, and in the grapple I boorded them, on the inſtant they got cleere of our ſhyp, ſo I alone became theyr priſoner, they haue dealt with me like thieues of mercie, but they knew what they did, I am to doe a turne for them, let the King haue the Letters I haue ſent, and repayre thou to me with as much ſpeede as thou wouldeſt flie death, I haue wordes to ſpeake in thine eare will make thee dumbe, yet are

they much too light for the bord of the matter, theſe good fellowes will bring thee where I am, *Roſencraus* and *Guyldensterne* hold theyr courſe for *England,* of them I haue much to tell thee, farewell.

So that thou knoweſt thine Hamlet.

Hor. Come I will you way for theſe your letters,
And doo't the ſpeedier that you may direct me
To him from whom you brought them. *Exeunt.*

Figure 7. Quarto 2 *Hamlet,* fols. L2v and L3r, detail. William Shakespeare (London, 1604–5). Photograph reproduced by permission of the Huntington Library, San Marino, California.

for italic type is also used in the letter for the names *Horatio, Rosencrans, Guyldensterne,* and *England.* Italics may mark Hamlet's signature, but not in a typeface that distinguishes it from other proper names or from the hand that has produced the formula of subscription. Moreover, the rest of the letter is printed in the same typeface as the rest of the play. Nothing in the typography distinguishes it as Hamlet's writing.

In the Folio, on the other hand, Hamlet's signature is printed in the same type as the rest of the text of the play and the same type as the names "Horatio," "Rosincrance, " and "Guildensterne" that appear in the letter; save for them, the entire body of the letter as well as the subscription is in italics (Figure 8). Do italics therefore mark the letter as *not* part of the play, or not part of the script produced by the hand that wrote the rest of the text? But in that case, to whom does the letter belong when the signature is not in the same hand as the letter but is instead marked the same way as the hand that produces the rest of the text?

In posing these typographic questions of character, I mean to situate Hamlet's hand in the history of handwriting and printing, remembering, for instance, that increasingly in the sixteenth century, and invariably by the close of the period, English royalty wrote their private correspondence in an italic hand, but remembering also that others, aspiring to this mark of privilege, signed their letters in italic, although the rest of their letter (whether written by themselves or by a secretary) usually remained in secretarial hand. Recall, too, that manuscripts of Elizabethan plays are usually written in secretary hand, except for the names of characters, stage directions, and the like, which are written in italic. Italic serves to mark what is not part of the script, and in some scripts such matters are written in Latin, observing the propriety of script to text. The playscript thus marks the extratextual in the same way that the private letter marks the proper name; its propriety therefore lies in being written in a foreign hand that serves as a mark of class (or class aspiration). The signature marks *différance.* I am assuming that the italic type used in the Folio and quarto texts of Hamlet's letter to Horatio corresponds to an italic hand, and I depend, too, on the fact that, whether in quarto or Folio (and not only in the case of *Hamlet*), the typefaces in letters and of proper names within them almost always play off the multiple scripts that characterize the handwritten letter. The letter—whether as a printed letter or as a printed playscript—marks Hamlet's name and signature as a textual property. In that case, it is perhaps worth returning to the letter to

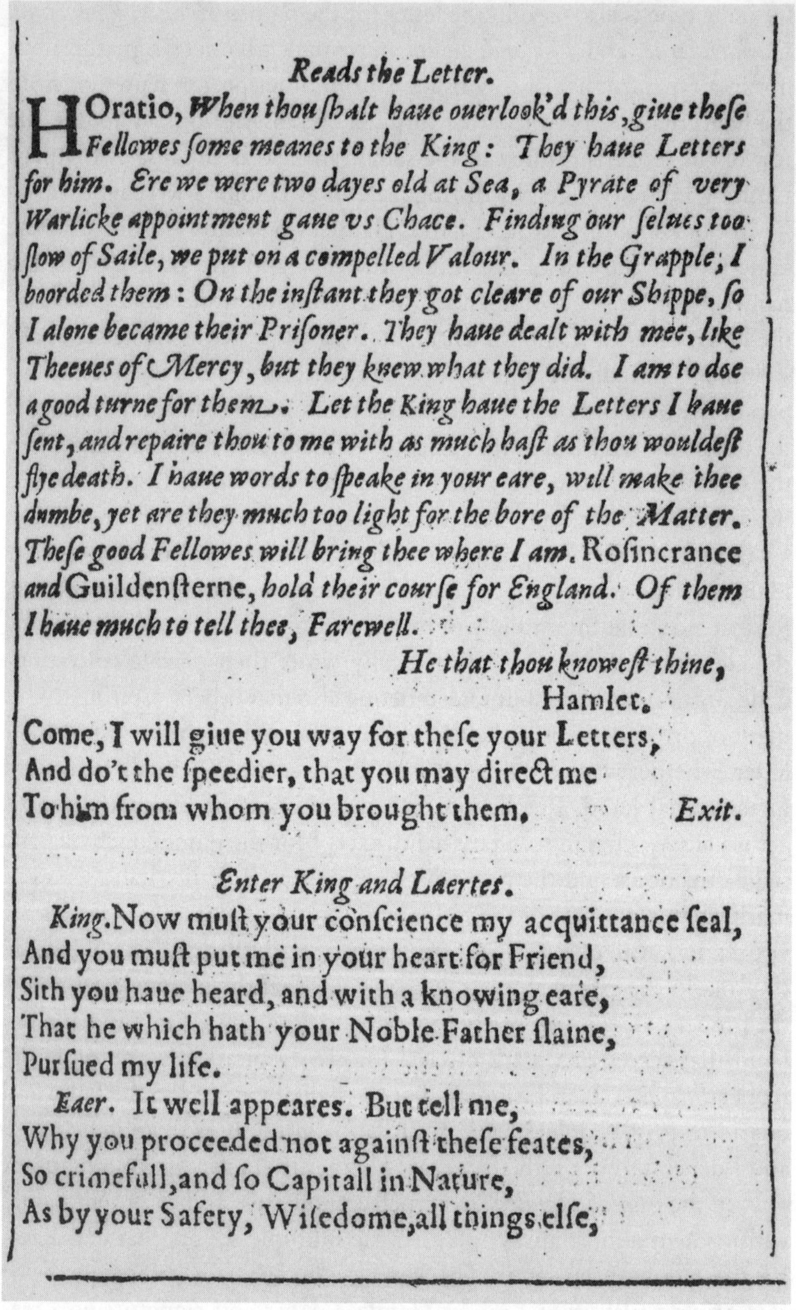

Reads the Letter.

HOratio, *When thou ſhalt haue ouerlook'd this, giue theſe Fellowes ſome meanes to the King: They haue Letters for him. Ere we were two dayes old at Sea, a Pyrate of very Warlicke appointment gaue vs Chace. Finding our ſelues too ſlow of Saile, we put on a compelled Valour. In the Grapple, I boorded them: On the inſtant they got cleare of our Shippe, ſo I alone became their Priſoner. They haue dealt with mee, like Theeues of Mercy, but they knew what they did. I am to doe a good turne for them. Let the King haue the Letters I haue ſent, and repaire thou to me with as much haſt as thou wouldeſt flye death. I haue words to ſpeake in your eare, will make thee dumbe, yet are they much too light for the bore of the Matter. Theſe good Fellowes will bring thee where I am.* Roſincrance *and* Guildenſterne, *hold their courſe for England. Of them I haue much to tell thee, Farewell.*

He that thou knoweſt thine,
Hamlet.

Come, I will giue you way for theſe your Letters,
And do't the ſpeedier, that you may direct me
To him from whom you brought them. *Exit.*

Enter King and Laertes.

King. Now muſt your conſcience my acquittance ſeal,
And you muſt put me in your heart for Friend,
Sith you haue heard, and with a knowing eare,
That he which hath your Noble Father ſlaine,
Purſued my life.

Laer. It well appeares. But tell me,
Why you proceeded not againſt theſe feates,
So crimefull, and ſo Capitall in Nature,
As by your Safety, Wiſedome, all things elſe,

Figure 8. Folio *Hamlet,* page 275, detail. William Shakespeare (London, 1623). Reproduced with permission from the Folger Shakespeare Library collection, Washington, D.C.

Claudius with which I began; in the Folio version of the letter, Hamlet's signature appears in the ordinary typeface of the rest of the play; the quarto letter, printed in the same type, has no signature at all. "Hamlet's character" is produced without the proper name.

What *can* a signature authenticate, especially in a culture that does not seem to place any particular value on the spelling of the proper name or on the hand in which it is written? A pedagogue complains, "[O]ur English proper names are written as it pleaseth the painter";[35] the proper name might be the prime example of what Claudius calls the "painted word" (3.1.53). For all writing exists within the sphere of the visible; indeed, it defines that sphere and with it the sociality of sight. This is the counterfeit order in which the hand participates. Claudius notes it when he reflects upon his "cursed hand," "Offense's gilded hand" (3.3.43, 58). As emphatic as Hamlet's insistence on the pictures of the brothers is the Ghost's remorse at his dispatch "by a brother's hand" (1.5.74). The brother's name we might suspect to be Cain, on whose brow, or so a writing master suggests, God wrote the first inscription,[36] the mark that descends as the benefit of clergy. The hand that writes is mystified in that social order where literacy would seem to ensure immortality, the order in which the individual is a mark like the signature. Is this why Claudius has a name that can only be read, but which no one in the play ever speaks? Guaranteeing the social order are two kings; Hamlet has the name of one, and the other withholds his name, or has it withheld, or has it in his hand. Or in Hamlet's: "So, uncle, there you are" (1.5.110), Hamlet writes on a pad that may be his mind—writes like the hand that writes the proper name "Cellebrino" on the title page of Eustachio Cellebrino's 1525 *Il modo di Imparare di Scrivere* (see Figure 9).

The signature is produced by the hand produced by writing. Hence, as hardly needs to be recalled, the six indisputable Shakespearean autographs reveal that he never spelled his own name the same way twice; he wrote them all in a secretary hand, the ordinary hand for a text, and had he signed in italic (and we do not know that he could not), the name would be no more his own, no more proper. Whether written in secretary or italic hand, the proper name is in the hand. Being *is* in the hand, but not as Heidegger alleged. For the individual subject is re-marked either way, produced by one hand or another.

David Browne, who styled himself King James's official Scottish scribe, attempted to face the problem of the authentic hand in an objection to his *New Invention, Intituled Calligraphia;* if all write fair, it had been

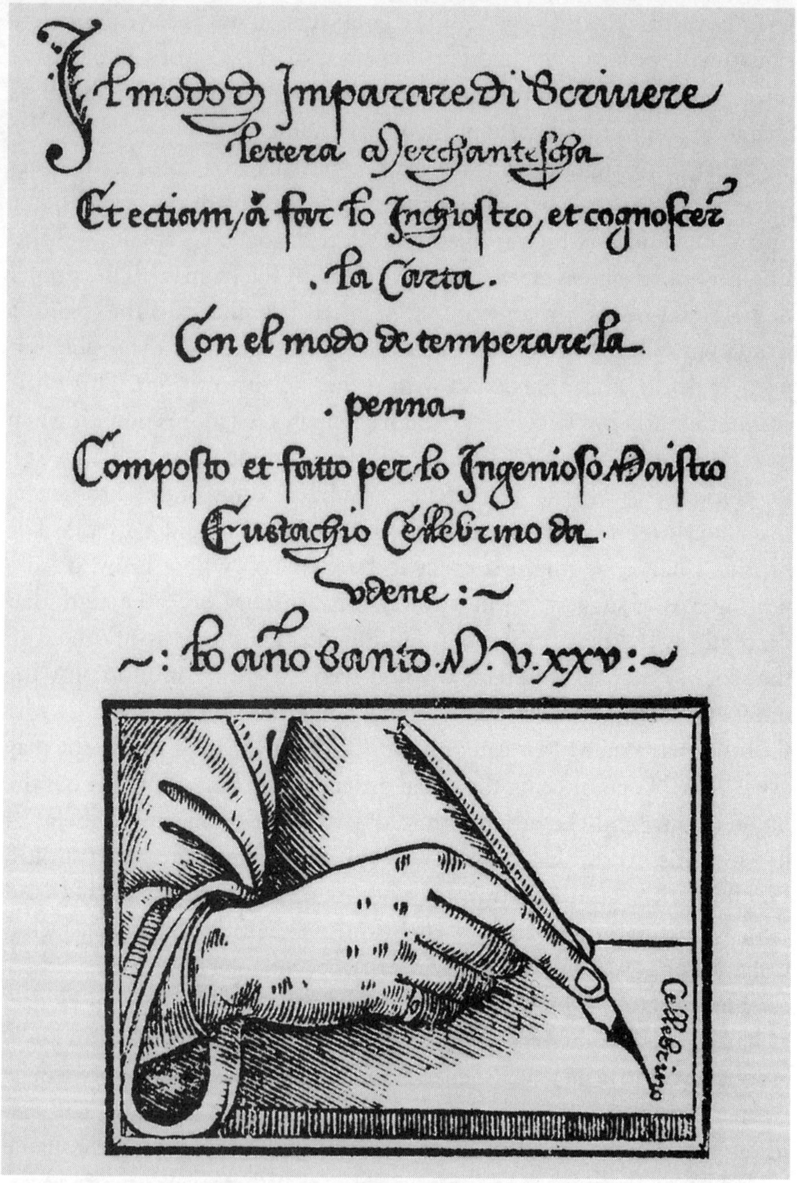

Il modo di Imparare di Scriuere
lettera Merchantescha
Et ectiam, a far lo Inchiostro, et cognoscer
. la Carta.
Con el modo de temperare la
. penna.
Composto et fatto per lo Ingenioso Maistro
Eustachio Cellebrino da
Udene :~
~: Lo anno Santo. M.D.XXV :~

Figure 9. *Il modo di Imparare di scriuere lettera merchantescha,* title page. Eustachio Cellebrino (1525). Reproduced from a collotype facsimile in *Eustachio Celebrino da Udene* (Paris: Pegasus Press, 1929) by Stanley Morrison. Reproduced with permission from the Folger Shakespeare Library collection, Washington, D.C.

objected, then all hands will be the same "and so make the Subscription of Evidence doubtfull" (188). Browne can only reply by pointing to "naturall disparity" or to the use of seals and witnesses. A lapsed hand, or an illiterate hand, is all that Browne can summon up against the charge. For *properly* employed, subscribing to the regime of copy and its royal impress, there is no propriety in the hand that signs, as one can see, for example, simply by perusing any collection of Elizabethan and Jacobean signatures that display the literacy of writers in their ability to sign or write in both italic and in secretary. These are facts about the hand that offend the Heideggerian character but that point to the being of the Shakespearean subject, to Hamlet bounded by the hand, the letter, a character who returns to life—to death—in a letter. What is a letter? Here is a typical Elizabethan definition. "An Epistle . . . or letter is nothing else, but a declaration, by Writing of the mindes of such as bee absent, one of them to another, even as though they were present."[37]

"Stand and unfold yourself" (*Hamlet,* 1.1.2). Letters (characters) are, literally, letters, and they stage presence, offering themselves, like Hamlet, as the "glass of fashion" (3.1.153), or, like the dead Hotspur, as "the mark and glass, copy and book / That fashioned others" (*2 Henry IV,* 2.3.31–32). "To make true diction of him, his semblable is his mirror, and who else would trace him, his umbrage, nothing more" (5.2.117).

Texts for life. "Do you see nothing there?" (3.4.132).

Texts for noting, tracing, copying.

Texts for nothing. "This nothing's more than matter" (4.5.173). Nothing more.

Perspectives: Dover Cliff and the Conditions of Representation

The Way to Dover

Act 3 of *King Lear* opens with a description that a nameless gentleman makes to the disguised Kent, a description of Lear blasted "with eyeless rage" (3.1.8).[1] Before we are offered the horrific spectacle of the king raging on the heath, we have this image of the king whom the storm would "make nothing of" (3.1.9). And virtually simultaneously, before the full force of Lear's expulsion from Gloucester's home becomes apparent, Kent voices the possibility that the movement of the play contains within it a counterforce. It crystallizes around Dover. Kent responds to the gentleman's annihilative vision; of his nothing he would make something, offering the hope of secrets to be revealed: the restorative forces of France, the return of Cordelia, the regaining of identity. Kent sends the gentleman, fortified with these hopeful words, with tokens "to Dover" (3.1.36); as if to answer the blinding storm and its "eyeless rage," he assures him of the possibility that he will "see Cordelia" (3.1.46) there. A compensatory pattern, initiated in this interchange and focused on the word "Dover," continues in the scenes that follow.

Thus, just as we are offered "Dover" as the possibility of a happy ending before Lear's agony on the heath, the word appears again after Lear has endured the storm. Gloucester directs Kent to "drive toward Dover where thou shalt meet / Both welcome and protection" (3.6.89–90). The king is borne sleeping to the place where he can escape the plots of death that threaten him. That direction and the reiteration of "Dover," however, are even more forceful in the scene that follows, Gloucester's blinding at the hands of Regan and Cornwall. Shatteringly, the path of escape from "eyeless rage" becomes the path to its realization. It is because Gloucester has sent the king to Dover that he suffers the inquisition of Cornwall and Regan:

Cornwall. Where has thou sent the king?
Gloucester. To Dover.
Regan. Wherefore to Dover? Wast thou not charged at peril—
Cornwall. Wherefore to Dover? Let him answer that.
Gloucester. I am tied to th' stake, and I must stand the course.
Regan. Wherefore to Dover?
Gloucester. Because I would not see thy cruel nails
Pluck out his poor old eyes

(3.7.50–57)

The pathos of the escape to Dover emerges in the repeated question "Wherefore to Dover?" Wherefore, indeed.

When Gloucester has endured what he would not see, Regan sends him to "smell / His way to Dover" (3.7.93–94). Gloucester's path, doubling Lear's, collapses the antinomy of "eyeless rage" and the hope of recovery. Gloucester emblematizes, literalizes, and makes fully horrific a path of fulfilled desire: the desire not to see. The desire and hope constellated around Dover sickens. In the next scene, Edgar, disguised as poor Tom, meets his father with his bleeding eyes, and Gloucester asks him to lead "i' th' way to Dover" (4.1.43). "Know'st thou the way to Dover?" (4.1.55), he asks, and asks again, "Dost thou know Dover?" (4.1.71). To Edgar's affirmative response, the old man describes the cliff that is his utmost desire, a verge from whose dizzying height he expects no return.

Either way—as the place where Lear will see Cordelia or the place where Gloucester will have the satisfaction of suicide—in these reiterations of "Dover," the word names a site of desire, of the hope for recovery or at least repose, of restoratives to answer "eyeless rage," or of the final closing of the eyes in a sleep without end. Lear will awaken in Cordelia's sight, perceiving himself deprived of that ultimate rest: "You do me wrong to take me out o' th' grave" (4.7.45). Before that, Edgar will have fulfilled Gloucester's request in a way that as strongly undercuts any hope that Dover might embody. For after Gloucester's reiterated questions to Edgar, the word "Dover" never recurs in *King Lear.* Instead of arriving at the place, we arrive at Dover Cliff only in the lines that Edgar speaks to his father in act 4, scene 6. In "Shakespeare Imagines a Theatre,"[2] Stephen Orgel argues persuasively for the imaginative weight and force of these lines, and I will not repeat his observations here. It suffices to say that Dover Cliff exists only in Edgar's lines and nowhere else in the play. The refusal to allow the word "Dover" to arrive at the place it (apparently) names, the failure, in other words, of the signifier to reach the signified—the failure of the sign—establishes the place that "Dover" occupies in the text. It is the place of illusion: the illusion of the desire voiced by Kent or Gloucester, the illusion of recovery, *and* the illusion of respite and end. Yet, to come to the central point that I wish to make here, Edgar's lines describing Dover Cliff establish themselves as illusion by illusionistic rhetoric. His description answers to a particular mode of seeing, and the limits that "Dover" represents in the text are the limits of representation themselves. Paradoxically, a speech that represents space in a realistic mode points to the incapacity of the stage—and of language—to realize what the lines represent.

Perspectives

Here are Edgar's lines:

> Come on, sir; here's the place. Stand still. How fearful
> And dizzy 'tis to cast one's eyes so low!
> The crows and choughs that wing the midway air
> Show scarce so gross as beetles. Halfway down
> Hangs one that gathers samphire—dreadful trade;
> Methinks he seems no bigger than his head.
> The fishermen that walk upon the beach
> Appear like mice; and yond tall anchoring bark,

> Diminished to her cock; her cock, a buoy
> Almost too small for sight. The murmuring surge
> That on th' unnumb'red idle pebble chafes
> Cannot be heard so high. I'll look no more,
> Lest my brain turn, and the deficient sight
> Topple down headlong.
>
> (4.6.11–24)

These lines begin ten lines into a scene in which the information given is, at best, ambiguous, Gloucester insisting that the ground he treads is flat and that he can hear no sea roaring. There is no evidence to his imperfect senses that he approaches the verge that suddenly looms in Edgar's lines; as Orgel argues, the evidence of the audience's eyes and ears would confirm Gloucester's denials. Still, an audience would also know that were we to witness a scene at Dover Cliff, Shakespeare's stage would have no way of representing that event save in the language of those on stage who could testify to such an arrival; in this scene, only Edgar could report the evidence of sight. The stage would be, whether we were at Dover Cliff or not, flat; language would tell us to see it otherwise.

Such had been Shakespeare's practice elsewhere. Thus, the Chorus before *Henry V* directly addressed the audience on the question of what the stage might represent and the possible transformation that the "wooden O" (Prologue, 12) could undergo, bringing something out of nothing. The limit of representation is the theme of the prologue to the play. Although the Chorus desires to show a "swelling scene" (Prologue, 4), all he can give is the "great accompt" (Prologue, 17), "flat unraised spirits" (Prologue, 9) in "little place" (Prologue, 16) offering themselves and their words to the multiplying capacity of the audience:

> Piece out our imperfections with your thoughts:
> Into a thousand parts divide one man
> And make imaginary puissance.
>
> (Prologue, 23–25)

The Chorus describes here a Shakespearean transaction regularly enacted: to allow the force of imagination to go beyond the limits possible on the stage and to take what the mind makes as the goal at which representation aims. Representation strives to be presentation; the audience credits the illusion as real event.[3]

Allowing words to become events on stage through the transformative capacity of images is the crucial Shakespearean metamorphosis to which the Chorus alludes. Banquo outside Inverness stops to observe birds building nests in the castle walls:

> This guest of summer,
> The temple-haunting martlet, does approve
> By his loved mansionry that the heaven's breath
> Smells wooingly here. No jutty, frieze,
> Buttress, nor coign of vantage, but this bird
> Hath made his pendant bed and procreant cradle.
> Where they most breed and haunt, I have observed
> The air is delicate.
>
> (*Macbeth,* 1.6.3–10)

Just as Gloucester cannot see the cliff, the audience can neither hear nor see Banquo's birds, but we credit Banquo's description and supply the sight he offers. When Edgar describes Dover Cliff, we might suppose that the lines work on similar principles. The reiterations of "Dover" seem to have been leading to the place as surely as the gentleman's lines in act 3, scene 1—describing the almost unimaginable scene of Lear in the raging storm, cursing and screaming as the storm unleashes its parallel rage—become the staged fact in act 3, scene 2. Kent exits in act 3, scene 1 to seek his master, and the empty stage then discovers Lear enacting what the words before had done. This transformation realizes the words; but on the other hand, the scene works in part because it has first been imagined and verbalized. What is staged has already been supplemented beforehand by the gentleman's lines. Language has been there before the act, and the scene is all the more potent because of what has come before it. "Dover" tantalizes us with these expectations, only to deny them.

The arrival at Dover in *King Lear* may be less overtly self-conscious about staging than the opening lines of the Chorus in *Henry V;* it is nonetheless much more incisive about the problems that such a moment represents. For in *King Lear,* the possibility of the creation of the illusion of place through language is entangled in the significance of that illusory place in the text.[4] To reach Dover means something crucial in the careers of Gloucester and Lear, and the testing of the limitations of representation collapses at one time both the questions about the stage's capacity to represent and the hopes and desires that have constellated around Dover Cliff. For unlike the imagined scenes that the Chorus of *Henry V* offers, the scene that Edgar paints is couched in a language of illusionistic rendering that is virtually unprecedented in Shakespeare. The representation of the real, the realization of representation, is in question. Edgar's description of Dover Cliff recasts a version of illusionistic representation upon which Renaissance painting depends. The lines offer a perspective on perspective.[5]

The theory of (Italian) Renaissance painting as presented in a treatise like Leon Battista Alberti's *On Painting* (*Della pittura,* 1436) depends on a few elements.[6] The viewer is imagined to be stationary. The surface of the painting is considered as a framed window, and the distance of the viewer's eye from the surface of the painting determines the distance into space of the painting, which is organized around a vanishing point that represents the horizon of vision and that is placed exactly correspondent to the fixed eye viewing the scene. All elements beyond the frame diminish proportionally until they reach the limit of vision that organizes the pictorial space.

Blind Gloucester is positioned to have this illusionistic experience. Edgar roots him to "the place" and insists, "Stand still." Between the spot where they are supposed to stand and the dizzying prospect, a series of midpoints are marked, dividing the space into mathematical segments. Birds appear the size of beetles; a man at this distance "seems no bigger than his head." Further down, they are even smaller; men become mice. The last objects seen are described in a kind of algebra that expresses a verbal version of a formula of proportion, a:b::b:c,

> yond tall anchoring bark,
> Diminished to her cock; her cock, a buoy,
> Almost too small for sight.

The diminution in scale is insistent. Equally important is the illusionism of this carefully constructed view, the truth of what is apparent: "Show," "seem," and "appear" are the operative terms in Edgar's account.

The exactitude of visual placement in Edgar's scene is remarkable. When Banquo draws our eyes to see his nesting birds, he fills every "jutty, frieze, / Buttress [and] coign of vantage" (*Macbeth,* 1.6.5–6) with scenes of procreation. These reflect his mind and his host's, and the moral and rhetorical pointing is telling.[7] But the audience to these lines is asked not to imagine an exact scene but to countenance the meanings read into it. We grant Banquo his sight because we measure his imagination by it. We need not see where the architectural elements are in relation to each other or where precisely each bird builds. Similarly, the Chorus of *Henry V* instructs: "Think, when we talk of horses, that you see them / Printing their proud hoofs i' th' receiving earth" (Prologue, 26–27). The scene he asks the audience to see derives its realization from a graphic art, the translation of words heard into the imprinting of an impression. The words stamp themselves on the mind so that what is seen as a picture is something like words as they come to be on a page. The Chorus focuses on a particular action here, just as Banquo does. But unlike in Edgar's vision, the emphasis is verbal, on the power of words to work on the imagination. By respecting the limits of representation and not insisting that the stage can go beyond itself, Banquo's birds or the horses of the Chorus can make their imaginary mark. But in Edgar's lines the power of images—"imaginary puissance," as the Chorus called it (Prologue, 25)—is pushed to its limits. Dover is to be realized, not simply to be imagined.

The moral meanings to be read in Edgar's description derive precisely from the attempt at passing from representation to actual presentation. Like Banquo's, his lines also measure the mind of the beholder. The lines comment, in their visual form, on the limits of possibility in the real and on the impossibility of the realization of language and desire. The real rests on an insubstantial basis. One sign of this is that Edgar's vision is fearfully reductive, not only in its mathematics but also in valuation: The birds metamorphosed into beetles or the fishermen turned mice are diminished on the scale of being. The "dreadful" trade of the herb gatherer is further horrific in his dismemberment: He has become nothing but a head. Intimated, then, in Edgar's lines is the notion that the creation of illusionistic space and a belief in it depend upon acts of annihilation. To make the scene plausible, it must draw toward the limits of visibility. Illusionistic representation depends upon reductions. The illusion of continuous space rests upon what cannot be seen, on exhausting the limits of sight and arriving at what is "too small for sight." Vision depends upon both blindness and invisibility; it rests upon a vanishing point.

These lines, spoken for the benefit of a blind man, establish him as the best audience for a mode of vision. Similarly, this diminishing scene is, like a painting, utterly silent:

> The murmuring surge
> That on th' unnumbered idle pebble chafes
> Cannot be heard so high.
>
> (4.6.20–22)

And seeing this way, Edgar feels that he will go blind and be drawn into the scene and be destroyed by it:

> I'll look no more
> Lest my brain turn, and the deficient sight
> Topple down headlong.
>
> (4.6.22–24)

Albertian notions of the continuity between the viewer's space and the space of the painting become a prospect of madness in which the conviction of illusion produces the annihilation of the viewer. Gloucester embraces this illusion and plunges into it. He has been convinced by the trompe l'oeil of representation, and his fall shows that he is the perfect audience for it.

Yet the effect of the scene, at least in retrospect, is to call representation into question. If the lines demonstrate that pictorial space is an illusion, they also show that words succeed only in perpetrating illusion. If they show that our eyes cannot be trusted, they do not, therefore, give us confidence that what we see subsequently can be believed. Nor do they restore faith in blindness, for they make blindness and sight coincident. When we return to Gloucester's initial perspective—the stage is flat, there is no roaring sea to be heard—we come back to a bare stage stripped of the possibilities that Edgar's language invoked. Gloucester's life is no "miracle" (4.6.55); rather, it is a cheat. And all miracles that we might have supposed to lie at Dover Cliff will be equally guilty of the charge of illusion. The scene, employing the language by which a convincing real space is created, shows up the power of the stage.

The perspective from the imagined cliffs of Dover is so unusual in Shakespeare that there is barely the linguistic evidence that such a scene lay within his knowledge.[8] Only in Sonnet 24 is the word "perspective" used with some possibility that it means what Alberti meant by it:

"[P]erspective it is best painter's art" (line 4). The sonnet describes how the beloved's picture has been inscribed in the lover's heart; it is a matter of the exchange of glances that transfers what is seen to what is within, this picture displaying the art of the painter and framed by the body of the seer:

> Mine eye hath played the painter and hath stelled
> Thy beauty's form in table of my heart;
> My body is the frame wherein 'tis held,
> And perspective it is best painter's art.
>
> (Sonnet 24, lines 1–4)

The more usual use of "perspective" can be found in *Richard II.* There, attempting to talk the queen out of her grief, Bushy offers this description of misprision:

> [S]orrow's eye, glazed with blinding tears,
> Divides one thing entire to many objects,
> Like perspectives, which rightly gazed upon,
> Show nothing but confusion—eyed awry,
> Distinguish form.
>
> (2.2.16–20)

Bushy's perspective is anamorphosis, the art of placing an object in a picture, which, to be seen correctly, must not be seen head on.[9] In anamorphic art, the spectator must be in two places at once to take in the picture. Only in the mind can the double act of seeing be reconciled. There is some possibility that the "painter's art" of Sonnet 24 is an optical illusion of this sort rather than the illusion of actuality, since it is about seeing through others' eyes and the discrepancy between what is seen without and within. "Now see what good turns eyes for eyes have done" (line 9), the final quatrain opens, and the "turns" may well be anamorphic metamorphoses. At any rate, the conclusion of the sonnet opens a distance between "painter's art" and knowing: "Yet eyes this cunning want to grace their art; / They draw but what they see, know not the heart" (lines 13–14).

It is striking to note that Bushy's version of misprision anticipates the Chorus of *Henry V* asking for what is seen to serve as the basis for multiplication; by not seeing what is on stage and taking single things as signs of more, the viewer can provide the false perspective necessary to the truth of theatrical illusion. The Chorus of *Henry V* thus implies that Shakespeare's is, regularly, a theater of perspective, but of the sort that Bushy describes, a stage where what is seen and heard invites one to go beyond the evidence of the senses. In this respect, a quintessential moment occurs at the end of *Twelfth Night* when the twins Viola and Sebastian are finally onstage together and in the Duke's sight. Orsino comments, "A natural perspective that is and is not" (5.1.209). The stage has made itself at that moment a multiplying glass; the opposing tendencies in the language and desires of the characters have been realized—as if naturally—when the twins face each other. This "natural perspective," however, is not Albertian. Rather, it issues in an art of multiplicity and not in an order determined by a vanishing point. The Chorus of *Henry V* is intent upon a mathematics in which a "wooden O," the theater-as-nothing, can contain all. In *King Lear,* nothing comes of nothing, and the very language that would seem (to us) solidly to locate the world slides into an abyss, an uncreating, annihilative nothingness.

In the scene that Edgar presents, two perspectives are in question: the one that can be associated with the optical illusion of anamorphosis—the theater, that is, as illusion and multiplicity—and another perspective, associated with representation (or illusionism), theatrical reality, and one-point mathematics. Ironically, the latter system, which we might be inclined to say shows the capacities of the mind and the reality of the material world, seems wanting. And it undermines even the first perspective, which is embedded in the notion that Edgar's *lines will give us a scene.* What is of further interest here is the fact that these two modes of perspective are crucial in understanding the history of the stage in Shakespeare's time; theatrical representation offers another perspective on Edgar's lines.

Two or three years before the production of *King Lear,* English audiences, at least those privileged to attend court theatricals, had first seen illusionistic scenery. From some contemporary eyewitness accounts, we know that these proved baffling, unconvincing. The distortions that Edgar enumerates as the enabling conditions of perspective—birds become beetles, men become heads—were all that Sir Dudley Carleton saw at a performance of Ben Jonson's *The Masque of Blackness.* Rather than seeing the representational necessity in what Inigo Jones had designed, here is what Carleton saw: an "Engine . . . which had Motion . . . in it the Images of Sea-Horses," and, he concludes, "The Indecorum was, that there was all Fish and no water." Carleton saw the elements, but not the design.[10] Unlike Edgar, he was in no danger of being absorbed in the illusion. He did not see it. Edgar's lines present the new convention of staging that was to challenge and ultimately supplant representation at the Globe. Gloucester's initial affirmation of the flat stage in which representation depends almost entirely on language is challenged by Edgar's pictorialism. Shakespeare in the scene is not only enacting a version of the familiar trope analogizing the arts, *ut pictura poesis,* he is posing one kind of stage against another. And, of course, he was implicated in both. From 1603 on, Shakespeare's company had worn the royal livery. By the time of *King Lear,* they not only continued to perform at the Globe but were also performing at court, where the King's Men took part in the masques that Jones was designing for the royal eye.

Those scenes, in fact, are the best evidence for Shakespeare's knowledge of Albertian perspective. Certainly, English painting until the 1620s conceived of the surface of a painting in terms more akin to anamorphic than to illusionistic perspective. Summarizing the qualities of the Elizabethan image, Roy Strong comments on the "schematic and episodic view of a picture's surface" and concludes: "Inscriptions, emblems, symbolic objects and whole inset scenes are meant to be read separately as well as together; they are not governed by the single perspective viewpoint as re-created by the artists of Renaissance Italy."[11] It was Inigo Jones's importation of Italian scene design that changed the conception of the surface of English painting, replacing an organization of two-dimensional surface coordinates with a three-dimensional hierarchy that invited the translation of surface positions into perceptions of depth. Subordination replaced coordination.

Edgar's lines cross and recross these pictorial paths. Hearing them, Gloucester kneels, addressing the "mighty gods," renouncing the world "in your sights" (4.6.34–35). What is *our* sight at that moment? What is our perspective on the scene? Edgar has presented an illusion one must be blind to see, he has disabled *at once* Gloucester's stage that depends on language and the stage that depends on pictorial illusion. The scene, summoning up the powers of representation, shows the limits of representation. Gloucester makes something of Edgar's nothing, and Edgar's imagined Dover is a working out of illusion that rests on nothing: silence, invisibility, blindness. Pictorial space is founded on the meeting of the eye and the vanishing point. Acceding to this representation, Gloucester passes through the vanishing point and topples down headlong into double blindness, for he has agreed to see what cannot be seen—as we do when we refer to act 4, scene 6 as the Dover Cliff scene or credit it with working miracles. The scene, however, insists that it is an illusion, and what it offers is an anatomy of the techniques of illusion—verbal and pictorial—upon which Shakespearean theater depends. The "eyeless rage" that beat upon King Lear's head and that would "make nothing of" him is visited upon Gloucester and upon the audience to the scene. "Nothing will come of nothing" (1.1.90), Lear had told Cordelia, and the anatomy of representation in act 4, scene 6 is spaced between the nothing of the vanishing point and Gloucester's assumption of Lear's "poor old eyes" (3.7.57). This is the space of representation. By invoking these nothings as the condition of representation, act 4, scene 6 shows just what we accede to in seeing *King Lear,* and it implicates the audience in its annihilative vision.

After Dover

In the late plays, the double perspective on perspective initiated in *King Lear* continues. The extraordinary theatricality of *The Tempest* is marked by the inclusion of a masque, which is dismissed as an "insubstantial pageant" (4.1.155) but which nonetheless manages to glance at the Globe, the greater globe, and court theaters with their painted scenes. These double takes on what the stage offers are complex reflections of Edgar's lines. Equally so is this example from *Cymbeline,* and with it we return perhaps to the scene itself. After Imogen has been separated from Posthumus, she participates in a departure she is not permitted to see. Pisanio recounts it to her, Posthumus on board ship, waving to the shore, seen until barely visible, or, as Imogen says in lines that echo Edgar's:

> Thou shouldst have made him
> As little as a crow or less, ere left
> To after-eye him.
> (1.3.14–16)

And then she continues:

> I would have broke mine eyestrings, cracked them but
> To look upon him till the diminution

Of space had pointed him sharp as my needle;
Nay followed him till he had melted from
The smallness of a gnat to air, and then
Have turned mine eye and wept.

(1.3.17–21)

As in Edgar's lines, Imogen imagines this prospect as little short of blindness, and the annihilative thrust of her sight is extended with the prick of her needle. Imogen reduces Posthumus to a gnat and then to thin air, as Prospero might say, finally to return to herself. For she, the play ultimately announces, is "the piece of tender air" (5.1.445). This is neither a simple affirmation nor a devastating annihilation. Rather, it is a fitting close to a play that plays on perspective and offers to our eyes—and to those onstage—repeated examples of the violence of vision and misprision, which nonetheless signifies the possibility we have of representing our desires or achieving them.

After "After"

You will be aware from the title of this final section that it comes as a supplement or coda, an opportunity to stand back from the critical procedures pursued thus far. It is another perspective, if you like. The structure of this essay perhaps invites this additional section, for you may have noticed that while the first section promised "the way to Dover" and the final section spoke "after Dover," the section between them is called not "Dover" but "Perspectives." The structure of the essay, thus, may have looked as if it took its model from Aristotle's notion of a well-formed plot—that is, with a beginning, middle, and end—but this essay has elided the middle. It has not arrived at the space its margins seemed to imply. The decentered center of this essay thus might invite some further perspectives at its close.

Edgar's lines about Dover Cliff enact a particular moment in the history of representation, the confrontation of anamorphic art and illusionism, public theater and court theater, the drama as text and the drama as spectacle. As I described these confrontations, you will have noticed certain remarks: about the failure of the signifier to reach significance, about the incapacity to realize the Real, about the rooting of the Real in the invisible and the imaginary. That is, you will have noticed a vocabulary that implies a Lacanian bias, that sees the desire represented in *King*

Lear—the desire for presentation to replace representation—as the representation of desire—an erotics of the text, in short. And perhaps, too, you will have noticed in the very double takes of perspectives on perspective a certain deconstructive play, an irreducible doubleness at the center—for example, in claiming that language supplements the scene (you can hear that two ways), supplements it *beforehand,* or in doubling blindness and invisibility, or in the indeterminacy of the undermining constitutive of Edgar's lines.

If you noticed these aspects of critical practice, you may have wondered where Lacan and Derrida fit within the confrontation within representation. Or perhaps you wondered about the representativeness of this moment in *King Lear.* What is its place in the history of representation?

These are enormous questions, of course, and they do not rightly belong in a coda to an essay. They are as much founding thoughts as afterthoughts. Having been raised, however, they cannot exactly be dropped.

So let us imagine what it would mean if representation had been haunted from its start by the confrontation enacted in Edgar's lines. We could begin with the anatomy of representation that Derrida offers in "The Theater of Cruelty and the Closure of Representation."[12] There, you will recall, he reads Antonin Artaud's attempt to describe a theater that would end the entire tradition of mimesis. Derrida sees Artaud's attempt as an impossibility that nonetheless points to the conditions of representation and that reveals the premises of representation. These premises are first, that representation is the illustration and embodiment of a text that is separate from the performance; second, that representation is *re*-presentation, making present again an action that could be really performed elsewhere (in real life); and finally, that representation is mere surface, simply something to be looked at.

For the sake of the confrontational structure of the argument about Dover Cliff, these three definitions could be reduced to two: on the one hand, a definition of representation that posits a Real that is other than the scene—the real of real life, or the real of the author's text—and on the other hand, a definition of representation as mere show.

A moment's thought will suggest that this dichotomy will not stand scrutiny. Mere show haunts all claims of representation. But, on the other hand, to treat representation merely as show ignores the human bodies performing actions and saying words. The real *is* somehow in the show.

This suggests another dichotomy, one that can be found in the classical formulations of representation and that has been repeated ever since. Plato, of course, banished representation as the imitation of an imitation, a show of appearances. But he also refused mimesis a place in the ideal republic because of its parasitical capacity, its ability to corrupt and, as he implies, to womanize the audience (*Republic,* 605d–e). Mimesis is dangerous not only because it is unreal but because it has real effects. The guardians cannot be actors, Plato says, because if they were to play parts, they could not play their part (394–95). There would be a confusion of roles. There is, as you can see from this presentation, a certain confusion in the position.

Aristotle defines tragedy, as everyone knows, as the imitation of an action. He seems, therefore, to hold to the notion of representation as the imitation of the real; indeed, there are several passages in the *Poetics* where he claims that plays need not be seen, that spectacle is inessential. What matters is the script; that is what is real. And the action imitated in the script is no mere copy of appearances. Ordered by the necessity of a beginning, middle, and end; structured through recognition and reversal—in these and in numerous other ways the script reproduces a principle of intelligibility more real than ordinary life. Yet, on the other hand, Aristotle also seems to think of representation as imitative in a much more naive and straightforward way. At least, when he offers an etiology of dramatic form, he roots it in a natural capacity for—and pleasure in—mimicry. "We enjoy seeing likenesses," he writes (1448b).[13]

Classical discussions of representation are motivated by a dichotomy. We could simplify it this way: On the one hand, representation is imitation, adequate or inadequate to the Real, however it is defined. On the other hand, representation is implicit in the real and functions the way a representative example does. Edgar's lines on Dover Cliff play out these definitions: Illusionism is on the side of imitation, anamorphic art assembles pieces of the real; it makes use, as the Chorus to *Henry V* suggests, of counters that enable multiplication. Could we then say that Lacan, who argues that desire voices the dictates of an Other and posits the Other as the goal of desire, favors a view of representation as imitation, always inadequate to the Real? And could we place Derrida on the other side of the dichotomy, rooting representation in the Real?

We could, if we could strip the Real of all its metaphysical assumptions. That project—as impossible as Artaud's—suggests, of course, Derrida's attraction to Artaud. In any event, it seems important to say that the concerns of Lacan and Derrida are pertinent to the classical dilemmas in accounting for the conditions of representation.

Where does Shakespeare's text stand in this conflict if not in the conflict? If we look again at the lines spoken by the Chorus of *Henry V*, we might notice now that the register of stage's inadequacy for representation is couched in very peculiar terms. If there is to be a "swelling scene," it can only take place through "imaginary puissance." The Chorus has another stage in mind: It represents the mind itself as a stage. Moreover, the Chorus represents the mind and stage as a body; the "flat unraised spirits" that work in a "little place" will swell elsewhere. The mind and stage are seen as a pregnant body, and re-production, as representation. In *that* representation, there is nothing before representation.

Yet we recall that the receptive space at which the Chorus aims is also described as a locus of impression, as if the mind were a blank pad ready for writing. And Sonnet 24 about painter's perspective records impressions "stelled" in the "table of my heart," where tables are tablets. Again, then, a scene of writing: "My body is the frame," the sonnet continues; if this is an Albertian frame, one perspective on representation encounters the other. What would it mean if the body were also a book and a picture? Would the opposition of real and representation hold? Could illusion and anamorphosis still be in conflict?

Would it help to see the two modes of representation as tropes? To see illusionism as metaphor, representativeness as metonymy? The tropes also cross the boundaries between them. For remember that Aristotle considered our delight in likenesses as the *natural* basis of mimicry; yet metaphor—which he defines as the ability to perceive resemblances—he calls a display of genius. And what if we looked at the politics of representation, along with its sexual politics? On the one hand, we have Plato's antifeminine charge against the theater, repeated in sixteenth-century antitheatrical tracts; on the other hand, the Chorus of *Henry V* imagines the mind and stage as a feminine receptacle. Plato's republic is an ideal world of coordinates, in which everyone is placed to play a part. Is this anamorphic art, with its feudal and chivalric representations? Inigo Jones's frames were meant for a royal eye, and they established a hierarchy of vision. Yet, one-point perspective ultimately—that is to say, historically—made every viewer sovereign; it is the pictorial mode coincident with the development of representative government.

Perhaps at this point, far too many perspectives on perspective have been offered. Perhaps the center will not hold.

And what about the margins? Prospero dismisses the masque in act 4 of *The Tempest* as insubstantial. Yet anyone who has ever tried to work out the syntax of the Revels speech (as it is called) stumbles on the crucial comparison, the one that either dismisses the stage as insubstantial when compared to the real, or dismisses the real as itself insubstantial, or grants to both stage and world whatever substantiality substance has.

> These our actors,
> As I foretold you, were all spirits and
> Are melted into air, into thin air;
> And, like the baseless fabric of this vision,
> The cloud-capped towers, the gorgeous palaces,
> The solemn temples, the great globe itself,
> Yea, all which it inherit, shall dissolve,
> And, like this insubstantial pageant faded,
> Leave not a rack behind.
>
> (4.1.148–56)

There are two "likes" in this speech, and no subject for the verb "shall dissolve"—no single subject, and thus no clear demarcation of what is being likened to what. Perhaps the "baseless fabric" is as far as we can go—the threads of the text that never will be unwoven. Perhaps, too, we might recall that "thin air" is the name of woman, as Imogen affirms the traditional etymology of *mulier,* "woman," from *mollis aer,* "piece of tender air." Representation again originates in reproduction in all its insubstantiality and in its embodiment, at the same time. Could this be what Wallace Stevens named, following Parmenides, "the nothing that is"?[14]

If this is what lies "after Dover," it had better be admitted that aftereffects undermine all openings, including the opening of this essay, which offers as the text of *King Lear* an interchange between a nameless gentleman and Kent, an interchange that occurs only in the quarto of the play, and not in the folio. Perhaps in the fact that there is not a *King Lear,* not one text but two, we can have a final perspective on the multiplicities of representation, a perspective on *original* representation apt for a playwright who never published any of his plays and who nonetheless allows the Chorus of *Henry V* to imagine performance embodied as printing—the printing that Shakespeare never in fact sought for his texts.

Shakespeare Writing Matter Again: Objects and Their Detachments

Writing Matter: From the Hands of the English Renaissance[1] was initially conceived as a Shakespeare book. The plan had been to develop the argument of "Shakespearian Characters: The Generation of Silvia," chapter 4 of my previous book, *Voice Terminal Echo* (and reprinted in this volume),[2] which had considered various instances of the coincidence of character in its scriptive and dramatic meanings from *The Two Gentlemen of Verona* and *Titus Andronicus* to *Twelfth Night, Hamlet,* and *Cymbeline,* among other texts. The point of such an exercise, of course, was to depsychologize character and to contest the transcendentalizing aims implicit in arguments for unique individuality. Character books, pedagogical books, and secretarial manuals were cited, the trajectory of the letter and the letter writer pursued in *Writing Matter.* The Shakespearean aim of the project only was realized in an essay, "Hamlet's Hand,"[3] which represents an initial attempt to read the manuals in which handwriting was taught alongside the play. More important than such connections was the work done in that essay and several others that argue the significant relationship between the textual situation of Shakespeare's plays and their representations of texts: the letters circulated, forged, and read.

The questions of who reads, who writes, and why always matters for understanding circuits of power and desire.[4]

I take this occasion to recall those earlier projects to encourage work that might further specify the connections among textual conditions, textual properties, and textuality in its broadest sense (in Shakespeare among others). Such work must be wary of supposing that seeing there is nothing but text necessarily evades transcendentalizing if it allows the admission (as both Jacques Derrida and Marjorie Garber would) of ghosts, if not quite spirits, into the machine. But it needs also to be wary of attaching substance to letters and thereby transcendentalizing materiality as an inalienable possession or the thing itself. Richard Halpern's account of handwriting in *The Poetics of Primitive Accumulation*[5] provides terms by setting textual production along the materialist path of a regulated volatility, a path to be connected to the commodity as an object of dispossession, volatized in exchange, fantasized and fetishized as possessions that, rather, possess their possessors. These are objects loosed from fixed property relations, signs that will not serve as the indexicals Sir Philip Sidney imagined characters bear onstage.

Plays by Shakespeare may have more letters in them than any other significant prop, props displaying (im)propriety. The circulation of letters is barely contained by the kind of empiricist gesture that counting might suggest. In the second act of *King Lear,* to take one example, Regan claims to have received a letter from Goneril a scene before the letter carrier arrives, and the delivery of the letter as later recounted by Kent describes a scene that cannot have taken place. In the letter as Regan reads it, Goneril tells her that she is about to arrive, something she could not possibly have written in act I when she dispatched the letter, since her decision depends on events subsequent to the posting of the letter. These dizzying refusals remind us of the "post" in "posting." They make plotting and retrospection coincident. If letters can arrive before they were sent, or vice versa, then before and after are—literally—preposterous. Letters, moreover, can find their proper recipients even when they are disguised and known to no one (how do Kent and Cordelia correspond?); they can convey true sentiments even when they are forged (Edmund does know his brother's character). Letters are the material form of uncanny knowledge, the vehicles of desperate idealizing hopes. Unfounded, they found modernity. Oswald, the fluid character most allied to the desacralizing regimes of modernity (as Halpern argues), unmoored from old property order and from gendered propriety as well (his service lubricates all sorts of promiscuity), is a postman, a secretary and letter carrier. When Edgar intercepts and kills him, he speaks for the first time in propria persona.

The circulation of letters in this play must be related to its textual condition; the fact that there are two *King Lear*s means only that there once were more than that and that no text of the play will ever be anything more than just that: one text among a number whose sum we can never total. Fifty at a clap, Lear exclaims, a piece of knowledge he gets from nowhere in act 1, scene 4—or from some (lost) text of the play or from the kind of knowledge the play intimates travels by the post. Nothing comes of noting.

In its foundational illusoriness, the play of the letter is to be related to the so-called scene at Dover where we look into an abyss we cannot see. Recently, both times an essay of mine on that moment was reprinted, its two final sections were omitted;[6] the punch line of the essay was thereby refused: that the double texts of *King Lear* will not even ground the deconstructive reading the essay offers and furthermore, that the play traffics in a scene of failed vision replicated elsewhere, notably in *Cymbeline* when Imogen's vision cracks seeing Posthumus sailing away. The effect of the Dover Cliff scene in *Lear* is intimately tied to the father-son pair and the pathos of blinded visionary patriarchy.[7] The founding spot where vision is annihilated may always be misogynistically understood as the dark and vicious place of begetting (Imogen points at Posthumus until he is nothing more than the tip of her needle, a gnat to be pricked, nothing more than a speck in the air). That the viewer in classic accounts of perspective is presumptively male—and that Imogen is not (or, rather, that the character is not while the gender of the player, a boy, refuses the modern taxonomy of diacritical gender difference, male and female)—suggests that the Oedipal drama of *King Lear* is as historically contingent as is the movement of the post. Literally.

Speculations: *Macbeth* and Source

This essay (or so its title suggests) poses a plurality of speculations against a presumed singleness of source; it glances, thereby, at a dispersal of origins. Source—in its heterogeneity—is its concern, aimed ultimately at locating Shakespeare's relation to *Macbeth.* But, it can be assumed, there is no immediate path to the author as the source of the text except through a relay of mediations, and by the end, even the supposed ultimate source—the author—must be considered within a heterogeneous dispersal.[1]

That dispersal might be termed "history," and this essay aims at a description of the place of *Macbeth* within some familiar historical determinations: its sources in Raphael Holinshed's *Chronicles,* its relation to the rule and rhetoric of James I, its proximity to Ben Jonson's *Masque of Queens.* Yet in alluding to such historical determinations as being heterogeneous, determinations become indeterminate. This essay is concerned with the openings within the hegemonic, and its trope for such situations is specular and speculative: to imagine that within the language of hegemonic imposition and superimposition, duplication opens a specter of uncontrolled resemblance rendering difference problematic—rendering, that is, determinate differences indeterminate.

Like Stephen Greenblatt in "Shakespeare and the Exorcists," in this essay in "the elephants' graveyard of literary history" (as he characterizes source study),[2] I am guided by the thesis that "history cannot be divorced from textuality, and all texts can be compelled to confront the crisis of undecidability revealed in the literary text" (102). Greenblatt terms this a "subversive" hypothesis (subversive of the territorial claims of history and literature), and I, too, am interested in examining the limits of subversion, the modes of representing officially discountenanced positions. In Greenblatt's study of the relationship between Samuel Harsnett's *A Declaration of Egregious Popish Impostures* and *King Lear,* the source practices a version of the exorcism it denounces; exorcists are exposed as theatrical imposters. Shakespeare welcomes what Harsnett has debunked, and the theater accrues a demonic power more frightening than Harsnett could imagine. For Greenblatt, this exchange crosses and establishes the borders between the source and literary representation; it displays an institutional economy. "The official church dismantles and cedes to the players the powerful mechanism of an unwanted and dangerous charisma; in return the players confirm the charge that these mechanisms are theatrical and hence illusory" (116). As described, this exchange characterizes a "cultural poetics" (103) that is apparently a closed system, an economics, thus, in which there is no waste. Yet Greenblatt adds a paradoxical twist to this paradigm: The theater practices an evacuation even more excessive than the official one and, at the same time, a surplus value—literariness—is founded in that self-revealed lack, the depiction of evil. Paradoxically, then, the theater's loyal gesture has a subversive edge; indeed, on that margin, it establishes its position.

What Greenblatt salvages from the elephants' graveyard is nothing less than the saving powers of theater, of Shakespearean theatricality in particular. His *King Lear* answers to "our need . . . our desire for spectacular impostures" (123). He wittily complains that deconstruction "is not satanic enough" (102). His criticism is properly satanic; from nothing, he produces the satisfaction of needs and desires. "If I have any fear, it is not of falling into hell, but of falling into nothing," Greenblatt quotes from John Wesley (102);[3] in Greenblatt's recuperation of the source in Shakespeare, we fall not into an abyss but, instead, into a satanic recouping of loss. Thus, for Greenblatt, *King Lear* offers the equivalent of devil worship: "[T]he force of evil in the play is larger than any local habitation or name" (122), and we are made to love what that theater produces: "The force of *King Lear* is to make us love the theater, to seek out its satisfactions, to serve its interests, to confer upon it a place of its own, to grant it life by permitting it to reproduce itself over generations" (122).

The inversion that Greenblatt practices may resituate the literary, but it does not ultimately call into question the value system upon which it rests. Greenblatt's *King Lear* is, in many ways, perfectly recognizable: Good and evil are not in question (nor is the greatness of *King Lear* or Harsnett's stylistic poverty); nor is there any question of the human desires the play engages. Not surprisingly, then, the play's "subversion" (its demonism) is congruent with the demonism officially exorcised. And theatricality takes on a transcendental function in its very negativity: It is the "life" breathed into the corpse of the elephantine source.

Greenblatt insists in the opening pages of "Shakespeare and the Exorcists," upon the modesty of his project: "[F]or me the study of literature is the study of contingent, particular, intended, and historically embedded works; if theory inevitably involves the desire to escape from contingency to a higher realm, a realm in which signs are purified of the slime of history, then this paper is written *against theory*" (101). Yet it could be argued, I think, that with "theatricality" Greenblatt has found that "universal, encompassing, and abstract problematic," which, he says, might be called theory, and which, if it is, he opposes. While the rhetoric of specificity has a Foucauldian ring, the practice of "cultural poetics" has its transcendental value (theatricality) and its metaphysical and humanistic investments. The situation in his text reveals, despite itself, a will to totalization. These are, of course, the charges that Jacques Derrida leveled at Michel Foucault in "Cogito and the History of Madness."[4]

I review Greenblatt's argument here to distance myself from a method that my own work certainly shares in some of its concerns and presuppositions, but also because Greenblatt's argument does not seem to me to go far enough in distinguishing itself from more conventional literary criticism. It seeks to preserve the very notion of literariness it calls into question; its subversion is most like that deconstructive reversal that does not, in fact, throw logocentric suppositions into question. Unlike Greenblatt, then, my concern in the pages that follow is with an *uneconomic* expenditure, with "an excess in the direction of the non-determined."[5] The direction I take, as these phrases indicate, is Derridean; it is also, I would argue, political.

The argument I make depends upon the notion that dominant discourses allow their own subversion precisely because hegemonic control is an impossible dream, a self-defeating fantasy. That defeat is marked by the self-division in Greenblatt's essay. More usually, that fantasy, I would argue, attaches itself to source, to the belief in an ultimate, and ultimately authoritative, origin. What I trace is an absolutist fantasy, and one that not only kings indulge. For literary critics, of various kinds, are prone to its lure as well: for example, when they suppose that there are certain unquestionable facts rather than allowing that what counts as factual is itself a discursive formation, or when they imagine for the text and its author some autonomy of intention. Greenblatt, for instance, assumes a literary intentionality in the Shakespearean text; I do not; rather, I regard the literariness of Shakespeare's texts as a literary-critical invention. Greenblatt opens his essay with a characteristic gesture toward the unquestioned reality of dates and facts, the local event that locates the Shakespearean text within a cultural economy. "Between the spring of 1585 and the summer of 1586, a group of English Catholic priests led by the Jesuit William Weston, alias Father Edmunds, conducted a series of spectacular exorcisms."[6] I mean to call into question the methods of literary critics and the practices of textual, historical, and formalistic criticism. The method I offer instead owes much to poststructuralism and, in this essay, to the work of Derrida. For it is Derrida's inquiries into questions of origin that inform my own.[7]

Derrida stages a version of that inquiry in his examination of Foucault's reading of René Descartes. For my purposes here, it is unnecessary to determine who reads Descartes correctly (I would argue, in fact, that such a determination is not possible). The argument hinges on whether a passage in Descartes introduced by *"sed forte"* is a feigned objection (according to Derrida's account) or a determining marker (as it is for Foucault).[8] Greenblatt would follow Foucault, I believe, in assuming that a text could be so historically saturated that a reading could reveal the historicity of the text. Derrida's alternate reading, even if only entertained hypothetically, shatters this notion of the historic decisiveness of any textual mark. The Foucauldian intervention in Descartes depends upon the possibility of constructing history as the history of meaning. It depends upon history as a rational concept. Whereas, for Foucault, the Cartesian text has all the force of an originary moment, a decisive break, for Derrida, the Cartesian text—as text—cannot be reduced to a historical determination; in its heterogeneity, it opens an interval between history and historicity-in-general. In his reading, Foucault has mistaken one for the other.

To invoke the name of Derrida in support of an argument that seeks to recover history—even history as a discursive formation—points to the central methodological issue of this essay. Derrida has far too easily been dismissed as unconcerned with history (Edward Said's denunciations are perhaps the most familiar), whereas history is for him a problematic matter precisely because it has been tied to certain metaphysical notions that will not bear close scrutiny. These include the idea of the present moment as one of complete self-presence, the idea of a past moment as one of sheer literality, and the idea of the future as the necessary outcome of such prior moments. As I have argued,

> [H]istory, as the word says, means narrative, and narrative means representation tied to principles of beginning and end that are part and parcel of the view of the world that rests upon concepts like Being and Presence, and such distinctions as inside and outside or body and spirit. *Différance,* Derrida writes, can replace the notion of origin or ground and, so doing, would open up a question that he terms *historial.* That neologism, as much as *différance,* is an attempt to provide terms for that for which there are no terms.[9]

As Derrida says in *Positions,* "history" is a term, like "writing," whose force he requires, although its metaphysical, ontological investments must be called into question. What is needed is "a history that also implies a new logic of *repetition* and the *trace,* for it is difficult to see how there could be history without it."[10] Indeed, Derridean "history" requires the full range of his nonconceptual concepts if it is to be reinscribed. To quote myself again: "History is the meeting of articulation, difference, and writing; history crosses paths with trace and supplement. These terms are not all the same, although their motion and meeting testify to the endless play in time of *différance.*"[11] The historic interval, or spacing, is a setting aside that refuses self-identity; the historical "moment" must be "marked twice."[12] It is neither unitary nor homogeneous.

Derrida's highly condensed statement suggests a number of things:

1. The historical moment—as a differential moment—must differ from itself and must defer its identity.
2. The critical activity of delineating a "moment" itself occupies differential relation to the moment marked, which it inevitably re-marks.
3. Thus, the necessity of double marking refers both to the "original historical moment," itself traversed by and constituted by difference, and to any subsequent moment of re-marking the "original."
4. Such re-marking therefore characterizes historicity-in-general, spacing, difference, and so on—all testifying to the failure of self-coincidence, which produces textuality and temporality.
5. Re-marking also defines the deconstructive project as a form of historicity and, indeed, as the attempt to re-mark the difference between history and historicity-in-general;
6. Re-marking, then, is the "new concept of history"[13] because it marks the break with the old metaphysical concept in an overturning that is not a reappropriation, since it permits the dissemination of the mark into the determined (historical) field without confining the mark to such determinations.

Andrew Parker offers a brilliant summary of these arguments, emphasizing the Derridean sense of history as refiguration, a temporality at one with deferral:

> Such a form of temporality elides the very "firstness" of the "prior" event, placing in question the possibility of an event that could be isolated in its self-contained moment of occurrence; as a *mélange* of proleptic and metaleptic relationships, deferred action would suggest that if our present understanding "normally" is dependent on the past as its determining ground, then the future would be equally predictive of the "pastness" of the past.[14]

Hence, in the essay that follows, history is limited by texts whose very determinations are indeterminate, texts, that is, that are determined precisely by their double marking: the overdetermination that renders any text a duplicate, a copy with no original. The issue of success/succession in *Macbeth* provides an image of this, indeed of the entire mirror structure that produces the otherness of Others, or of other moments (the past, the future), in short, the otherness-of-the-present or of the self as it (fails to) coincide(s) with itself.

Derrida sums up his historical concerns in *Positions:* "Must I recall that from the first texts I published, I have attempted to systematize a deconstructive critique precisely against the authority of meaning, as the *transcendental signified* or as *telos,* in other words history determined in the last analysis as the history of meaning, history in its logocentric, metaphysical, idealistic . . . representation."[15] The statement comes, as is well known, in the midst of Derrida's most extended confrontation with Marxist critics and in the midst of a struggle to define his political position. In "Between Dialectics and Deconstruction: Derrida and the Reading of Marx," Parker has, once again, brilliantly explored these issues. His call, "to construe the political *otherwise,*" I take to be exemplary.[16] If Derrida objects to Marxists, as he does to Foucault, for their metaphysical investment, for their belief in Marxism as a decisive and grounded discourse (it must be noted that these accusations do not keep Derrida from endorsing certain Althusserian arguments or, indeed, from being willing to call himself a materialist), his critical "position" represents a politics that insists on the (inevitably limited) recognition involved in taking positions. It is usual to complain that Derrida's refusal to be "for" or against" is an implicit endorsement of the status quo; however, Derrida's argument is that taking such a position (taking sides) in no way alters the dualistic, logocentric suppositions upon which position taking is posited. That, in effect, is the argument I rehearsed above in relation to Greenblatt's essay, which ends by denouncing political totalitarianism and yet by endorsing what might be called a literary totalitarianism.

I argue, then, that to think of history as heterogeneous dispersal, as I attempt to do in this essay, is a political act precisely because it calls into question those modes of "logocentric, metaphysical, idealistic . . . representation" that ascribe determinate force to hegemonic rhetoric and that assume that ideological inscriptions really have the power they claim. It is instead the argument of this essay that ideology is haunted by what it excludes, subverted by what it subordinates. Yet the argument does not assume the possibility of some other mode of discourse (an Althusserian dream of science, for instance, "outside" ideology), for to do so would be to replace one form of idealism with another. And thus, in this essay, the terms that must be used—referring us to texts and authors and events—can only be taken as tropes, speculations with counters that discourse fills but that cannot be contained; halls of mirrors in which resemblance does not halt. In that respect, this essay might be called "The Mirror of Kings." Although the argument I make seems to me congruent with the thesis of my *James I and the Politics of Literature,*[17] there is a shift of emphasis in this essay. In that book, I was interested in mapping strategies of representation shared by Jacobean authors and their monarch. This essay looks at the dark side of representation. The emphasis now is on the "re" in representation, the haunting specter of duplication that unmoors texts and events from a positivistic view of history or literature. What is *real,* then, is the "re," perhaps itself a recovery of the nothing into which things slide. Latin *res* ("thing") lies behind French *rien* ("nothing").

"Shakespeare deals freely with his source," so Frank Kermode writes, considering the relationship of *Macbeth* to Holinshed. "The actual words of Holinshed are closely followed, notably in IV.ii, but Shakespeare deals freely with his source, making Duncan old and venerable, instead of a young and weak-willed man. This is part of the general blackening of Macbeth's character."[18] Geoffrey Bullough marvels at "Shakespeare, with that wonderful memory ever ready to float up, albeit unconsciously, associations from reading or hearsay."[19] Thus, these critics affirm, Shakespeare moves freely in Holinshed, drawing on many narratives to fashion his "composite picture," as Bullough calls it.[20] And whereas, in Holinshed, Duncan is both a good king and a weak one, and Macbeth is at first loyal and then traitorous, Shakespeare—so the common line has it—recombines and simplifies his materials to offer a saintly king and his villainous murderer and thereby makes differences clear-cut. Holinshed's narrative, because it motivates Macbeth's rebellion by allowing for defects in Duncan's rule (Duncan bars Macbeth's right to succeed to the throne, after all), makes an about-face when Macbeth turns tyrant; his earlier service to the king is labeled "counterfet."[21] Shakespeare, according to Kermode, does not have Holinshed's problem; his Macbeth is "blackened" from the start. The start? Where does a "composite" text begin?

Such a question, I would argue, must be raised before the common assumptions about Shakespeare, implicit in these descriptions of the relationship of *Macbeth* to Holinshed, can begin to be investigated. For the assumption about the autonomous imagination of the author is allied to a description of a text remarkable for its moral clarity and its political conservatism—a description that may reveal more about the critics than about the play.

To test these commonplaces, let us take as an example Duncan's musing on the treacherous thane of Cawdor:

> There's no art
> To find the mind's construction in the face:
> He was a gentleman on whom I built
> An absolute trust
>
> (1.4.11–14)

These lines, cut short by the entrance of Macbeth, are generally seen as an index to the innocence of Duncan's mind. What is their source? In Holinshed, Duncan's words are spoken by a witch. She prophesies that the "trustie servant" of King Natholocus, who has come to her on his ruler's behalf, will murder his monarch. The king, she says, will be killed by one "in whome he had reposed an especiall trust."[22]

Duncan's lines, especially as they have usually been read, suggest clear-cut moral differences. Yet that other habit of Shakespearean composition, its "free" association, might lead one to ask if it is significant that Duncan voices lines spoken elsewhere by a witch. The question resonates if one allows another echo to sound, the reverberations of the witches' greeting of Macbeth—"All hail Macbeth! hail to thee, Thane of Cawdor! / All hail, Macbeth! that shall be King hereafter" (1.3.49–50)—reverberations that come to occupy Duncan's mouth. Just a few lines after the witches' all-hailing, messengers from the king arrive, bid to "call" Macbeth "Thane of Cawdor: / In which addition, hail, most worthy Thane" (1.3.105–6); a scene later, Duncan names the king to be, "Our eldest, Malcolm; whom we name hereafter" (1.4.38). The text of *Macbeth* is itself "composite," redistributing the witches' lines.

Is it to be accounted to the *free* dealing of the author's mind that Duncan's lines have their source—in Holinshed and in the play—in the mouths of witches? We might notice, too, that where Duncan swerves from the lines in Holinshed describing a king *reposing* his *special* trust, he substitutes the *activity* of *building* an *absolute* trust, and recall that Shakespeare drops Holinshed's description of Macbeth as master builder of Dunsinane, virtually the only incident from Macbeth's career not duplicated in the play, and allows Duncan instead to comment on the architecture of Inverness, thus permitting Duncan's to be the constructing mind. In short, the absolute differences and moral clarity that critics have found to be Shakespeare's are, at least in these instances, Duncan's. Monarch of the *absolute,* Duncan constructs differences against the demonic source of his lines, spoken by a witch and to a figure that serves as a model for Macbeth. Duncan's musings on the betrayal by the thane of Cawdor have always been allowed the ironic echo that extends to the newly named thane, Macbeth; the lines, I would suggest, might also be thought of as self-reflective. "There's no art / To find the mind's construction in the face;" has not criticism—with scarcely an exception—succumbed to Duncan's glassy surface?[23]

That surface is cut into again if we return to the source of Duncan's lines in Holinshed. For Holinshed also describes King Duff as one "having a special trust in Donwald,"[24] the loyal retainer who slays him. Holinshed's King Duff is a haunted and sleepless figure who sends his trusty servant to try to discover the cause of his disease. Donwald, the servant, finds a witch "rosting upon a woodden broch an image of wax at the fier, resembling in each feature the kings person" (480). The king's illness is the result of this demonic voodooism, spectral identification, and he is restored to health as soon as Donwald destroys the waxen image. It scarcely needs mention that Holinshed's King Duff is—except for the line that Duncan speaks—a version of Macbeth. Does the specter of identification drawn from the composition of Holinshed in *Macbeth* signify in the play? Both Duff and Donwald are versions of Macbeth. Duncan is a further spectral emanation of a source less intent on *absolute difference* than on resemblance. After King Duff is cured, he celebrates his recovery by making a "spectacle" (481) of hanged rebels. Among them are Donwald's kin, and the loyal retainer who cured the king by destroying his specter turns on the king who has made the spectacle. Similarly, *Macbeth* opens with reports of Macbeth fixing a rebel head upon the battlements (1.2.23) and closes with his severed head displayed by Macduff (5.9.20); it is a plot inscribed and generated within specularity: In each instance, a supposedly saintly king has let another do his dirty work.

As another example of specular contamination, consider this episode from Holinshed: King Kenneth, successor to King Duff and murderer of Duff's son and heir, suffers guilt and sleeplessness; he is told by prophetic voices that he will die and that the heir he has named will not succeed to the throne. His murder is accomplished by Fenella, avenging the death of her son, another child killed by the guilty monarch. Knowing "that the king delighted above measure in goodlie buildings,"[25] she constructs an elaborate tower covered with engraved flowers and other images. "In the middest of the house there was a goodlie brasen image also, resembling the figure of king Kenneth" (487) holding in his hands a golden apple that, if plucked, activates crossbows aimed at the taker. The king succumbs to the lure and is killed. Whose career is this in *Macbeth,* Macbeth's or Duncan's?

Macbeth looks in his conscience, torn by demonic representations and by Duncan's furthering of their designs. In soliloquy, he produces the saintly king, but as a mirror:

> This Duncan
> Hath borne his faculties so meek, hath been
> So clear in his great office, that his virtues
> Will plead like angels.
>
> (1.7.16–19)

Duncan's polished surface: is it the representation of an absolute power or the mirror of resemblance?

Duncan articulates and constructs absolute difference, but equivocation arises from the source. "People wished," Holinshed writes,

> the inclinations and maners of these two cousins to have beene so tempered and enterchangeablie bestowed betwixt them, that where the one had too much of clemencie, and the other of crueltie, the meane vertue betwixt these two extremities might have reigned by indifferent partition in them both.[26]

Similarly, Lady Macbeth fears her husband "is too full o' th' milk of human kindness" (1.5.17), and, as Harry Berger has persuasively argued, the opening scenes of the play enact an elaborately concealed hostility between Duncan and Macbeth, scenes, that is, of rivalry between characters who represent (in Holinshed's words) the "indifferent partition" that "reign[s]" in *Macbeth.*[27] "Have we eaten on the insane root, / That takes the reason prisoner?" (1.3.84–85), Banquo asks after the witches appear. The "insane root" lies in the source; in Holinshed, Duncan disables the rebels by feeding them a poisoned brew that puts them to sleep. "Look up clear," Lady Macbeth counsels her husband (1.5.71), and he looks in a mirror, to find Duncan, "clear in his great office" (1.7.18). Succession in the play can never take place except in a mirror. Macbeth invents the sainted king; he is not visible in the lines he speaks. After Macbeth kills him, he reports that Duncan's silver skin was breached with golden blood (2.3.110).[28] Such images are the obstacles that Macbeth finds in his path; they are also the source of his own legitimation when he comes to occupy Duncan's place. Macbeth succeeds as the king of the image repertoire in *Macbeth.*

Thus, when one looks to the most apparently straightforward scene of the transmission of source—the recasting of Holinshed's conversation between Macduff and Malcolm in act 4, scene 3—what one discovers is that something has come between the source and the scene. What blocks the way of transmission is the text of *Macbeth* itself; Malcolm and Macduff repeatedly echo words and phrases that have come before, words most often heard in Macbeth's mouth. Resemblance, not difference, dominates the text; Macbeth attempts unpartnered to occupy alone what occupies him, to the end "wrought / With things forgotten" (1.3.151).

"People wished the inclinations and maners of these two cousins to have beene so tempered and enterchangeablie bestowed betwixt them," so Holinshed writes; is that desire, articulated in the source, also Shakespeare's? The chance and wayward associations of his "wonderful memory"? The floating of his unconscious? A conscious design? To consider these questions, another source must be considered, the occasion of the play, for it is equally a critical commonplace to see the author of *Macbeth* succumbing to the exigencies of history and to regard the play as a royal compliment: Edward the Confessor touches for the king's evil as James, reluctantly, did; Banquo fathered James's line.[29] Moreover, the text of *Macbeth* that we have derives from a court performance. Could Shakespeare have represented the contaminations of spectral resemblance before James I? Intentionally? Secretly? These questions about source lead to what Fredric Jameson might call the *political unconscious* of the play, a determined heterogeneity rather than the freeplay of the mind.[30] What, we need to ask, are the political conditions of representation in which *Macbeth* is located?

The text of *Macbeth* offers one index to these conditions, for it is, as

Stephen Orgel has remarked, a palimpsest, combining at least two versions of the play.[31] One version dates from the time of the Gunpowder Plot, which is alluded to, for instance, by the Porter's use of "equivocation" in the play (act 2, scene 3; and also, at 5.5.43, by Macbeth). Another version from several years later is marked by the additions of songs from Middleton's *The Witch,* a play presumed to postdate Jonson's 1609 *The Masque of Queens.* From act 3 on, if not before, the text of *Macbeth* shows signs of tampering: transposed scenes, cut lines, wholesale interpolations of songs and dances. The menacing powers of the witches are trivialized, and to reduce the impact of their show of kings, they propose to "cheer . . . up" Macbeth:

> Come, sisters, cheer we up his sprites,
> And show the best of our delights.
> I'll charm the air to give a sound,
> While you perform your antic round;
> That this great King may kindly say,
> Our duties did his welcome pay.
> (4.1.127–32)

Who is "this great King" to whom compliment is paid, if not the monarch in the audience? The text alludes to the presence of King James in this compliment as well as in the formal accommodations that make the text of *Macbeth* masquelike. But even these trivial lines of jaunty welcome to the king enact a curious play of resemblance. For example, Kenneth Muir, the editor of the Arden edition of *Macbeth,* takes "this great King" to refer to Macbeth. One king slides into the other, a type of diffusion that can be remarked elsewhere in the latter half of *Macbeth,* in the withdrawal of Lady Macbeth and her replacement with Lady Macduff or in the English scenes with their echoes of Scottish horror. As the play proceeds, we see less of Macbeth and hear more of him. The presence of King James in the text of *Macbeth,* however much it disturbs the original and irrecoverable designs of the play, also seems to be written within them. Might we say that the earlier relationship between Macbeth and Duncan is reenacted between Macbeth and King James? That there is room in the text for only one king? That these two monarchs are haunted by spectral identification? A mirror, literally, provides an answer to these speculations. In the show of kings, Macbeth looks into the mirror in which James I is reflected:

> [T]he eighth appears, who bears a glass,
> Which shows me many more; and some I see,
> That two-fold balls and treble sceptres carry.
> Horrible sight!
>
> (4.1.119–22)

Disturbing the notion of clear-cut difference in this confrontation is, once again, the problem of source, for the show of kings is provided by the "filthy hags" (4.1.115), and however much their subsequent jauntiness seems to diffuse the spectacle, it retains its disturbing power. Steven Mullaney has written wonderfully about this moment, about the alliance of the demonic to a linguistic excess. As he says, in that mirroring moment,

> genealogy and prophecy are made manifest in the visible display, but there is another genealogy in the air as well, one heard rather than seen. Juxtaposed to the projection of James's line, the witches' riddles complicate its complimentary gesture with what amounts to a genealogy of treason and equivocation.[32]

Where earlier Duncan spoke witches' words, here the king is transported on stage in the witches' show, caught within speculation. Where earlier Duncan bestowed gifts and titles to "name" a "hereafter" already named, here James is asked to "kindly say" that the witches' "duties did his welcome pay." The king lives to bestow, as James indicated when he titled his treatise on kingship the *Basilikon Doron,* the royal gift.[33] His gifts were his presence and the heir he produced; presentation that is re-presentation. There is an economy of speculation.

Is the show of kings subversive? Do its spectral identifications implicate Shakespeare in a revolutionary politics? Could such a politics evade the reflections of a mirror that catches the king onstage and off? Is there an autonomous realm available for representation that would not be caught within representation? That realm of autonomy, Franco Moretti suggests, is coincident with sovereignty imagined as "a power . . . having its origin *in itself.*"[34] When James represented that power, as in the sonnet prefatory to the *Basilikon Doron,* he declared himself a god by announcing that "God gives not Kings the stile of *Gods* in vaine"; the king who gives all has been given his power as a *style* and as an echoing name. The king stands *in the place* of the "heavenly King," his "Lieutenant."

Duncan dresses Macbeth in borrowed robes as well, making a voodoo version of himself. "Remember," James counseled his son and heir, "the throne is Gods and not yours, that ye sit in."[35] Presenting himself, claiming all his kingdom as his own—the kingdom was his body and his wife, he declared on more than one occasion—James also saw himself as representation, a king on stage, whose behavior offered a living "image" of himself. Royal existence is representation. "Let your owne life be a law-booke and a mirrour to your people" (30), James urged his son in the book in which he similarly presented himself, counseling him to present himself as the "vive image" of his "vertuous disposition" (51). Offering himself to parliamentary inspection, the king was fond of declaring that his breast was a crystal mirror, both a reflecting surface and a transparent one. What could one's "owne life" be in such formulations of identity—even absolute identity—as reflection? Would not this hall of mirrors include the notion of "a power . . . having its origin *in itself,*" whether we were to attach that idea of autonomy to the king or to the sovereign author of *Macbeth*? Could there be an end to these speculations, or a source?

Ben Jonson's masques for King James frequently depend upon such absolutist assertions, and they are our best guide to the conditions of absolutist representation in the Jacobean period. When Jonson wrote a masque celebrating James's birthday in 1620, *Pan's Anniversary,* the king was cast as Pan, for Pan means "all": "Pan is our all, by him we breathe, we live, / We move, we are."[36] Yet included in the spectacle that Jonson offered the king were disturbing reflections of himself and his courtiers, particularly in the figure of a court ape outrageously parodying the court. Jonson showed James how to view the attack by reprimanding the parodist in the masque. "Your folly may well deserve pardon because it hath delighted," he is told; "but beware of presuming, or how you offer comparisons with persons so near deities. Behold where they are that have now forgiven you, whom should you provoke again with the like, they will justly punish that with anger which they now dismiss with contempt" (131–36). The court and its parodist face each other in this moment to regard one another within the spectacle of "comparisons" and resemblances; the derisory spectacle is to be seen with derision. James must forgive all if all reflects him and if he is the ultimate source of all representation. In Jonson's masques, the representation of the king's claims to totality offers the possibility of endless replications within the system of reflecting power in which the king was placed.[37]

This can be demonstrated, too, in *The Vision of Delight* (1617), a masque, as its title suggests, about vision. For in it, the spectacle of the king's Arcadia on stage, the image of the realm perfected, is presented by the antimasque figure of Fant'sy. Fant'sy's realm is, in the antimasque, the suspect terrain of wayward dreams:

> Dreams of the maker and dreams of the teller,
> Dreams of the kitchen and dreams of the cellar;
> Some that are tall, and some that are dwarfs,
> Some that are haltered, and some that wear scarfs;
> Some that are proper and signify o' thing,
> And some another, and some that are nothing.
> (55–60)

What sort of dream does Fant'sy present when the antimasquer presents the king? He offers this climatic vision of his realm in the masque proper:

> Behold a king
> Whose presence maketh this perpetual spring,
> The glories of which spring grow in that bower,
> And are the marks and beauties of his power.
> (189–92)

Is this vision of majesty a tall dream, too? Are not the confusions of Fant'sy's antimasque speech also to be found in the mirror image of the king and his imagined Arcadian state? What kind of spectacle does he present? One that signifies one thing, or many, or even nothing? The impropriety of making Fant'sy the purveyor of the royal image dallies with double meanings and with the subversions that lurk in the mirror of resemblance.

Pan's Anniversary and *The Vision of Delight* can be offered as examples of the proximity of royal compliment and its subversion, which Jonson managed before his monarch's eyes. We can come closer to the source of *Macbeth* if we look at the Jonsonian masque that stands somewhere behind the masquelike movement that the play ultimately takes. *The Masque of Queens* is particularly apt for consideration here because, as in *Macbeth,* central to its concerns is a contention between royal and demonic powers and, specifically, the question of the source of power.

Jonson's *Masque of Queens* is palpably dualistic in design. It opens with "a foil or false masque" (12) in which eleven witches invoke their Dame. She arrives, and the witches join together as "faithful opposites" (120) to "disturb" the entertainment and, more frighteningly, to oppose the accomplishments of an "Age of Gold" (129) and return all things to chaos. The Dame proposes their plans in these words:

> Let us disturb it then, and blast the light;
> Mix hell with heaven, and make Nature fight
> Within herself; loose the whole hinge of things,
> And cause the ends run back into their springs.
> (134–37)

Gathering together the elements necessary for their powers, the Dame attempts to raise a spirit to accomplish their task. She fails, and in the midst of their frenzied dances, loud music and a sudden change of scene usher in Perseus, the figure of Heroic Virtue, announcing the arrival of Fame; she, in turn, brings on a consort of twelve heroic queens, who end the masque in dancing. Virtue has triumphed over vice; as Jonson notes at the climactic change of scene, the hags vanish "scarce suffering the memory of such a thing" (337).

"Scarce suffering": barely permitting, but yet, not entirely effacing. For, as is apparent even in a brief summary of the action of the masque, the forces of good and evil bear a striking resemblance—twelve hags, twelve queens—and the structure of the two halves of the masque is also broadly parallel: invocations, arrivals, dances. Dualism would seem to be a mirror effect. In *The Masque of Queens,* moreover, language passes through the mirror, overriding differences. Although ostensibly the two parts of the masque are related only by opposition, and although the second half of the masque removes all traces of the first, the language of the masque is seamless. Its central trope, in fact, involves sources and origins, suggesting an overriding power. Jonson announces that the argument of the masque is "true fame bred out of virtue" (6); yet breeding, arrival, and origination are everywhere apparent in the masque, throwing the relationship between the two parts into question. Does the second come from the first? Has the Dame's unsuccessful attempt to raise a spirit issued in the arrival of Heroic Virtue? Is there a beginning principle?

Here, in any event, is the seamless thread: The witches arrive, claiming they "come . . . from" a landscape replete with death (45–54), and as they try repeated charms, naming all their instruments (owls, baying dogs, toads, voodoo images, and the like), they raise their Dame. More invocations follow, filled with snatching, gathering, plucking, choosing, biting, sucking, getting, and making: a depletion and a dismemberment of nature to reconstitute it in the specter they would raise. The earth is made a grave, they bury (230) what they have gathered and seek to make it rise again, reconstituted. Here, the language of birth that underlies all these activities is made explicit:

> Dame earth shall quake,
> And the houses shake,
> And her belly shall ache
> As her back were brake
> Such a birth to make
>
> (240–44)

At first they are unsuccessful—"our labor dies! / Our magic feature will not rise" (269–70)—and they attempt again their "magic birth" (298). Instead, the House of Fame rises "in the place of" (338) the witches' hell, as the stage direction indicates. Perseus declares himself the "parent" (356) of Fame; Fame arrives acknowledging her "father" (431) and announcing that she will "draw . . . forth" (439) the twelve queens, who sing in celebration of "Fame that's out of Virtue born" (487) and "this famous birth" (500).

These continuities would seem to confirm the Dame's design, mixing hell with heaven, loosing the "whole hinge of things," and making endings fetch their origins in chaotic beginnings—the scarce-remembered, almost vanished traces of a design that the masque replicates even as it replaces it. Why should this specter of resemblance be in the masque? The answer, we may assume, has to do with absolutist power. Power in the masque is figured as origin-giving. Perseus is both parent and strength (356); like the witches, he makes life from death: "When Virtue cut off Terror, he gat [i.e., begat] Fame. / . . . when Fame was gotten Terror died" (351–52). He, as much as the witches, needs to dismember to make. Powers of making depend upon depletion. And this, too, is how the masque itself is constructed, "scarce suffering" the memory of the displaced hags but not entirely effacing them. Jonson's making is thus also in question. Although Perseus points to the columns of the House of Fame as "men-making poets" (362), the poet of the masque is at pains to disavow his powers, telling his reader (Prince Henry) that the masque's invention comes from the queen (9–10), that the decorum of the masque derives from Horace (7–8), that the queens and witches are drawn from the storehouse of classical and contemporary books that he has perused, and that even the spectators give life to his designs: "[A] writer should always trust somewhat to the capacity of the spectator, especially at these spectacles" (95–96).

The privileged spectator here is the king, of course, and the spectacle is designed to mirror and bring forth his mind. Hence, when Perseus presents the twelve queens, he ends with the king, and although Bel-Anna (Queen Anne's role in the masque) is the highest of queens, she must submit "all her worth / To him that gave it," the one who has "brought forth / Their names to memory" (402–4). The pronoun may refer to the poet; a few lines later, it means the king, source of all "increase" (410), conferring the bounty on all which is "contracted" (412) within himself. The king, Perseus says, will "embrace" the "spectacle" (414–15). From a "spectacle of strangeness, producing multiplicity of gesture" (17–18), as Jonson describes the antimasque of witches, arises "the strangeness and beauty of the spectacle" (466), the genuine masque of queens. What the text produces is referred to the king's eye.

What lives in the king's eye here, as in *Macbeth,* is genealogy, what he produces; here, as in *Macbeth,* the king lives to bestow, to give gifts that are contracted within him and that are extended without. Royal absolutism is coincident with full ownership and extension over all so that nothing and no one has autonomy except the king; yet this means that, like Duncan, his absolutism also signifies opacity. The king who gives all is appropriated by what he appropriates. Building and constructing all in his all-embracing view, his power is his blindness. His power lies in a mirror whose reflections cannot be controlled; they are speculative investments that may deplete the all-giver. Duncan and Macbeth meet for the first time in the play, and Duncan voices the depletion involved in giving, the horrific sense that their exchanges are spectral identifications, transfers like the voodoo magic between the king and his replica:

O worthiest cousin!
The sin of my ingratitude even now

Was heavy on me. Thou art so far before,
That swiftest wing of recompense is slow
To overtake thee: would thou hadst less deserv'd,
That the proportion both of thanks and payment
Might have been mine! Only I have left to say,
More is thy due than more than all can pay.
(1.4.14–21)

The more he gives, the less he has; his wish: "would thou hadst less deserv'd." A few lines later, Duncan attempts to name the "hereafter" despite Macbeth's success, "so far before."

On 27 August 1605, in the course of a visit James and his family made to Oxford, they were welcomed to St. John's College by a learned show, a Latin entertainment hailing the fulfillment of fate's prophesied genealogy (the line of Banquo) embodied in the king and queen and their heirs. The lines were spoken by three woodland creatures, "quasi Sibyllae," they are called, boys masquerading as numinous female powers, all-hailing their monarch:

Fame says the fatal Sisters once foretold
Power without end, great Monarch, to thy stock . . .
And thus we greet thee: Hail, whom Scotland serves!
Whom England, Hail! Whom Ireland serves, all hail![38]

So, too, the witches greet Macbeth, so Duncan gives addition to the new thane of Cawdor. Banquo wonders if the witches can speak true, but the echoes go back further. The witches' all-hailing inaugurates Macbeth's career by appropriating a moment of royal compliment. From the start, the mirror of representation respects no boundaries; the show of kings staged for the mutual benefit of Macbeth and King James occurs *within* these representations. There is no source, not even a sovereign author, outside of representation; there is no end or beginning to these speculations.

Within *Macbeth,* the menacing heterogeneity of uncontrolled duplication that threatens the autonomy of power is embodied in the witches. In the anxiety about women in the play we might find a further reflection of the disturbing questions raised about the sources of the Shakespearean imagination.[39] Jonson's *Masque of Queens* is instructive in that regard as well, for in order to represent sovereign power, woman's control over nature and birth are ascribed to the king. Perseus declares his power—to give birth—and refers it to the king's bounty. Yet what is presented to the monarch's eyes is a pageant of armed women to replace the army of hags, a haunting version of the king's declaration of patriarchal appropriations. Questions about a power that "lies like truth" (*Macbeth,* 5.5.44) menace men's words and their assertions of authority. Kings and authors, then, are menaced.

In *Macbeth,* the heterogeneity of the female as Other is implicated in scenes of writing and reading that may reflect on the Shakespearean signature and its sources. "The King hath happily receiv'd, Macbeth, / The news of thy success" (1.3.89–90), Rosse reports, describing Duncan as reading:

> and when he reads
> Thy personal venture in the rebels' fight,
> His wonders and his praises do contend,
> Which should be thine, or his.
>
> (1.3.90–93)

Contention over ownership of the text, however, is, as Rosse goes on to say, "silenc'd," rendered undecidable; the text that Duncan attempts to master instead masters him, news of success that cannot be controlled:

> silenc'd with that,
> In viewing o'er the rest o' th' selfsame day,
> He finds thee in the stout Norweyan ranks,
> Nothing afeard of what thyself didst make,
> Strange images of death.
>
> (1.3.93–97)

Within the "selfsame" ("th' selfsame day") a specter of swallowed difference rises;[40] Duncan discovers Macbeth "in the rebels' fight," "in the stout Norweyan ranks," and he finds himself implicated in Macbeth's acts. They meet in "strange images of death" which neither the monarch nor his general fears. And so Rosse's report of the king and Macbeth locked in contention for the interpretation of a text ends with Duncan's submission to what "came post with post" (1.3.98), the news of Macbeth's success and the specter of succession passing from king to rebel: the king impressed with the letter. Two scenes later, the scene of reading is repeated, literally. Macbeth sends his wife a letter, which he has "thought good to deliver thee," as if he were giving birth to the word as his child. "Lay it to thy heart," he orders (1.5.10–14). Lady Macbeth looks in her heart and finds Macbeth "too full o' th' milk of human kindness" (1.5.17); whose milk does she find in the word, hers or his? King James declared that his gifts to the nation were their very "nourish-milke" and that he was the kingdom's "loving nourish-father";[41] the patriarch as male mother, greedily sucked dry. Reports of Macbeth's success, Rosse says, were "pour'd . . . down before" (1.3.100) the king, delivering what they "bear":

> As thick as hail,
> Came post with post; and every one did bear
> Thy praises in his kingdom's great defence,
> And pour'd them down before him.
>
> (1.3.97–100)

And in his letter to his wife, Macbeth relates and conflates the earlier scene, "came missives from the King, who all-hail'd me, 'Thane of Cawdor'; by which title, before, these Weird Sisters saluted me" (1.5.6–8). The letter circulates, and male attempts to appropriate power encounter a heterogeneity in their attempted representations; an alliance between women and their words. Macbeth's letter suppresses the success the witches have promised to Banquo, just as the play organizes itself around the conflict between Macbeth and Macduff and around the succession from Duncan to Malcolm. Its mirroring structure represents an absolutist fantasy surpassed by the witches' show.[42]

The hypermasculine world of *Macbeth* is haunted—as is *The Masque of Queens*—by the power represented in the witches; masculinity in the play is directed as an assaultive attempt to secure power, to maintain success and succession, at the expense of women. As is typical of many of Shakespeare's tragedies, the play is largely womanless, and family relationships are disturbed; Duncan and Banquo both have heirs, but no wives; Macbeth and Lady Macbeth have no surviving children. Macbeth's one fully gratuitous act is the murder of Lady Macduff and her children, an act in which Macduff is fully complicit; he has abandoned his wife, and she accuses him of betrayal. He allies himself with Malcolm in a scene in which the future monarch displays his credentials first by presenting himself as excessively libidinous—and Macduff willingly responds as a virtual procurer to satisfy his lust—and then as excessively chaste; either way, masculinity and power are directed against women. When Macbeth is finally defeated, he is replaced by two men who have secured power in the defeat of women. Indeed, not only has Macduff abandoned his wife and family, but his very birth represents a triumph over his mother's womb, the manifest fantasy of being self-begotten that also deludes Macbeth in his final encounter. To mark the new powers in Scotland, the battle concludes with Siward's celebration of the ritual slaughter of his son. It is not Macbeth alone who opposes generativity or wishes to eradicate its source. Good and bad Scots alike are bent on securing power, and that means to seize fully the terrain of women. For Scotland is a bleeding mother in the play, and the Scots' aim is to "bestride our downfall birthdom" (4.3.4). "It cannot / Be call'd our mother, but our grave" (4.3.165–66), Rosse goes on to say. Birth and death are, in these paradigmatic utterances, man's downfall, the limits of beginning and end; they survive his successes, unlimited limits. The seizure and defeat of women is a bid for immortality, for a power that will never fade.

The shape of that fantasy is revealed in the mirror scene: A line of kings is propagated in the mirror. Males produce males, just as Banquo and Duncan seem capable of succession without the interference of women. "Look in thy glass, and tell the face thou viewest / Now is the time that face should form another"; so the third sonnet opens on the prospect of a duplication of images that might be called—if we follow Luce Irigaray—a determining patriarchal fantasy, the glassy facade of "the sovereign authority of pretense."[43] Macbeth looks in the mirror and sees his reflection in the line that extends to James; not in the mirror is Mary Queen of Scots, who haunts the patriarchal claims of the *Basilikon Doron,* who is the mother on whom James rested his claims to the throne of England, and whom he sacrificed to assure his sovereignty.

Men may look in the mirror, may have their being in the mirror; but in *Macbeth,* the specter of duplicates is in other hands. The spectacle of state here, or in *The Masque of Queens,* is the witches' show. All masculine attempts at female deprivation—including Lady Macbeth's desire to unsex herself—are robbed of ultimate success. Mortality cannot be killed. What escapes control is figured in the witches; emblematically bearded, linguistically ambiguous, they represent, in Harry Berger's brilliant phrase, the textual "display of withheld surplus meaning."[44] Their words stretch out "to th' crack of doom" (4.1.117), an ultimate fissure in which both Macbeth and Malcolm have their place hereafter.

Confronting source—and end—the play registers an excess, unsettling in its indifferent and repetitious production, one king after another, a Malcolm for a Macbeth, raised on the body of woman, embodied in the text. The partnership of indifference begins (and ends) in rivalry over the letter, Duncan's reading of Macbeth, Lady Macbeth's reading of Macbeth's letter, or Banquo's confrontation with the witches:

> You seem to understand me,
> By each at once her choppy finger laying
> Upon her skinny lips: you should be women,
> And yet your beards forbid me to interpret
> That you are so.
>
> (1.3.43–47)

Their beards and fingers on their lips forbid interpretation and point beyond an order of words and utterance to an excess at the source. Generators of the text, they suggest that the male fantasy of *Macbeth* may have as its counterpart the fantasy of the autonomy of the artistic imagination—Prospero's fantasy in *The Tempest,* for instance, when he displays his power in a masque whose deities are all female—and they caution the critic who would describe the play as the free workings of a mind playing with its sources.[45] At the furthest reach of speculation, they intimate that the mirrors in *Macbeth* represent a meeting of authority and author swallowed in its source. That textual situation might be named Volumnia.

The Anus in *Coriolanus*

This essay was originally written for a plenary session at a meeting of the Shakespeare Association in 1994. Indeed, in 1996 its delivery there was noted in an essay by Cynthia Marshall, who takes me to task for my mode of delivery, for some of the language used in this essay, and for my distribution on that occasion of an image that, she reports, "clearly shocked some members of the audience."[1] *While I have not included the supposedly offensive image here (and Marshall might be shocked to discover that a woman drew it), the text of this essay remains close to the original version as delivered.*[2] *Uncensored, this essay probably cannot receive the G rating that Marshall seems to think appropriate for texts or images aimed at adults (in this, she resembles other regulators who are worried about the Internet and TV and who are incapable of distinguishing violence from sexuality); nonetheless, it may yet register as a necessary intervention in Shakespeare studies.*

In a paragraph on the names in *Coriolanus* in the section of comments following his essay "*Coriolanus*—and the Delights of Faction," Kenneth Burke notes that "though the names are taken over literally from Plutarch, it is remarkable how tonally suggestive some of them are."[3] If

Volumnia's name speaks volumes, the "tonal suggestion" of the name of the hero is equally remarkable. "In the light of Freudian theories concerning the fecal nature of invective," Burke writes, "the last two syllables of the hero's name are so 'right,' people now often seek to dodge the issue by altering the traditional pronunciation (making the *a* broad instead of long)."[4]

Burke on the whole is suspicious of psychoanalytic readings of the play, yet that is the route that seems to him to indicate the "rightness" of the anus in Coriolanus, and it is therefore of some interest that avowedly psychoanalytic readings of *Coriolanus* by Janet Adelman and her followers (among whom I would include the author of *James I and the Politics of Literature*) stay within the domains of orality in the play, richly symptomatic as they are, and on a number of registers.[5] Only Stanley Cavell, in the postscript to his essay "*Coriolanus* and Interpretations of Politics" in his volume of essays on Shakespeare, *Disowning Knowledge,* picks up where Burke left off.[6] It is perhaps worth remarking that just as Burke's note on the anus occurs as part of a set of comments appended to the body of his essay, Cavell's afterthoughts come in a similarly well-positioned postscript. Pursuing a route from the oral to the anal, Cavell takes Coriolanus's "horror of putting in his mouth what (. . . in his fantasy) comes out of the mouths of others" as an indication that what is involved in Coriolanus's disgust at the "rank-scented meinie" (3.1.65, to recall one of the phrases of his delicious invective) is "imagining that in incorporating one another we are asked to incorporate one another's leavings, the results or wastes of what has already been incorporated."[7]

Cavell finds support for his analysis in the fable of the belly offered by Menenius Agrippa in the opening scene of the play as he attempts to placate the revolting plebians who are clamoring for food. This is an apt site, it seems to me, since Cavell's speculations take up precisely what Menenius's tale omits; his alimentary allegory leaves out any mention of elimination, presenting the belly as a site of distribution, as if without a remainder. Yet the language used to describe the belly is undeniably anal: It is the "sink o' th' body" (1.1.121) according to the First Citizen, a "gulf" in the accusations against the belly voiced in the allegory (1.1.97); even in Menenius's defense, the belly is left, after distributing flour to all the parts of the body, with nothing but "bran" (1.1.145), uneatable refuse. In the allegory, then, the belly assumes the position of the anus, receiving what is normally expelled; a closed economy is imagined in which waste is consumed.

Ingestion and evacuation, inside and outside, change places. That equivocation, however, shapes the delivery of the fable. It is to be noted, for instance, that what Menenius offers his listeners is "a pretty tale" (1.1.89), and the telling of it he describes as a "venture / To stale't a little more" (1.1.90–91). The economy of speech, even, as here, in an attempt at pacification, takes the form of an offer of words as if they came from the anus, a stale tale. Indeed, Menenius interrupts his tale with a belly laugh, "a kind of smile, / Which ne'er came from the lungs, but even thus—" (1.1.106–7), a bodily gesture that may as easily be a fart as a belch. This speech, however gentle or good-humored it appears to be, is directed against the plebians as much as are the invectives that Coriolanus hurls. To put it crudely, Coriolanus hurls shit at the plebians because he experiences their words as shit hurled at him; Menenius's stale tale is a euphemized and seductive version of this. To Coriolanus, the strength of the plebians lies in their breath, and he imagines war as one way "to vent / Our musty superfluity" (1.1.224–25). "Vent" (or Menenius's stale venture) and "superfluity" are terms that recur in the play and that seem to point to a disposable excess, to the waste products to which Cavell refers. Burke's and Cavell's argument, therefore, seems apt: One site of the anal economies of the play is speech. I would add, however, as some indication of the extent of this economy, that the social processes of the play are insistently about evacuation (banishment) and entrance, often across forbidden thresholds, and suggest that the equivocations of inside and outside in Menenius's fable have their counterparts in the mirroring locations of Coriolanus. Accused of being the enemy of the people, he joins the enemy after his banishment.

These ins and outs are not all that explicitly anal, and perhaps one ought not put these matters more crudely than the play seems to. That, at any rate, is the position that Cavell takes. It follows from his desire to hold on to his thesis (indebted to Adelman) that the primary circulation in the play is oral; for him, this is not only a psychological datum but the basis for political communion. "The very suggestion of the element this postscript invokes," he writes, "is apt to stifle what the body of my essay takes—correctly I persist in thinking—as fundamental in the play, namely the circulation from mouth to mouth of language" (170). Curious figures insist upon themselves in this formulation: the worry about stifling, the question of what is fundamental in the play. The fear is that the fundament might indeed be fundamental.[8] (Cavell's language recalls the birth of Gargantua, forced to emerge from Gargamelle's ear after her vaginal canal is blocked when her fundament collapses, emitting turds that some take at first to be her baby.)[9] Cavell goes on to suggest—as perhaps this allusion to Rabelais does, too—that it is difficult to think about these matters without joking, and his tone, in considering "the element" his postscript invokes, is much like Menenius's in his civilized fable of the belly. Trying to maintain the proper tone, Cavell writes, with delicate philosophical distance, that such matters appear "in the part of the world I know, mostly in slang, or jokes, . . . and in expressions rejecting the words of others by asking what they are trying to hand you, or by naming the product as the droppings of horses or bulls" (170). It would almost seem for Cavell that the only place the anus exists is *in language* and that it can only be spoken through these circumlocutions, displacements perhaps akin to those in *Coriolanus.* Cavell worries the question of how to "allude to the fecal issue" (a pregnant phrase to which I will return) "in unprotected prose" (175). He worries, to put it bluntly, about covering his ass, and he confesses to shame, embarrassment, and the need to find a way of preserving the decorum of civility in the play's "assessments":

> It was coming to see more unprotectedly that Shakespeare's *Coriolanus* is itself exactly in struggle with this question of explicitness and naming . . . that I was shamed into making my embarrassment (of style, say) more explicit in this note. The implication is that to avoid risking one's critical balance in traversing this play is to avoid a measure of participation in the play's assessments of the balance civilization exacts. (175)

Embarrassed assessments: Is the anus perhaps more inescapable than Cavell imagines, more than just the locus of shame and shit? Once one has granted the possibility that oral and anal exist in a substitutive relationship in the play, can one still hold on to an uncontaminated sphere of orality or attempt to write in a language that would avoid—or even void—the anus? Cavell attempts to do so as a way to secure the play as a civilized document and as a site for a liberal politics of speech. But, I argue, this involves a misreading, not only of the body economies of the play, however phantasmatic they may be, but also of a body politic more absolutist and exclusionary than Cavell seems willing to imagine. And beyond that, it involves anal economies that go beyond the regions that Cavell would keep in place.

Recall, for instance, that Menenius, however much his first speech offers itself as a tactful, persuasive utterance, later in the play, in dialogue with the tribunes, reports himself as "one that converses more with the buttock of the night than with the forehead of the morning" (2.1.50–52). This important association of nocturnal pleasure with the buttocks is immediately followed by lines in which Menenius "spend[s] [his] malice in [his] breath" (2.1.53) attacking the tribunes as those who have an altogether different relationship, he claims, to their posteriors: "When you are hearing a matter between party and party, if you chance to be pinched with the colic, you make faces like mummers, set up the bloody flag against all patience, and, in roaring for a chamber-pot, dismiss the controversy bleeding, the more entangled by your hearing" (2.1.72–77). While this exchange secures the association of shit and invective, it also opens around the anus the dynamics of pleasure and pain that many readers will recognize as crucial throughout the play. Further substitutions seem at hand: for instance, a route from the bleeding bowels of the tribunes to the orifices of Coriolanus's body, the wounds that he is obliged to and refuses to display when he stands for the office of consul. To pursue this point would necessarily extend the standard psychoanalytic equation of words, mouths, and wounds. And in terms of a more immediate reading of the play, it suggests that we reconsider what it means when a character who "converses . . . with the buttock of the night" can, a bit later in the same scene (2.1.142ff.), tally up and locate every hole in Coriolanus's body, a body whose wounds, after all, Coriolanus refuses to display in public.

These speculations suggest that it is time, as Gail Kern Paster has urged, to stop protecting Shakespeare from "anal contamination,"[10] time to open the question of anal erotics. Paster goes some way in this direction in the third chapter of *The Body Embarrassed.* Noting the early modern attachment to enemas and the conceptualization of sexual release as a purgation congruent with bloodletting and other procedures meant to ensure humoral balance, Paster forthrightly locates a homology between sexual pleasure and anal pleasure, in a word, the sexual pleasure of the relaxation of the sphincter as shit passes through it. Indeed, for some Renaissance authors that Paster cites, including Sir John Harington, author of the resonantly punningly titled *Metamorphosis of Ajax,* the pleasures of the privy exceed those of coitus, especially when the latter is attached to the body of a female whore: "Harington's praise of the privy suggests . . . that in metonymic exchange between whore and privy, the privy gains in innocence as well as desirability at the expense of the corrupted female body," Paster comments (155). Furthermore, by locating early modern toilet training in the maternal domain, Paster points to the privileged site in which oral commands and anal performance are intimately linked, making oral/anal substitutions all the more likely, as might be assumed as part of the pedagogic relationship between Coriolanus and his mother; the spitting of blood from Hector's wound that Volumnia imagines in a substitutive relationship with the milk from Hecuba's breast (1.3.40–43), and by analogy her own, in this light can as easily figure in an exchange in which the refuse from the mouth takes the place of anal evacuation, where the bloody breast anticipates the ulcerated bowels of the tribunes. "The blood I drop is rather physical / Than dangerous to me" (1.5.18–19), Coriolanus claims. And we might add here that the scene at the breast also involves another substitution: The hurling mechanism of blood is both phallicly and anally assaultive.

This substitution gives some reason to extend the understanding of anal eroticism that Paster offers; she sees "the privy as a displacement for the female body" (160), defecation as a substitute for vaginal intercourse. Terms like "sink" and "gulf" easily make these connections, and my point is not to dispute the analogy but to suggest that the model of substitution and displacement deployed by Paster (on good psychoanalytic warrant) inevitably assumes a proper and singular form to sexuality and closes off other possibilities too quickly. Paster as much as admits this when she describes anal eroticism of the Elizabethan sort as a site of "greater psychic intensity than we consider normal today" (114). "Today," she comments, "we associate any sexual use of the laxative purge with the practice of anal intercourse among male homosexuals"; Elizabethan practices, she implies, were "abnormally" more widespread (135). Yet following Paster's reading, it would seem that purgatives and anal intercourse were only male practices then and now and that they constituted a form of heterosexual intercourse manqué. The very logic of displacement suggests otherwise. And although Paster is far more forthright than Cavell, there is a certain amount of modern, civilized, knowing occlusion going on in her chapter "Covering His Ass." Why not covering *her* ass?[11] Paster misses the opportunity to pursue those questions when she analyzes Titania's love for her ass.[12] Nor does she engage the question asked by Jeffrey Masten: "[W]hat would 'anality' mean—would it exist—as a psychoanalytic structure" in these historico-cultural contexts?[13]

Why should the pleasures of the anus only be thought of in terms of its evacuative function? Answers are not far to seek. Anal eroticism, as described by Freud, involves infantile fantasies of anal birth ("fecal issue," to recall Cavell's nice phrase), in which the delivery of the stool stands for the delivery of the baby and in which the anus seems, therefore, to function in the way Paster takes it to, as a substitute vagina.[14] In *Homosexual Desire,* a groundbreaking study that first appeared more than twenty-five years ago, Guy Hocquenghem titled a chapter "Capitalism, the Family, and the Anus," describing the ways in which the Oedipal organization of modern society depends upon the sublimation of the anus; anal control secures the most private site of the body, the place where one learns what is one's own, what must be kept clean, what must be kept out of circulation.[15] Part of the way this is done is through the Freudian phantasmatics of the anus as substitute vagina; another way is through associating the anus entirely with its excremental functions, so that lack of control, as in violent speech, comes to be seen as an unruly insistence by that which should be kept hidden and private. The privatization and sublimation of the anus suggests to Hocquenghem why homosexuality threatens society, because whether or not homosexuals perform anal sex, homosexuality affirms the anus as a site of desire. It thereby threatens the proprieties of modern economies of all kinds: individual and social boundaries and principles of regulation. If we inflect Hocquenghem's arguments in the direction of the Elizabethan period as Paster describes it, where anality is not a delimited phenomenon, this suggests that the modern economies—psychic and capitalist—that Hocquenghem describes are not yet in place in Shakespeare's world. The anus may not need *or have* the civilized covering that Cavell assumes.

To further this point, it is apt, now, at last, to cite the lines from the play that have motivated this inquiry from the start, Aufidius welcoming Coriolanus to the enemy camp:

> . . . that I see thee here,
> Thou noble thing, more dances my rapt heart
> Than when I first my wedded mistress saw
> Bestride my threshold. . . .
> . . . .

Thou hast beat me out
Twelve several times, and I have nightly since
Dreamt of encounters 'twixt thyself and me—
We have been down together in my sleep,
Unbuckling helms, fisting each other's throat—
And wak'd half dead with nothing.
(4.5.116–19, 122–27)

It is clearly no overstatement to regard these lines as sexual or to see a relationship between the wedded mistress (whom, Aufidius assures Coriolanus, he loved: "Know thou first, / I lov'd the maid I married" [4.5.114–15]) and the nocturnal enemy now crossing the threshold like a bride, or between the fisted throat and the vagina. But, to follow the argument I have been presenting, this scene of fisting also must be read as a displacement of anal sex to the mouth.

If Aufidius's dream participates in the substitutive equation of mouth and vagina, one needs to note that the ordinary word used for the vagina in the play is "womb," a word that also means "belly" and "bowels." When, at the end of the play, Coriolanus stages an attack on his native place—that is, the site from which he first emerged, his mother's womb (5.3.123) as much as the city of Rome—that act realizes what he says outside the gates of Antium, the enemy city: "My birthplace hate I, and my love's upon / This enemy town" (4.4.23–24). It has often been noted that Coriolanus has two names, one his family name, the other the name of the Volscian town of Corioles that he single-handedly defeats, and it is perfectly easy to read his assault on Corioles, his bloody emergence alone from its walls, as a rape and birth fantasy. But if Coriolanus has these two relations, one origin in the maternal, natal womb, and the other in the enemy's place, that fantasy of second birth involves an unnatural site of origination: the enemy's gates, which open to release him, bleeding. The play here traffics in a fantasy of origination in an alternative to the "natural" site, a fantasy of anal birth. And more than that: The site of Coriolanus's love, after all, is the enemy town, and the enemy whose threshold he crosses like a longed-for bride, or fuck buddy.

This makes further sense of the standard psychoanalytic perception that Aufidius and Volumnia are versions of each other, lovers and enemies; the erotic intensity of Coriolanus for Aufidius, the man explictly named as the object of his "soul's hate" (1.5.10), is obviously equivalent to the fully ambivalent feelings he has toward his mother. At the end of the play, after all, she kills him as much as Aufidius does, and her final taunt convincing him not to invade Rome—that he is a foreign "fellow" born of a Volscian (5.3.178)—has its counterpart in the maternal sadism of Aufidius calling Coriolanus "boy" (5.6.100). Adelman sees in Aufidius an alter ego, a brother, and a father figure; but in fact, Coriolanus has plenty of substitute fathers: Menenius, who appropriates the language of paternity, and his general Cominius, under whom he serves. Both of these relations are also eroticized: Coriolanus, for instance, embraces Cominius on the battlefield

> [i]n arms as sound as when I woo'd; in heart
> As merry as when our nuptial day was done,
> And tapers burn'd to bedward!
>
> (1.6.30–32)

And Menenius explicitly names himself Coriolanus's "lover" (5.2.14)—a term that, however much the Arden editor, for instance, would like to translate it as "friend," will not be capable of de-eroticization once we recall Coriolanus's own description of

> [f]riends . . . ,
> Whose double bosoms seem to wear one heart,
> Whose hours, whose bed, whose meal and exercise
> Are still together, who twin, as 'twere, in love
> Unseparable.
>
> (4.4.12–16)[16]

As for his relationship with Aufidius, however much it might be thought of as being within the family—insofar, that is, as Aufidius is the Volscian "mother" of Coriolanus, say—it is also important to recognize the intense eroticism of their relationship, which the terms "alter ego" or "brother" diffuse but which is evident not only in the dream that Aufidius reports but also in the comments of the servants who witness their embrace: "Our general himself makes a mistress of him" (4.5.199–200), the third serving man comments in lines that are perfectly ambivalent about whether it is Coriolanus or Aufidius who is in the so-called female position, as ambivalent about position as is the case in the imagined scene of mutual fisting. In short, the parallelism between Volumnia and Aufidius, the casting of male-male relations within the terms of gender-differentiated ones (husband and wife, man and mistress) as the sites of Coriolanus's hate and love, of a simultaneous embrace and rejection, establishes these loves/hates in the endlessly substitutive locus of womb/bowel.[17]

Moreover, as doubly born, Coriolanus himself is doubly gendered, as Cominius reports when he narrates the life of Coriolanus (2.2.82–122), which passes through an "Amazonian" phase (2.2.91). This further complicates the division between natural and unnatural, with female and male as "mothers." One site for these meetings that complicate gender difference and the meaning of the natural is the anus, as both "natural" (i.e., a bodily site shared by men and women) and yet as "unnatural" (because it produces "nothing," to recall Aufidius's lines). This is what I think makes for the "rightness" of the anus in Coriolanus, for it suggests that the anus is the *productive* site for the character in the play and is not merely to be read within the Freudian trajectories of shame and sublimation. Coriolanus's career of attempted self-authorship represents a desire to become a machine, to "live" in some realm that is not the biological. The fantasy of the play thus involves a dream of authoring and of self-authoring that transgresses even the transgressive desire that the play suggests in its equation of womb and bowels. For in making the loves of Aufidius and of Volumnia parallel, in equating hetero and homo desire *and its betrayal,* the play looks beyond these forms of sexuality, or perhaps it imagines an "inhuman" sexuality that would not be subject to betrayal. This is a form of reproduction glimpsed in the sonnets, in the artifices of image production. Aufidius's dream may be Shakespeare's, too.

PART III

Rebel Letters: Postal Effects from *Richard II* to *Henry IV*

> In the beginning, in principle, was the post, and I will never get over it. But in the end I know it, become aware of it as our death sentence.
>
> —Jacques Derrida, *The Post Card*

On Deposit

Marjorie Garber offers a breathtaking start. Writing of the thematization of writing in Shakespeare, she asks, of act 4, scene 1 in *Richard II,* what is a deposition? "A 'deposition' is both a forced removal from office and a piece of testimony taken down for use in the witness's absence (as well as the term describing the lowering of Christ's body from the cross—Richard's view of the event). Richard here deposes at his own deposition."[1] Garber notes an undoubtedly repressed textuality in this scene, a repression so strong that the text itself remarks it. After Richard deposes himself, he asks, "What more remains?" (4.1.222),[2] and he is answered that he must read the document that details his crimes. So doing, he will be "worthily deposed" (4.1.227). Richard refuses to read the document and to turn his deposition into the written deposition demanded of him.

What he refuses to do in the play, he does, however, in Raphael Holinshed's *Chronicles.* There, according to a parliamentary document, he reads "a bill drawne of the said resignation, that he might be perfect in the rehearsall thereof," a bill that he in fact "desired to have . . . drawne" (37).[3] He insists, in Holinshed's account, that his recited resignation be letter-perfect; when he deposes himself, he reenacts a textual inscription. In Holinshed, then, the double meaning of deposition is explicit, and the duplication of terms points to the assumption that writing acts as a guarantee. The letter has a fixity and a permanence into which Richard inserts himself: "[F]or the more suertie of the matter, and for that the said resignation should have his full force and strength, himselfe therefore read the scroll of resignation" (37). Richard does not merely read the scroll; he signs his resignation: "And for more record of the same, here openlie I subscribe and signe this present resignation with mine owne hand" (39).

Shakespeare's scene seems to be constructed in the repression of the double meaning of deposition apparent in Holinshed. And when Richard declines to read, he launches an attack on writing, refusing to "ravel out" his "weaved-up folly" (4.1.228–29). "Weaved-up" offers an etymology for "text" that stresses its fabrication; as Richard describes it, a text that unkings him cannot be a sure text, for it unspeaks itself. Rather than that text, he asks his accusers to look at an (imagined) book that would describe their rebellious acts; if it contained "the deposing of a king" (4.1.234), that text would be "marked with a blot, damned in the book of heaven" (4.1.236). The text (for the imagined text is the very text the rebels would have him read, deposing him), as Richard describes it in his response, is therefore, by definition, a rebel text. Letters are not sureties or guarantees; to find oneself inscribed means to have been offered up to undoing.

Instead, Richard delivers (has already delivered) himself in speech:

> Now mark me how I will undo myself.
> I give this heavy weight from off my head
> And this unwieldy sceptre from my hand,
> The pride of kingly sway from out my heart.
> With mine own tears I wash away my balm,
> With mine own hands I give away my crown,
> With mine own tongue deny my sacred state,

With mine own breath release all duty's rites.
All pomp and majesty I do forswear;
My manors, rents, revenues I forgo;
My acts, decrees, and statutes I deny.
(4.1.203–13)

Yet the speech that Richard delivers in which he undoes himself is, in fact, derived loosely from the bill in Holinshed; although hardly letter-perfect, Richard's speech of resignation is a version (a rewriting, as it were) of the written deposition he refuses to read in the play:

> I resigne all my kinglie dignitie, majestie and crowne, with all the lordships, power, and privileges to the foresaid kinglie dignitie and crowne belonging, and all other lordships and possessions to me in anie maner of wise perteining. . . . And I renounce all right, and all maner of title of possession. . . . And also the rule and governance of the same kingdome and lordships, with all ministrations of the same. . . . And also I renounce the name, worship, and regalitie and kinglie highnesse, clearlie, freelie, singularlie and wholie, in the most best maner and forme that I may.[4]

Richard's speech insists on his "own," yet his words have been written already. His speech (in both meanings of the word) enacts a textual suppression and makes claims for the propriety of speaking. "Mark me how I will undo myself"; the written mark marks him, and the command "hear me" appears in a textualized form, as if audition were an act of inscription. "Are you contented to resign the crown?" Bolingbroke had asked, and Richard replies: "Ay, no; no, ay; for I must nothing be; / Therefore no no, for I resign to thee" (4.1.200–202). Whereas in Holinshed, Richard signs when he resigns, here that doubled mark is marked in the duplicity of his response. Rather than the supposedly confirmatory doubling of Holinshed, Richard speaks within a textual duplicity. Saying yes and no at once, blotting himself out and insisting on himself, Richard speaks as if "resign" meant both to give away and to write again. In his duplicitous speech it does. So doing he speaks within a writing that lacks the monumentality and permanence of the text as represented in Holinshed.

Richard's deposition "speech" enacts a version of the repression of textuality to which many Shakespeareans have succumbed (not least in speech-act and metatheatrical analyses of the history plays).[5] For a representative instance, consider Terence Hawkes's *Shakespeare's Talking Animals.* Guarding against the possibility that we might misapprehend Shakespeare's plays as literature, Hawkes describes his book as a set of essays concerned with the ways in which the plays exhibit "a deep and almost certainly defensive commitment to language in its oral dimension: to the ideal as well as the idea of man as the animal that talks."[6] No doubt: Shakespeare's audience was not highly literate, and literature, as the institution we readily name, does not apply to the Shakespearean text. But no doubt, too, a relationship to an emerging textuality is marked throughout the plays. Shakespeare writes scripts that can, as the instance of Richard's deposition begins to exhibit, repress that relationship. That repression, I argue, serves an ideological function, and I would add "ideology" to Hawkes's listing of the "ideal" and "idea" of the oral. Hawkes almost admits as much when he describes the "Tudor 'revolution'" as "the establishment of the king as the vital and unifying communicative link between man and deity and man and man" (75), but by not interrogating that claim, his argument repeats an attitude toward power (textual power) in the plays: an insistence on living breath ("the vital and unifying communicative link") rather than the claims of the text on speech—in this instance, the text of Holinshed repressed in the deposition speech; the text of that speech (the script that the actor "reads" as he speaks); and the thematization of those linked repressions in the representation of textuality that Richard makes in his refusal to read the rebels' document. In these multiple repressions, I argue, can emerge a notion of the text in Shakespeare and its relationship to the ideology of the second tetralogy.[7]

The ideological construction of textuality in Richard's speeches in the deposition scene—or their repetition in Hawkes—are instances of what Derrida calls logocentrism, confining "writing to a secondary and instrumental function: translator of a full speech that was fully present (present to itself, to its signified, to the other, the very condition of the theme of presence in general), technics in the service of language, spokesman, interpreter of an originary speech itself shielded from interpretation."[8] As Derrida argues, such characterizations of writing are not neutral (although they formulate writing as, at best, a neutrality, a representation that would ideally efface itself before living speech). Rather, the hierarchization of voice and writing (in temporal as well as evaluative terms) attempts to guard speech from the incursions of writing—precisely, then, the attitude of Richard refusing to read the deposition or of Hawkes in his "defensive" characterization of the primacy of oral communication. "Such is the breath of kings" (1.3.215); however, that speech is invaded by what it would deny. This is palpably so, in the play's citations of Holinshed, but it is also more generally so, as Derrida argues, since such incursions are systematic: They found speech (in an unfounding of the logocentric denials of writing). "Writing did not reduce the voice to itself, it incorporated it into a system,"[9] for, as Derrida demonstrates, from Plato on, discussions of writing that have attempted to secure its merely secondary, derivative, fallen nature have been haunted by the possibility that writing is as originary as speech (and if so, that there is then no origin). He points "to the tradition that has always associated writing with the fatal violence of the political institution" (36), a *usurping* incursion upon nature, life, breath.

Richard would ally writing to rebellion against the sanctity of the monarch and the breath and life of the king. But, as Derrida argues, such representations of power are ideological constructions couched in the devaluation of the very instrument that is allied to power and makes it possible: writing. Introducing a selection from the Shakespearean editor William Warburton's inquiry into the origins of language, Derrida exposes the ideological construction in which writing merely "befalls" power; rather, he insists (and demonstrates that despite itself, Warburton's text insists) on the complicity of writing and power.[10] The relationship is, at one and the same time, effaced (in the logocentric devaluations of writing) and productive of the text. As Warburton writes the history of writing from hieroglyphics to phonetic transcription (a history toward writing effacing itself, since phonetic writing should efface itself before the sounds it represents), he also writes a history of script as an instrument of concealment, secrecy, and power. The very arbitrariness of the relationship between phonetic script and sound (that is, that which should make script "invisible") is part of what makes script insistent and primary. It is not merely that phonetic script fails to provide a system that merely translates sound into another medium; script usurps voice ("mark me").

> A writing made to manifest, serve, and preserve knowledge—for custody of meaning, the repository of learning, and the laying out of the

archive—encrypts itself, becoming secret and reserved, diverted from common usage, esoteric. Naturally destined to serve the communication of laws and the order of the city transparently, a writing becomes the instrument of an abusive power of a caste of "intellectuals" that is thus ensuring hegemony, whether its own or that of special interests: the violence of a secretariat, a discriminating reserve, an effect of scribble and script.[11]

Derrida's summary of Warburton's enlightened horror also characterizes Hawkes's attitudes, his attempt to rescue the Shakespearean text from the hands of the literary establishment. Warburton locates the moment in which the "fall" into phonetic writing occurred: in Egypt, when the king's secretary devised a script for the king that would not have the limits of hieroglyphics, a script for letters of state, "whence the name *epistolic:* '. . . as the government doubtless sought to keep the invention secret.'"[12] The Shakespearean text, as the deposition scene indicates, bears this duplicity too: It registers, in Richard's speech, the logocentric devaluation of writing as it is allied to an ideology of power; yet it also is a written text (Shakespeare and Holinshed usurp Richard's "own"). Logocentric ideology, at one and the same time, effaces its relationship to that which establishes its power.

"What more remains?" Richard's refusal to read the deposition is not the end of the deposition scene, and the remainder of the scene exhibits the relationship between the oral deposition (invaded by the mark) and the repudiation of the rebel text. For Richard does agree to read—himself, in a mirror—as if to affirm the presence of the body and the voice.

> I'll read enough
> When I do see the very book indeed
> Where all my sins are writ, and that's myself.
> (4.1.273–75)

For Hawkes, such reading is tantamount to a confession of failed kingship: "[H]e commands a mirror to be brought so that, as ever, he can look inward, not communicating directly with the world, with reality, but with himself alone, like a reader who studies alone, without communicating outside the realm of the printed page, abstracted from the warmth of oral-aural contact."[13] "Such 'writing,'" Hawkes concludes, reviewing moments in the play in which Richard is attached to script, "measures the extent to which, under that king, the vivid island language has indeed been grossly reduced" (103). But if, as I have been suggesting, the deposition scene stages relationships to a suppressed textuality, this scene of reading, in which Richard attempts to claim his "own" in the mirror, is, I argue, the most explicit register of that suppressed textuality, a textuality that is one with power, not its fallen debasement.

For when Richard looks in the glass, that text refuses to confirm what he sees there. It deposes him, too, beguiling him with a false image; it refuses to deliver the present or to offer an outer image that corresponds to what Richard supposes he will see:

> Give me the glass, and therein will I read.
> No deeper wrinkles yet? Hath sorrow struck
> So many blows upon this face of mine
> And made no deeper wounds? O flattering glass
> Like to my followers in prosperity,
> Thou dost beguile me!
>
> (4.1.276–81)

Richard's reading in the mirror disputes the solipsism that Hawkes sees there. Rather, the mirroring reflection insists on a primacy that undoes the lived reality of the body and the voice. Moreover, even that lived reality is presented as textual: Sorrow should have furrowed his brows, imprinting them. And the mirror is like the gaze of some other upon him (the flatterers of the past); it does not allow Richard to eye himself. The circuit of one's own—everything that is entailed in what Derrida calls presence—is shattered in this glass. Richard looks upon a mirror for magistrates and finds himself displaced and deposed by the image, by the usurping secondarity of the reflection: the mirror or the text (the equation is a Renaissance commonplace, of course),[14] which refuses to be merely a reflection or to efface itself as writing supposedly does in its relation to speech. The mirror, in every sense of the word, makes Richard a subject—subject to the disseminative dispersal of a textuality that refuses simply to mirror "reality." Rather, the signified face is the signifying face. In the glass, Richard reads himself through a textual citation:

> Was this face the face
> That every day under his household roof

Did keep ten thousand men? Was this the face
That like the sun did make beholders wink?
Was this the face that faced so many follies
And was at last outfaced by Bolingbroke?
(4.1.281–86)

Richard's "self-discovery" is so entirely a matter of citation that the mirror offers him a version of Christopher Marlowe's Doctor Faustus when he looks in the glass. The flattering voice of the past includes, then, an author that Shakespeare would put behind him. Richard is written within literary history. And the relationship between Richard and Bolingbroke is signaled in the kingly title they share at this moment, as the hollow crown passes from one to the other; depositioning describes the relationship of signified to signifier.

This is, as Derrida claims, an economy of death.[15] When Richard deposes, he is put on deposit, a virtual corpse as the glass shatters, an actual corpse as the play ends. "Mark, silent king" (4.1.290), Richard directs Bolingbroke, pointing to the shared economy of a shattering textuality, for the *silent* king is no avatar of the oral-aural. "There lies the substance" (4.1.299). There is no referent for "there." All shadow, no substance. By the end of the play, Bolingbroke, who, as much as Richard, turns the word against the word, is buried in the casket of textuality: "[W]ithin this coffin I present / Thy buried fear" (5.6.30–31). As Garber comments about the deposition scene: "He is already a voice from the past, and the disembodied voice, the ghost of Richard II, will haunt the rest of the tetralogy with increasing power."[16]

But the subsequent plays are also haunted by what is put on deposit in the deposition scene: the alliance of kingship with the repression of textuality, and the ways in which the play both supports that logocentrism and undermines it. The rebel letter that Richard reads is disseminated and displaced in the play that follows. It is the circuit of that letter, put on deposit in *Richard II* and posted in *1 Henry IV*, that I pursue here. It takes the breath away.

The Factor of Truth

Confirming Richard's logocentric alliance of writing with rebellion, the rebels in *1 Henry IV* are associated with writing. The king holds councils or confers privately with Prince Henry; he receives messengers with news; he listens to stories. But when the Percies are alone, Worcester offers to "unclasp a secret book" to his nephew (1.3.188), the book that inscribes, in Hotspur's words, "a noble plot" (1.3.276), one that will save the Percies from "the detested blot" (1.3.162) that threatens to "fill up chronicles in time to come" (1.3.171). Worcester does not reveal his plot to Hotspur; rather, he promises to "send you written" (1.3.261) his plan, and the scene ends with his assurance that the rebellion has been "ruminated, plotted, and set down" (1.3.271). Hotspur is told, "No further go in this / Than I by letters shall direct your course" (1.3.289–90), and, as if in confirmation of this textualization of rebellion, the next time Hotspur appears, he enters *"solus, reading a letter"* (2.3.0). When the rebels meet, their scene together (act 3, scene 1) takes as long as the drawing of their indentures (3.1.80, 140, 258). "I'll haste the writer" (3.1.141), Glendower promises the impatient Hotspur, and when Mortimer agrees to hear his lady sing in Welsh, he justifies the delay: "By that time will our book, I think, be drawn" (3.1.221). And so the scene ends: "[O]ur book is drawn; we'll but seal / And then to horse immediately" (3.1.262–63). At the rebel front at Shrewsbury, Hotspur receives *"one with letters"* (4.1.12), and as the battle is about to begin, the post arrives again: "My lord, here are letters for you," a messenger says; "I cannot read them now" (5.2.79–80), Hotspur responds. Between these, an entire scene between the Archbishop of York and Sir Michael serves merely to display other rebels in a flurry of letter writing. "Hie, good Sir Michael; bear this sealèd brief / With wingèd haste" (4.4.1–2), the scene opens, and the Archbishop is still beseeching Sir Michael to speed as he exits to "write again / To other friends" (4.4.40–41).

Logocentric devaluation of writing is furthered by the contents of these rebel letters. Letters are so true to rebellion that they are rebellious, as shattering as the glass that Richard reads. This is apparent when Hotspur reads the first of the letters to arrive: "'But, for mine own part, my lord, I could be well contented to be there, in respect of the love I bear your house.' He could be contented—why is he not then?" (2.3.1–4). Hotspur deciphers the equivocal and prevaricating letter; yet, true to the rebel form, he answers the letter with the letter: "Is there not my father, my uncle, and myself; Lord Edmund Mortimer, my Lord of York, and Owen Glendower? Is there not, besides, the Douglas? Have I not all their letters to meet me in arms by the ninth of the next month?" (2.3.23–28). Taking up the letter writer's devaluation of the "plot" as "light" (2.3.12), Hotspur counters, "[O]ur plot is a good plot as ever was laid" (2.3.15). When the messenger arrives with the first letter at Shrewsbury, it reveals Northumberland's "sickness"—he too "could be well contented to be there" and is not; by the time of the battle, none of the letter writers named in Hotspur's response to the letter of act 2, scene 3, save the Douglas, has arrived. The Archbishop of York's dispatches are letters betraying the rebel plot. The indentures drawn with Owen Glendower secure nothing, like the map of England that the rebels also carve up, with Hotspur opposing the "deep indent" (3.1.104) of the River Trent and wanting to redraw the line on the map and on the land. The rebels depend on letters, and it is only letters that arrive at the battlefield: Death is their destination.

From his father's letter, Hotspur learns the "truth" of the conventional definition of a letter, "the messenger and familiar speeche of the absent," as Angel Day defines the letter in *The English Secretorie;* "a declaration, by Writing of the mindes of such as bee absent, one of them to another, even as though they were present," as William Fulwood puts it in *The Enemy of Idlenesse.*[17] Northumberland's letter represents and delivers his absence. This is true to the etymology of "epistle"—"upon (the occasion of) sending"—for the epistle is a dispatch put into the hands of time. And as the epistolary handbooks of which Day and Fulwood are late exemplars, make clear, letters have so little to do with their senders or receivers that they may be copied from a collection like Day's or Fulwood's, to be sent as the occasion dictates. Thus, while it is true to say that the rebel letters of *1 Henry IV* contain betrayal, it is also true to say that within the epistolary tradition of the letter, they could not do otherwise. Conveyers of absence, they cannot assure presence, neither the presence of sender nor of receiver. Nor could the words in the letter be one's own. To be true to the structure of the letter, in fact, they must be capable of dissemination. Hotspur seems entirely circumscribed by the letter. As he countered the rebel letter of act 2, scene 3 with the letters of his coconspirators, so he responds to his father's letter by making the lying letter into a surety: "I rather of his absence make this use: / It lends a lustre" (4.1.76–77). Hotspur *calculates* with his father's absence; as the Douglas puts it, "[W]e may boldly spend upon the hope of what / Is to come in" (4.1.54–55). He counts on time, the occasions that dictate letters upon which they are written. Absence is put on deposit to deliver a temporal remainder. The rebels have not yet "read / The very bottom"

(4.1.49–50) of the letter, not until Hotspur dismisses the second letter carrier at Shrewsbury: "O gentlemen, the time of life is short!" (5.2.81). Soon, it is over. Soon, that is, Hotspur and his coconspirators are only "blots" in the chronicle of time.

In part, this alliance of the rebels and writing can also be found in Holinshed. There the rebels draw up a set of "articles" and "by their writings and seales confirmed the same."[18] Letters are sent abroad, and at the battle of Shrewsbury, documents are delivered into the king's hand. But in Holinshed, unlike in Shakespeare, the king also reads and writes: "But the king understanding their cloaked drift [the letters', which, as Holinshed comments, put a plausible face on the rebellion by detailing faults of the king], devised (by what meanes he might) to quiet and appease the commons, and deface their contrived forgeries; and therefore he wrote an answer to their libels" (42); indeed, they are able to meet him face to face at Shrewsbury because the king sends "letters . . . under his seale, that they might safelie come and go" (43). In Holinshed, then, the king is as deft as Shakespeare's Hotspur in deciphering the "cloaked drift" of writing; but like the rebels, too, he puts his guarantees into writing. Shakespeare's Henry IV does not read or write; the text of *1 Henry IV,* like the deposition scene in *Richard II,* seems complicit with an ideological and logocentric suppression of any connection between power and writing.

The king's, it appears, is a world of speech. He knows what the rebels

> have articulate,
> Proclaimed at market crosses, read in churches,
> To face the garment of rebellion.
>
> (5.1.72–74)

But never on stage does he read or write in reply. Rather, he sends Blunt to parlay with the rebels (act 4, scene 3), and he meets them in conference. The Percies do not trust the king's word ("well we know the king / Knows at what time to promise, when to pay," as Hotspur puts it [4.3.52–53]), but they cannot produce his lying script. Rather, they offer the evidence suppressed in *Richard II* of the king naming Mortimer his heir. When they refer back to the past as written—and that means to *Richard II*—they cannot find Bolingbroke in his words. He was and is, for all his speech, a "silent king." Hotspur recalls his meeting with Bolingbroke, quoting lines from the earlier play:

"Look when his infant fortune came to age,"
And "gentle Harry Percy," and "kind cousin"—
O, the devil take such cozeners!

(1.3.251–53)

Yet the cozenage Hotspur takes Bolingbroke to task for has no textual support; Bolingbroke does not say "kind cousin" to Hotspur in *Richard II* act 2, scene 3; misquotation of a nonexistent text is another rebel inscription. "My heart this covenant makes, my hand thus seals it" (2.3.50), Bolingbroke had told Hotspur; but there is no writing in that hand. "Look how we can, or sad or merrily, / Interpretation will misquote our looks" (5.2.12–13); thus Worcester defends the lie that condemns Hotspur to death. Characteristically, Worcester, who had first unclasped the "secret book," sees his face as an inscription and sees seeing as reading. Rebel textuality is allied insistently to cozening texts that can only be misquoted.

Even in the most "oral" scene between the rebels—at Owen Glendower's, where the lady sings a seemingly untranscribable song—Glendower goes out of his way to insist that he is no illiterate magician, proclaiming his education and his literacy. And, as Mortimer hears his lady sing, he can praise her by claiming that her "tongue / Makes Welsh as sweet as ditties highly penned" (3.1.205–06). The rebels occupy a world that is always being textualized. A scrivener prepares a document offstage, and rebel speech turns speech into text. Unlike the rebels, the king, it appears, has no offstage secretaries writing letters or preparing articles for him. No reader of letter manuals, with their insistence on the etymological link between "secret" and "secretary," the king has no ties to script and its capacity to betray the writer. Hotspur dies midsentence at Shrewsbury, and Hal fills the absence, the living replacement of the dead letter.

That, at any rate, is how it may appear. For, as in *Richard II,* royal scenes of inscription and writing and reading have been replaced with scenes of speaking. Among their own, the rebels write; with the king, they speak. (Indeed, written "articles" in Holinshed are articulated in the scenes at Shrewsbury.) The play, from this evidence, would appear to be intent on an ideological project to secure the king's breath. Yet in his first words in the play, Henry represents himself as a breathless figure:

So shaken as we are, so wan with care.
Find we a time for frighted peace to pant

And breathe short-winded accents of new broils
To be commenced in stronds afar remote.
(1.1.1–4)

And Hotspur's "cozenage" is a charge that sticks; Henry himself, speaking to Hal, points to his kinship with the rebel leader. And in the first scene, his dearest wish is that one Harry might replace the other. Such echoes in the play are commonplace in the criticism of *1 Henry IV,* and I do not plan to detail them here.[19] What does need to be remarked, however, is the way such relationships between the king and rebels share a textuality. The king may not be represented as the rebels are, literally engaged in inscription; but his very "being" is written: Recall his sealing hand in *Richard II.* Note that the king's charge that the rebels have "face[d] the garment of rebellion / With some fine color that may please the eye" (5.1.74–75) describes their false writing in the same terms as the king had used to depict his performance to Hal:

I stole all courtesy from heaven,
And dressed myself in such humility
. . . .
Thus did I keep my person fresh and new,
My presence, like a robe pontifical,
Ne'er seen but wond'red at.
(3.2.50–51, 55–57)

This also echoes the equation of writing with defacement in Holinshed (42). In such metaphors, the king is literally invested, clothed in the garments of textuality within the logocentric devaluation of writing. Hotspur may appear in the battlefield besieged by letter carriers; the king on the battlefield is the letter: "The king hath many marching in his coats" (5.3.25). "What art thou / That counterfeit'st the person of king" (5.4.26–27), the Douglas demands, and is answered, "The king himself." Henry's being is counterfeit; his person impersonation. The garb he wears—his presence—is a disseminative textuality.

Thus, the ideological structure of the play is not quite as dualistic as it first appeared to be. The rebel attachment to letters is the literalization—in letters and writing—of the textuality that marks the king, a textuality so secret that it is proclaimed openly. The emperor only has clothes: the naked body of the letter. "Has it ever been doubted that writing was the clothing of speech?" Derrida asks,[20] and is not such "exteriority" the attempt to secure being, life, presence against that which founds and unfounds them? In *1 Henry IV,* logocentric devaluation is everywhere haunted by what it represses, constituted by it. The king is never "in" in his words. He sees himself in Hotspur, and Hal as Richard: "[I]n that very line, Harry, standest thou" (3.2.85), "thou, the shadow of succession" (3.2.99). For Hal truly to succeed his father, he must replace Hotspur; the line that will continue is a line of script. Hal finishes Hotspur's sentence on the battlefield, as we noted before, but not to replace death with life; rather, to continue the line.

This is how Hal assures the king that he will "be more myself" (3.2.93):

> I will redeem all this on Percy's head
> And, in the closing of some glorious day,
> Be bold to tell you that I am your son.
> When I will wear a garment all of blood,
> And stain my favors in a bloody mask,
> Which, washed away, shall scour my shame with it.
> (3.2.132–37)

To be himself—to be the king's son—Hal must pass through the form of Hotspur, face and body clothed in Hotspur's blood. The "shame" here includes that textualization, and the washing away is the effacement of that which makes Hal himself. At the end of the line, the "closing of some glorious day," Hal will come into his own by this violent act of appropriation and effacement; he will emerge unblotted, as if no passage through textualization had taken place. It is not merely the metaphors of garment and mask that support such a reading of these lines. Hal continues:

> Percy is but my factor, good my lord,
> To engross up glorious deeds on my behalf;
> And I will call him to so strict account
> That he shall render every glory up,
> Yea, even the slightest worship of his time,
> Or I will tear the reckoning from his heart.
> (3.2.147–52)

As much as Hotspur receiving the letter of his father's absence, Hal calculates here on the making absent of Hotspur as the necessity behind his becoming present. Yet presence here is a coin that circulates; what Hotspur has engrossed (bought up and monopolized as his own) will be Hal's own. Such ownership is as dubious as Richard's claim to speak his own. The agency here is explicitly that of the letter. "Factor" is an agent, doer, maker, author. And "engross" has as its primary meaning the large and clear secretarial hand of the professional scribe preparing a legal document. Hotspur is Hal's secretary, writing the script in which he will be written—written true, legal heir, on the line—so he will be accounted. To be engrossed is to be named in a document, written in a list of accounts; it is the "reckoning" that will occur on the day of reckoning when the violent effacement of Hotspur will "face" Hal's garment as he passes from one text into another and thereby into his own. Hal replaces Hotspur, his presence posited upon absence; he enters into textuality. The "deeds" of this "strict account" are written deeds in a legal register, an account book in which no one has his own.[21]

Hotspur. O, I could prophesy.
But that the earthy and cold hand of death
Lies on my tongue. No, Percy, thou art dust,
And food for—
Prince. For worms, brave Percy.
(5.4.82–85)

The hand of death on Hotspur's tongue is a hand writing; Hotspur's final sentence, spoken as if in another's text, names Percy in the third person. Only in writing can Percy say of/to himself, "Percy, thou art dust." The Prince, completing the sentence, enters into that reckoning.

Such reckoning is how Hal is characterized throughout the play, and nowhere more so than in his soliloquy at the end of act 1, scene 2. Debates about Hal's character have always had to come to terms with that speech and its uncanny echoes in the king's self-presentation in act 3, scene 2. "Hal's justification of himself," Stephen Greenblatt comments, "threatens to fall away at every moment into its antithesis. . . . Although we can perceive at every point . . . the potential instability of the structure of power, . . . Hal's 'redemption' is as inescapable and inevitable as the outcome of those practical jokes the madcap prince is so fond of playing."[22] In the speech, truth and falsity are allied as they are in the rebel letter, and, indeed, the images throughout the speech—economic, sartorial—are the images of the letter. Hal as "bright metal on a sullen ground" (1.2.200) offers himself as Hotspur takes his father's letter of absence and puts it on deposit for the final reckoning. As stamped coin, Hal's value is written.[23] And Hal's promise to "pay the debt I never promisèd" (1.2.197) depends upon the "factor" of engrossment elsewhere. "By how much better than my word I am, / By so much shall I falsify men's hopes" (1.2.198–99); better and worse, true and false, exist in a counterfeit relationship to each other. And genuine "being," sunlike majesty, does not escape the textual order of simulation, eclipsing, clouding over a "heliocentric concept of speech."[24] "Yet herein will I imitate the sun" (1.2.185). In which case, being itself would be counterfeit, the metaphor of truth, majesty, sun, revealed as the veil of truth.

The economy in which Hal offers himself is written within the metaphors in which writing is regularly devalued as the violent and rebellious letter incapable of truth. This is also the language of Hal's truth. If there is something "inescapable" here, as Greenblatt contends, it is not the play's inevitable support of constituted order.[25] It is, rather, the inevitability of textualization. Hal's reckoning here plays with his being absent, with the possibility of his insertion within a script. If Hal draws our assent, it is because he speaks within the truth of the already written, within a historical destiny that has written his lines.[26] He does not, as a character, know the future. He speaks, rather, within its already writtenness, charactered by the histories that proclaim his success and his succession. That is the inevitability in Hal's lines, a reckoning within a reckoning that has already been written. The present in which Hal speaks is "awhile" (1.2.183), and the future arrival as and into "himself" is one that "betters" his word only by falsifying it. It maintains a structure of veiling in which unveiling and re-veiling/revealing are one: "reformation, glitt'ring o'er my fault" (1.2.201). The structure, that is, is that of writing, in which truth is offered in the metaphor of (un)veiling, in which that veil, that metaphor, offers "the familiar acrobatics of the metaphor *of* the truth."[27] The glittering truth is put on deposit.

And it is delivered at Shrewsbury. "Glittering in golden coats like images" (4.1.100) is Vernon's phrase for the king and his troops, "gorgeous as the sun" (4.1.102), none more so than Harry "like feathered Mercury" (4.1.106), the trickster-god of the crossroads, where death and writing engross reality, like Hermes, the letter carrier of the gods. So Abraham Fleming offers his *Panoplie of Epistles* (1576):

> I give counsel to passe & respasse, to view and review, to take down and put on, to exercise and use, such weapons as he shall finde in this our Panoplie or house of furniture, and he shall feele him selfe in short space, fenced and strengthened to the purpose, against ignorance that ougly monster of many heades, an enimie of order, and a friend of confusion.[28]

Fleming's letters are "warlike weapons," and the writer presents himself as "a *Mercurialist*" rather than a *"Martialist"* (5v). Or, rather, like Hal, as both—for instance, when he challenges Hotspur to single combat, speaking the rebel's praise "like a chronicle," making but "a blushing cital of himself" (5.2.57, 61). "Dispraising praise . . . / . . . became him like a prince indeed" (5.2.59–60). In the structure of giving and taking away, in a structure of the violence of the letter, Hal is *like* himself, present in "a 'dialectic' of protention and retention that one would install in the heart of the present."[29]

> At hand, quoth pickpurse. (2.1.46)

To summarize: The logocentric ideology of *1 Henry IV* is produced in a linking of two counterprocedures. The rebels are insistently attached to script literally, while the king is not; and concurrently, the king is attached to script metaphorically. Hal's historical destiny in the play is the destiny of the letter; he will come to be, he already is, inscribed in the histories that assure his arrival. "To send, to destine, to dispatch";[30] Derrida writes these as a series of appositions, and they concur in the career of the prince, whose telos is also within the scope of a Derridean equation: *"telos:* acquittal, exemption, payment, cost, expenditure, fee" (56). Hal arrives at the point where his scripted being and his being scripted coincide: in the engrossment that puts him in the hand of the letter (so that his deeds are in the script of another) and puts that letter in his hand (so that when he speaks the end of Hotspur's final sentence, his speech is within that text). The exchange, the arrival into his own, takes place through the agency of death.

But is there only death within this economy? "Engross" not only designates a script, it also means corporeal enlargement, life. The word also implicates Falstaff lying "dead" beside Hotspur as Hal completes his sentence, as the letter arrives. Falstaff evades the arrival in an equation of the counterfeit orders of death and life: "'Sblood, 'twas time to counterfeit. . . . Counterfeit? I lie; I am no counterfeit. To die is to be a counterfeit . . . ; but to counterfeit dying . . . is to be no counterfeit, but *the* true and perfect image of life indeed" (5.4.112–18). Counterfeit in all this is Falstaff's claim to "true" existence; truth is produced in the "lie" and life itself is the "perfect image of life." Falstaff's evasions are written within the economy that embraces Hal and that Hal embraces. Indeed, from his first words to Falstaff, Hal is writing him within his script:

> Unless hours were cups of sack, and minutes capons, and clocks the tongues of bawds, and dials the signs of leaping houses, and the blessed sun himself a fair hot wench in flame-colored taffeta, I see no reason why thou shouldst be so superfluous to demand the time of the day. (1.2.6–11)

Hal here performs a reckoning, writes a bill; at the opening of act 2, scene 4, such reckoning is transferred to Francis, whose rebellion he incites with the hopes of a thousand pounds, and to Hotspur, inflamed with death: "his eloquence the parcel of a reckoning" (2.4.96–97). In these "trim reckonings" (to cite Falstaff's definition of the word "honor" [5.1.134] and the airy order of speech),[31] Hal's speech scripts others within the order of writing that also claims him and that he (dis)claims.

The Purloined Paper

"Text" and its synonyms, as they have appeared this far in this essay, are Derridean terms; yet as I have argued elsewhere, the terms also ramify in their bibliographical meanings.[32] This inquiry into the representations of textuality within the Shakespearean text may also forward a consideration of the text—literally. Indeed, this might be the moment to return to the deposition scene in *Richard II* and to detail the bibliographical difficulties it entails.[33] I choose, however, to stay with *1 Henry IV*, a text regarded generally as an unproblematic one. "The two 1598 quartos of *1 Henry IV* are . . . among the cleanest and best printed of all the Shakespeare quartos," David Bevington comments in his 1987 Oxford edition;[34] they are the copytexts for all modern editions of the play, the Folio having been set up from Q5 and exhibiting changes that reveal "literary meddling"[35] without any authoritative source in authorial manuscripts or playhouse practices. Yet there is one F1 emendation accepted in virtually all modern editions, and I would like to examine it here. It may be one of only two moments when a piece of script is in Hal's hands, when, perhaps, he reads. The episode in the editorial tradition, to be examined here, participates precisely in the countermoves that I have described as structuring the logocentric ideology of *1 Henry IV.*

In Q1, the tavern scene (act 2, scene 4 in F1) closes like this:

Prince. This oylie rascall is knowne as well as Poules: goe call him forth.

Peto. Falstaffe: fast asleepe behind the Arras, and snorting like a horse.

Prince. Harke how hard he fetches breath, search his pockets.

He searcheth his pocket, and findeth certain papers.

Prince. What hast thou found?

Peto. Nothing but papers my Lord.

Prince. Lets see what they be, read them.

Item a capon.	2.s,ii,d.
Item sawce.	iiii,d.
Item sacke two gallons.	v.s,viii,d.
Item anchaves and sacke after supper.	2,s,vi,d.
Item bread.	ob.

O monstrous! but one halfepeniworth of bread to this intollerable deale of sack? what there is else keepe close, weel read it at more advantage; there let him sleepe till day, ile to the court in the morning. We must all to the wars, and thy place shal be honorable. *I*le procure this fat rogue a charge of foot, and *I* know his death will bee a march of twelve skore, the money shall bee paid backe againe with advantage; bee with me betimes in the morning, and so good morrow Peto.

Peto. Good morrow good my Lord. *Exeunt*

F1 prints this scene almost word for word, and with numerous variants in the accidentals: pointing, capitalization, and spelling. Its major substantive change is this: before the reckoning, Peto's name is inserted as the reader of the tavern bill; and a second speech heading below the list returns "O monstrous" to the Prince. Modern editions follow the Folio emendation; Peto (or sometimes Poins) reads the paper.

The emendation appears unarguable. "Read them" sounds like a command to someone; it is parallel to "Search his pockets." As Bevington comments in a note to line 516, "The omission of a speech prefix . . . before some quoted document to be read or proclaimed is not unusual."[36] The Folio "meddler" is simply spelling out the obvious. Or is he? As A. R. Humphreys remarks in his Arden edition of *1 Henry IV,* the one change that we can be certain of between the first staging of the play and the 1598 quarto was the substitution of names: Falstaff for Oldcastle, Peto for Harvey, Bardolph for Russell.[37] A couple of slips, where the original names still appear in the text or in the speech headings, is evidence that someone went through the text and, in all but those few instances, made the changes. Thus, the absence of a speech heading for the reading of the tavern bill could mean that it had not been read originally by Harvey, for it has not been changed to Peto in Q1. The F1 emendation, according to this argument, would be unwarranted. It would be, even by an admission that Bevington makes, "literary meddling," his charge against the F1 changes in speech headings in act 2, scene 2: "They [the headings in that scene] read like literary meddling, and, in this important detail at least, do not inspire confidence in F1's report of staging or assignment of speeches."[38] Yet Bevington trusts F1 at the end of act 2, scene 4. Fredson Bowers, on the other hand, does not; he believes what Q1 presents: "[T]he lack of a speech-prefix before the inventory and before Hal's subsequent speech . . . indicates that Hal reads."[39]

Bowers believes that Q1 represents a textual emendation caused by stage history. He claims that in the original version of the play, Poins was to have been left alone on stage with Hal at the end of the scene, another prank started in picking Falstaff's pocket. Then, according to Bowers, when the play was staged, it was found that the actor playing Poins was needed to take another part in act 3, scene 1, and so Peto was called upon to end the scene with Hal. Since it is hard to believe that Peto could read the tavern reckoning, Bowers argues, Q1 made Hal the reader; a proper edition of the play should therefore emend the scene so that Poins is the reader of the bill. Q1, in short, is not a reliable text for the end of act 2, scene 4; undoubtedly, erroneously, it does have Hal read.

Among modern editors, only John Dover Wilson in the Cambridge text has Poins read the reckoning, although his argument is based on the assumption that the manuscript behind Q1 had the speech prefix *"Po"* for Poins, which was mistaken for *"Pe"* for Peto.[40] (Dover Wilson's argument makes more sense than it might appear, since an italic *e,* which would be used in a speech heading, looks very like a secretary *o,* which would be the hand in which most of the text was written and would also be the ordinary hand that a scribe wrote; it will not explain how the Prince comes to name Peto in the text of his speech, however.) Moreover, as Dover Wilson and Bowers point out, the emendation from "Peto" to "Poins" has good precedent. Malone did it; Dr. Johnson applauded it: "What had Peto done that 'his place should be honourable' or that he should be trusted with the plot against Falstaff? Poins has the Prince's confidence and is a man of courage."[41] And Bowers concurs: "Dr. Johnson's instincts were sounder than the present-day veneration for a theatrically altered text that violates the propriety of character and of situation as Shakespeare had conceived it. An editor . . . can at least give back to Hal his proper companion Poins, and keep Peto exclusively where he belongs . . . as a member of Falstaff's party."[42]

Dover Wilson and Bowers indulge fantasies about restoring Shakespeare's lost original text (so, too, do Stanley Wells and Gary Taylor in their Oxford edition of the plays, in which "Harvey" appears at the end of the scene—and as the reader of the bill).[43] Bowers's elaborate argument about stage history and its role in shaping Q1 is quite clearly bent on saving Hal from being sullied with low companions like Peto; it is shaped by the royal contempt that can be read in the play. The Petos of the world, Bowers insists, cannot read without being risible. Shakespeare cannot originally have wanted the prince to have ended the scene in his company. Modern editors, on the whole, are willing enough to leave Peto there, and reading, as he does in F1; but they, too, share similar suppositions. The prince must not read. And perhaps the editorial emendation in F1 is a result of the ideological construction of scenes of reading in the play; rebels read, but royalty do not.

There is one further point in favor of Poins that both Bowers and Dover Wilson enlist: the Dering manuscript, a composite of both parts of *Henry IV* put together for a private performance in the early 1620s.[44] There, Poins shares the stage with Hal at the close of act 2, scene 4. But not because the playscript has some access to Shakespeare's original; in Edward Dering's editing, the part of Peto has been eliminated from the play entirely. Moreover, in the Dering manuscript, although Poins is there with Hal, no speech heading precedes the tavern bill. Hal, apparently, reads it; the Dering manuscript transcribes Q5, but with an eye to performance (the substitution of Poins for Peto in the scene is clear evidence of that); yet it allows Hal to read the reckoning. The manuscript does not, therefore, support Bowers's argument; it does, however, lend support to Q1.

This moment at the end of act 2, scene 4 is, then, a genuine textual crux, and the editorial problem it represents is fully complicit with the constructions of textuality within the play. Were Hal to read—and to read the reckoning that literalizes the accounting and calculating that marks his scripted being throughout the play—he would have crossed the line into rebel territory. The reckoning he began in his first exchange with Falstaff, reading him as if he were a tavern bill, would be realized literally, the purloined paper in his hand. And the robbing of that pocket would find its echo on the battlefield with Hotspur:

> O Harry, thou hast robbed me of my youth!
> I better brook the loss of brittle life
> Than those proud titles thou hast won of me.
> (5.4.76–78)

Not the proud titles, but the mean calculations that keep the body alive, would accrue to Hal in the robbing of Falstaff's pocket. "He fetches breath" (2.4.505) and searches his pockets.

If someone else reads at the end of act 2, scene 4, then Hal is protected from script. "What there is else, keep close; we'll read it at more advantage" (515–16). His hands are clean, although the lines could mean that he has read and puts further reading on reserve. The purloined papers are put into another "rebel's" pocket, at hand when the pickpurse demands it, secret otherwise (as script is in the occulted orality of the royal word). Ransacking the corpus of Falstaff, the monstrous body yields paper—rebel text—a reckoning of items consumed and payment due. Food for worms.

In act 3, scene 3, the jest comes home, for Falstaff produces prodigious lies about what was in his picked pocket. Hal reveals that he knows just what was there, and Falstaff confronts him:

> **Falstaff.** . . . You confess then, you picked my pocket?
> **Prince.** It appears so by the story.
> (3.3.161–62)

Hal confesses nothing, nor does he produce the paper. Rather, he reproduces it as speech, as the story. The heir apparent deals only in appearances; script has become the trim reckoning of air, a story. Logocentric ideology suppresses the text—history and the instability of the manipulable, deceiving, lying letter that goes under the name of truth. Yet a moment after this oblique confession, Hal closes the scene with the one clear admission of the order of writing that goes hand in hand with power:

> Go bear this letter to Lord John of Lancaster,
> To my brother John; this to my Lord of Westmoreland.
> Go, Peto, to horse, to horse.
>
> (3.3.186–88)

The Commodity of Names: "Falstaff" and "Oldcastle" in *1 Henry IV*

Alternative Shakespeares: Political Shakespeare, Puzzling Shakespeare, Reinventing Shakespeare, Bad Shakespeare, Shakespeare Reproduced, Shakespeare Revealed: These are not only the names of recent books but new names for the author central to the canon of English literature. These renominations, aimed at unsettling that centrality—or showing its complicity with the institutions of modernity—raise the worry that the name is only resecured for further institutional appropriation. This situation can be glimpsed too in the editorial work associated with the Oxford Shakespeare (produced under the aegis of Stanley Wells and Gary Taylor), whose inclusion of two plays called *King Lear* in the 1986 one-volume *Complete Works* begins the work of destabilizing the texts that have gone under the magisterial name—but, as I have argued elsewhere, only begins it.[1] For the point is not (as Wells and Taylor seem to think) that the Oxford Shakespeare has given readers another play to add to the canon but, rather, that it provides further evidence for the canon's contingency, for Factitious Shakespeare.

The pages that follow continue that argument by pursuing another editorial decision made in that volume: the printing of *1 Henry IV* without the name "Falstaff." My argument attends necessarily to bibliographic details—to the evidence that the play once had the name "Oldcastle" in it and to the argument that it ought to again—but its implications are broader. Denying "Falstaff" to its readers, the Oxford Shakespeare could seem to be taking away a textual support for the canonical edifice. Paradoxically, I will be arguing on behalf of "Falstaff," but in order to remark the improprieties of the proper name and the instability of its textual properties. Thus, although the argument that follows is directed against an Oxford editor, it aims to further his project and to offer criticism another tool—a (de)foundational one—for dismantling Shakespeare.

Preparing the way for the decision enacted in the one-volume Oxford Shakespeare, in 1985 Taylor published an essay, "The Fortunes of Oldcastle," in which he argued that editors must restore the name "Oldcastle" in their editions of *1 Henry IV.* "Oldcastle is what Shakespeare wrote; . . . Oldcastle is what Shakespeare meant; . . . Oldcastle is what his contemporaries understood," Taylor summed up his case, continuing, "If editors nevertheless refuse to restore Shakespeare's name for the character, then they might as well confess that they care more about an artificial *post hoc* consistency than they do about the integrity of the individual work of art."[2] Parts of Taylor's argument are indisputable: There was once—in its original performances—a play by Shakespeare in which a character named "Oldcastle" appeared; we know that because of the documented evidence that Shakespeare was compelled to change the name because it had given offense, presumably to Oldcastle's descendants, Sir William Brooke, Lord Cobham, the Lord Chamberlain at the time of the play's initial performance, and his son, Sir Henry Brooke;[3] moreover, as many before Taylor have pointed out, the part involves Puritan posturing, claims to vocation, and biblical allusions—all apt for Oldcastle, a proto-Protestant martyr celebrated in such texts as John Foxe's *Acts and Monuments.* Given such evidence, Taylor's case seems compelling, and the editorial whimper that no one had ever thought of restoring the name—that no text of the play from its first printing on has ever had the name in it—is nothing but what Taylor calls it, pusillanimity in the face of tradition, a slavish worship of transmission of the sort that one finds in edition after edition until the advent of the New Bibliography sent editors back to the beginning and to the possibilities of restoring "what Shakespeare wrote." Here, Taylor claims, the choice is clear: We know the author's original intention, we know the original reading; how can we ignore what we know? "What says Monsieur Remorse?" (1.2.109).[4]

The case presented thus far is, in Taylor's terms, external: It depends upon secondary knowledge about a performed version of the play that may—or, as I will be arguing, may not—be identical to the first printed versions. It depends upon facts about a historical Oldcastle who may—or may not—be the referent for the play's pious lines. Taylor's further external arguments are equally open to suspicion. Noting persistent references to the name "Oldcastle" and arguing from them for the possibility of the retention of that name in subsequent performances of *1 Henry IV*, Taylor refuses to take seriously the possibility that the play called *Sir John Oldcastle* and not *1 Henry IV* is meant in the instances he cites. Taylor's belief that no one could have confused Shakespeare's play with Philip Henslowe's property is belied by the evidence of the 1664 Folio and its subsequent reprintings until Nicholas Rowe, which include *Sir John Oldcastle* as Shakespeare's. Moreover, even if a version of the play with Oldcastle in it was staged subsequent to the 1598 printing of *1 Henry IV*, there is no way of knowing whether its text was the same as the one that was printed; the argument that follows insists that the Oldcastle version of the play cannot have been identical to the one with Falstaff in it.

Taylor, however, has, or claims to have, internal evidence as well to support his argument that the earliest texts of the play are identical to that original performance save for the change of names, in which "the integrity of the individual work of art" was violated by the forced removal (the censorship) of the original names by yet another external agent. Two places in *1 Henry IV*, he argues, give evidence that nothing but the name has been changed. "The only verse line in which the character's surname appears," Taylor writes, "would be metrical if a three-syllable name had originally stood in place of the two-syllable 'Falstaff'" (85). The line in question occurs at the end of act 2, scene 2, when the prince turns to Poins after they have easily robbed the robbers:

Prince. Got with much ease. Now merrily to horse:
The thieves are all scatter'd and possess'd with fear
So strongly that they dare not meet each other;
Each takes his fellow for an officer!
Away, good Ned—Falstaff sweats to death,

And lards the lean earth as he walks along.
Were't not for laughing I should pity him.

Poins. How the fat rogue roared.

(2.2.99–106)

"Away, good Ned, Oldcastle sweats to death": Thus Taylor would have the line read. That way it would have ten syllables, the ten syllables we are to suppose it originally had. But would it be a more metrical line by the addition of that extra beat? Certainly not a more regular one: "Oldcastle" interrupts the iambs, while the line with "Falstaff" in it, although short by one syllable, is regular; the caesura before the name functions as a weak beat, and the accent on "Falstaff" occurs where one would expect it to be in a line of iambic pentameter. To claim that Shakespeare's line only is metrical with "Oldcastle" in it is to argue that it is the number of syllables in a line that makes it metrical, that Shakespearean versification is simply a matter of arithmetic.

That assumption is palpably incorrect; the line is metrical either way. There is, in short, no internal proof here that originally the line had "Oldcastle" in it. Moreover—and this is something Taylor only glances at in a footnote, something that editors only put in small type at the bottom of the page—these lines are printed as prose in the earliest editions. "The Quarto sets the whole speech as prose, but it is clearly verse," Taylor notes (85 n. 4). *"As Pope; prose QqF"* the Arden lemma reads. Ever since Alexander Pope rearranged these lines as verse, editors have succumbed to his relineation as if it discovered the essential poet buried in the prose. "Shakespeare may have intended verse but failed to make the lines clear," A. R. Humphreys comments about the end of act 2, scene 2 in his Arden edition (xx); "the comic narrative stimulates him to metre while the wit-play stays in prose." That "comic narrative," in Humphreys's account, is nothing less than the destiny of the English nation, embodied in Prince Hal, the future Henry V; as Hal escapes from his low companions and turns the tables upon them, he must "naturally" rise to verse. Versification assures us of the moral purity of the princely robber, and the lines are snatched away from the prosaic compositor who misunderstood the stimulant that moved the author's hand to stray into something that looked like prose. Humphreys divines Shakespeare's divine(ly) right intentions. Humphreys's comments follow upon Pope's agenda in his edition of Shakespeare, to give Shakespeare the poet's pretensions, rescuing him from the depredations of the actors and the printers. Printed as verse, some—but scarcely more than half—of these lines have ten syllables; some of them even scan. These lines are only "clearly verse" because they have been printed that way ever since 1725. Taylor's internal evidence here lies not in the text but in that slavish respect for tradition he so abhors.[5] "*Nature* and *Homer* were, he found, the *same*."[6]

Taylor's second piece of internal evidence is a pun, when the Prince names his companion "my old lad of the castle" (1.2.41). The phrase certainly depends upon the fact that Oldcastle was once the character's name. But does it secure the argument that in the original staging the character named Oldcastle was so addressed? While one could argue that the pun works better after the name had been changed—in which case it would allude to the suppressed name—it is perfectly possibly that the text originally had this rather lame pun. Taylor himself, however, provides a way of adjudicating this issue, although it undermines his argument. Looking to the plays in which Falstaff figures—*1 Henry IV, 2 Henry IV, Henry V, Merry Wives of Windsor*—Taylor notices in each of them a moment in which a space is opened in which Oldcastle's censored name is recalled. This is most palpably the case in the epilogue to *2 Henry IV* with its insistence that Falstaff is not Oldcastle, but it is equally the case in moments in the other plays when the character's name is forgotten—when, for instance, Fluellen needs to be prompted to supply the name of "the fat knight with the great-belly doublet" (*Henry V,* 4.7.50),[7] or when Mrs. Page claims to Mrs. Ford that she has forgotten the name of the knight who has supplied her husband with a page. "I have forgot his name," Fluellen says (4.7.52); "I can never hit on's name," Mrs. Page insists (*Merry Wives of Windsor,* 3.2.21).[8] Each time, as memory lapses, a pause occurs, and then the name "Sir John Falstaff"; each time, as Taylor powerfully argues, the audience is reminded of another name that cannot be recalled, made to recall what the play cannot.

The pun on "Oldcastle" could be like these moments, for what makes the pun possible is the fact that "old lad of the castle" is not a proper name but, as the Arden editor puts it, "a cant term for roisterer" (*1 Henry IV,* 1.2.41 n). Oldcastle is not named in the term; the pun depends upon the dispersal of his proper name. Of course, this possibility is there either in an original version in which "Oldcastle" is the character's name or in the Falstaff version. But what if *1 Henry IV* gave evidence, as the later plays do, of the forgetting of Falstaff's name—and with it the recall of a version of the play with "Oldcastle" in it? "What says Monsieur Remorse?"

From the start, he desires another name:

> **Falstaff.** Marry then sweet wag, when thou art king let us that are squires of the night's body be called thieves of the day's beauty: let us be Diana's foresters, gentlemen of the shade, minions of the moon; and let men say we be men of good government, being governed as the sea is, by our noble and chaste mistress the moon, under whose countenance we steal. (1.2.23–29)

From the start, he has many names: "Sir John Sack—and Sugar" (1.2.110); "Sir John Paunch" (2.2.63); "Ribs . . . Tallow" (2.4.109). Sir John does not seem to have a proper name. What it is has been forgotten.

When he plays the king, he attempts to summon up the name of the sole companion his son must not cast off, that one "virtuous man" he has "often noted" in the prince's company. "I know not his name" (2.4.414). The prince prompts his recollection, and soon the swelling belly delivers the name: "[A]nd now I remember me, his name is Falstaff. If that man should be lewdly given, he deceiveth me" (2.4.419–21). The joke is so good that it comes again, after the prince and his companion switch parts. Now the prince, speaking as his father, singles out a monster. "I would your Grace would take me with you: whom means your Grace?" Falstaff, playing the prince, interrupts; to be answered: "That villainous abominable misleader of youth, Falstaff, that old white-bearded Satan" (2.4.454–57). Twice, then, a pause interrupts the production of the name; first, to supply the virtue lacking in the old name; then, to dispel the possibility that the new name has quite effaced the old, "that old white-bearded Satan." From the start, Falstaff says, he wishes that he and the prince "knew where a commodity of good names were to be bought" (1.2.81). As they exchange parts in this play within the play, they jostle over the name the boon companion has acquired thanks, if not to Diana herself, then to her Lord Chamberlain. He too puts in a disguised appearance in the play, clothed, like "Oldcastle," in the guise of a pun, in the possibility that the proper name can be dispersed. "What ho! Chamberlain!" Gadshill calls (2.1.46)—Gadshill, the setter of the robbery, the thief whose name also is not quite proper, since it also names the place of the robbery; "'At hand, quoth pick-purse'" (2.1.47), the chamberlain, arriving, replies to the thief's call, his first line a citation of a proverb. He does not own the line; it is not properly his. Is it the Lord Chamberlain's line, a line that belongs to the hand that struck out "Oldcastle" and that allowed the name to be recalled, but only in a proverb? "My old lad of the castle; . . . is not a buff jerkin a most sweet robe of durance?" (1.2.41–42). "What says Monsieur Remorse?"

The gaps, the multiple names, the glances at the queen and her chamberlain—these, I would argue, are as compelling as the instances that Taylor cites for the plays with "Falstaff" in them; like them, they make the argument that the *1 Henry IV* we have is not the play that originally had "Oldcastle" in it but a text revised to re-mark the censored name and even the agents of that censorship.[9] The outside has entered the inside, and the external agents of censorship and suppression cannot be distinguished from the hand writing. The absent name is marked by "damnable iteration," as Falstaff calls it (1.2.88); it is paralleled by a censorship represented in the play when the king forbids mention of another name:

Hotspur. He said he would not ransom Mortimer,
Forbade my tongue to speak of Mortimer,
But I will find him when he lies asleep,
And in his ear I'll holla "Mortimer!"
Nay, I'll have a starling shall be taught to speak
Nothing but "Mortimer," and give it him
To keep his anger still in motion.
(1.3.217–23)

Instead, to keep the censors at bay, another name is insisted upon:

Falstaff. No, my good lord; banish Peto, banish Bardolph, banish Poins—but for sweet Jack Falstaff, kind Jack Falstaff, true Jack Falstaff, valiant Jack Falstaff, and therefore more valiant, being as he is old Jack Falstaff, banish not him thy Harry's company, banish not him thy Harry's company, banish plump Jack, and banish all the world. (2.4.468–74)

"I do, I will," the prince responds. And so does Gary Taylor.

What Taylor proposes is not restoration but censorship of the texts we have. This is most apparent when Taylor turns to what the text would mean were "Oldcastle" to appear in it. The claim is that just as the lexical substitution would restore an originary text, so the name would secure and fix historical referentiality. "Oldcastle" in the text would be the real historical Oldcastle; his lines would now refer us to that figure—he would be that figure—and it would be apparent that Shakespeare's depiction of him was a scoffing representation of the Protestant martyr.[10] "Oldcastle really was a soldier," Taylor writes; "Sir John's appearance at the King's side, in the council before the battle of Shrewsbury (5.1), would therefore not have seemed as incongruous with 'Oldcastle' as it does with 'Falstaff'" (93). What "really was" enters the text, securing congruity, despite the representation of Sir John in the scene. Its meaning would be contained within the historical referent; the play would be delimited to a singular history. History, in this way of thinking, always is one and the same: It is the locus of truth—of incontestable facts; meaning is likewise univocal. Oldcastle—in the play, in real life—"really was" a Protestant martyr, and his depiction in the play once he has his proper name would confirm Taylor's suspicion that Shakespeare was a papist (100). All of Taylor's claims meet in the final sentences of the essay; Oldcastle's name secures, in Taylor's words, "the recovery and the restoration of the original authoritative *logos*" (100). What's in a name? another Shakespearean character asks. Taylor's answer, the original, singular *logos,* in fact covers many names. In the place of "Oldcastle" one could read "God," "Shakespeare," "History," "Meaning"—multiple names for the singular origin supposedly to be found lodged in "Oldcastle." For Taylor, all these are one and the same. Such is the phantasmatic nature of the so-called proper name.[11]

These restorations, made in the name of "the integrity of the individual work of art" and, congruously, "the integrity of the individual"—call him Oldcastle or Shakespeare—relentlessly reduce multiplicity to singularity. This text of *1 Henry IV* is the one and only text, unrevised. The character's name is likewise fixed, referring to the real. But in these claims, Shakespeare's hand is being held firmly in the censor's grip, for the exterior has violated the very integrity Taylor wishes to secure; claiming to free Shakespeare—and to allow him artistic autonomy—

Taylor ties him to a singular historical referent and to a singular meaning. Through the proper name, all sorts of propriety are secured in the transcendental name of the *logos.* Scorning the priesthood—the editors—who idolatrously worship the received, transmitted text, Taylor's restoration would return editors to the one true faith, making the author central to the canon of English literature his scribe. "New *Presbyter* is but old *Priest* writ large."[12]

The evidence reads otherwise. The play *1 Henry IV* is written not with one hand but with two. It opens upon the scene of censorship, punctuates its referentiality at the very moment it names Falstaff and with him the suppressed name of Oldcastle. When it puns upon "Oldcastle"—or assigns Gadshill a name that is also the name of the place of the robbery—it disperses the proper name and punctures the fantasies of propriety that Taylor would secure. History enters the text, and the writer is in history, but not as some stable ground of singular meaning and determination. The historical is a field of contestation and submission, and so too is the Shakespearean text. And while Taylor's restoration claims to ground the text in history, his historical restoration would remove the traces of the history that produced the earliest texts of *1 Henry IV.* It would stop history in the *logos.* It would produce a cleaned-up text, one in which there could be but one meaning.

So doing, Taylor repeats something that can be seen in the text of *1 Henry IV* after it was submitted to the censors. For, as editors regularly note, the text of *1 Henry IV* is a remarkably clean one, one made proper by the demands of the censors that a cleaned-up text be produced to replace the offending one.[13] In Taylor's account, only the names have been changed (John Jowett supplements the argument by seeing the suppression of an original Harvey and Russell as congruent changes in the text).[14] Yet if only the names had had to be changed, the compositors might have been told to perform a simple act of mechanical substitution of names. The clean text of *1 Henry IV,* however, does not suggest that behind it stood authorial foul papers; rather, it suggests a scribal transcription. The clean printed text suggests that there was more to changing the text than changing the names, that the foul papers had grown so foul in revision that they had become illegible, or that the author had rewritten so much that only a fair copy would do.[15] Yet here and there in the margins of *1 Henry IV,* a stray "Russell" and "Harvey" put in an appearance, signs that the copiest (a scribe who might also have been the author) or the compositor, busily attending to much else, had lapsed in the performance of the merely mechanical task of substituting new names for the old ones. And once, even, "Old." appears in the margin, not, as it happens, in *1 Henry IV* but in its sequel. Its appearance, which Taylor takes as further support for his argument that "Falstaff" was once "Oldcastle," that the two characters are identical, in fact embarrasses his case,[16] not merely because it suggests that more was involved in printing the play than substituting the name, but in its very insistence on the name that was supposed to be suppressed. The Lord Chief Justice addresses Sir John: "I think," he says, "you are fallen into the disease, for you hear not what I say to you." And the fat knight replies: "Very well, my lord, very well. Rather, and't please you, it is the disease of not listening, the malady of not marking, that I am troubled withal" (*2 Henry IV,* 1.2.117–21). Not marked out, in the margin, is the speech prefix "Old." for this speech in defense of not marking. "Old." remains—thanks to whose hand?—to mark what the censor, inside the play and outside it, would have marked out. This double structure of the mark re-marks the proper name, denying it all the properties of an originary *logos;* the name is written within a dispersal that refuses selfsameness, a history of marking and re-marking. It is produced and erased at once, remembered and forgotten in a relationship between the margin and the text, the outside and the inside, that never can be stabilized through some originary meaning, some fixed history, some text restored to singular propriety, an inside protected against all time from the outside. This mark, intentional or inadvertent, rebellious or accidental, original or secondary, re-marks the limits of Taylor's originary designs upon the Shakespearean text, a lapse in the mechanisms of censorship made in whatever name.

Hal's Desire, Shakespeare's Idaho

The *Henry IV* plays are, no doubt, history plays, yet their relationship to at least one kind of history—the history of sexuality—has gone largely unexamined.[1] The reasons for this are not all that difficult to understand. Sexuality is often thought to be nothing other than heterosexuality, and, especially in relationship to the central drama of these plays—the prince's ascendance to the throne—there is little to be said on that score. The fact that women are exiguous in this political plot could make the plays available to the kind of gender analysis that takes as foundational and virtually transhistorical the exclusion and subordination of women (assumptions that shape the argument of Phyllis Rackin's *Stages of History*);[2] such analyses often also assume that gender relations are always already structured invidiously by an equally transhistorical heterosexuality. Thus, to raise, as I will be doing here, questions around the history of sexuality might have consequences for how one understands the historicity of gender and might lead, even by way of such unpromising texts as the *Henry IV* plays, to the prospect of a more fully inflected reading of gendered difference.

The history of sexuality is by no means a field that is so established that one can refer to it in an offhand fashion, however. For my purposes here, since I am using his title, *The History of Sexuality,* the name of Michel Foucault might be invoked (along with other historians who advocate social constructionist views, among whom Jeffrey Weeks might be cited as of particular importance),[3] especially for a set of pronouncements in *The History of Sexuality*[4] which I take as guiding assumptions: that the regime of heterosexuality is a modern one, that it came into existence at the same time as (if not slightly later than) the identification of a sexual identity formation called homosexuality, and that the early modern period in which Shakespeare wrote did not know such distinctions. Rather, Foucault audaciously argues that sexuality per se is a modern phenomenon (the argument may be familiar by now, but it remains remarkably counterintuitive to many); whereas the Renaissance and ages before had managed marriage relations between men and women as a means of conveying property, title, and privilege—a host of social relations that Foucault calls "alliance" in *The History of Sexuality*—these sociolegal ties are not the site for sexuality, if by that term one means a supposed personal core that defines individual desire and structures identity as a consequence of such desires. In the nineteenth century, Foucault argues, a vast sexual science was developed; from its panoply of sexual possibilities (masturbators, zoophiles, sadists, masochists, and fetishists of every imaginable variety) emerged the dichotomy in which everyone is presumably straight or gay and in which object choice alone defines sexuality. (The confusions around these suppositions, and the reasons to be skeptical about them, are a central subject of Eve Kosofsky Sedgwick's immensely powerful *Epistemology of the Closet.*)[5]

What Foucault's argument implies in terms of a reading of the *Henry IV* plays within the history of sexuality is that the absence of women from the central drama of the play—which might, now, be recast as Hal's desire to arrive in his father's place—does not make the plays simply available for a reading of homosexuality in them. Such an alternative reading would be as deeply anachronistic as any that mistakes the management of gender relations in Shakespeare for an account of heterosexuality in the Elizabethan age. Gay readings of Shakespeare have been made, of course, particularly in relation to the sonnets, from Oscar Wilde's *Portrait of Mr. W. H.* on; however, the history of criticism on the sonnets (the academic formation being, as it happens, virtually coincident with the history we are considering here) has in large measure been characterized by massive evasions of the erotics of the poems or, more recently, as in Joseph Pequigney's *Such Is My Love,*[6] by dehistoricized banalizations of them. (Pequigney is to be credited, however, with pointing out that the ways the sonnets have been "universalized" has involved treating them as the repository for timeless wisdom about love, the timeless and the universal always turning out to be nothing other than the heterosexual.) In reading male-male relations in the *Henry IV* plays, I will be arguing that the syntax of relations mapped in the sonnets can also be found in the plays, not to argue (as Wilde does in *The Portrait of Mr. W. H.*) that these texts participate in some transhistorical homosexuality but to seek to understand how male-male relations in the plays—relations that are or that *could be* construed as sexual—are to be read before the modern regimes of sexual identities can be presumed as reference points.

Luckily, powerfully suggestive ways of addressing such questions have been provided before. Alan Bray's *Homosexuality in Renaissance England*[7] and the reading of Shakespeare's sonnets in Sedgwick's *Between Men: English Literature and Male Homosocial Desire*[8] provide necessary analytic tools for this enterprise. Sedgwick's importation of the social scientists' term "homosocial" provides literary critics with a crucial lexical item to describe male-male social relations that can, but need not, be sexual. Bray's book is keenly attuned to the fact that its title advances an anachronism that its every page seeks to address. "To talk of an individual in this period as being or not being 'a homosexual' is an anachronism and ruinously misleading," Bray writes (16); rather, he focuses on terms available in the period, particularly on "sodomy" as the nearest word in the Renaissance lexicon for what moderns might call homosexuality. In doing so, he agrees with Foucault, who points to sodomy as that which ruins alliance, sodomy thereby comprising a range of sexual practices all bent on frustrating the marital tie and the presumption that marriage exists only to ensure legitimate sexual acts: those leading to procreation. Memorably, Foucault labels sodomy an "utterly confused category" (101), and one of Bray's aims is to show that the term includes a wide range of sexual practices. It would limit and confuse things to assume that the modern homo-hetero distinction gives one much analytic purchase in dealing with a sociosexual order that found "sodomy" a term capacious enough to include bestiality, adultery, rape, and prostitution, to name only some of the possible kinds of debaucheries that are not organized in terms of the distinction of gendered object choices. (This is not to imply that sodomy occupies an archaic register utterly unavailable to us now—the term and some of its ancient confusions survive into modernity in U.S. law—nor is it to imply that something like an archaeology of the homo-hetero distinction cannot be traced in the Renaissance, a point to which I will return.) Even more to the point of a reading of the *Henry IV* plays—indeed, this is crucial—is Bray's insistence (fully congruent with Foucault's pitting of sodomy against alliance) that these sexual possibilities register only in particular social circumstances: Sodomy names a crime, not a behavior, and sodomites were likely to be accused as well of treason, atheism (or Roman Catholicism, virtually the same thing in Renaissance England), sedition, and the like. Whereas alliance is part of a social fabric, sodomy destroys it.

As Bray argues in the crucial third chapter of *Homosexuality in Renaissance England,* because sodomy was demonized, it necessarily existed at some distance from actual sociosexual relations (think of the work that the word "communists" used to do or that "terrorists" does now). There is every reason to suppose that those accused of being sodomites did what others did as well. For, as Bray suggests, in a world that has not assumed that people make sexual choices on the basis of excluding one gender or the other, it seems likely that members of the same sex will be having sex with each other, and in ways so ordinary as to be virtually unperceived—necessarily unperceived, if the only label for such relations was sodomy and if sodomy was a world-destroying practice. Bray assumes, in fact, that the very structures that assured order and provided conduits for power in the Elizabethan age were the sites for practices that might be called sexual, that hierarchies and social differences were maintained or created by sexual relations. It is, to complicate Bray's point, perhaps more accurate to say that upon these sites something that retrospectively would be called sexuality fastened. In this culture, servants regularly slept together or with their masters, as did pupils with their teachers. Indeed, Bray argues, the hierarchies of public life (which, in effect, almost always means male-male relations of the sort featured in the *Henry IV* plays) were oiled with such sexual possibilities if not virtually requiring them as part of relationships of patronage; in fact, in "Homosexuality and the Signs of Male Friendship in Elizabethan England,"[9] Bray claims that as the social order swerved farther from the social ties summarized under the word "friendship" (ties that could include patronage relations, diplomatic bargaining, and influence trading of all sorts), the acts that constituted evidence for sodomy came to be increasingly indistinguishable from those that maintained the normative ties. Bray argues that changes in the social structure in sixteenth-century England that marked the breakdown of an older social order are the largest context in which this crisis of definition occurred. The ties of friendship were no longer those uniting gentlemen. Thus, whereas Henry VIII had instituted the Gentlemen of the Privy Chamber as his bedfellows, and his companions were nominally aristocratic, by the end of the century, in *The Arte of English Poesie* (1589), George Puttenham could imagine that a social climbing poet might claim such a position too. Henry VIII, he reports in the eighth chapter of the first book of that volume, made Sternhold groom of the privy chamber for versifying the psalms, and what the king did, Puttenham holds up as an example for Queen Elizabeth I.[10]

It is in such a context that one can see how euphemized it is to speak of the sonnets to the young man as bids for patronage—as Arthur Marotti does[11]—as if a desire for favors meant only money or position. One can also see that however sexualizable these social relations are—and the language of the sonnets is hardly desexualized—these are not poems about homosexual relations; nor are they about sodomy. The poems are not written with any assumption about exclusive identities, and in that respect it is useful to recall that the first group urges the young man to marry, an injunction that is not seen as an alternative to the young man's relations with the speaker of the poems. Nowhere are the suggestions of sexual relations between men taken to constitute the antisocial behavior of the sodomite. If anything like sodomy does appear in the sonnets, it is in relation to the so-called dark lady of the final poems, a woman with whom promiscuous, nonmarital sex occurs; this is seen as debauched and transgressive sex, not least because it threatens to destroy the relation between the sonneteer and his beloved young man. That conflict, seen in these terms, is not one between homo- and heterosexuality.

Sedgwick's reading of the sonnets, which seeks to vacate the modern lexicon of homo-hetero difference to describe far more labile desires that cannot be captured by those labels, begins to offer tools for further differentiating and relating male-male and male-female sexual relations. Like Bray, she sees that male-male sexual relations need not be read as outside the normative systems that promote male interests at the expense of women (the homosocial order can be a patriarchal one and can seek to erase women, allowing them no function beyond serving as conduits for relations between men); tellingly, she argues that as homosexuality becomes more visible and differentiated in the modern period, men who choose other men as sexual partners become subject to annihilative pressures congruent with those placed upon women. Misogyny and homophobia, though hardly reducible to each other, are nevertheless inevitably intertangled. But these relations will not be the same in different historical periods, nor is there an easy calculus to map these volatile relations; the history of sexuality provides necessary leverage for any understanding of the historicity of gender and of gender relations.

It is from this cautionary position that I would mention one final frame for reading the *Henry IV* plays, one way critics of Renaissance literature have recently adduced "homosexuality" in Shakespeare. I have in mind arguments about cross-dressing, where the presence of the boy actor beneath the woman's clothes has been taken to mean that the only sexual desire that exists in Shakespeare is homosexual desire. Despite major differences in their arguments and approaches, for instance, this is a point of agreement between Stephen Greenblatt in "Fiction and Friction"[12] and Lisa Jardine in *Still Harping on Daughters.*[13] When Jardine conveniently forgets that women formed a considerable portion of the audience for plays, she leaves out something that must complicate the circulation of desire in the theater (antitheatricalists, in fact, worry more about promiscuous debauch among men and women than anything else). An account like Greenblatt's betrays a complicity between misogyny and male-male desire, since it assumes that male-male desire can only batten on, even as it opposes, male-female desire. In these accounts (and others as well), transvestism is taken to reveal a homosexuality that is claimed really to be a heterosexuality manqué; the assumption made (even by feminist and gay affirmative critics, who should have no interest in making such arguments) is that the only difference upon which desire moves is gender difference, a position ably dismantled in Michael Warner's "Homo-Narcissism; or, Heterosexuality."[14] Against such claims, one would want to argue that in a culture, like Shakespeare's, that did not make the homo-hetero distinction, the availability of either gender as a sexual partner cannot be understood through our modern categories (themselves, it hardly needs to be said, suspect). Valuable at a theoretical level would be the point that Marjorie Garber argues in *Vested Interests,*[15] that the transvestite is a necessary and foundational third term—or third sex—that disrupts the more usual plotting of sexual difference in terms of binaries and dichotomies. (Their bankruptcy is further suggested by the structuring contradiction that treats men and women both as opposites and yet as "made for each other.") Although Garber's third term may be questioned for its own normalizing and stabilizing effects—she allies it, for example, with the Lacanian Symbolic and, thus, implicitly with the law—she nevertheless points to a highly impoverished way of thinking about gender that, one could argue, is a consequence of the simplification that the hetero-homo distinction makes. In the Elizabethan period, it is, I believe, arguable, just for starters, that boys are a different sex—neither men nor women—so that there are at least three genders in the period and a corresponding geometrically increased number of sexualities. These cut across the binarism of gender, but they also are structured by (or violate) other boundaries—of age and status, most notably. It is these crossings that provide much of the excitement in the sonnets, when the older, often abject sonneteer addresses the young man, whose youth may place him in the position of his pupil but whose money and social status makes him the older man's master—make him that unless, of course, the young man is, as Oscar Wilde in *The Portrait of Mr. W. H.* and others since have sometimes thought, a boy actor, pretending to more than he has and also possessed of a beauty that seems to feminize him, casting him as the cross-dressed master-mistress. This is a cross-dressing that he seems virtually to embody, though, as Sedgwick argues, however much it makes him a "dumb blonde," it also renders him "exaggeratedly phallic. . . . He represents the masculine as pure object."[16] From such observations, Sedgwick delivers a sweeping summary that points the path for the inquiry that follows. "Gender and genitals we have always with us," she writes (perhaps a bit overconfidently, but one has to start somewhere), "but 'family,' 'sexuality,' 'masculine,' 'feminine,' 'power,' 'career,' 'privacy,' 'desire,' the meanings and substance of gender and genitals, are embodied in times and institutions, literature among them" (47).[17]

The opening scenes of *1 Henry IV*[18] locate Hal's career—his desire for the throne—in the context of others' desires for his arrival there. First, we catch the king in a narcoleptic moment, having virtually forgotten his wayward son and recalling him only as he spins out the fantasy of the son he desires, Hotspur. The king's wish—that "some night-tripping fairy had exchang'd" (1.1.86) children, so that Hotspur might be his Harry—conditions the plot of replacement brought to a close at Shrewsbury, when Hal steps into the place of this desired alter ego. How phantasmatic this desire is, both on the part of the king and his son—and therefore how much it might exceed the requirements of paternal succession and royal inheritance and bring the homosocial distribution of power between men onto a sexualizable terrain—is suggested by the degree to which the king's wish resonates with another royal plot of desire, the one in *A Midsummer Night's Dream.* There, Oberon defeats Titania in order to possess the Indian boy, a changeling like the desired son in Henry IV's fantasy; the fairy king desires him as a companion, not as a successor, however, and this begins to suggest that the paternal fantasy of producing mirror children (the imaginary terrain described by Theseus in *A Midsummer Night's Dream* as the paternal power of duplication, the ability to figure or disfigure the wax impression of the child)[19] may be as opposed to the maternal and to procreation within marriage as Oberon is. Such image production also conditions the reproduction of the figure of the fair young man in the sonnets from the moment when the possibility that the young man will marry and reproduce is abandoned.

In the second scene of *1 Henry IV,* another voice is heard yearning for Hal's arrival, and it too offers a model for the legitimate heir based in a rebellious—and self-duplicating—alter ego. Falstaff, like the king, desires the prince's arrival, perhaps even more insistently, as is suggested by the refrain that punctuates the first words he addresses to Hal in the play: "I prithee sweet wag, when thou art king . . . Marry then sweet wag, when thou art king" (1.2.16, 23). Falstaff's desire for Hal to be a king of thieves is only a hair's breadth from the king's desire for his son to equal or to replace the rebel Hotspur; for him to legitimize the king's desire by being illegitimate; indeed, for Hal to arrive in his father's place by being as illegitimate as his father, a usurper and a rebel himself, once was. Falstaff's longing and its echo of the royal desire baffles the commonplace critical distinction between good and bad fathers in the *Henry IV* plays, complexly intertwining legitimate and illegitimate desires: paternities and surrogate sonships, heirs and rebels. The territory of desire does not seem safely contained by the homosocial and patriarchal orders.

Not that Falstaff is presented in any direct way as a sexual partner for Hal. It remained for Gus Van Sant, in his translation of the relation between Hal and Falstaff into modern terms in the film *My Own Private Idaho* (1991), to realize these possibilities. There, Falstaff, now called Bob, is the leader of a gang of street kids, many of them hustlers, and including Scott, the mayor's son. This latter-day Hal affirms the supposition of his companion—his Poins, the narcoleptic Mike—that he has had a "thing" with Bob; Bob, he says, loved him. Van Sant's film does not present this unequivocally as a sign of a homosexual relationship; rather, he explores the permeable borders between homo- and heterosexuality, and in ways that are suggestive for reading Shakespeare and the cultural situation in which he writes, one that has yet to invent these supposedly opposing forms of love and desire. While, to follow Bray, in Elizabethan culture, sex could maintain male-male hierarchies and function as a site of exchange, in the film the cash nexus that defines prostitution allows for sexual crossings that need not testify to choices of identity. Thus, although Mike is a hustler, he also loves Scott and wants to have sex with him for that reason, while Scott claims that he only sleeps with men for money. Indeed, Scott's use of this claim functions as a site of refusal of homosexual identity even as it allows him to have homosexual sex. In this context, Scott's conversion to "normalcy" is markedly different from Hal's in one respect: It involves the assumption of heterosexuality, acquiring a wife, and renouncing not merely Mike's and Bob's company but also, indeed more importantly, sex with men. It remains like Hal's conversion, however, in one respect: It is a site of betrayal.

No such renunciation, in fact, marks Hal's arrival, and no wife appears at the end of *2 Henry IV.* This suggests that the *Henry IV* plays are far less direct in their depiction of sex and sexuality than Van Sant's film is, in part because the sexual domains that characterize modernity have yet to come into existence and therefore will not define the transformation or self-realization of the prince. This means that what could be called sexual in the plays will not be represented along axes that correspond to modern definitions. It helps to recall Bray's arguments at this point: that sodomy in the period will always be voiced through or alongside other charges and that the possibility of making sodomy visible depends upon its being attached to a social disruption that cannot be ignored. The king sees "riot and dishonour stain" (*1 Henry IV,* 1.1.84) his son's face; he sees Falstaff as the blot on his son's character, the mark made where the paternal impression should be. One sign of the ways this illegitimate mark gets connected to the paternal impression can be found in the lines Hal speaks at the moment of his arrival into his father's place, at the end of Part 2, for he can see no difference between the dead father and the companion he is about to cast off (Van Sant goes even further, allowing Scott to declare his Falstaff a better and more beloved father even as he rejects him, a declaration that therefore functions to mark Scott's "conversion" to heterosexuality as a self-betrayal motivated by social regulation):

> My father is gone wild into his grave,
> For in his tomb lie my affections;
> And with his spirits sadly I survive
> To mock the expectation of the world,
> To frustrate prophecies, and to raze out
> Rotten opinion, who hath writ me down
> After my seeming.
>
> (2 *Henry IV*, 5.2.123–29)

Harry replaces Harry here (5.2.49) as he had replaced another Harry at the end of Part 1 ("Harry to Harry shall, hot horse to horse, / Meet" [4.1.122–23]), and the Lord Chief Justice, *chosen* as father now in place of both the king and Falstaff, is the father only of the newest self-simulation, the artificial paternity that the king first dreamed, the position that Falstaff assumed. Hal is still bent, as he was in his first soliloquy in Part 1, on the mockery of expectation and the falsifications that are coincident with his truth, and this double erasure and the announcement of a new father figure is one more suspect legitimizing gesture. The parallel between this moment of arrival and the defeat of Hotspur at the end of Part 1 is another. All these suggest that the plays continually negotiate Hal's career in terms of relations between men.

In his first soliloquy in *1 Henry IV* and in the fulfillment of his promise to the king that he will prove himself the king's true son by taking upon himself the form of Hotspur's honor, Hal composes an image of himself in which he is at once both Harrys: Hotspur and his father, legitimate and illegitimate at the same time. Doing so, he makes himself the very simulacrum that the king sees in act 3, scene 2, when he reflects on how much alike they are (144–52). Hal's offer to redeem himself and prove himself the king's true son involves taking the form of Hotspur, the very shape of a royal desire that is all too like Falstaff's illegitimate desire for Hal. (In *My Own Private Idaho,* one further way such complexities are translated is by having Scott appear for the reconciliation scene with his father dressed in his most outrageous street hustler guise: denim jacket, naked chest, slave collar. When he goes down on his knees and buries his head in his father's lap, momentarily it looks as if a blow job is about to occur, thereby recalling the first scene in the film after the opening title sequence, which begins with Mike receiving a blow job and ends with him telling lies about his father.) Indeed, Hal's description of how he will replace Hotspur offers another version of the razing and replacement imaged when dead king and boon companion stand in for and erase one another to produce the final Harry at the end of the pair of plays:

> I will redeem all this on Percy's head,
> And in the closing of some glorious day
> Be bold to tell you that I am your son,
> When I will wear a garment all of blood,
> And stain my favours in a bloody mask,
> Which, wash'd away, shall scour my shame with it.
> (*1 Henry IV,* 3.2.132–37)

Hal's promised redemption involves a restaining and scouring that produces not exactly himself but, as he goes on to say, an exchange like the one his father dreamed of: "I shall make this northern youth exchange / His glorious deeds for my indignities" (3.2.145–46). This shameless deed rewrites Harry's brow as unspotted only by casting the northern youth as the locus of his glory; that the lines also promise to "engross" (3.2.148) these deeds further implicates this rewriting in the one that Part 2 brings to a close, when Hal's gross companion is cast off, leaving engrossing Hal once again supposedly unstained.

The rewriting here—the staining and erasing—aims at legitimizing the illegitimate. This is a political project, to be sure, but that in no way guarantees—the opposite, in fact—that it will not be played out in a bodily register. Hal can engross, but unlike his fat companion, his body fails to serve as the register of what he has done. Falstaff's *gross* body is not Hal's *engrossed* one, and the "base contagious clouds" (*1 Henry IV* 1.2.193), "the foul and ugly mists / Of vapours" (1.2.197–98) that figure

Falstaff's flatulent body[20] suggest a form of anality—sodomy—that Hal's anal economies seek to overcome.

Hal's arrival—easily exposed as calculating and as involving the defeat of Hotspur and, even more insupportably, the casting off of Falstaff—remains, for all that, something readers of the play may be expected to desire. How this is so depends on recognizing the mechanism the play produces to engage such desires, the way the desire for arrival serves as an endless dissimulation of legitimate and illegitimate desires. In this context, it is worth recalling arguments made by William Empson, more than fifty years ago, in a few pages in *Some Versions of Pastoral* that have never received the critical attention that they deserve.[21] Empson forthrightly notes the register of desire that I believe must be taken into account. The prince has been cast in the part of the fair young man of the sonnets, he writes, and "Harry has no qualities that are obviously not W.H.'s" (108). Falstaff's desire, even what is made of the father's desire, is, in this light, not to be distinguished from the desire of the sonneteer, always ready to take upon himself the faults of the faultless young man:

> Henry's soliloquy [at the end of act 1, scene 2] demands from us just the sonnets' mood of bitter complaisance; the young man must still be praised and loved, however he betrays his intimates, because we see him all shining with the virtues of success. (104)

In his soliloquy, Hal makes up to the audience by promising to cast off his bad company (by the end of Part 2, as we have seen, his father makes up part of that disreputable crew). As Empson observes, Hal gives one further twist to the dynamics upon which the male-male relations in the sonnets depend: It is the prince, speaking in the position of the young man, who proclaims his own perfection and dumps his faults upon those who love and desire him. Empson concludes, "We have the central theme of all the sonnets of apology; the only difference, though it is a big one, is that this man says it about himself" (105).

How Hal's self-love and corruption get a saving translation is suggested, for instance, in Falstaff's repeated claims that the prince has corrupted him. For the truth he points to is that no one in these plays is innocent, that predation is endemic, increasingly and overtly so in Part 2. From the first scene in Part 1 in which they are together to the final repudiation, Falstaff stands to be abused. It is often said that we desire Falstaff's resurgence (given in his resurrection at the end of Part 1, half promised in the epilogue to Part 2), but if so, it is because that is his condition throughout the plays; comebacks are his forte. Falstaff teaches us to see the prince as a sweet wag; he also shows us a thousand ways to prevaricate, to keep believing in the prince as he keeps letting Falstaff down. Somewhere along the line, the abuse of Falstaff becomes the lure of the prince—or, at least, that is what the plays count on, and numerous readers who acclaim the prince's arrival in his father's place attest to this effect. The equation of good and bad fathers at the end of *2 Henry IV* is supposed to work to secure our love for Hal. Ideally—ideologically—at least, that is how desire is being channeled to fulfill the play's legitimizing political project. This is more or less what Hal declares in his first soliloquy, positioning the audience to assume the stance of the sonneteer, to love him despite his faults. If this makes us Falstaff, it is the Falstaff of an exchange like this one:

Prince. Sirrah, do I owe you a thousand pound?
Falstaff. A thousand pound, Hal? A million, thy love is
worth a million, thou owest me thy love.
(*1 Henry IV* 3.3.134–36)

This declaration of love is protected from being read at face value: Falstaff is once again being shamed, caught out this time lying to the Hostess and defrauding her (Hal can even, for a moment, appear to be the protector of women, a stance given the lie in *2 Henry IV,* act 5, scene 4 when the Hostess and Doll Tearsheet are sent off to prison). As Empson says, "the more serious Falstaff's expression of love becomes the more comic it is, whether as hopeless or as hypocrisy" (109); his love can always look like a form of rapacity. Nevertheless, the complex trajectories of Falstaff's declaration of love cannot fail to remind one of the structure of the sonnets. Indeed, as I remarked earlier, the royal desire for simulation participates in that project too. For, from the moment (at Sonnet 17) that the possibility is abandoned that the young man might, through marriage, be the source of an ever-fresh supply of duplicate young men, the sonnets seek to propagate the young man through the writing of his perfected image: the image declared perfect despite all the faults and failures revealed. Henry IV never specifies what stains his son's brow; although he characterizes him as a "young wanton, and effeminate boy" (5.3.1) in *Richard II,*[22] little afterwards would suggest that Hal is spending himself in the company of women (no bawdy houses for him, nor does the king ever think about a marriage for his son). Even in *Richard II,* Hal's "loose companions" (5.3.7) are highway robbers and tavern companions, a low-life milieu that appears as exclusively male as the public world of court and battlefield. These are the sites of struggle for Hal, and in them, the plays seem to occupy the terrain of Sonnets 18–126, with their production of an image of perfection and the tainted rebounds of that desire, the desire that I have suggested rebounds upon king, rebel, and tavern companion.

That criticism has not followed Empson is thus perfectly understandable, since it would require seeing how its celebrations of Prince Hal might come close to a love only Empson seems to have had no trouble naming. If one follows Empson and historicizes the connection he makes between the prince and the fair young man, one must see that what keeps the play from making more overt the love relation between Hal and his fat companion is the proximity of their relation to sodomy: the terms "stain," "riot," and "rebellion" suggest as much. The scandal of the play lies in suggesting how close that illegitimate desire might be to the usual workings of male-male relations, patriarchy in the play written, as we have seen, within the register of the sonnets' fantasies of duplicative inscription.[23] Hal, we know, is stained with riot, and the king fears he might join the rebels. His blot is embodied in Falstaff, his rebellion in Hotspur: They wear two of the faces of what the period calls sodomy. The very facts that Hal's misdeeds are never specified and that his riots are allied to Hotspur's rebellion but are supposed to be enacted in his relations with Falstaff place his "shame" on that unspeakable terrain. It is arguably that "shame" that Hal scours when he dispatches Hotspur. Yet the defeat of Hotspur at the end of Part 1 importantly marks Hal's path toward becoming the son the king desires; it even points ahead to the end of *Henry V,* for it is a Hotspur-like Hal who woos a wife (like Hotspur's, named Kate) in the voice of a plain soldier. Around Hotspur the plays negotiate an image of masculinity that serves to define the boundaries of what is allowable in relationships between men and between men and women. Hotspur, I argue, serves as the site for the production of a misogyny and an incipient homophobia—an incipient heterosexuality—that serves both purposes.

In this context, it is important to note the purposes that Lady Percy serves in the *Henry IV* plays. Though she appears in Part 1 largely to be abused and in Part 2 to memorialize her dead husband, she nonetheless functions between men, in Part 1 thereby legitimizing Hotspur's alliance with the rebel Mortimer by making it a family affair. (In Part 2 she is so much a part of the political atmosphere of the play that her fiction of an ideal Hotspur serves to encourage his father once again to betray the rebel cause.) Under the modern regimes of the supposed exclusiveness of male-male and male-female desire, it would seem as if Hotspur's wife guarantees his heterosexuality. Yet what she guarantees is alliance, and the figure of Hotspur is troubled—in his relations with women and with men—with the specter of effeminization.

This is explicit in the narrative that Hotspur offers to explain his refusal to behave as a vassal should, to explain why he has not given up his prisoners to the king; in making his excuse, Hotspur fastens on a courtier who arrived on the battlefield speaking "holiday and lady terms" (1.3.45), talking "like a waiting gentlewoman" (1.3.54), perfumed and taking snuff. Hotspur reports himself "pester'd with a popinjay" (1.3.49). How threateningly reversible this might be is suggested when Lady Percy calls her husband a paraquito (that is, a parakeet) (2.3.86) when he refuses her embraces in the name of his love for his horse and the masculine camaraderie of the battlefield. This is Hotspur's relation to Kate throughout Part 1; his exactions rebound, however, echoing his father's when Northumberland chastens the ranting Hotspur for what he calls his "woman's mood" (1.3.234). In that mood Hotspur is as impoverished in his vocabulary as the Welsh woman Hotspur would have his wife echo; he would train a bird—a starling—to parrot nothing more than "Mortimer" (1.3.221–2); the Welsh woman, Owen Glendower's daughter, can presumably say no more English. What Hotspur's father attempts with his son, Hotspur exacts with his wife in that scene among the rebels in Wales. When she calls him a paraquito, she speaks with his father's voice.

These representations of Hotspur serve at least two functions in *1 Henry IV.* As the site of a contradiction in the production of "proper" masculinity, Hotspur is, on the one hand, the locus of a normative misogyny defended against women and effeminization (a masculinity linked to that older order of aristocratic arms bearing, founded in the exchange of women that solidifies ties between men). But on the other hand, Hotspur is also a rebel; hence, the contradictory nature of the site he occupies, for what he achieves as a normative image is subject to the rebound accorded to him as rebel; thus, rebellion wears the face of femininity and theatricality. Hotspur's masculinity—emblematized by his devotion to his horse—is secured by the supplementary addition of a wife that assures that the all-male rebel world in which he thrives could not be tainted by the effeminacy of a perfumed courtier or of a man like Mortimer, who loves his wife too much. But what secures him is also what threatens to make his heroism a sham and his masculinity a performance guarding against what it is always in danger of revealing.

In *My Own Private Idaho,* Van Sant transfers the Welsh scene of *1 Henry IV* and the wooing scene at the end of *Henry V* to Italy,[24] and he has Scott fall in love with a woman whose native language is not English. Carmela has been taught English by Mike's mother, the figure he seeks and never finds in the movie. This suggests that Scott replaces Mike by way of the mother and the mother tongue. The heterosexual object has been produced for him by the woman also responsible for Mike's existence. At this juncture in Van Sant's film, Mike is as much Hotspur as he is Poins, and the killing of Hotspur, robbing him of his youth, is here, as it is with Falstaff/Bob, a matter of breaking a heart; in both cases, with Mike and with Bob, this is accomplished by making a heterosexual choice. (The conflation of Bob and Mike is suggested by our first glimpse of Mike in the film, wearing a shirt that has the name *Bob* on it, a crossing of identities that suggests how Shakespearean Van Sant's film is even when its text is not.) Carmela, like the Welsh woman Hotspur would have his wife be and yet whom he fears will emasculate him as she has Mortimer, further troubles Scott's assumption of heterosexual masculinity. Produced by Mike's mother and as a kind of Mike substitute, Carmela suggests that Scott's assumption of heterosexuality obeys cultural compulsions, not necessarily incompatible desires. (The English in which they communicate is not Carmela's mother tongue.) This is conveyed, too, by the fact that the scene in which Carmela and Scott are shown having sex is shot in the same way as the earlier scene in which Scott and Mike have sex with Hans. By shooting these scenes as a series of stills, Van Sant refuses either of them the teleological narrativity associated with sexual identity as culminating in the "mature" form of heterosexuality. It also suggests that the three-way—for money, supposedly—is another opportunity for Mike and Scott to have sex with each other, Scott having only once agreed to sleep with Mike without money being in question. But money is also in question with Carmela; when she appears with Scott in the funeral scene at the end of the movie, she forms part of his retinue as she had in the restaurant scene in which

Scott finally rejects Bob. Carmela functions as an acquisition and as part of Scott's inheritance, a guarantee of his newfound respectability like the three-piece suit he wears; she has cash value. The film thereby suggests that compulsory heterosexuality is a form of self-prostitution for the sake of "normalcy."

In the film, Scott is not, as Hal is in Shakespeare's play, at the center; Mike is, and what is plotted is not his arrival. Rather, this is a road movie whose path is recursive, a journey backwards to a mother who is never found, and forwards to a future that remains indefinite. Although Mike hopes to find his mother working at a hotel aptly named The Family Tree, the movie relentlessly works against the patriarchal plot; Mike's brother is also his father, and the incestuous relationship is thus as recursive as his journey on a road that he continually revisits and that has no end. That Mike is a narcoleptic has its Shakespearean resonances, for Van Sant is remembering what Shakespeare forgets: the mother, of course, but also Poins, one of those Shakespeare characters who simply disappear. The movie remembers him, prompted, in part, by Orson Welles's film *Chimes at Midnight* (1966), to which Van Sant pays continual homage and in which Hal is positioned repeatedly between Poins and Falstaff; if part of Van Sant's rewriting of Welles involves making explicit homosexual relations—which Welles tends to represent either phobically (for example, he represents Henry IV's desire for Hotspur as son as part of his "sick" behavior) or in euphemized ways (as free-for-all polymorphous perversity or as filial relationship)—through Mike, Van Sant offers a figure that holds up for scrutiny the lie that men cannot love men (a line Scott delivers) or that heterosexuality and homosexuality are necessarily mutually exclusive identities. Van Sant's "Poins" thus also rewrites Welles's, who is cast as a dark angel and a rival to Falstaff. Welles "remembers" him by having him point, at the end of *Chimes,* to the casket containing the body of Falstaff while uttering his name with total indifference to his fate.

In his remembering, Van Sant recasts Mike/Poins as the good angel Scott abandons (another Bob, as the name on his shirt testifies). This rewriting of Welles insists on the homoerotics that bind Scott and Mike, Hal and Poins/Hotspur. If we return now to the *Henry IV* plays and their plots of replacement to consider how Harry reproduces Harry—how Hal replaces Hotspur—we might note that the point of crossing is erotic attraction and rivalry. While Hotspur, in his woman's mood—

playing out in the sexual sphere what counts as rebellion in the political sphere—suffers no womanish man to compromise his masculinity, it is in the throes of such hypermasculinity that he wishes to meet Harry on the battlefield, "Harry to Harry," "hot horse to horse" (the slight asymmetry in Hotspur's phrase perhaps registers his attempt to maintain his advantage in the relation):

> Come, let me taste my horse,
> Who is to bear me like a thunderbolt
> Against the bosom of the Prince of Wales.
> Harry to Harry shall, hot horse to horse,
> Meet and ne'er part till one drop down a corse.
> (*1 Henry IV,* 4.1.119–23)

Hotspur responds here to Vernon's heavily eroticized depiction of Hal, vaulting "like feather'd Mercury" (4.1.106), his thighs tightly clenching the horse beneath, throned as Hotspur would be on his roan, the male horse he straddles. This is an image of Harry-as-Hotspur fully to be achieved when his rival lies dead at his feet. From Hotspur, Hal seeks a proper masculinity, a sexuality that will permit relations with men not tainted with effeminacy. But, as Empson suggests, some of this supposed achievement is marred immediately when Falstaff wounds the dead Hotspur in his thigh, delivering a counterfeit death blow that suggests that Hal cannot take from Hotspur what he most desires. The thigh wound is a sexual wound, Empson suggests, no doubt with a handbook like Jessie Weston's in mind, and that Falstaff can deliver it suggests what defeating Hotspur entails, what was being resisted, and where the charge of male-male erotics lies. If in his defeat of Hotspur Hal becomes the Phallus, it is, to quote Judith Butler, to reveal that "the Phallus is always already plastic and transferable,"[25] which is to say that it is not in any way the natural consequence of having a penis, that it is no one's (and no one gender's) property, and that as a construct it is movable and thereby contestable. How Hotspur's relation with Kate might redound upon Hal is suggested finally when he woos his Kate in *Henry V;* within the *Henry IV* plays, in which Hal is never seen involved with women, the moment closest to these occurs in an exchange with Poins in Part 2, the only other scene in the tetralogy in which a marriage is proposed for Hal, with Poins's sister, or so Falstaff claims. Hal's rejection of Nell constitutes a refusal to legitimize his relation with Poins through marriage with his sister: "Do you use me thus, Ned? Must I marry your sister?" (2.2.131)—such is the rebuff Hal delivers to the man he knows down to the peach stockings he wears.

The refusal to legitimize his male companion along the axis of alliance is not the same thing as the supposed differentiation of hetero- and homosexual object choice enacted when Scott chooses Carmela instead of Mike, although it is very likely that the scene between Hal and Poins conditions Van Sant's understanding of the relationship between Scott and Mike. In the *Henry IV* plays, the regimes of homo- and heterosexuality are only incipient, and more to the point is the remark the Hostess makes about Falstaff in *2 Henry IV,* that "he will spare neither man, woman, nor child" (2.1.16–17), that he is "a man queller, and a woman queller" (2.1.51–52), hence Hal's gift to him of the page boy who presciently promises to "tickle [the Hostess's] catastrophe" (2.1.59—but hence, too, Falstaff's relations with Doll and the Hostess). Falstaff's sexual tastes are those possible for any man.[26] Yet that these possibilities are not necessarily indifferent, but can be threatening, is suggested both by Hotspur's relation to his wife and the effeminate courtier and by Hal's negotiation of his relations with men, particularly with Hotspur and with Falstaff. One place this is especially clear is a theatrical scene that Hal imagines in *1 Henry IV,* in which his "damned brawn shall play Dame Mortimer" (2.4.107–8). Dame Mortimer is Hotspur's wife, but she is also the effeminized Mortimer, and for a moment Hal entertains the possibility that Falstaff might play Dame Mortimer, the woman, the feminized man to Hal's Hotspur. Hal imagines Hotspur and his wife in the same reductive mode that he does in his savage baiting of Francis—the show he does stage while awaiting Falstaff's arrival—all of them reduced to a trim reckoning. The scene participates in complex routings of identification and difference that exceed Hal's economizing, however, and we should note that Falstaff is made into a trial Kate only *after* Hal has (parrotlike) imitated her voice.

> "O my sweet Harry," says she, "how many hast thou killed today?" "Give my roan horse a drench," says he, and answers, "Some fourteen," an hour after, "a trifle, a trifle." I prithee call in Falstaff; I'll play Percy, and that damned brawn shall play Dame Mortimer his wife. (2.4.103–8)

This deflection of cross-gender identification has not been noticed by critics, who have all too easily read Falstaff *as* a woman, on the basis of his "gross" body and his corpulence, a reading first offered by W. H. Auden[27] and more recently by Patricia Parker.[28] Not only would one want to caution against the potential misogyny and homophobia of this connection, but one would also want to add that the size of the body is as much an index to class negotiations as it might be to gender and sexuality.[29] Here it would be worth mentioning, of course, that the ambivalences around Hotspur as chivalric and effeminate mark a crucial moment in bourgeoisification. Hal's new regime of trim reckonings (the predations of the engrossing arriviste that write themselves as civilized restraint) would cut the body down to size; it is mobilized against decaying aristocratic corpulence—the fat body that will come to be the body of the malnourished poor—and the woman's body. As Empson brilliantly noted, the point at which the eulogies for Falstaff and Hotspur cross comes when Hal summons up the *weight* of their bodies. Critics who repeat Hal's agendas in act 2, scene 4 as the truth of Falstaff's "female" body—rather than seeing it as a reflex against his own identification as a woman—or who associate Falstaff's loquacity with the female tongue, are like Hotspur in act 3, scene 1, policing Kate's language and sexuality. Hal's imagined scenario with Falstaff is no more benign; he recoils from the possibility of crossing gender, and he attempts to put Falstaff where he was a moment before. That recoil must be read if we are to interrupt the route from such grossness to femininity that has been understood as a "normal" connection, or even as one that psychoanalysis makes available as the truth (infantile Falstaff now seems to be the mother's body).[30] It is true that Falstaff claims his womb undoes him, that he compares himself to a sow that has overwhelmed her children; it is true, too, that Falstaff is the sole adult male in any Shakespeare play to don drag. Feminization, as in Hal's fantasy play with the brawn as Dame Mortimer, may be part of the casting off of the character, the slurring together of an abjected femininity whether male or female, but it also represents the attempt to distinguish male and female as sexual objects. It is just that distinction belied by Falstaff when he fails to know the difference between men and women. Falstaff's "femininity" is not written within the misogynist masculinity of a proto-heterosexuality and homophobia. I do not mean to idealize Falstaff's sexual capacities or to suggest that his relations to women can be shielded from charges of misogyny; he makes both Doll and the Hostess sites of continued demands and repeated frauds. What is to be noted is only that, unlike Hotspur (or the "ideal" Hal), Falstaff is no supporter of rigidified gender exclusivity. It is the presumed difference between sexualities that Falstaff's body breaches.

Hal first casts Falstaff as Dame Mortimer as part of his attempt to cast him off. When Falstaff arrives, Hal attempts to shame the cowardly liar, the monstrous bed-presser. Falstaff catches Hal out; his truth that he robbed Falstaff makes the difference between lying and truth telling moot. And to the charge of bed-pressing, the fat knight has a devastating response, pointing to skinny Hal's pitiful endowment: "[Y]ou starveling, you eel-skin, you dried neat's-tongue, you bull's-pizzle, you stockfish . . . you tailor's-yard, you sheath, you bow-case, you vile standing tuck!" (2.4.240–44). His thinness, in these charges, as David Bevington glosses these lines in his 1987 Oxford edition of *1 Henry IV,* carries the accusation of "genital emaciation."[31] Falstaff points to the phallus Hal lacks just as at the end of the play he will mock the one Hal has from Hotspur. The old bed-presser knows where to get the prince.

So much Hal all but testifies to in his first exchange with him. To Falstaff's irrelevant question about the time of day, Hal replies that the time would be of interest to his fat companion only were the "blessed sun himself" to appear like a "fair hot wench in flame-coloured taffeta" (1.2.9–10). Hal, we know, thinks *he* is the blessed sun, and in this line the sun is male; Hal imagines himself as cross-dressed.[32] Hal places this imaginary woman between himself and Falstaff, this imaginary locus of self-identification between them. It looks as if the only desire Hal can acknowledge is male-female desire. It looks as if that is how he acknowledges his relation with Falstaff. Yet the lines intimate the kind of sexual pleasure Hal does have, just as they further suggest why Hal's other alter ego, Hotspur, has a wife *and* protests against feminization. As with the master-mistress of Sonnet 20,[33] this initial exchange with Falstaff suggests that the prince can be used elsewhere and otherwise, that if his prick is of no concern (as the sonneteer says of the fair young man in that sonnet), this does not exhaust the sexual possibilities. If this seems too crude a supposition, one can point to the ways in which their status difference, which should place Hal on top, is crossed by the age difference that has made Falstaff Hal's tutor and mentor. These crossings of age and status are the sexual locus for the rebound that Hal attempted in his reduction of Francis to a single parrotlike word ("Anon, Anon," Hal's line too, in his economizing). In Part 2, Hal and Poins appear *as* Francis, and Falstaff has no trouble recognizing the two serving lads, and this is the last we see of Poins. When Van Sant rewrites the taffeta wench into a hustler in black leather he is not very far, after all, from Shakespeare.

Are Hal and Falstaff bed companions? It is perfectly clear why the plays can never answer that question directly. For while the king could sleep with men, he could not be a sodomite. Hence, in *Henry V,* when one of the king's betrayers turns out also to have been his bedfellow, it was their physical intimacy that was supposed to have kept Scroop ever from turning traitor to the king. His crime is not what he did in bed. Although Hal is forever casting off his companions, it is not bedfellows per se that are called into question. There is no reason, therefore, not to suppose that Hal and Falstaff were bedfellows, too. In what situation, after all, does Falstaff ask his first question, "Now, Hal, what time of day is it, lad" (*1 Henry IV,* 1.2.1)? If he is just waking up, what is Hal doing? What should be made of the fact that the next time we see Falstaff asleep (at the end of act 2, scene 4), Hal is in his pockets? What *is* Hal talking about when he charges Falstaff with being an exorbitant "bed-presser" (2.4.238)?

There is no absolutely definitive way to answer such questions, but not because the plays give evidence for the modern supposition that a line can be drawn between homosocial and homosexual relations. That Hal has a bedfellow in *Henry V*[34] is publicly announced as the scene opens (2.2.8); with whom a man sleeps in the climb for power is not private knowledge, nor has sex been cordoned to the area of the private as in the modern phantasmatic.[35] We do not know whether Hal sleeps with Falstaff, though, and this points to one way in which the plays police male-male sexual behavior. For even if, on the one hand, it would be unremarkable for men to be sleeping with each other, it would be unspeakable if the wrong men were, if the sex between men was not conducive to maintaining social hierarchies and distinctions. What is at stake comes as close to being made explicit as is possible in that scene in which Hal confronts Scroop as he casts off the treasonous "English monsters" (*Henry V,* 2.2.85). The monstrosity of the treasonous bedfellow is a way of naming sodomy, and it must be to the point that in the next scene of *Henry V,* Falstaff's death will be described in lines in which the Hostess has pilfered the final page of the *Phaedo* for her account of how Falstaff's body, like Socrates', grew colder and colder as she moved her hand up his legs;[36] the corrupter of Harry's youth is also the father of philosophy. What Hal's sexual relation with his bedfellows was is all but spelled out when Henry V declares that Scroop knew "the very bottom of my soul" (2.2.97) and held the "key" to Hal's treasure, "almost might have coin'd me into gold / Would'st thou have practis'd on me for thy use" (2.2.98–99). The description returns us once more to the sonnets—

> So am I as the rich whose blessèd key,
> Can bring him to his sweet up-lockèd treasure,
> The which he will not every hour survey,
> For blunting the fine point of seldome pleasure.
> Therefore are feasts so solemn and so rare,
> Since seldom comming in the long year set.
> (Sonnet 52, lines 1–6)

—to the very lines that echo Hal's first soliloquy or his father's later ministrations on the economies of royal image production. In *Henry V* Hal attempts, Hotspur-like, to cast off the revolting male lover who makes the king a queen. One inheritance that critics and readers have from such moments is a resistance to seeing any possibility of male-male sexual relations in Shakespeare plays unless one man is wearing a dress. But what this account of the *Henry IV* plays might suggest is that, rather than continuing what is by now a zero-sum game of looking at cross-dressing in the comedies as the sole locus of male-male sex in Shakespeare, it is about time to follow the historical paths opened by Foucault and by Bray and the critical paths enunciated by Sedgwick and by Empson. There is no way of knowing in advance where they might lead.

Nor do I mean to suggest that such work has not begun; I would instance Joseph A. Porter's recent book on Mercutio;[37] it, as does Bray's essay "Homosexuality and the Signs of Male Friendship in Elizabethan England," suggests that the representation of friendship in Shakespeare (Hamlet and Horatio, Macbeth and Banquo, Brutus and Cassius, and the list goes on) would be one site that needs to be rethought. One might look again at Antonio and Bassanio, and begin to take stock of how Portia's assumption of masculinity might be read as a response to the threat that that relation poses rather than as a further instance of the slide from the homosocial into sexual territory (as if only a woman or femininity could guarantee the slide). One would want, in a similar vein, to look again at Sebastian and Antonio in *Twelfth Night;* one would have more to say about the end of the play than Stephen Greenblatt does in *Shakespearean Negotiations* when he expresses pity for "poor Antonio . . . left out in the cold"; and one would want to contemplate under what guise and at what cost "Orsino does in a sense get his Cesario" (93). It is a pleasure to record that such thoughts are now thinkable. I would instance Valerie Traub's "Desire and the Difference It Makes," which articulates female desires in Shakespeare plays, desires that cannot be read within the matrices of the compulsory heterosexuality that conditions much feminist Shakespeare criticism, as well as Elizabeth Pittenger's "Dispatch Quickly: The Mechanical Reproduction of Pages,"[38] which allies the unruly woman—Quickly in *Merry Wives*—with the scandalous mating of males that ends that play.

The *Henry IV* plays are, undeniably, history plays, but they are mixed-genre plays, too, and the lines of similarity to the comedies are not surprising. But it is not just the histories and comedies that require further investigation. One might want to think about the substitutive logic of a play about lieutenants that lands Cassio in bed with Iago, his leg flung across him, or about Shakespeare's play about the economies of empire and gender, to ponder not only Prospero's relation to the transvestite Ariel but also his horror at, and inability to punish, that conspiratorial pair separated in *Twelfth Night* but rejoined in *The Tempest,* Antonio and Sebastian. These are characters Shakespeare could not let go of; Antonio is a byword for the sonneteer. Male-male sexual relations were not an early phase in the playwright's development that he outgrew, nor were such relations the marginal tastes of his culture. Students of Shakespeare—at all levels—have to be reminded continually of ways Shakespeare is not our contemporary. In this context, it is important not to enlist him as an unquestioned supporter of the modern regimes—themselves highly imaginary—of hetero- and homosexual difference.

Appendix

I conclude this essay by reprinting an exchange with Nigel Wood, the editor of the volume in which this essay was first published, *Henry IV* (London: Open University, 1995).

Nigel Wood: You suggest that Hal sacrifices the sexual or libidinal side of his character to assume the necessary public image of the king. Hal is, though, a fictional construct. Could you summarize the general problematic about the economies of power and desire that you find in *Henry IV*, and the part that the representation of Hal plays in it?

Jonathan Goldberg: This question has two parts, and I would want first to say that its initial premise is not, in fact, quite what my essay argues. Rather, the question implies a familiar humanist reading of the plays (it can be found, for example, in Derek Traversi's *Shakespeare from Richard II to Henry V* [Stanford: Stanford University Press, 1957] or in Norman Rabkin's essay on *Henry V* in *Shakespeare and the Problem of Meaning* [Chicago: University of Chicago Press, 1981]) that understands them within a modern liberal framework. In such readings, there is the supposition that a personal, private self is the locus of a privileged and valued realm of freedom secured against the impositions of the social, that the drama portrayed in Hal's development represents the sacrifice of that interiority for the necessary impoverishments of the assumption of a public personality. (It is this view, incidentally, that governs the strategies of representations of the king in Kenneth Branagh's film of *Henry V* [1989].) My essay seeks to discover where the sexual inheres, what its inevitable entanglements with power are; that is, it does not regard the sexual as separable from the social, nor does it imagine that the regimes of privacy assumed in your question have much purchase in the plays (privacy, rather, is a construct, a site for performances that serve eminently political purposes, as can be seen in Henry IV's soliloquy about sleeplessness in *2 Henry IV*, act 3, scene 1, for instance, or even in his opening display of guilt and the desire for a pilgrimage to Jerusalem in *1 Henry IV*, a desire voiced to mobilize a project of national unity and canceled by the end of the speech). As Foucault details in the introductory volume of his *History of Sexuality* (trans. Robert Hurley [New York: Random House, 1978]), sexuality is, within the modern constructions of the individual, a privileged locus for the personal, private, and deepest truths about the self. These are the regimes of sexuality that Foucault aligns with modernity, and my essay follows his arguments in exploring the historicity of sexuality; in effect, this entails both tracing some of the paths to modernity and also noting the differences that obtain in a period yet to organize itself through the modern distinction between hetero- and homosexualities. For the fact that modern regimes of sexuality cannot be found in Shakespearean texts does not mean that the topic cannot be broached or that representations of sexual behavior will not be entangled with and function across a range of public and political axes. Thus, sex between men will not be represented as sex per se but within various normative bounds that secure the social order. One would be the emulation between Hal and Hotspur in Part 1, a desire for there to be one Harry who serves both as the site for the image of chivalric accomplishment and as the rightful heir to the throne. This identificatory drive carries with it a strong sexual charge and also contributes to the production of gender in the play, to discriminations between masculinity and femininity. It is, of course, more familiar to modern readers to recognize that relations between men and women are to be read politically; Hal's career in the *Henry IV* plays is largely imagined in terms of male-male relations, but Hotspur's relations with his wife (who is related by blood to Mortimer, the supposed legitimate claimant to the throne) are a site for the management of women, their subordination to the masculine designs of power. Thus, if there is some "sacrifice" performed in the plays, it has to do with the attempted consignment of a figure like Kate to the spheres of domesticity (a parallel to this would be the baiting of Francis the tapster that Hal performs in Part 1, and the attempts through him to manage unruly underclass desires), a carving out of public space as an exclusively aristocratic, or at the most, proto-bourgeois, masculine preserve. *Henry V* in a number of ways—given that the claims to France rest on female inheritance and are secured by marriage—makes it clear that women play a part in public life and that marriage is a public and political sphere. This raises some possibilities for female empowerment in the plays as I discuss in the longer version of this essay that appears in *Sodometries* (Stanford: Stanford University Press, 1992), although the energies of the plays—especially the *Henry IV* set—attempt to discount them. And the plays, in continuing to have their focus on male-male relations, open those relations as the most complete sphere for male self-realization. Since, as I suggested above, the modern division between hetero- and homosexuality cannot easily be read into the plays, one task of the essay is to see to what extent male homosocial relations can be construed as (potentially) sexual, where sexuality between men can be admitted (e.g., Henry V's bedfellow) and where it must be occulted or recoded (Hal's relations with Falstaff and Hotspur, whose riot and rebellion, were they to be made explicit as sexual behavior, would produce the image of sodomy, an impossible conjunction given the legitimating processes of the play, but one that nonetheless haunts Hal's career). The focus of my essay is thus on the imbrications of a legitimating process that has not ruled out spheres of desire but seeks to manage them. It thus seeks to read even in Henry IV's desire to reproduce himself in his heir a ground that is potentially a sexual one. (Indeed, in Orson Welles's *Chimes at Midnight* [1966], a major source for Van Sant's Shakespearean representations in *My Own Private Idaho* [1991], the king's desire for Hotspur-as-heir is cast in a strongly erotic mode, in part to deflect the possibility that Hal's relationship to his surrogate father might also be read this way. Van Sant "misreads" Welles in order to make such relations explicitly sexual.)

NW: It is a fairly universal conclusion that Parts 1 and 2 of *Henry IV* were probably conceived as different kinds of play and not as a compact unit. Does this not question the validity of a reading that regards them both as figuring a single process?

JG: This question supposes that a critic's loyalties must be first and foremost to the integral formal qualities of a work of art; it is, of course, true that the two parts of *Henry IV* are two different plays, though it seems equally clear to me that Part 2 represents a sequel to Part 1 that serves a number of different functions, not least the exposing of some of the mechanisms of ideological production in Part 1, the failures of a supposed benign theatricality. (For a breathtaking argument along these lines, see Jonathan Crewe, "Reforming Prince Hal: The Sovereign Inheritor in *2 Henry IV*," *Renaissance Drama*, new series, 21 [1990]: 225–42.) It seems clear, too, that however different the four plays that comprise the second tetralogy are, they are also committed to a historical narrative. This need not be regarded as seamless, of course, and the plays, as they succeed each other, no doubt are filled with a variety of arrières-pensées and retrospective rewritings. (Indeed, that process seems to me to be insistently thematized, as when Hotspur misquotes *Richard II* in *1 Henry IV*, act 1, scene 3, when Falstaff labels all of Justice Shallow's memories lies in *2 Henry IV*, act 3, scene 2, or when Hal tells the unabashed lie that he does not know Falstaff as he falls on his knees before him at his coronation.) Some of this process of self-censorship and forgetting no doubt arises from the textual history of the plays and the fact that the version of *1 Henry IV* that survives has been obliged to "forget" Oldcastle in order to satisfy the mechanisms of censorship, and yet it continually reminds us of the name it is has been refused (as

I argue further in "The Commodity of Names: 'Falstaff' and 'Oldcastle' in *1 Henry IV*," *Bucknell Review* 35 [1992]: 76–88 [reprinted in this volume]). So one answer to the question, within the formal terms proposed, would be the appeal I have been making to the fact that the plays, if not in prospect then at least in retrospect, are conceived of as a unit, if not quite as a formal unity. This is not to suggest, of course, that such retrospection would easily accommodate itself to the shibboleths of formalist criticism. In this respect, it is worth emphasizing the fact about the textual history of *1 Henry IV* glanced at above—there is equally telling evidence to adduce for *2 Henry IV*—that makes it difficult (to say the least) to maintain formalist notions of the integrity of *any* Shakespeare play given the multiplicity of Shakespearean texts and the history of revision that marks them. Indeed, the retrospection *in the plays* might be said to thematize their textual instability.

I could answer this question in opportunistic terms, saying that this essay was written for a volume on the *Henry IV* plays and that therefore I was already assuming the possibility of writing about the plays without regard to formal differences. But to be more principled: The method of this essay, and, I would venture to say, of most work done since the heyday of formalist criticism, has other priorities than the so-called text itself; indeed it regards the "text itself" as a construct of critical procedures rather than an incontestable fact and regards formalist criticism as itself devoted to and motivated by many other things besides its supposed object. That is to say, agendas that seek to secure the literary against other supposedly extraneous questions are themselves as "externally" motivated as any other form of criticism, motivated by political and institutional aims that need to be scrutinized and that are imbricated in a history of the production of the "intrinsic" literary object. Once such an argument is granted, there is nothing more or less legitimate about considering the framework for posing the consideration of the text at an immanent or at a contextualizing level of inquiry.

NW: In Stephen Greenblatt's "Invisible Bullets" essay (in his *Shakespearean Negotiations* [Berkeley and Los Angeles: University of California Press, 1988]), the close of Part 2 is read as staging a disjunction between the perception of a royal authority based on stage-managed theater and the inevitable obeisance it exacts by its power and our need for "truth." Some might miss a wider political perception in your piece. How would you claim a priority for your position?

JG: Like the first question, this one also seems to me to be asking more than one thing, since it seems to assume that Greenblatt's essay is *eo ipso* political while an essay located in the history of sexuality would not be and would need to defend its politics and "priority" (thus, it seems to me that the question recirculates some of the assumptions I addressed in answering the first one, that sexuality would not be a political/social domain). I would have to say, too, in answer to the question, that the version of the political that Greenblatt offers is one that I would want to question, since its false dialectic of subversion and containment is, as is by now widely recognized, entirely committed only to the second of those terms and cannot imagine any site of subversion that is not produced and controlled by dominant forces. In Greenblatt's reading of *2 Henry IV* as a play that exposes the predations of power (a reading I find persuasive, though I am not moved to sympathize with those in power, as Greenblatt is, or to identify with them, as he does), what seems questionable to me is his belief that the exposure of the political and ideological serves to secure it. Greenblatt's essay thus posits, as your question nicely captures, something it constructs as "our need": a need to be bamboozled and mystified, to be placated and pleased, a need for what Greenblatt calls "imaginary identification." I take it, however, that the phrase is more exact than it might be meant and that therefore it can be seen through as an ideological effect. Indeed, since I also take the phrase to expose an equally imaginary ego investment, a psychoanalytic argument could also be marshalled against it (i.e., a psychoanalytic argument that took seriously the imbrication of ego formations that take place under the aegis of an Other, and that granted a history to the unconscious and thereby recognized that the Other cannot be detached from sociohistorical loci of power).

The political impulses that might therefore be read in my piece start from the positions outlined in answer to the first question: the imbrication of sexuality and power, the multiple crossings of their paths, the impossibility of their full containment either by our modern (and themselves highly questionable) labels of hetero- and homosexuality or the equally imaginary spheres of private and public as absolutely sealed off one from the other. Rather, I take it, following Foucault, that they are produced by each other, and in ways that will not secure them. What I understand this to mean, to return to the topic at hand, is that containment is a dream of absolutist power (it is also the dream of formalist criticism), and while there are many mechanisms within the apparatuses of power that work toward closure and containment, a criticism that affirms those mechanisms *as the political* has sold short the possibilities of the political and of political criticism. Thus, while I am not interested in claiming *priority* for the position that I argue in my essay, I would want to say that its attempt to uncover the relationship of the plays to the history of sexuality means to redescribe the sphere of the political to include relations that many definitions of the political and many attempts at social theory ignore. It is, to say the least, a remarkable fact that a new historicism that claims major allegiances to Foucault operates as if his volumes on the history of sexuality were beside the point. And it is, by now, equally well understood that the nonrelationship of much new historicist work to feminism also marks a serious historical liability in the approach.

NW: In the opening chapter of your *Voice Terminal Echo* (London: Methuen, 1986), you favor the resurrecting of the Renaissance idea of *copia* (as it was understood in Terence Cave's *The Cornucopian Text* [Oxford: Clarendon Press, 1979]) as an opening up of a text to multiple and fragmentary readings in order to replenish them and defer fixed meaning. Do you still find that approach appealing (post-Derrida?), and if so, are there any limits on plurality you would observe?

JG: Oddly enough, then, some of the sentences toward the close of my answer to the last question lead to this methodological point. I would say that I remain a post-Derridean critic, though I would now be far more skeptical of the procedures of *Voice Terminal Echo* than I was able to be when I wrote the book. It now seems to me that to stay within a region of textuality, even if the aim is to expose a general economy of textuality, can look too much as if the textual is being secured against the historical, political, and social. It was for that reason that in *Writing Matter* (Stanford: Stanford University Press, 1990), I sought to explore textual practices (specifically, handwriting) at a level of material production and to position that activity within institutional sites and within a history of social transformation. I sought there to scrutinize the regulatory regimes of management of the hand and also to see what might escape them. (Thus, the argument was not on the side of containment, though it did not wish to ignore the massive forces involved in regulatory regimes.) Elsewhere, for example in "Dating Milton" (in *Soliciting*

Interpretation, ed. E. Harvey and K. Maus [Chicago: University of Chicago Press, 1990]), I have tried to articulate a post-Derridean sense of the historical and political, one that might find in the non-self-presence of the historical moment possibilities of the sort that Raymond Williams offered when he saw that any moment is split among residual, dominant, and emergent forces. While these seem to me rather overly tidy labels for forces that ought to be conceptualized relationally (viewed as discrete and separable, they can only be mobilized retroactively, and therefore they seem to bear with them a teleology that one could easily question, especially if one were to note that emergents must therefore emerge into dominants and that residuals must once have been dominant), the terms, like the Derridean notion of the nonpresence of presence, do divide the present and refuse to contain it. (Thus, the argument works against the new historicist paradigm of containment and its frequent recourse to empiricist evidence, the exact day and date of an event as some sort of guarantee of historicity.) Having said all this, the main modification to my earlier work would certainly involve taking much more seriously the limits to what you call "plurality." I think I still believe in the utopian possibilities of deconstructive reading, that is, the ways in which such readings allow one to move beyond the impasses of ideological reinscription, but I also recognize the complicities between such "pluralism" and, as far as I am concerned, suspect political agendas that go under the same name (Derrida's recent work on Europe would be implicated in this statement, to take one example). Still, the work in this essay, and in recent writing in the history of sexuality that I have been conducting, is everywhere enabled by deconstructive habits of reading and analysis, which still hold out for me vital tools for *contesting* hegemonic relations of power and the production of meaning.

"'What? in a names that which we call a Rose': The Desired Texts of *Romeo and Juliet*"

Fredson Bowers provides a good place to start. Commenting on a reading in *Romeo and Juliet* adopted by editors from Alexander Pope to George Lyman Kittredge, by John Dover Wilson in the Cambridge edition and by John E. Hankins in the Penguin, the reading that has Juliet say that "a rose by any other name would smell as sweet" rather than "a rose by any other word would smell as sweet," Bowers writes: "[T]his *name* got put into the received texts in early days when no distinction was made between bad and good authority, and it has remained ever since, although it is completely wrong."[1] Bowers continues, after explaining the bibliographical logic of his absolute judgment,

> I once read a musical criticism in which Winthrop Sargeant used the violinist's treatment of a single phrase in the opening of Beethoven's Violin Concerto as a touchstone to show whether the violinist really understood the Concerto throughout. In somewhat similar manner, I use this choice in *Romeo and Juliet* of *name* for *word* as a touchstone to distinguish a textually untrained editor from a good one. (122)

Bowers's judgment follows upon the orthodoxy of the New Bibliography. "Name," the bad reading preferred by bad editors, derives from the bad quarto of *Romeo and Juliet;* "word" is from the good quarto, and a good editor will know the difference and will know therefore that there really is no choice to be made. (The Folio text is of no importance to editors, since it is derivative, based largely on Q3, which descends from Q2; the Folio diverges from Q2 unauthoritatively.) With the clear choice between Q1 and Q2 before them, who, to paraphrase the question that Random Cloud asks in "The Marriage of Good and Bad Quartos," would want to be bad when they could be good?[2] Who would want to defile a good text by marrying it to a bad one?

Bowers's absolute judgment ("it is completely wrong") is based on the absolute difference between good and bad; yet his touchstone, with its appeal to the authority of the music critic Winthrop Sargeant—a name that suggests its own *military* authority?—is rather disconcerting. It likens the "trained" editor to a performer; it makes editorial judgment indistinguishable from interpretive choice. Although Bowers inveighs against "some unspecified literary way" in which "name" has been thought "superior" to "word" (120), his musical analogy introduces taste into the sphere of judgment. Unwittingly, Bowers provides me with my argument here: that bibliographical logic cannot be divorced from desire and that the editorial aim, to give us "What Shakespeare Wrote" (the title of the essay by Bowers from which I have been quoting), cannot be separated from a desire to clothe an interpretation with authority. Shakespeare's editors belong to the tradition of performance, and not merely on the basis of Bowers's analogy, as I shall suggest later in more detail. But even here one must pause over the way Bowers's analogy undermines the absolute logic involved in choosing the good before the bad, for, as we know, bad texts only have the authority of performance behind them; they are not "what Shakespeare wrote."

At this point, it might be appropriate to have before us the texts upon which Bowers would have us win our editorial stripes. The 1597 quarto (Q1) of *An excellent conceited Tragedie of Romeo and Iuliet* reads:

Iuliet. Tis but thy name that is mine enemie.
Whats *Mountague?* It is nor hand nor foote,
Nor arme, nor face, nor any other part.
Whats in a name? That which we call a Rose,

By any other name would smell as sweet:
So *Romeo* would, were he not *Romeo* cald,
Retaine the diuine perfection he owes:
Without that title *Romeo* part thy name,
And for that name which is no part of thee,
Take all I haue.

(D1v)[3]

In the 1599 quarto (Q2) of *The most excellent and lamentable Tragedie, of Romeo and Iuliet* the speech reads:

Iuliet. Tis but thy name that is my enemie:
Thou are thy selfe, though not a *Mountague,*
Whats *Mountague?* it is nor hand nor foote,
Nor arme nor face, ô be some other name
Belonging to a man.
Whats in a name that which we call a rose,
By any other word would smell as sweete,
So *Romeo* would wene he not *Romeo* cald,
Retaine that deare perfection which he owes,
Without that tytle, *Romeo* doffe thy name,
And for thy name which is no part of thee,
Take all my selfe.

(D2r–v)

And finally, to cite the lines as they appear in Brian Gibbons's New Arden edition, which shares Bowers's editorial supposition that Q2 is a good text, based on Shakespeare's foul papers, one whose readings therefore are to be preferred:

Juliet. 'Tis but thy name that is my enemy:
Thou art thyself, though not a Montague.
What's Montague? It is nor hand nor foot
Nor arm nor face nor any other part
Belonging to a man. O be some other name.
What's in a name? That which we call a rose
By any other word would smell as sweet;
So Romeo would, were he not Romeo call'd,
Retaine that dear perfection which he owes
Without that title. Romeo, doff thy name,

And for thy name, which is no part of thee,
Take all myself.

(2.2.38–49)[4]

Gibbons chooses "word" rather than "name," and in every other place in which the two texts offer alternatives, Q2 is the basis for his text. He, presumably, would earn Bowers's applause; he has garnered praise, in fact, from Stanley Wells, who sums up the usual New Bibliographical suppositions.[5] The 1597 text is, Wells writes, "a 'bad' quarto" while Q2 "was set up mostly from Shakespeare's working papers," although, he adds, unfortunately, they had not "been tidied up for use in the theatre," as the 'bad' quarto had been; thus Wells commends Gibbons's composite text, especially for making use of the theatrical evidence of Q1, as revealed in the stage directions that Gibbons derives from Q1, but Wells confirms Bowers's opinion for the choice of Q2 as the basic copytext. Not that Gibbons relies only on Q2; even Bowers admits that there are moments when an editor cannot help preferring bad readings to good ones (120); Wells notes some one hundred Q1 readings adopted by Gibbons. One of them, as should have been clear from the citations already, occurs in this passage, and Wells applauds it. It involves, in his words, "the restitution of a phrase" ("nor any other part") at 2.2.41. For, Wells insists, the bad quarto is a much "maligned predecessor"; the reporter sometimes remembered what the Q2 compositor left out. Such, he claims, is the case at line 41, "nor arm nor face nor any other part," the last part of which appears only in Q1—which Gibbons has "restored" in his conflated text.

Gibbons at this point has not merely incorporated a Q1 reading. For to choose Q1's version of this line poses difficulties for the passage as it appears in Q2, "nor arme nor face, ô be some other name," with its following half-line, "Belonging to a man." Wells does not comment on what Gibbons has done here, which is to reverse the two phrases found only in Q2, thereby producing line 42: "Belonging to a man. O be some other name." Wells's silence is not surprising, however, for Gibbons's line has a long if not a New Bibliographical tradition behind it. As the apparatus in the Arden edition reveals, Gibbons reproduces an emendation that Edmond Malone made to solve this supposed textual crux, and it has to be asked whether, in giving his readers what Malone wrote, Gibbons has delivered what Shakespeare wrote. It is, to say the least, rather startling to recognize that such well-known Shakespearean lines were written by Malone. Wells's "restitution" implies, however, that what Malone wrote, Shakespeare really wrote. (Bowers's silence about a standard emendation that lies so close to his touchstone may be supposed also to endorse this choice.) This must be one of those moments when an editor is driven to choose a bad reading that has somehow not found its way into a good text.

If one supposes that what Malone wrote is what Shakespeare wrote, one must then ask how Q2 managed not to reproduce the author's manuscript. John Jowett, who also reprints Malone's lines in the new Oxford edition of the complete works, attempts an explanation.[6] Sharing Wells's supposition that "Q1 simply omits a verse line, as elsewhere," Jowett argues that "its unique 'nor any other part' is especially significant as it makes sense of material in Q2 which it does not itself print." He admits, however, that "Q2's deficiency and mislocation have no obvious cause." What must be assumed, he argues, is that the manuscript was particularly illegible at this point and that the phrases that found their way into Q2 were marginal additions. Perhaps, Jowett opines, "nor any other part" at a cursory glance by the compositor seemed simply to be "Nor arme nor face" written a second time—foul papers have such repetitions; such, at any rate, is the claim offered to explain other features of the text supposedly behind Q2—and thus the compositor, this time recognizing and eliminating a repetition, was faced with the stray half line "Belonging to a man," which he then misplaced. In offering this solution, however, Jowett conveniently forgets the other half-line, "ô be some other name," and its misplacement.

Throughout his commentary, Jowett seems haunted by the specter of Alice Walker, who rewrote and relocated the lines (in a reading adopted by Dover Wilson and G. I. Duthie in their Cambridge edition):

Juliet. 'Tis but thy name that is my enemy.
Thou art thy self, though not a Montague.
O be some other name! What's Montague?
It is nor hand, nor foot, nor arm, nor face,
Nor any part belonging to a man.
What's in a name? That which we call a rose
By any other name would smell as sweet.
(2.2.38–44)[7]

"Clearly," Wilson comments in his notes to this line—what a relief that something should be clear at this point!—"Clearly Q2 here derives from a corrected passage of Q1 in which the collator's marginal additions from the foul papers have somehow got misplaced." Adopting Walker's reading, Wilson explains that her decision to render the line as "Nor any part belonging to a man," omitting "other" before "part," was based on the supposition that the actor's memory anticipated "other" in "By any other name." Walker's rearrangement gives us a metrical line—which Shakespeare surely wrote!—and avoids the repetitions that befoul the memories of actors and the bad texts they reconstruct. Jowett is haunted by this argument, for his own, as he admits "is analogous to Walker's but does not depend on the hypothesis of Q1 copy for Q2." Admit that hypothesis, and Q1 might not be so 'bad' after all (at any rate a bad quarto would have to be admitted to stand behind the good). It might allow—as it does in all the editions Bowers scorns, including Wilson's—the repetition of "name" rather than the alternative "word."

For here one must face the well-known and extremely disturbing fact that Q1 does lie behind Q2 (that Q1 "contaminates" Q2, as the standard terminology of editors from Pope to Wells would have it). For a stretch of some hundred lines in act 1, scenes 2–3, Q2 reprints Q1, as is clear not merely by the virtual coincidence of words in this passage but by the replication of typographical peculiarities and other features of the accidentals.[8] Editors have wrestled with the question of the further extent of Q1's influence on Q2, and the answers have ranged from Dover Wilson's assumption that Q2 is in large part based on marked-up Q1 copy[9] to the more widely shared belief that Q1 was occasionally—and indeterminately—consulted by the Q2 compositor.

It is in terms of an assumed relation between Q1 and Q2 that Duthie explains the lines we have been examining.[10] Duthie argues that corrections in Q1 misunderstood by the compositor account for Q2's omission and mislocation of lines. In his reconstruction, Duthie supposes that the scribe marking up Q1 inserted "Belonging to a man" directly beneath "Nor arme, nor face" in Q1. Cramped by the interlinear space, he added the remainder of the line, "ô be some other name," in the righthand margin, drawing a line from those words to the place in the text where they belonged. Unfortunately, that line went through "nor any other part," and the compositor replaced that phrase with the marginal insertion. "The conflation, traditional since Malone, is I believe, correct,"

Duthie concludes (14)—a conclusion implicitly retracted, however, when he came to edit the play with Dover Wilson and adopted Walker's reading, one even more seductive since it preserved Q2 phrases in their proper order and also managed to eliminate memorial corruption. Duthie's initial solution to the problem seems to me ingenious, and far more elegant and cogent than Jowett's. Why, then, does Jowett not adopt it; why, indeed, does he offer his troublingly analogous reconstruction?

The answer seems to be that Duthie and Walker both assume that Q2 is bibliographically derivative, while Jowett wants, insofar as possible, to make the authority behind Q2 authorial. If something has gone wrong in the text at this point, it can only be the illegibility of the manuscript that will account for it. In the manuscript that Jowett reconstructs, two things are supposed: first, that it will allow the Q2 misreading; second, that it will not explain the Q1 reading, for in Jowett's story, a phrase that is in Q1 is missing in Q2 because the manuscript could not be read. The assumption is, therefore, that no authorial manuscript lay behind Q1. The further assumption, of course, is that there was always—in the manuscript Jowett dreams of—one possible version of these lines: the one that Malone wrote.

Duthie's reconstruction assumes a marked-up Q1, but it need not rest upon that supposition. It will also allow for a manuscript marked up in precisely the same way. To believe that, however, would produce a different manuscript from the one Jowett wants. It would be a manuscript that vested authority in the Q1 reading, making Q2 a failed attempt to understand authorial revision of lines that once authoritatively stood as they appear in Q1. Perhaps what makes Jowett nervous is not merely the fact that he too rearranges the lines as Duthie does, but also the fact that his account assumes authorial revision; for Jowett, however, the marginalia were produced before Q1 was, in a single manuscript of the play. But to follow Duthie's argument—and to allow it its analogical force as an explanation of the state of the manuscript behind Q2—could lead one to assume that the manuscript of the play was revised and that such revision occurred after the state of the manuscript authoritatively represented by Q1.[11]

When questions about Shakespeare's text—or texts—become questions about the manuscript—or manuscripts—behind them, we pass, inevitably, into the sphere of desire, the desire for the missing object, which, in certain post-Freudian accounts, defines the nature of desire.

("To strip the veil of print," Bowers's well-known phrase,[12] sounds uncannily like the scene Sigmund Freud described in *Beyond the Pleasure Principle,* watching his grandson play the 'Fort! Da!' game of disappearance and reappearance.) That we are dealing with a textual desire, or the desire for a text, in no way disturbs this psychoanalytic paradigm, for, as Jacques Lacan insists, the unconscious is structured as language, and the search for the absent Other is undertaken in language; the words spoken in desire come from the illusory place of the Other and are spoken toward the desire of restitution, to find the Other in one's words. It is of more than passing interest that this passage in *Romeo and Juliet,* where textual desire is enacted on the bibliographical scene, is also a moment of Juliet's desire for Romeo, enacted also as a textual desire: "O Romeo, Romeo, wherefore art thou Romeo?" "O be some other name"; be "word" instead of "name"? There is, perhaps, a complicity of desires here. But more of that in a while.

To return to strictly bibliographical questions. We seem to be faced with two possible accounts of the phantasmatic object behind the texts of *Romeo and Juliet.* In one of these—the version offered by Wells and Jowett—Q1 is a corrupt text, marked by omissions that are restored, or whose restoration is attempted, by Q2. The only full source of the play is the author's holograph, and the only text with access to it is Q2. In the other version of textual transmission, Q1 serves as the copy for Q2, and it has been marked up by consulting the author's manuscript. Implicit here, then, is the supposition that readings in Q1 might be authoritative not merely because the actors remembered what the Q2 compositor missed but also because they remembered a version of the text that did not coincide with the manuscript behind Q2. At least, that is implicit in my analogical extension of Duthie's reconstruction to a different Shakespearean manuscript. I do not think a marked up Q1 will explain Q2, and I am convinced by those who have argued that Q1 can, at best, have been consulted only sporadically by the Q2 compositor.[13] The lines we have been examining could represent one of those moments of consultation, but, as others have shown, in the hundred or so lines where consultation is certain, we know that Q1 lies behind Q2 precisely because the texts of Q1 and Q2 are virtually identical for these lines, particularly in matters of punctuation, typography, and the abbreviations used to name the characters. At those points, Q1 was treated as authoritative, and it did not need to be marked up. However, if the lines in Juliet's speech in Q2 arose from a marked-up text, as Duthie argued, the only marked-up text in question could have been the manuscript. If he is right, that manuscript would initially have contained the lines as they appear in Q1.

From a New Bibliographical standpoint, such an argument is inadmissible. It returns us to the bad old days that Bowers attacks, when authority between good and bad had not been established and the bad quartos were considered to be early drafts of the plays. This is, for example, the opinion of P. A. Daniel in the introduction to his 1874 enface edition of Q1 and Q2. Yet his understanding of Q1 is, in fact, rather complex; for him (and, I must add, for me too), Q1 is a mixed text, sometimes authoritative, sometimes memorial reconstruction; "in its more perfect portions," Daniel writes, it "affords conclusive evidence that that 'copy' underwent revision, received some slight augmentation, and, in some few places, must have been entirely re-written."[14] In the modern orthodoxy (confirmed by Harry Hoppe in *The Bad Quarto of Romeo and Juliet*),[15] where Daniel saw revision and augmentation, we are to see omission. Q1 is a memorial reconstruction of a cut Q2. There was always only one *Romeo and Juliet.*

But which one? The one supposed by Jowett, or the one I have supposed based on Duthie? Bowers, one can be sure, would find it "completely wrong" to desire to return to the bad old days when anything was possible; the streamlined efficiency of the New Bibliography promised that would never happen again. It stands for order and economy, for logic and rationality. It knows the difference between good and bad. It has its machines, and its mechanistic view of compositors as machines, always making the same mistakes. And, as Bowers admits, it also has its proponents, like Dover Wilson, who somehow know the rules of the game and always make the wrong choices. The reason for that situation is not hard to explain, however; for all the supposed rationality of the New Bibliography, there inevitably comes the moment of unreasoned choice, the making of editorial decisions. The work of reason, moreover, is directed at a phantom, a lost text, always reconstructed on principles that will never be fully explained rationally. What, then, is a good New Bibliographer to do, producing a substitute object on the basis of a lost one?

For the passage we have been examining, Hoppe and Richard Hosley in their editions of the play make (in their terms) the only "rational" choice; they abandon the phantom for the material fact and reprint Q2 without Malone's "restitution." For, as Hosley comments, "it is not entirely clear that Q2 is corrupt."[16] No editor before Malone conflated the texts; either the Folio (and thereby the Q2 reading) or the Q1 reading appears in the early editions.[17] What Malone wrote, Hosley argues, is not what Shakespeare wrote, and Malone can never be proved right in his emendation. Q2 is what Shakespeare wrote, and it therefore should be reprinted as it stands. This is Hosley's argument. I may have erred in assuming that Bowers would approve of Gibbons's text; perhaps the decision made by Hoppe and Hosley would be more to his liking. Nonetheless, few editors have emulated their rigor, and their reasons are not far to seek. Q1 haunts all editions of *Romeo and Juliet;* it even haunts Q2. And there is no way of knowing when it might not be authoritative.

This fact has lead to the bibliographical commonplace that Q1 is the problem facing the editor of the play. "The bad first quarto of 1597 may fairly be said to pose the chief editorial problem in *Romeo and Juliet,*" Hosley opens an essay on "The Corrupting Influence of the Bad Quarto on the Received Text of *Romeo and Juliet.*"[18] "Most, though not all, of the problems in *Romeo and Juliet* derive from the existence of the first edition," Wells opines, hedging the case a bit. I submit that the real editorial problem is Q2, not merely because it authorizes Q1 in some always undecidable manner, although that is bad enough. If we once admit that what Malone wrote, conflating Q1 and Q2, is what Shakespeare wrote, then Bowers's touchstone disappears. If lines in this speech were revised—as both Jowett and Duthie suppose, however opposed their notion of the manuscript may be—how is one to know where the revision stopped? Now, in fact, in the account thus far given, the situation is relatively simple. Choose my version of Duthie, and one chooses a manuscript that existed in two states, temporally separate. State one lies behind the "more perfect portions" of Q1; state two authorizes Q2. There are then two *Romeo and Juliet*s, an earlier and a later one. Conflation of the two may be permissible, however, since Q2 appears to be a conflated and corrected text. One might then choose "word" instead of "name" on the supposition that it is the substitute that has ultimate authorial validity. So, too, one might choose Malone's lines as the best way to restore a Shakespearean revision. One would not, in this scenario, be returning to what was always there, the one and only *Romeo and Juliet* that Jowett and Wells desire; but one would at least be restoring the author's final intention.

I want to argue, however, that it is precisely the author's final intention that Q2 does not deliver. This fact about Q2 is, from a slightly different vantage point, agreed upon in deriving Q2 from foul copy that offers moments of incoherence that are especially evident in the first and second shots that Q2 reproduces at several points in the text. Editors, who want to give their readers what Shakespeare wrote, usually baulk at such moments and choose one version of what Shakespeare wrote, deciding which is best, what Shakespeare would finally have chosen had he only gotten his papers into order for the acting company. There is nothing wrong in editors so doing, so long as they do not fool themselves into thinking that in eliminating variants they are giving their readers what Shakespeare wrote or that they are privy to final intentions. Editors have good authority for what they do; their practice derives from the playhouse, however, and not from the text. No actor could possibly deliver Romeo's final soliloquy as represented in Q2, for example; it offers several versions of the same lines, and an actor will have to choose among the alternatives. So, too, do editors choose. Their texts are scripts for performance, as Bowers unwittingly revealed in the analogy that accompanied his touchstone. The authority for an editor at such a moment is not Q2, for it does not choose. The authority for editors is Q1. It represents a version of the play in which choices have been made and redundancies have been removed. I submit that we know what Q1 is, and that we can recognize it as the legitimating ancestor for edited versions of *Romeo and Juliet.* In that sense, Q2 is the real problem. An editor may not wish to make the same choices as Q1 has, but few editors will rigorously reproduce Q2. Rather, they do what Q1 has been accused of doing: They cut Q2, they emend it, they rewrite it. Q1 haunts editors of *Romeo and Juliet* because it is the dark specter of their own practice.

On its title page, Q2 announces it is *"Newly corrected, augmented, and amended."* Although one need not take this claim literally, its multiple terms do suggest that Q2 gives evidence of a range of kinds of revision. Q2 claims authority in the sundry performances of the play as acted by the Lord Chamberlain's Men. No mention is made of the author's hand, nor is his name offered on the title page. In this, it is not unlike Q1, which also vests its authority in the playhouse. My point here is not to call into question the supposition that foul papers lie behind Q2 but to ask what their relationship might be to the playhouse. Wells, we recall, assumes that they would have been "tidied up"—edited, in a word—for the players. I want to argue against that supposition. I submit that what stands behind Q2 is a manuscript that offers an anthology of possible performances of the play, one of which is captured by Q1. Q2's relationship to that version of the play is complex; it corrects its errors—I am not denying that, in part, Q1 may be an unreliable text—but Q2 also augments and amends the text printed in Q1, making additions and changes. Q2 is a different version—or rather, different versions—of the play. It is a selection from or an anthology of a number of productions of *Romeo and Juliet,* one of which was close to the performance represented by Q1, close enough to allow Q2 to use Q1 as its authority at some points. At some moments, such as the lines we have lingered over, Q2 offers an augmented version of Q1. But we do not know when the augmentation took place; that is, we do not know whether Q1 chose to omit lines or whether such a choice would have been impossible because the lines had not yet been written. There is no way of knowing whether new lines in Q2, including "Thou art thy selfe, though not a *Mountague,*" as well as the problematic "ô be some other name / Belonging to a man" were cut in the Q1 performance or added subsequent to it. Nor is there any way of knowing whether Q2 was offering substitute lines or lines meant to be added. For not only is there no way of knowing which of the two manuscripts hypothetically reconstructed lies behind Q2, but also there is no guarantee that those two possibilities are exhaustive. I am now proposing that they are not. And in this, as in much else that I have been arguing, I follow Random Cloud, who writes, "[W]e must countenance Shakespeare's writing of *Romeo and Juliet* as extending over some time and running through several different phases, and perhaps in several different manuscripts, each perhaps with its own characteristic aesthetic, offering together several finalities" (429).

The basis for this argument lies in Q2, although one must look to lines other than those about the rose for further confirmation—at Romeo's final soliloquy, for instance, or the variant sets of lines spoken by Romeo at the end of act 2, scene 2 and by Friar Laurence at the opening of act 2, scene 3.[19] For although in those cases it is clear that Q1 has made choices among possibilities left open in Q2, we have no way of knowing whether these options were there from the start—in an original, untidy manuscript—or whether they resulted from later additions. For Q2 offers different kinds of revisionary processes, some of which may represent first and second thoughts in an initial draft of the play and some of which may represent different versions in different performances of the play from season to season. It is possible that there once may have been one *Romeo and Juliet,* but insofar as Q2 is derived from foul papers, it suggests that there was always more than one *Romeo and Juliet;* these variants, I would argue, were "tidied up" only in performance, but not in a manuscript replete with second thoughts and alternatives. If, in performance, selections necessarily were made from the authorial multiplicity, subsequent performances also occasioned further revision; there is no guarantee that such revision was authorial or that playhouse decisions necessarily were authorial either. All these versions, authorial or not, remained in the untidy and burgeoning manuscript—or manuscripts—left, once again, for the performers to choose among. The manuscript(s) became an anthology. And it is some version of that anthology that Q2 preserves.

Q2 thus represents a very complicated situation, combining both original multiplicity with temporally spaced revision. And there is no way to tell them apart; in those revisions, deletions as well as additions were made and substitutes were tried out.[20] As is clear from the remarkable coincidences between Q1 and Q2, much of the play remained unrevised. Many of the revisions are of the sort found in other instances of Shakespearean revision: a word changed here or there. Q2 is considerably longer than Q1, and it displays several moments when different versions of speeches or longer and shorter alternatives were offered, or when different characters might be allowed to speak versions of the same lines. Jowett and Wells assume that Q1 has omitted lines genuinely preserved in Q2, but there is no evidence for that except in the retrospective recasting that gives authority to a fuller version; in the case we have been examining, that fuller version is the product of editorial conflation. When Jowett hears a line in Q1 as incomplete without its Q2 addition, there is no way of knowing if he is right. "It is nor hand nor foote, / Nor arme, nor face, nor any other part" does not necessarily cry out for "Belonging to a man." I submit that here, as with many of the supposed "cut" moments in Q1, it is equally possible that Q2 has added to Q1. Furthermore, even if Q1 cuts material found in Q2, that is no argument against its authority. Q2 has to be cut in any performance (or edition) of the play. And although it prints various versions of scenes and lines, we do not know that it prints them all. Because it is often too full for the sake of performance, for all we know, it has made choices too. After all, there are lines in Q1 that are not in Q2, and Malone's conflation testifies to the desire to credit some of them as being authentically Shakespearean. On the other hand, as Hosley remarked, there is nothing obviously wrong with "ô be some other name / Belonging to a man." Lines that have been conflated ever since Malone may, in fact, be alternatives. Perhaps, as Walker's rewriting of the lines suggests, this speech of Juliet's was made of movable parts. And if so, that would be the case elsewhere. Editors who reproduce Malone's version operate under that supposition, but so, too, do Hosley and Hoppe when they imagine that in choosing Q2 they have not made a choice. If that is the case, I would argue that where Q1 and Q2 differ in terms of substitutions that can be explained by revisionary processes, we have no way of knowing which version is earlier or later. Nor am I convinced that such distinctions count in terms of authority.

The substitution of "word" for "name" is one of these moments. The fact that Q1 has "name" does not necessarily mean that that was the earlier reading; it could mean that "word" and "name" were alternative possibilities in the script or scripts behind Q1 and Q2. Both might be authorial; either might not be.

What these two versions of the lines intimate is that there were as many more *Romeo and Juliet*s as we might imagine within the plausible life of the play in Shakespeare's time. An editor of the play, at least one following New Bibliographic protocols, will choose one of them, just as any actor playing Juliet chose one of the alternatives. There never was a final *Romeo and Juliet,* a single authoritative or authorial version of the play. There were only versions, from the start. As scripts to be acted, they presumed multiplicities and contingencies, the conditions of the theater. Q1 and Q2 in their very different ways both tell us that any single performance differed from other performances, just as every text of *Romeo and Juliet* differs from every other one. An edition can never give us what Shakespeare really wrote, because we have no evidence suggesting there finally was such a definitive thing. There is scarcely a Shakespeare play—even those that survive in only one text—that does not give evidence of existing in multiple versions. An editor seeking an alternative to the protocols of the New Bibliography might choose not to choose and would thus risk producing the virtually unreadable texts of *Romeo and Juliet,* opting for the "infinitive" text. In its editorial apparatus, such an edition would give alternatives as alternatives; it would mark up the texts to allow for as many performances as the editor deemed plausible. Such a text is utopian, and, in truth, it might be no more than a composite of all the different editions of *Romeo and Juliet* that have ever been or that ever will be.[21]

These editorial alternatives animate Juliet's lines. On the one hand, they manifest a powerful, utopian sense of an identity that is separable from its verbal representation, a sense that Romeo remains Romeo no matter what he is called. Although this could appear to be an idealistic fantasy—like the editorial dream of reconstructing the lost manuscript—it is not, for it does not assume that the identity of Romeo is identical to *any* verbal form. Treated textually, it is a version of the phantasmatic object known as *Romeo and Juliet,* a play that is itself in every possible version and variation. In this understanding, whether one chooses "word" or "name" is indifferent. Romeo remains Romeo, and *Romeo and Juliet* remains itself in all its alternatives. This is the version of the play that I have been assuming, a play without a fixed text, without a stable "name" or "word." The phantasm in Juliet's imagination is no single manuscript; rather, it is an unfixed one. It is as incapable of stabilization as the form that Juliet assumes when she becomes a living corpse, dead and alive at once. This is the dream that Romeo and Juliet share, that they will somehow survive themselves and live beyond their deaths.

Juliet's desire, however, is proved wrong, or at least, unsustainable. Romeo chooses to see her dead. Romeo, moreover, cannot take another name; he is inescapably a Montague, she a Capulet. Their marriage, like the marriage of good and bad quartos, will not survive; they are done in by the inexorability of their identities, by family trees as relentless in their hold upon the characters as the stemmata of bibliographers are when they insist upon the true generation and filiation of the text. The play, then, seems ultimately to be on the side of the New Bibliography; it will not allow the desire for variation to be realized. It insists that a rose cannot be called by another name. Thus, New Bibliographers succumb to the textual effect that produces the dead corpses of Romeo and Juliet.

However, this is not the final textual situation. When Juliet addresses Romeo—"O Romeo, Romeo, wherefore art thou Romeo?" (Gibbons, 2.2.33)—she assumes his name even as she desires it to be abandoned.

At that complex moment, the two assumptions thus far described as antithetical function at once. Jacques Derrida, in an extraordinary essay on the play, paraphrases Juliet's lines and their implicit argument: "Romeo is Romeo," he writes, "and Romeo is not Romeo. He is only himself insofar as he departs from his name; he is only himself in his name. Romeo can be named himself if he abandons his name; he only is named himself on the basis of his name."[22] And, as Derrida goes on to argue, what is true of Romeo is equally true of the play. The theatrical life of *Romeo and Juliet* is predicated upon the dual possibility that allows the play to be itself in each of its subsequent different performances. The self-remarking textuality of Juliet's lines is consonant with the play's theatricality. Romeo and Juliet, the characters in the play, do not sustain a life-in-death; but the play does; it remains, in all its versions, Derrida writes, as a "still living palimpsest" (533).

What is the name of the rose in *Romeo and Juliet*? What word would secure the possibility of real invariant existence despite textual variation? The rose that Juliet names has many names. Not least of all, it names the very literariness of the text, its relationship, to go no further, to *The Romance of the Rose,* or to all the works of literature in which women are flowers, as Juliet is, immured in the Capulet garden. At the very moment when she insists that a rose is a rose is a rose, Romeo has abandoned one rose, Rosaline, who has the name of the rose quite literally, and has substituted Juliet for her. Juliet names herself in naming the rose; names herself otherwise in this substitution. In Juliet's speech, then, the very example of unchanging identity despite substitution is belied by the substitution that Romeo has made in choosing her as his rose. The rose has been replaced, and Juliet has Rosaline's part. Her inexorable identity rests upon substitution and replacement. The difference between Juliet's multiple textual desire and her singular textual devastation disappears in a textuality that has embraced both sides of the question; Juliet's lines, in a manner that exceeds the very logic of her desire, act out the conflicted and opposing notions of textuality represented by Q1 and Q2.

In act 4—in either version of the play—Juliet's simulated corpse is covered with rosemary (Gibbons, 4.5.79, 95 stage direction);[23] in lines found only in Q2 (Gibbons, 2.4.201–8), the Nurse reports that Juliet has been dallying with the letter "R," joining Romeo and Rosemary through it: "Doth not rosemary and Romeo begin with a letter?"[24] The letter "R" travels through the play, linking Rosaline and Romeo, Romeo and

Juliet; the names of the rose are Rosaline, Romeo, Rosemary, and Juliet. Proper names and ordinary words are linked in the letter, joined in substitutions. There is no selfsame rose here; nor is there elsewhere in the canon, in plays that this one anticipates, not through the actors' contaminated memories but within authorial memory, substitution, and revision. In *Love's Labors Lost,* Rosaline will name a dark lady; in *As You Like It,* Rosalind will name the master-mistress. "From fairest creatures we desire increase, / That thereby beauties *Rose* might neuer die": So open Shakespeare's sonnets, that collection of variations upon the name of the rose.[25] The names of the rose are multiple: They name the possibilities of erotic experience as Shakespeare imagined them. *Romeo and Juliet* unfolds what is folded in the supposed identity of the letter "R," differences within the same. At the end of the play, the letter arrives, in the miscarriage of Friar Laurence's letter, "stay'd by accident" (Q2; Gibbons, 5.3.250), a necessary "accident" for the letter to become literature, and for the play to be enacted over and over again, each time different, each time the same.[26]

It would be possible, although it would take another essay, to trace the trajectories of the letter through the variations in the two texts of *Romeo and Juliet* and to examine the conflicted notions of textuality that circulate in them. Such an inquiry would find that Q2 insists upon a multiplicity of textualizations; many letters, in the various senses of the word, cross its paths.[27] Yet it would not be possible finally to line up the alternatives through the alternative texts. In the moment we have been examining, for example, the repetition of "name" in Q1 would seem to be on the side of an invariability belied by Q2's variant "word"; but Q2, with "ô be some other name" has not reduced the repetition of "name" when it offers its substitute "word," for it also has added a "name" even as it substitutes a "word." So too with other changes: In Q1 Juliet ends by offering all she has, while in Q2, echoing the line that had declared "Thou art thy selfe, though not a *Montague,*" Juliet correspondingly offers "all my selfe." Any editor who thinks that Q1 is memorially contaminated with all its repeated "name"s and "part"s must face the new repetition added by this variant or by the echoing phrase "thy name." In a play that often considers the question of replacement and obliteration—and often figures that question through the possibility of erasing one word and putting another in its place (take "banish" as an instance)—any adjudication of the question of whether a repetition represents memorial contamination or compositorial error or whether a substitution represents an authoritative change must remain suspended.[28] The notion of ownership in Q1's "Take all I haue" migrates to "Belonging to a man" in Q2. This displacement of ownership belies the possibility of the self-identical, self-owned text or proper name. It is finally impossible to know what belongs to *Romeo and Juliet* and what does not.

"I am not my name. In other words, I could survive it. But from the first it is destined to survive me. It thus announces my death to me." Thus Derrida writes (532), teasing out the implications of Juliet's lines as they are unfolded in the play. The death that the proper name announces to its bearer is the life of *Romeo and Juliet* in its multiple texts and multiple representations.

One more word: The title of this essay begins with a quotation, one more naming of the rose: "What? in a names that which we call a Rose." The line is yet another variant, this time from the Folio,[29] and its aberrant form has been explained,[30] once again on the basis of nonexistent marginalia; this time a marked-up copy of Q3 must be posited to explain how a question mark wandered to replace an "s" and an "s" found itself where a question mark should be. I have no desire to embrace the Folio reading as authoritative or to begin now an examination of that text of *Romeo and Juliet.* But I let the line remain at the head of this essay as a reminder of what I have been arguing: that the singular text is the phantasmatic object of a textual desire that is realized only in the deformations and multiplications of that desire in its textual manifestations. I let the line stand, since it erringly offers the plural "names" by which we truly name the rose. If this essay has a real title, it is "The Names of the Rose."

Romeo and Juliet's Open Rs

Since the mid-1970s, *Romeo and Juliet* has become the Shakespeare play assigned to more U.S. high school students than any other. *Julius Caesar* has been usurped; the sexual revolution has replaced the civics lesson. Yet given the conservative nature of most high school curricula, one can only assume that the play is taught in formalist terms (the young versus the old, night versus day, love versus society, and so on) and toward a valuation of a kind not limited to high school lesson plans. Typical in this regard might be these sentences from Brian Gibbons's introduction to his Arden edition of the play (1980):[1]

> The lovers are from the outset withdrawn in an experience of sublime purity and intense suffering which renders them spiritually remote from other characters and the concerns of the ordinary world. The single clear line of ideal aspiration in love is set against the diversified complex intrigues which proliferate in the ordinary world, and contact between the two has tragic consequences.

In such an estimation (it recurs as the thesis in the thirty-five pages of his introduction given over to—ominously—"The Play"), Gibbons seems to be doing little more than echoing the closing lines of the play, in which the prince intones, "never was a story of more woe / Than this of Juliet and her Romeo" (5.3.308–309) as his response to the offer of Montague and Capulet to raise a monument to the dead pair of lovers:

Montague. For I will raise her statue in pure gold,
That whiles Verona by that name is known,
There shall no figure at such rate be set
As that of true and faithful Juliet.
Capulet. As rich shall Romeo's by his lady's lie,
Poor sacrifices of our enmity.
(5.3.298–303)

Predictably enough, Gibbons finds in this moment that the "artifice of eternity" (74) is being erected, the statues symbolizing for him "the alchemical transmutation of worldly wealth, property, earth, into the spiritual riches of the heart and the imagination" (76).

In such estimations of the "purity" and transcendentality of their love, and, by extension, of Shakespeare's art, mystifications are set up to obscure what can as easily be read in the lines: that the corpses of Romeo and Juliet continue to have a social function; indeed, that they make possible the union of the two opposing houses. Moreover, this union, and more generally its social function, is as long lasting as the name of the city in which their monument is erected, while the material value of the statues, insisted upon as Montague and Capulet vie in their offers, is tied to that contingent temporality, to a future that cannot be predicted or controlled however much these grasping and still rivalrous fathers would try to do so. Reading the lines this way, one can hear them echoing against the concerns in the play, voiced over and again, about the possibility that names and words might be unmoored and uncontrollable, subject to accidents and to determinations that no artifice of eternity can secure. One could also see that the three men speaking at the end of the play are bent upon securing the social order through the dead couple, and one could extend this back to the entire play, reading the love of Romeo and Juliet as imbricated in rather than separated from "ordinary" life. The idealization of the lovers, to be brief, serves an ideological function. The marriage of their corpses in the eternal monuments of "pure gold" attempts to perform what marriage normally aims at in comedy: to provide the bedrock of the social order; or, to speak somewhat more exactly, the heterosexual order.

Yet what is solidified in this final set of gestures is indicated just before, when Capulet offers his hand to Montague and calls him "brother" (5.3.295). For, to speak more exactly, what the ending of the play secures is a homosocial order,[2] and it is that configuration that continually triangulates the relation of Romeo and Juliet, adding in every instance a third term that gives the lie to the shelter of their love: Romeo and Paris as possible husbands, still fighting over the body of Juliet in the final scene of the play; Capulet and Paris as the patriarchal couple trading Juliet between them; Romeo and Tybalt as enemies and yet as lovers, joined and divided by Juliet. The functioning of the patriarchy (the "brotherhood" of Montague and Capulet at the end of the play, the surrogate sonship that extends from Capulet to Paris), as well as its misfunctioning (if rivalry and enmity are that—an easily disputed point), is tied to the love of Romeo and Juliet. Indeed, what makes their love so valuable is that it serves as a nexus for the social order and can be mystified as outside it. The sexual revolution replaces the civics lesson indeed: With the myth of love as a private experience, the personal is disconnected from the political.

One would think, therefore, that feminist criticism that has engaged the play would speak against the formalist project that I have conveniently fetched from the account offered by Gibbons; to a certain extent it has, and valuably, by excoriating patriarchal violence in the play. But it too dreams of the ideal world that Gibbons imagines. I take as typical the opening sentences of Coppélia Kahn's discussion of the play: "*Romeo and Juliet* is about a pair of adolescents trying to grow up. Growing up requires that they separate themselves from their parents by forming with a member of the opposite sex an intimate bond which supersedes filial bonds."[3] This seems ready for high school use; the play is translated effortlessly into modern (at any rate, 1950s) terms. The tragedy of the play implied in these opening sentences has to do with the failure of Romeo and Juliet to grow up into the mature couple that has separated itself from parental bonds. Mystified, thereby, is the fact that at the end of this ideal trajectory lies the transformation of the couple into their parents; what they rebel against is also what they become. These blandly descriptive sentences reek of prescriptiveness, most notably when growing up is allowed, indeed required to have, only a single heterosexual trajectory. The term "homosocial" has already begun to suggest how far this might be from *Romeo and Juliet,* and Kahn's rewriting of the play to suit her normalizing plot could not be clearer. For rather than breaking the filial bond, Romeo and Juliet reensure it; it is the brotherhood of Montague and Capulet that they secure. And such would have been the case too had the play been the comedy Kahn desires, in which boys would arrive at manhood free of the phallic aggression and fear of women that deforms the patriarchy, for even in this benign state they would not leave behind the institutional site of marriage upon which patriarchy rests. Were the social order to work properly, Kahn implies, it would effortlessly produce heterosexuality. Shakespeare, she believes, critiques patriarchy because it does not make growing up easy; his art is on her side.

In the pages that follow, I seek not to enlist Shakespeare for the projects of a formalist and heterosexist agenda but rather, following Eve Kosofsky Sedgwick, to suggest that the homosocial order in the play cannot simply be reduced to a compulsive and prescriptive heterosexuality, that sexuality in the play cannot be sheltered from sociality, and that sexuality in the play cannot be found enshrined in an artifice of eternity because neither the social work the play performs nor the play itself (a formalist phantasm) can be thought of in those terms.

Accounts of the sort that I have been invoking rest upon the value of the love between Romeo and Juliet, upon treating it as a unique manifestation, the locus of all kinds of intensities and transcendentalities (the perfection of the individual and, concomitantly, of the work of art). In so doing, critical estimations could be said to follow a path the play itself marks out, for at the opening of the play, Romeo is in love, but not, as it happens, with Juliet. Rather, he is in love with Rosaline, and from the opening of the play, Romeo is being solicited to forget her and pass on to some more responsive object. The critics, that is, manage to do what Romeo is told to do. "Forget to think of her" (1.1.223), the peacemongering Benvolio counsels his friend—his "fair coz"—a lesson he reiterates in less-than-exalted terms: "Tut man, one fire burns out another's burning" (1.2.45). It is a lesson Romeo learns; to Friar Laurence's worried query, "Wast thou with Rosaline?" Romeo replies, "I have forgot that name, and that name's woe." "That's my good son" his "ghostly father" returns (2.3.40–43): Benvolio and Friar Laurence have been preaching Romeo the same sermon, a lesson in forgetting that, at least in the first scene of the play, Romeo protests that he cannot learn, but a lesson that, once accomplished, arguably involves the very transformation that Benvolio counsels: not so much a forgetting as a replacing, a substitution. Seen in that light, Juliet as replacement object is inserted within a seriality rather than as the locus of uniqueness and singularity. The play offers reasons to think about the relationship in these terms, not least when Juliet on the balcony ponders Romeo's name and likens it to the rose that remains itself whatever it is called (2.2.38–49). Is Juliet that rose, and, thereby, Rosaline renamed? What would the consequences be of thinking of her as the newest avatar of Rosaline in the play? What, moreover, would follow from the other identification implied in Juliet's lines, one that locates Romeo in the place of the rose and thus also in Rosaline's place? At the very least, a recognition would follow that desire might not be determined by the gender of its object, that the coupling of Romeo and Juliet is not a unique moment of heterosexual perfection and privacy but part of a series whose substitutions do not respect either the uniqueness of individuals or the boundaries of gender difference.

These implications can be read from the start, in Benvolio's gentle solicitations of his "fair coz"; as the play opens, Benvolio knows where to find Romeo because he shares with him a like condition, "measuring his affections by my own" (1.1.124), keeping his distance as Romeo keeps his, weeping at his sorrows, displaying thereby a "love . . . that . . . / Doth add more grief to too much of mine own" (1.1.186–87); one heart vibrates to the other's:

Romeo. Dost thou not laugh?
Benvolio. No coz, I rather weep.
Romeo. Good heart, at what?
Benvolio. At thy good heart's oppression.
Romeo. Why such is love's transgression.
(1.1. 181–83)

"Love's transgression" here refers indifferently to the effects of Rosaline upon Romeo, dividing him from himself, and the affection, the love of Benvolio for him, marked as it is, at once, by the strongest indications of identification and distance. His counsel, that Romeo forget Rosaline, is tantamount to a desire for him to remember himself and his friend; his counsel to replace Rosaline with some other flame is undertaken in the belief that a happy Romeo would be a happier companion.

The situation with Rosaline cannot help but recall the initial sequence in Shakespeare's sonnets, where the sonneteer urges the young man to marry in order to further solidify bonds between men. In those poems, as Sedgwick astutely observes, the woman is barely present; she is no more than the conduit for firming up the patriarchy and guaranteeing the young man's place within a social order in which all the most heavily invested relations are those between men. The woman in these poems is no one in particular, simply anyone whom the young man would marry, and she poses no threat to the men or to the love that the sonneteer proffers. Rosaline would seem to be in much the same situation; she has no lines in the play, and if she ever is onstage—at the ball at the Capulet's to which she has been invited, for example—her presence is unmarked and unremarked. Benvolio's desire that Romeo replace Rosaline with some more willing young woman seems to operate within the assumption that such a woman could occupy the position of the woman in Sonnets 1–17, a nonentity who would guarantee that Romeo fulfilled his debt to society and yet remained available for the comforts of friendly solicitations. Such assumptions, it might be supposed, are also at play when Friar Laurence breathes a sigh of relief that his "son" has not transgressed with Rosaline, and he hastens to legitimate Romeo's relation with Juliet by arranging their marriage. If these plans presume a smooth transition from one love to another, they also make clear that from the start Romeo's condition is not one in which love exists in the privatized domain to which commentators assign it. Romeo's absence is remarked by his parents as the play begins; his friend's counsels make clear that love affects their relation too; and Friar Laurence moves quickly to legitimize the relationship through the institution of marriage.

In this context, it is worth noting that Romeo's initial oxymoronic descriptions of love are occasioned by the signs of the street fight that opens the play; that is, he reads his emotional state as the reflection of the public brawl. This is only to say from another vantage point that love, from the start of the play, is implicated in the social order, not separate from it. Thus, if from one vantage point, it might appear that in moving from Rosaline to Juliet, Romeo moves from an unproblematic love to a disruptive one, the plot of replacement seems, rather, in either case to recognize the sociality of desire. The difference between Romeo's two loves—of comfort and despair?—is crossed from the start, and both loves work to secure and to disrupt the social order; both loves are "transgressive." Both loves are forbidden, a fact made clear when we recall the moment when Rosaline is first named in the play: Her name appears on the list that Romeo reads of those invited to the Capulet's ball; she is Capulet's "fair niece" (1.2.70). "My only love sprung from my only hate" (1.5.137): Romeo may be, for Juliet, her first transgressive desire, but she is, for Romeo, the second in his pursuit of forbidden loves. When Juliet delivers her speech about Romeo and the name of the rose, she inserts him into the series in which she already participates as Romeo's substitute love, a new Rosaline with a different name. (It is worth noting that the Rosaline figure in Shakespeare's source has no name.)

Placing him in her place, however, Juliet follows a textual track marked out earlier. For while one can argue, as I have, that the negotiations around Rosaline resemble those in the initial sequence of Shakespeare's sonnets, one moment in which those poems are recalled might suggest that the configuration is not quite the one I have already described. Romeo's complaint about Rosaline is that she is unresponsive, chaste as the moon; refusing to be "hit / With Cupid's arrow" (1.1.206–207). She is armed against love, even against "saint-seducing gold" (1.1.211): "O she is rich in beauty, only poor / That when she dies, with beauty dies her store" (1.1.213–14). These are recognizable complaints from the initial sonnets, but there they are directed at the young man who threatens by a kind of usury to make waste. These charges are also laid at Rosaline in the lines immediately following those quoted above, when to Benvolio's query, "Then she hath sworn that she will still live chaste," Romeo replies, "She hath, and in that sparing makes huge waste." In these respects Rosaline duplicates the young man who seems to have a patent on a beauty that the sonneteer cannot imagine located anywhere but in him and a progeny of young men who will duplicate and keep forever in circulation his unmatchable beauty:

> Looke what an unthrift in the world doth spend
> Shifts but his place, for still the world injoyes it
> But beauties waste hath in the world an end,
> And kept unusde the user so destroyes it.[4]

If Rosaline is, in this respect, in the place of the young man of the sonnets, the connection is furthered by her name, for it is possible to suspect that in the sonnets her name is his; in the very first poem he is named "beauties *Rose*" (Sonnet 1, line 2). Hence, when Juliet ponders the name of the rose—a name that might as well be hers or his—her lines operate in this sphere of gender exchange, too.

On the one hand, this could explain why the figure of Rosaline is so unthreatening in the play, why Romeo's grief over her can be so easily incorporated in homosocial relations; she is so little a woman that she might as well be a man, so little a woman that all she does is consolidate relations between men and serve as a conduit for them. Yet before one endorses this reading, one would also have to add: She is as much a forbidden love as Juliet is, and she is as threatening, too. If, that is, Rosaline, and the infinite replaceability of the rose, intimate the smooth workings of a homosocial order that gives women a place only in order to erase them, the transgressive danger spied in this love—even if it is between men and so secured—is what the period might call *sodomy*. Moreover, that transgression—of alliance, of the ties of the patriarchal organization and distribution of property and entitlements—while usually thought to occur between men, can also take place between a man and a woman. Locating Rosaline as the young man, in short, might as easily place her in the sphere of the homosocial as in the space of less containable and less socially approved desires. It is here that one might suspect that the name of the rose—like the name "Rosaline" as it travels in Shakespeare's plays to characters in *Love's Labors Lost* and *As You Like It*, where Rosalind's other name, of course, is Ganymede—plots a trajectory from the fair young man to the dark lady. For it is of course the case that the threatening sexuality that the dark lady represents—outside marriage and thus promiscuous and dangerous to the homosocial order—is closer to sodomy than almost anything suggested in the poems to the young man. Yet one must think of these sets of poems in a complementary and displaced relationship rather than, as in Joel Fineman's account, as marked by the uncrossable diacritical markings "homo" and "hetero."[5] Just as the threat to Romeo's masculinity that Juliet represents when he declares himself effeminized by her—valor's steel gone soft (3.1.111–13)—might be read within the dynamics of the dark lady sonnets (Juliet assuming Rosaline's guise in that transformation), so can it also be read as suggesting another movement across gender: If Romeo is feminized by her, she perhaps is masculinized. Hence, at the moment when Romeo spies Juliet on the balcony, he declares that the sun has replaced the moon; the moon earlier is Rosaline's celestial counterpart, mythically allying her to Diana. Is the sun, then, male, and is Juliet Romeo's Apollo?

Such a question returns us to the position of Rosaline as fair young man and to the possibility that Juliet's gender is equally destabilized, and we are thereby led to ponder desires that are not governed by the gender of objects and that are not allied to the formations of gender difference as the homo-hetero divide imagines them.[6]

Such a way of reading the play is anathema to heterosexualizing readings of *Romeo and Juliet* and of Shakespeare in general. Thus, when Janet Adelman, for example, declares that the tragedy begins at the moment when Romeo announces his effeminization—

> O sweet Juliet,
> Thy beauty hath made me effeminate
> And in my temper soften'd valour's steel.
> (3.1.115–17)

—because it signals the breakup of male-male relations in the play, solidified by their aggression toward and fear of women, this marks a tragedy that she regards as inevitable when comedy takes the form of male bonding or, worse, as it seems in Adelman's account, when male bonding can extend itself to the transvestite actor.[7] In those instances, Adelman opines, Shakespeare's plays indulge in the supposition "that one need not choose between a homosexual and a heterosexual bond" (91), a belief that she terms a fantasy that stands in the way of maturity and male development, which must culminate in heterosexuality. Otherwise, the plays might suggest "the fantasy that the relationships [with transvestite actors] are simultaneously homosexual and heterosexual—a simultaneity that threatens to become uncomfortable when, for example, in *As You Like It* we hear that Orlando has kissed Ganymede-Rosalind" (86). We, it is presumed, do not like it, and the reason seems to be that anything other than heterosexuality is repellent.

However much arguments like Kahn's or Adelman's expose the misogyny of Shakespeare's plays, their enforcement of heterosexuality and gender difference belies energies in the plays that cannot be reduced to the erasure of women. For if one thinks of Rosaline or of Juliet assuming the place of men, or of Romeo taking up a feminine position, those differences only read invidiously within the logic of a compulsory heterosexuality. When Rosaline is imagined as hoarding herself and refusing to open her lap to gold, she is, like the young man and like the dark lady, imagined as sexually autonomous and sexually self-fulfilling. Insofar as

Juliet takes up the position of Rosaline, their difference is marked by a single word. The woman who says no has become the woman who says yes; "Ay" is Juliet's first reported word (1.3.43) and her first word in the balcony scene (2.2.25), and the locus of her subjectivity is her assent to desire, her active solicitation of sexual experience (see, in this respect, her play on "Ay" and "I" in 3.2.45–51). When she thinks about having sex with Romeo, she imagines cutting him up into little pieces (3.2.21–25); whether this marks her as (in the favored terms of Kahn's analysis) phallically aggressive or not, it suggests that the diacritical markings of gender are transgressed in the play, something also to be seen earlier in the same soliloquy, in which the solicitation of Night, a maternal figure, is transformed into the scene of an enactment of a "strange love" (3.2.15) in which Romeo first is Night and then lies "upon the wings of night / Whiter than new snow upon a raven's back" (3.2.18–19). In this "purification" and masculinization of her beloved not only has he become—as she was—the brightness of day, but he also takes Night from behind; strange sex indeed.

It is, of course, arguable that the transgressions of gender that masculinize Juliet (or Rosaline) participate in misogyny (either by way of erasure or by an excoriation of active sexuality, as occurs most often in the play through attacks on the Nurse), but this move across gender also allows a subject position for women that is not confined within patriarchal boundaries. That is to say, it is only by seeing the energies in the plays that are not dictated by a compulsory heterosexuality and gender binarism that one can begin to mark their productive energies. In the case of *Romeo and Juliet,* as I have been suggesting, this means to put pressure on the heterosexualizing idealization of the play and on the magical solution it arrives at over the corpses of the young lovers. It is, in short, to make them available for forbidden desires that really do call patriarchal arrangements into questions. Readings of the plays, written from whatever position, that seek to enforce a compulsory heterosexuality must be complicit with the domestication of women and with the scapegoating of men (often by palming off the ills of heterosexuality on homosexuality). Such readings need to be opposed, and not merely on ideological grounds; "heterosexuality" and "homosexuality" are profound misnomers for the organization of sexuality in Shakespeare's time. As this essay has been suggesting, gender and sexuality in *Romeo and Juliet* do not subscribe to the compulsions of modern critics of the play.

So much Juliet's lines on the name of the rose prompt us to think, especially, as I have been suggesting, in the identifications across gender that they allow and in the ways they open trajectories of desire that cross gender difference. If the rose is most literally Rosaline's name respelled, it is, with only the slightest metaphorical force, Juliet's as well, since not only is she Romeo's newest rose, but she is herself locked within "orchard walls . . . high and hard to climb, / And the place death" (2.2.63–64), a dangerous flower to be plucked. As I have been suggesting, and as this description does too, she is dangerous because the desires she represents are closely allied to forbidden sexual acts more usually thought of as taking place between men. Juliet is most explicitly a flower when she has apparently been taken by death. "The roses in thy lips and cheeks shall fade" (4.1.99), Friar Laurence tells her, and this is what her father sees; "the sweetest flower of the field" (4.5.29), he tells her husband-to-be, has been taken already, not, as is the case, by Romeo but by death: Death has "lain with thy wife. There she lies / Flower as she was, deflowered by him" (4.5.36–37). Such imaginings of the sexual act as taking place in the wrong place ("the place death") and with the wrong partner only further the sense that the sexual field in which desire operates in the play is the forbidden desire named sodomy. The ungenerative locus of death allies the sexual act to the supposedly sterile and unreproductive practice of usury associated with the young man and with Rosaline's self-hoarding and waste, themselves as suggestive of sodomy as they are of masturbatory activities. If the living-dead Juliet is the flower deflowered, the usual deformations of the signifier that works to make these connections in the play—the name of the rose—finds a further point of transformation (of nominal difference and identification) at her funeral. Friar Laurence orders rosemary to be strewn on her supposed corpse (4.5.79) and the stage direction at line 96 suggests that it is done: *"Exeunt all but the Nurse and musicians, casting rosemary on Juliet."* Juliet's living-dead status could be taken to prevaricate in bodily terms between the generative and ungenerative desires whose paths cross each other in the play; much as she has and has not been deflowered by death, her union with Romeo is, from the end of the second act of the play, legitimated by marriage and continues to summon its allure from the unspeakable terrain of sodomy. If in her balcony speech Juliet joins herself to Romeo through the name of the rose—the name that connects them both through the cross-gendered figure of Rosaline as well—at her funeral the name has been transformed to rosemary. But this too has been anticipated by the vagaries of the signifier, or so the Nurse reports in lines that seem to have misheard the balcony declaration and to send those lines about the rose along the route to the rosemary cast upon Juliet:

> **Nurse.** Doth not rosemary and Romeo begin both with a letter?
> **Romeo.** Ay, Nurse, what of that? Both with an "R."
> **Nurse.** Ah, mocker! That's the dog's name, "R" is for the—No, I know it begins with some other letter; and she hath the prettiest sententious of it, of you, and rosemary, that it would do you good to hear it.
> (2.4.202–208)

The circuit of desire moves through the letter R, linking Romeo, the rose, Rosaline, rosemary, and Juliet, whose name begins with some other letter but is not misspelled in this sequence, proper and improper at once like the name Rosemary attached by her to Romeo and through the rosemary to her living-dead body, or like the forbidden fruit (whose other proper name we will, in a moment, confront) that can be domesticated behind the orchard walls.

The Nurse's lines deform the lovely alliteration of the letter R; she hears in it not only the growling of a desire that is less than transcendentally human—the bestial bark—but also something else. In his note on 2.4.205–6, Gibbons allows Phillip Williams to complete the Nurse's unfinished sentence: "[T]he Nurse just stops herself from saying the word *arse*—'with a somewhat unlooked-for show of modesty.'"[8] Another name for alliteration, apt here: assonance; another name for the movement of the letter R and the cross-couplings it allows, the *open Rs*. Gibbons goes where the nurse does not, immodestly allowing the unspeakable, and not just in the margins; the word is pronounced outside the garden walls as well:

> **Mercutio.** If love be blind, love cannot hit the mark.
> Now will he sit under a medlar tree
> And wish his mistress were that kind of fruit
> As maids call medlars when they laugh alone.
> O Romeo, that she were, O that she were
> An open-arse and thou a poperin pear!
> (2.1.33–38)

The medlar, whose other name, open-arse, is this secret now pronounced, is a member of the rose family (check Webster's if you don't believe me).[9] Gibbons allows the open-arse into his text (it appears in no quarto nor in any early edition of the play), an instance, in which, as he puts it in the textual introduction of his edition, he has "retained" an "archaic" form (25) unwarranted by his copytext.[10]

I don't want to be detained here by the textual crux of 2.1.38, much as it would communicate with the other moment that has animated this discussion—the passage on the rose, which also has a famous textual problem around the very issue of the proper name or word that makes possible the open Rs of this text—or the nurse's assonance, available only in Q2, a text of the play remarkable for its self-remarking textuality.[11] Rather, I would simply notice that in this scene Mercutio begins by conjuring Romeo, naming him by his proper—which is to say, entirely generic—names ("Romeo! Humours! Madman! Passion! Lover!" [2.1.7]), and that when these (im)proper names fail to raise him, Mercutio tries a more (in)direct approach, naming him by calling him up in the name of Rosaline: "In his mistress' name / I conjure only but to raise up him" (2.1.28–29). If the lines imagine Romeo rising to occupy this place, they deal at once in an identification between Romeo and Rosaline and with Romeo's desire for Rosaline. These meet in that conveniently open place that the Rs mark, the open-arse that also hits and deflects the mark (much as both Q1 and Q2 fail to deliver what Gibbons and most modern editions now allow Mercutio to say). Mercutio's line about a blind love that does and does not hit the mark recall Benvolio's counsels earlier about the deflection of Romeo's desires from Rosaline (1.1.203–205), and they also suggest that the path of the deformations of desire away from her never leaves the spot that she marks, which is precisely the unnameable crossing here (in the modern text) not left blank or marked out or marked over. The locus of anal penetration, of course, is available on any body, male or female. Mercutio's conjuring also conjures him into the magic circle, an O that is not, as most commentators would have it be, the vaginal opening, for this is how Mercutio voices—through Rosaline—his desire for Romeo; it is his version, that is, of Benvolio's more benign voicing of the place she can occupy between men.[12] Mercutio is calling Romeo up for him, as he does throughout the opening acts of the play, a deflection of Romeo's desire from the unresponsive beloved to one who, as much as Juliet later, wants to share a bed with Romeo (where Mercutio would lie is suggested by the solitary bed he goes home to, the "truckle-bed" [2.1.39] that lies under one placed above it).

As Mercutio conjures Romeo up in his generic names and then deflects those names through the name of Rosaline, he calls up his relationship to Romeo. The secret name of Romeo in the play, as Joseph Porter has convincingly argued, is Valentine, the otherwise nonexistent brother for Mercutio named only in the list of those invited to the Capulet ball that the illiterate servant cannot read, and that Romeo does, *"Mercutio and his brother Valentine"* (1.2.68).[13] It resonates (assonates) with another name down the list, *"Signior Valentio and his cousin Tybalt"* (1.2.71). This second Valentine, as invisible elsewhere in the play as the first, participates in a cousinship that, like the brotherhood of Mercutio and Valentine, may name properly what cannot be said. This male couple resounds in Tybalt's charge that Mercutio is Romeo's "consort" ("Mercutio, thou consortest with Romeo. / *Mercutio.* Consort?" 3.1.44–45) and in Mercutio's dismay at Romeo's declaration a few lines later that he would rather make love than fight with Tybalt. Tybalt, after all, is someone that Mercutio characterizes as ill-equipped to handle a sword; if Romeo is his man, as he declares (3.1.55), then, Mercutio opines, Romeo will follow him, taking him, it would seem, from behind. If Mercutio counsels Romeo to prick love for pricking (1.4.28), it is, it appears, because he fears that his Valentine has received the "butt-shaft" (2.4.16) of love, that Rosaline, armed like Diana, has hit his mark, that the boy love has come to the depth of his tail and buried his bauble in that hole rather than in his (see 2.4.90–100). To return to the scene of conjuring, then, is to register Mercutio's rivalry for a place that anyone might occupy and to recognize his projection into Rosaline's place as his own, as his way, that is, of occupying the magic circle or owning, to vary the metaphor slightly, the desires named by the open Rs in the text.

That these desires can be named variously, and never properly, Mercutio's lines further intimate when the secret name is one that maids trade among themselves in private. Female secrecy is broached in those lines and appropriated to a secret about transgression that does not respect gender difference. If there is, in this context, something to be said about the textual crux at 2.1.38, it is perhaps best suggested by John Dover Wilson's gloss in the Cambridge edition of the play (1955) on the reading that is adopted by Gibbons (and by a number of other editions, most recently by Stanley Wells and Gary Taylor in their 1986 Oxford

Complete Shakespeare). Q1, as noted above, has "open *Et caetera*" at this point, while Q2 prints "An open, or thou" (D1v). Dover Wilson argues that a compositor or scribal error is responsible for "or" (as a misreading of manuscript "ers," the presumption that leads Gibbons to "retain" a reading not found in any printed text but assumed to have been in Shakespeare's hand). In writing his note on the crux, Dover Wilson conveniently ignores the comma in Q2 that might, like the Nurse's unfinished sentence, indicate that Mercutio leaves unsaid what needs not be said (the alternative name for the medlar is about as available as anything, an open secret not to be said more openly). This allows him to dispose of the possibility that "or" means "or" rather than being a misread arse. "He speaks," Dover Wilson opines, "of the fruits [the ripely rotten apple and the popping pear] as complementary not alternative so that 'and' not 'or' is required" (151). "And" introduces, anglice, the "bad" Q1 evasion of the more forthrightly named Rs. For Dover Wilson, this is what is proper and required at this spot, that her arse and his poperin complement each other. In other words, Dover Wilson reads "and" to mean "or" (inserts "and" in his text so that it does so) since "or" might mean "and"; "or," were it to be there, might offer an "alternative" that Dover Wilson will not allow, the possibility that either member of the couple could assume either position. This is perhaps the scandal that the whispering of the maids is about or that can be heard as Juliet swallows the potion in order to get Romeo in the grave before Tybalt does:

> O look, methinks I see my cousin's ghost
> Seeking out Romeo that did spit his body
> Upon a rapier's point! Stay, Tybalt, stay.
> (4.3.55–57)

In those lines Juliet assumes Mercutio's rivalrous position, while Tybalt functions for her—as he had for Romeo and as he does earlier for Juliet in a scene that prevaricates over and also enforces the identity of her cousin and her lover (3.5.65–125)—as the switching point for an identification that breaches love and enmity, friend and villain, death and life, the open arse and the open grave of transgressively (un)productive desires. What these moments share—and they structure the trajectories of desire imagined in the play—is the recognition that anyone, man or woman, might be in the place marked by the open Rs of *Romeo and Juliet.*

Under the Covers with Caliban

My task here is to consider the gay text, and I begin with a caveat: If by "gay text" one designates a text in terms of the presumed sexual identity of its writer or of the characters represented, the term functions as a kind of legislative, normative category, and the critic's task is reduced to asking questions about how the author's sexuality affects the text or to finding the gay character in the text. In these acts of discovery, a regulatory definitional apparatus always is in place. Moreover, to think of a gay text this way constitutes a marginalizing gesture: Only texts that fit the criteria can properly be called gay texts, and what this inevitably means is that most texts are not. Instead, I take Eve Kosofsky Sedgwick's stunning program in *Epistemology of the Closet* to be a far more productive route in asking what a gay text is. In her cogent formulation, there is no question of knowledge in modernity that is not structured by the homo-hetero problematic, and this means that the question of the gay text is not to be reduced to one of identity.[1] Rather, it is always a relational question, and it figures everywhere. This formulation is vital, especially in the situation that concerns me here, the consideration of a text produced in an era that handles the homo-hetero divide very differently from the way our own does, since those identity categories were unavailable in the Renaissance (but the range of sexual experiences was not)—a consideration, of course, by a critic who writes now and whose task must be shaped by modern protocols of knowledge. Indeed, the aim of these pages is not merely to read *The Tempest* but also to ponder its editorial and critical production, that is, to measure its status as a modern text. In exploring questions of sexuality in *The Tempest* enabled by recent work in feminist and gay/lesbian studies and in engaging with earlier accounts of the play produced from other vantage points, my critical stance does not entail charges of blame or ignorance; instead, it measures future possibilities. I should add immediately that this essay does not pretend to cover all the sexual elements in the play; rather, it aims to tease out, largely on the basis of textual evidence of the bibliographic kind, some implications occasioned by, although not limited to, the figure of Caliban.

Caliban first appears in the text of *The Tempest* when his birth is recounted in the dialogue between Prospero and Ariel in act 1, scene 2. To Alden T. Vaughan and Virginia Mason Vaughan, I owe my awareness that this moment is accompanied by a crux, hitherto uncommented upon, in the Folio text of the play, its sole authoritative source. In their *Shakespeare's Caliban,* they print the lines as follows:

> Then was this Island
> (Save for the Son that [s]he did littour heere,
> A frekelld whelpe, hag-borne) not honour'd with
> A humane shape

depending on the Folio text and, for the bracketed *s* in *[s]he,* on an emendation, which, they note, Nicolas Rowe first supplied.[2] This bibliographic information will, of course, be found in most modern texts of the play (e.g., Frank Kermode's New Arden edition, Stephen Orgel's Oxford text), and it undoubtedly was the context in which the lines are cited in *Shakespeare's Caliban* that made the Folio text and Rowe's emendation suddenly seem urgent. The Vaughans are considering the question of whether or not Caliban is regarded as human in the play; they take these lines as establishing that he (unlike his mother, presumably) is the first "humane shape" to inhabit the island.[3] What is striking in this context is the fact that, at least as printed throughout the seventeenth century, this moment in the play ascribes his birth to a mother who has—and only for these lines describing the moment of parturition, since elsewhere there is no question of the gender of Sycorax—become male in gender. If Caliban is born human, he is born from a mother who is not merely inhuman (littering is not a human form of giving birth) but whose inhumanness the text would seem to be underscoring by the impossible gender change that takes place at this moment. Were one to take the male pronoun seriously, it would necessarily call into question at least one biblical definition of the human: man, born of woman. Caliban's humanity would not be assured if his mother were not a woman.

That it is possible to take the Folio line seriously (i.e., not simply to regard *he* as a printer's error that Rowe corrected) is attested by the textual history of the play in the seventeenth century. For if this is merely a mistake, it is remarkable that it was not until Rowe's 1709 edition of Shakespeare that it was caught. As is argued by Matthew W. Black and Matthias A. Shaaber, "the three later folios are not imperfect reprints of F1, F2, and F3 respectively, but critical editions in exactly the same sense that Rowe's is a critical edition."[4] The anonymous editors of 1632, 1664, and 1685 each consulted the previous folio for the basic copytext, much as Rowe based his text on F4. Each, moreover, was unlikely to have had much, if anything, in the way of authoritative textual material in support of emendations to the previous texts. That is, in most cases, changes in the subsequent folios (when they are not new errors) are emendations, many of which modern editors happily accept, that can be chalked up to common sense, to what Black and Shaaber refer nicely as "the fitness of things" (25). This is to say that a "mistake" of the kind that appears at this moment in the F1 text of *The Tempest* is exactly what one might have supposed would have been caught in one of the seventeenth-century folio printings of the play, which, Black and Shaaber argue, are especially good at correcting obvious typographical errors (even if some new ones inevitably were also introduced) as well as correcting the kind of solecism the misgendering of Sycorax would seem to represent.

The fullest modern collation of these lines occurs in Kermode's edition: "282. son] Sunne F2; Sun F3, F4. she]Rowe; he F, Ff,"[5] and it suggests something that an examination of the seventeenth-century texts further reveals: that these lines were not printed unchanged from edition to edition (the pronoun *he* remains constant); that instead of correcting the "obvious mistake," a possible new mistake was introduced in the lines, the replacement of F1's *Son* with the *Sunne* of F2 modernized in spelling to *Sun* in F3 and F4. A possible mistake, that is, unless the change from *son* to *sun* was an attempt to locate birth from a male at an appropriately mythological level, where such an event could happen (Zeus gives birth to Athena, for example); if so, the response to the lines seems less to register the "wrongness" of the gender as to want, somehow, to accommodate it. This is, of course, mere speculation on my part, and it is possible that *son/sun* is an indifferent variant (although, given the insistent modernization of the text from edition to edition, this is not all that likely). What is clear, at any rate, is that changes in punctuation (which serve, in fact, to confuse the sense of the lines, another sign that the "obvious" mistake of *he* for *she* was not perceived as such), in capitalization, and in the spelling of "frekelld," "hag-borne," and "humane," to bring the text in line with modern orthographic practices, make it evident that these lines were not merely reset from folio to folio; in every instance there is change, and therefore, in every instance there was the opportunity to change *he* to *she*.[6] That Rowe first did it, then, is not quite to be ascribed to common sense, nor is it the case that Rowe was the first editor to have felt that these lines needed to be changed. He was simply the first to think that "he" should read "she." (Actually, this is not quite accurate: although Rowe first made the change in a Shakespeare edition, John Dryden and William Davenant have "she" in their *The Tempest: Or The Enchanted Island* [1670].)

How, then, to account for the persistence of this "error" in seventeenth-century editions of *The Tempest*? Perhaps by appealing to the "fitness of things" that Black and Shaaber invoke, the fitness, that is, that necessitates that the monstrous offspring of a witch (in these lines bestially born, whelped and littered, and freakishly marked, freckled, a maculate conception) must be prodigiously and unnaturally mothered. But perhaps, too, by seeing that this gendered change has its counterparts elsewhere in the play. Stephen Orgel has described some lines from Prospero's narration of the past to Miranda earlier in this scene as articulating a birth fantasy on his part.[7] In these lines, if one follows Orgel's reading of them, Miranda's saving presence on board their vessel of exile is turned by Prospero into the instrument by which he gives birth:

Miranda. Alack, what trouble
Was I then to you!
Prospero. O, a cherubin
Thou wast that did preserve me. Thou didst smile,
Infused with a fortitude from heaven,
When I have decked the sea with drops full salt,
Under my burden groaned, which raised in me
An undergoing stomach to bear up
Against what should come.

(Orgel, 1.2.151–58)

"Burden," Orgel notes, "is the contents of the womb," while "groaning" "is a lying in." In these lines, as is the case throughout the play (as Orgel argues in the introduction to his edition and in his crucial essay "Prospero's Wife," which preceded it), Prospero does his best to efface and to denigrate women and to appropriate their powers to his own; in this he would seem to mirror the monarch of the time, whose misogyny was accompanied by proclamations of his female creative powers as "nourish-father" to the nation.[8] James I's formulation makes him, at once, nursing mother ("nurse" derives etymologically from Middle English "nourrish") and father; Prospero's lines to Miranda place him even less equivocally in the female position, as the one with a burdened and delivered womb, while (and perhaps in some tension with the erasure and appropriation of the female) Miranda is in the angelic position, spirit to his matter, strength and fortitude to his tears; she seems not merely responsible for "infusing" him but also for his final erection, as he reports himself "raised" and bearing "up." The lines, therefore, much as they appropriate femaleness (or, more specifically, maternal function)[9] from Miranda, also seem to be giving and taking maleness to and from her. As Orgel remarks, concluding the section of "Prospero's Wife" on "The Marriage Contract," "The women of Shakespeare's plays, of course, are adolescent boys" (57), and, he continues, this may help explain Shakespeare's identification with nominally female characters; so, in this instance, these gender dislocations might be relocated by remembering the fact that Miranda was played by a boy and that thus, these exchanges between genders are nonetheless exchanges between persons of the same gender.

In the context of such an argument, the gendering of Sycorax as male at the moment of her delivery of Caliban mirrors Prospero's seizure of female territory, and it also mirrors the stage that Orgel reminds us only appears to offer a world of "hes" and "shes." Rowe's emendation, then, especially as it is printed by the Vaughans, "[s]he," nicely brackets and subordinates the female to the male. Their proper bibliographic form is Prospero's plot in small.

And yet nowhere, save in the line Rowe emended, is Sycorax anything but female. If the line in F1 is not a mistake, its "fitness" would lie not along the naturalizing lines that would remind us that under the covers (beneath their costumes) all Shakespeare's actors were genitally male but, rather, in "fitting" monstrous birth to monstrous womb. Orgel's suggestion that Prospero indulges in a birth fantasy and, by extension, encroaches on female/maternal powers is borne out, and not merely in the lines from act 1, scene 2 cited previously. It can be seen in many of the assumptions of his power, whether he is delivering Ariel from a tree—something Sycorax, he claims, could not do, and in which he acts as a midwife in a scene reminiscent of the birth of Adonis from Myrrha, his incestuous mother:

> It was mine art,
> When I arrived and heard thee, that made gape
> The pine and let thee out.
>
> (Orgel, 1.2.291–93)

—or uttering lines, in the monologue in act 5, scene 1, originally spoken by Ovid's Medea, lines that mark his closest moment of identification with Sycorax. If, then, the male gendering of Sycorax is to be explained, one route would lie through the identification of magicians in the play, cutting across the denials that structure Prospero's assumptions (or those of Kermode's introduction to the New Arden edition, with its detailed discriminations between black and white magic). But it has to be remembered that Prospero has two seemingly opposing but actually congruent gender strategies in the play: One involves strongly marking gender difference and denigrating females (this is especially the case with Sycorax, but it is there when Prospero turns on Miranda and calls her his foot); the other is through the erasure of gender difference, the subsumption of women into his part, as in the lines we have already considered, in order to produce identification. A critic like Peter Hulme struggles in *Colonial Encounters* to drive a wedge between Prospero's play and *The Tempest.* In much the same way, to read the crux about the gender of

Sycorax as a further instance of the appropriation of female under the sign of male and the erasure of gendered difference is to fold one play into another and thereby to subscribe to a patriarchal phantasm.[10] If, then, one were to treat F1's mistake as not mistaken, it would be with the aim of preserving and exploring what is monstrous in this moment rather than seeing it as part of the way Prospero's seamless power overrides all opposition, including gendered difference. A simpler but, I think, equally important point to be made is this: The genital identification between adult male actor and boy actor is not necessarily a bottom line; that boys could play women's parts has everything to do with the fact that there was a strong gender identification between boys and women. Boys are only genitally male, although the fact that they are not genitally female must also have meant that their identification with or as women was not based in genital equipment. In other words, it is not a simple matter of looking under the covers to sort the genders in Shakespeare and to reduce them to one. It may be more to the point that the Shakespearean stage offers three genders, that the boys playing women are neither simply male nor simply female.[11]

Sycorax's violation of the biological function that differentiates males and females cannot, then, be equated with Prospero's violation of that same boundary from the opposite direction. The interchangeability of genders that is the result of the one-gender model that Thomas Laqueur has detailed (and that stands behind the historicizing of gender in a number of new historicists' thinking, including that of Orgel and Stephen Greenblatt) works, as it were, only in one direction.[12] If under the cover (beneath the appearance of external difference), women "really" are men (genitally), then it is the cover that ensures difference, the social trappings of gender and, in the case of women, the very flesh, which cannot simply be removed. (Women and men are only the same in the one-gender model at the level of anatomical drawing, at a level of abstraction that does not ramify to the social distinctions maintained between genders.) If at the moment that Sycorax performs the uniquely female act of giving birth and, in so doing, encroaches on territory that Prospero claims for himself, then her monstrosity is registered as gender change and recorded in the form that her offspring takes. Were Sycorax to serve as a mirror of Prospero at this moment, it would not be, therefore, in order to bolster the assurance of male power, the subordination and incorporation of the female within the male; rather, it would be to suggest something quite different: not the opposite of female monstrosity (for that opposition is included in the masculinist plot) but a monstrosity gendered here as male at the maternal site and even more equivocally in the shape of what is delivered, Caliban. *Is* he human? Is he *properly* male?

I don't know whether such questions vexed Sir Arthur Quiller-Couch and John Dover Wilson in their editorial labors for their 1921 Cambridge edition of the play,[13] but Dover Wilson is quite adamant about the inappropriateness of the lines we have been considering. Here are the lines in the Cambridge edition:

Then was this island,
(Save for the son that she did litter here,
A freckled whelp, hag-born) not honoured with
A human shape.
Ariel. Yes: Caliban her son.
Prospero. Dull thing, I say so: he, that Caliban
Whom now I keep in service.

(1.2.281–86)

And here is Dover Wilson's comment on them:

> (1) This passage is a violent digression. (2) Omit it and the context flows straight on. (3) The F. has a comma after "in service," which is absurd. . . . Is it possible to avoid the conclusion that these five lines are an addition, a piece of patchwork, designed to compensate for a rent elsewhere in this section? The reason for their introduction is not far to seek; Caliban is to enter at 1.321, and this is the first mention of his name! (83)

Dover Wilson, as is well-known, argued (unconvincingly to most subsequent editors) that F1 preserves a text of *The Tempest* reworked for court performance and that this is especially apparent in act 1, scene 2, where Prospero's prolix narrations replace an earlier play that dramatized what he narrates. Nonetheless, this is the only passage that Dover Wilson explicitly and vehemently declares to be not merely awkwardly covering over the earlier text but spurious and in need of excision. All this, I would add, without even addressing the "she/he" problem that is dutifully noted elsewhere in the edition. That is, I assume that it is the monstrous birth of Caliban in this passage that exercises Dover Wilson, an eruption that unnaturally secures his presence at this moment in the dialogue and creates a moment of awkwardness between Prospero and Ariel as they describe the conditions of the island when Prospero arrived to find Ariel confined in a tree. The "violent digression" provokes a violent response: "Omit it," Dover Wilson suggests, to make up for "a rent elsewhere" by making another cut here. And to what end? So that the discussion will flow "straight on"; so that the relationship between Prospero and Ariel will not be interrupted and (as I have already suggested), even worse, be echoed when the birth of Caliban parallels the birth of Ariel from the tree; so that one might not hear in Prospero's threat to "rend an oak / And peg thee in his knotty entrails" (Orgel, 1.2.294–95) a repetition not merely of Sycorax's act but also of her mode of delivery: The tree to which Prospero would return Ariel is gendered male, and the spot in which Ariel would be confined is "his knotty entrails."

What exercises Dover Wilson here is perhaps more evident in the gloss supplied for 2.2.163–64 (Cambridge edition lineation): "*An abominable monster!* Exclamation perhaps caused by a glimpse of Caliban from behind, as he bends to kiss Stephano's foot." The Vaughans, we might recall, cited the lines describing Caliban's birth in order to argue that however monstrous Caliban is, he is nonetheless human, and they detail for pages the various configurations that haunt this claim: Caliban as tortoise or fish as well as the more general claims about his bestiality, monstrosity, demonic origins, and the like, not to mention the stage traditions in which Caliban has appeared in various non- or subhuman forms. Nowhere, however, does the play seem to suggest that Caliban is particularly monstrous when seen from the rear, and although what Dover Wilson presumably has in mind is the degradation and abasement of his offer of service to Stephano (as compared, presumably, with the propriety, in the Cambridge editor's eyes, of his service to Prospero), this political abjection is described in charged physical terms. This is Dover Wison's fantasy, his glimpsing of a monstrosity that I would, now, be willing to credit—not as a "fact" but, rather, as a consequence of the line of associations that I have been pursuing here: Caliban born from a male mother, a witch, born monstrously and as a monster, born in a manner that is echoed in the threatened return of Ariel to his origins in the entrails of a tree; Caliban, in short, as sodomite.

To make this case one wishes that the conjunction of witchcraft and sodomy had been the subject of sustained historical scrutiny.

Arthur Evans's *Witchcraft and the Gay Counterculture*[14] is the only book with these ambitions, and it is deeply flawed by its desire to prove a transhistorical identity between witches and homosexuals as part of an ages-long subversive counterculture. While there is little to be said for this thesis, some of Evans's references to moments in which the two crimes coincide are indisputable, as when, for example, the inquisitors in Avignon in 1582 condemned fornication between men and succubi and between women and incubi as sodomy.[15] As Jeffrey Richards notes in his recent survey of sexual dissidence in the Middle Ages, by the mid-thirteenth century, "homosexuality became an inevitable concomitant of accusations of heresy and witchcraft," no doubt thanks in part to the papal bull, *Vox in Rama* (1233), from which he quotes this description of the witches' sabbath: "those present indulge in the most loathsome sensuality, having no regard to sex. If there are more men than women, men satisfy one another's depraved appetites, women do the same for each other."[16] E. William Monter, in his several studies of the Inquisition in various locales during the sixteenth and seventeenth centuries, has supported these linkages, noting, for instance, that of fifty-eight witches convicted in Fribourg in the early seventeenth century, eight were condemned as sodomites (there seems to have been no distinction between male witches and sodomites); accusations of witchcraft, sodomy, and infanticide, Monter further concludes, circulate differentially, as ways of policing the category of the "unnatural."[17] What makes this connection easy can be gleaned from one description of a sodomite as someone "committing heresy with his body,"[18] for it suggests how the bodily act of witchcraft—sex with the devil—that preoccupies Prospero and many other commentators might easily overlap with the category of sodomy (not least because witchcraft was most usually a charge leveled against women, sodomy against men). Paul Brown has commented on Prospero's sexual obsessiveness and his desire to regulate others' sexuality, and this feature of the character—the way his "project" plays out in the realm of sexual behavior—perhaps bears comparison with the fevered imaginations of those who described the supposed goings-on at the witches' sabbath. As G. R. Quaife summarizes, these scenes regularly included "anal and oral sex, homosexuality, bestiality, mutual masturbation, group sex and incest."[19]

These connections do not exist solely on the Continent and in practices sponsored by the Catholic church. As Retha Warnicke has pointed out, the first person condemned under the sodomy statute passed in England in 1533 (the statute that made sodomy a felony rather than a matter of church control), Walter Lord Hungerford, was found guilty not only of having sex with his male servants and with his daughter but also of having plotted against the king with the help of witches.[20] This particular configuration is, in certain respects, no surprise: Sexual crimes in the period are always linked to state crimes; heresy, in Reformation England, translated into papacy (so much so that the law against sodomy was repealed during Mary's reign), and this, in turn, translated into treason. Warnicke summons up the 1540 case against Hungerford in the context of her study of the fall of Anne Boleyn, and it is her argument that it was the queen's delivery of a monstrous, abortive fetus that sent Anne Boleyn to the block. Warnicke details the "sexual heresy" that surrounded these events, in which charges of incest, adultery, and sodomy (between the queen's supposed lovers), followed upon this monstrous birth. The fetus, that is, did not just represent the queen's infidelity to the king and therefore her treason; the other sexual charges followed upon it and served to explain the monster. We are close here, I think, to the imagination that links the witch Sycorax with the monstrous Caliban.

Here, as with charges of heresy on the Continent, we are not dealing so much with an equation as with a relay from witchcraft to sodomy, and indeed with a point of some contention in the literature on witchcraft. For while the witches' sabbath was often viewed as a feverishly sexual event, there was much debate about whether actual physical union between a (mortal) witch and the devil was possible and, if so, whether such unions were capable of producing offspring. (Reginald Scot, in arguing against these sexual possibilities in *The Discoverie of Witchcraft* [1584], nonetheless provides a fair sampling of the arguments made on both sides.) Even such a debate about the impossibility of such sexual acts must necessarily traffic with notions of sodomy, either because they involve acts that frustrated sexual reproduction within marriage (witches were regularly assumed to have the power of causing impotence, often by making a man's penis vanish; the sodomitical wasting of seed or its implantation in improper vessels both link to accusations of witchcraft, since those who thought that the witch could not have intercourse directly with the devil argued that human male semen was conveyed by the devil to the witch) or because the sex acts of witches, like those of sodomites accused of bestiality (the charges are not usually distinct), were thought capable of resulting in monstrous births.

In *Homosexuality in Renaissance England*, Alan Bray pursues the consequence of these (non)connections, pointing both to the ways sodomy overlapped with demonism (in terms of assumptions about destructiveness, heresy, and the like), especially in the "persistent motif that the child of the witch's diabolical union is a sodomite," and also to the ways witchcraft and sodomy diverged.[21] One of his main examples for the latter point is, significantly for the discussion here, Michael Drayton's "Moone-Calfe." The term, of course, is applied repeatedly to Caliban in *The Tempest* to indicate his monstrous, abortive nature. In Drayton's poem, the familiar topos of the world, the flesh, and the devil is presented in an allegorical narrative in which the devil fathers on the world monstrous offspring, twins who are masculine-feminines, androgynes and hermaphrodites.[22] The male twin is explicitly a sodomite, and the devil, frightened by the monster (line 170), appears to share the divine disgust at the sin of Sodom (lines 317–24). Bray argues that, in so doing, Drayton's devil is expressing a commonplace, that sodomy could be viewed with horror by the devil because it seemed to go beyond even his domain. That is, insofar as demonic offspring were nonetheless the product of heterosexual unions, sodomy suggested a form of sexual relationship that exceeded what was already a kind of demonic parody of proper sex. Strange as this point might seem, it is, in fact, made in the *Malleus Maleficarum*, that handbook of beliefs about witchcraft, in which it is claimed that "nowhere do we read that Incubi and Succubi fell into vices against nature," for sodomy, the writers claim, is a sin of such "very great enormity . . . that all devils, of whatsoever order, abominate and think shame to commit such actions."[23] Sodomy and witchcraft cannot be equated; they touch at a border of abomination and of the unspeakable.

In this context, it is worth recalling, too, that the pregnant wombs of condemned witches were opened to reveal within them horrific and deformed spawn. These assumptions are most fully in play around the trial of Anne Hutchison in early-seventeenth-century New England. Charges of heresy are materialized in her body as well as in her followers', who are also revealed as witches by their abortive and monstrous offspring (one of whom, like Caliban, is described as having horns, claws, and scales): "Mistris Hutchison . . . brought forth not one . . . but . . . 30. monstrous births or thereabouts, at once; some of them bigger, some lesser, some of one shape, some of another; few of any perfect shape, none at all of them (as farre as I could ever learne) of humane shape."[24] Next to the birth described by this Puritan minister, Sycorax's "littering" is almost demure, and the declaration that her offspring bears a human shape is almost humane. Yet he is also insistently called monster and "mooncalf" as she is never anything but a witch, whose crime Prospero cannot name.

If Dover Wilson's recoil at the "abominable monster" is then a recoil at what is most abominable—the sin beyond all others—he turns from ass kissing (metaphorically, to spell out what foot licking means in this scene) to even more unspeakable acts, literalizing in his presumed view of Caliban's bottom the horror he sees him performing. Ass kissing is of course the devil's kiss, the sign the witch makes of her devotion to her master. It is the sign of a political allegiance, just as Caliban's is. There is, however, another moment in the play that prepares and makes "fit" Dover Wilson's reaction to the abominable monster. Here is how Prospero describes what Antonio did:

> bend
> The dukedom yet unbowed—alas, poor Milan!—
> To most ignoble stooping.
>
> (Orgel, 1.2.114–16)

Dover Wilson's gloss on Caliban inadvertently glosses these lines, and the implications here are complex, not least because "Milan" is at once the name of Antonio and of Prospero in the substitution that has as yet not quite differentiated one from the other (as the rightful holder of the name, it is in Prospero's interest not to make that distinction). The lines thus represent the submission of Milan to Naples as either Antonio's voluntary or Prospero's enforced violation. Here Dover Wilson's reading of Caliban's abject position finds a more immediately plausible object: This scene of "ignoble stooping" invites a view from the rear; indeed, it suggests that Milan has been taken from behind, mastered anally. Moreover, the connections between sodomy and treason make this implication utterly unexceptionable (not that any editor, so far as I have found, has ever commented on the lines describing Antonio's behavior).[25]

Dover Wilson's reading of the scene of Caliban's submission to Stephano thus ramifies to one way betrayal of political propriety is registered in the play as sodomitical submission. It also connects back to the scene of Caliban's origins with which we began. Finally, it connects to the episode in the play that readers of *The Tempest* will recognize as alluded to in the title of this essay, a scene in which Caliban is represented as anally receptive and as anally productive. In act 2, scene 2, Trinculo creeps under Caliban's gaberdine. "Misery acquaints a man with strange bedfellows" (Orgel, 2.2.38), he remarks as he does so, using the word that refers to same-sex sleeping partners. Stephano comes across this four-legged figure and assumes that "this is some monster of the isle" (2.2.63). Yet the monstrosity here (the term is used over and over again in the scene), while initially registered by Trinculo in terms of the animal/human nature of Caliban and by Stephano in terms of the Mandevillian man of Ind, lies in what Stephano finally sees, Trinculo and Caliban making the beast with two backs, "an incarnation of the monstrous in lovemaking," as David Sundelson comments, not distancing himself from what he takes Stephano's attitude to be.[26] Stephano euphemizes the situation when he regards the four-legged creature before him as doubly mouthed, though he marks one mouth as forward and the other as backward. The exchange of mouth and anus here fits nicely with a figure whose name respells "cannibal" and with the colonialist tradition that regarded New World inhabitants as cannibals and sodomites.[27] At the moment when Trinculo emerges at Stephano's command to "come forth" (Orgel, 2.2.98; the line echoes Prospero's delivery of Ariel as well as his first command to Caliban [1.2.315]), Stephano asks: "How cam'st thou to be the siege of this mooncalf? Can he vent Trinculos?" (Orgel, 2.2.101–2). The excremental vision of birth here also seems to imagine that Caliban has swallowed Trinculo and now is delivering him whole (cf. Jonah and the whale; Rabelais's experience inside the body of Gargantua). The alimentary canal and the birth canal meet in the fantasy of anal delivery that we have already seen in Prospero's threat to return Ariel to the entrails of the tree from which he was delivered. It is this scene that realizes the mistake about Caliban's origins that the seventeenth-century folios repeated and that Rowe corrected. Here a male mother, the mooncalf who is the abortive and monstrous child of the witch, gives birth anally. Orgel is one of the few editors to at least record that "siege" means "excrement" and "vent" defecate. Only George Steevens, in a note to the line in his 1778 edition of the play, registers (phobically, to be sure) any sense of what is going on here: "*Siege* signifies *stool* in every sense of the word, and is here used in the dirtiest."[28]

The scene of male delivery in act 2, scene 2, therefore, stages what is implicit in the gendering of Sycorax as male at the moment she is described as giving birth to Caliban. While it is not my point here that future editors of *The Tempest* ought to follow the Folio reading, mere notation of Rowe's emendation seems an inadequate response to what, if my argument is convincing, is, at the least, a highly overdetermined error in the Folio text. To simply print "she," adopting Rowe's reading as what the line was supposed to have read, has consequences. For, as I have been suggesting, Prospero traffics in fantasies of male birth, too. That the play realizes these fantasies, doubly, on the body of Caliban (as the one who gives birth and as the one who is so born) represents the kind of deflection and displacement to be found throughout the play: the location of abomination anywhere but in the figure of Prospero.

To suggest some of the further ramifications of the crux that has occasioned this essay, I want to turn now to a *recognized* crux in the play (one that involves textual and sexual issues) and to place beside the problematic "he/she" of act 1, scene 2 "a reading whose time has come," to cite the final words of the "bibliographic coda" to Orgel's "Prospero's Wife" (64). Having teased out "the absent, the unspoken," in his essay—instances centering on the suppression of women in the play (and it is my concern now to consider those silences next to the unspeakable terrain that this essay has been exploring)—Orgel ends his essay by endorsing the bibliographic evidence presented by Jeanne Addison Roberts, that Ferdinand's lines during the masque in act 4, scene 1, "So rare a wondered father, and a wise, / Makes this place paradise" (the reading to be found in all previous twentieth-century editions of the play), originally read "So rare a wondered father and a wife / Makes this place paradise" (this is the reading adopted in Orgel, 4.1.123–24).[29] Orgel summarizes Roberts's findings in his note to line 123: "[E]arly in the print run, the cross-bar of the f broke, transforming 'wife' to 'wise.' Several copies of the Folio show the letter in the process of breaking"; this explains why most copies of the Folio read "wise," why the variant "wife," when recorded, has seemed merely a variant, and hence why most modern editions of the play read "wise." Orgel's endorsement of Roberts's work is not made merely on the bibliographical grounds that "wife" is what the Folio text read originally and authoritatively; it is also part of a "collaborative" effort of the kind that he remarks on throughout his essay, the understanding that what makes for the "rightness" of a reading is never simply the facts but the climate in which they are available and visible. Orgel's reading marks a time, then, in which feminist readings allow one to see things that were formerly invisible, and the restoration of "wife" in these lines thus restores Miranda to the scene of celebration. It marks her presence, whereas the traditional reading had absented her from Ferdinand's rapt response, which begins, after all, "Let me live here ever" (Orgel, 4.1.122).

I thoroughly support this reading and find Roberts's bibliographic evidence compelling; nor would I, for a moment, wish to dispute the feminist impulses arguably to be found in her essay (it is not an explicit thematic) and affirmed in Orgel's. Nonetheless, the crux that these lines represent, especially in the context of the argument that I have been presenting here, requires some further consideration. In "Prospero's Wife," Orgel claims that the variant "wife" was lost before Roberts found it: "[A]fter 1895 the wife became invisible: bibliographers lost the variant, and textual critics consistently denied its existence until Roberts pointed it out" (64). This is not, in fact, quite true, and therefore there is a question of choice in twentieth-century editions, for the variant *is* recorded (e.g., in Morton Luce's 1901 Arden edition and in Northrop Frye's Penguin text);[30] it is simply not adopted. Kermode has it both ways: He places a question mark after noting the variant and recommends "further inquiry" but ends his gloss by commenting that "the true reading may be *wife* after all." Kermode does not have before him the evidence that Roberts did; he relies, instead, on the easy mistake of confusing "f" and long "s" in the printing process and, lacking hard evidence, he can only allow "wife" in his note, not in the text. Horace Howard Furness in the 1892 variorum edition of the play cites with approval one Grant White, who opines that to print "wife" here would "degrade the poetical feeling of the passage," and he then goes on to make the revealing comment that in his own copy of F1 he cannot tell by looking whether the line reads "wife" or "wise"; how he comes to print "wise" fully supports Orgel's contention that we see only what we are prepared to see. "Personally," Furness writes, "seeing that I much prefer *wise,* I incline to believe that it is 'wise' in my copy."[31] Presumably, editors after Furness who print "wise" have shared his preference.

What preference is this, however? Not the one Kermode records in his note—"[W]e may think that in this Adam-like situation, Ferdinand must have said *wife*"—nor the preference to be found in all eighteenth-century editions, from Rowe on, which, in fact, print "wife." Rowe probably did not emend the line on the basis of consultation of a Folio text that read "wife"; his emendation was made on what Orgel in "Prospero's Wife" calls "logical grounds" (63), the logic, presumably, that Kermode suggests: that it is difficult to believe that at the moment of his bethrothal and in the context of a declaration of a desire to live in paradise forever, Ferdinand would not include Miranda in this sentiment.

It is this logic, however, coupled with the fact that eighteenth-century editors invariably print "wife," that must lead us to ask what time has come when the line reads "wife" in Orgel's edition. Eighteenth-century editors, who assumed that Shakespeare wrote "wise," were not restoring his intended meaning but were, instead, modernizing the text, indeed, in ways that I would argue parallel the normalizing of gender that Rowe first performed in assigning a feminine pronoun to Sycorax at the moment of her delivery of Caliban. The eighteenth-century readings of the play, that is, are not feminist interventions; they put "wife" there to assure the domestic relationship and the propriety of Ferdinand's remarks. They make the wife present in order to police the male-male relations between Ferdinand and Prospero; Ferdinand's celebration of his "father" is only saved from excess within the context of marriage. This must be granted at least as a caveat against the assumption that restoring "wife" restores a woman to the text; "wife" is not Miranda's name but her function. While she has been given the illusion that she has freely chosen Ferdinand, she marries him as part of her father's designs. (Ferdinand is Prospero's choice, and it is his desire that his daughter enacts and legitimizes.) As Orgel astutely argues, Prospero's aim in marrying them is to legitimize what Antonio did, placing Milan beneath Naples; now Milan will not fall to "ignoble stooping" because of the marriage alliance. What this further assures is the propriety of male-male relations, and it manages the hierarchy between Naples and Milan by having a woman come between the men. What Rowe and his followers presumably heard in Ferdinand's lines as they were presumed to appear in the Folio was the admission that Ferdinand's desire for Prospero repeated Antonio's for Alonso.

This "danger" is not entirely removed when the correct reading is restored. "And a wife" is, at best, an addition, and "so rare a wondered" seems primarily, if not exclusively, to refer to Prospero; as "wife," Miranda is in the lines but not named, and she is clearly in a subordinate relationship to her husband-to-be and to her father. Moreover, as Orgel notes, as do other editors as well, "wondered," as an adjective describing Prospero, echoes Miranda's name, which is subject to such punning elsewhere in the play. If "wondered" means someone who can produce wonders, then Prospero's magic show and his magical daughter are equated: They are both wonders that he produces. What Ferdinand is celebrating in the lines is Prospero's art and his production of a child, his male maternity. Miranda is, as it were, already in the phrase "rare a wondered," and her separation out in "and a wife" is almost as redundant and self-referential as the line would be if it read "and a wise." Putting "wife" in the line—as presumably Shakespeare did—hardly ensures Miranda's independence or her existence outside of patriarchal arrangements being celebrated here as Prospero hands her over to his chosen son-in-law.

The difference between eighteenth-century texts and the original Folio reading "and a wife" is that Rowe and his followers presumably believed that, by supplying "wife," the intensity of the male-male bond had been diluted and made acceptable, whereas F1 does not quite have those guarantees. In the sex/gender system in which Shakespeare writes, the choice between male and female lovers is not an exclusive one, as it comes to be in the eighteenth century; the fact that in these lines these two relations come together as one and that the emphasis is on the father (he gets the adjectives; he comes first in Ferdinand's utterance) is marked too by the verb form "makes": Father and wife are here a single entity. Rowe and subsequent eighteenth-century editors emend "makes" to "make"; this separation, this grammatical propriety of making father and wife two subjects, furthers the work of heterosexual propriety. Shakespeare's more fluid grammar cannot be taken unequivocally to be making father and wife a single subject, but it cannot be ruled out either.

Hence, the modern reinsertion of "wife" in this line does not by itself mean that some time of enlightened gender relations has necessarily come when the woman is put back in the lines. Now, of course, that is not Orgel's argument either; it is only within a certain climate of reading that the line would have feminist force. But, to my mind, it is not enough simply to get Miranda back into this line; a feminist reading of the lines might well involve a critique of the limits under which she appears here (as that appendage called wife) and might seek to underscore the work that heterosexual arrangement is being called upon to do: that is, to make acceptable male arrangements that might otherwise give (homophobic) critics pause. The lines, of course, also have a caution for the gay critic; to note that F1 here marks the difference between the properly homosocial and the overcharged and dangerously sodomitic (which it seeks to situate everywhere but in Prospero's relations with men) through the body of a woman means that one cannot simply celebrate Shakespearean sexuality for the ways in which it takes male-male and male-female relations in stride, as complementary and not as mutually exclusive. There are hierarchies of power in these lines, between father and children, between men and women. To Ferdinand's ecstatic lines Prospero replies, "Sweet, now, silence!" a gentle and affectionate command at which some editors have balked (Dover Wilson assigns the line to Miranda), although Orgel quite usefully points out that men do call each other "sweet" in Shakespeare.

Dover Wilson refuses to print this display of male-male affection, but like all other modern editors, he prints "wise" here too (the "variant" "wife" does not appear in the Cambridge edition). This returns us to a question raised earlier: Why have modern editors preferred "wise" to "wife"? It is not, presumably, because it allows the eros of the situation between Prospero and Ferdinand to be registered. Indeed, when Grant White claimed that printing "wife" would constitute a degradation of "poetic feeling," I think that one can see that the presence of "wife" for him would necessarily introduce a sexual element and thus mar poetic feeling between men, which presumably cannot ever be supposed to have an erotic component. Here Kermode's remark on the Adam-like situation of Ferdinand-in-paradise could be further glossed. In his line, Prospero is, as it were, the sole source of Miranda, just as in the biblical myth woman comes from man. This is the paradisial version of what, were Sycorax male, would be the abomination of Caliban's monstrous birth, and it is a component of the version of the misogyny that led Andrew Marvell to write, "Two Paradises 'twere in one / To live in Paradise alone,"[32] and, indeed, of the ages-long Christian tradition that lays the blame for the Fall on woman and yearns for the time before the creation of Eve, when Adam's only playmate was his creator. White's recoil at "wife" is a response to these yearnings for a paradise of male solitude. Kermode's more tempered remark about Ferdinand in paradise participates in eighteenth-century normativizing heterosexualization.

The time that has come, when "wife" appears in these lines, certainly disputes the virulent misogyny of White; it remains in danger, however, of simply reproducing heterosexuality and thus also insisting upon limits for women (they were meant for marriage) and for men (their relations could not ever be sexual ones).

It thus seems necessary to recognize the limits of interventions in the name of feminism or of gay affirmation that can be made by way of the Shakespearean text; nonetheless, within its modest limit as a political move, Orgel's restoration of "wife" and his declaration that it is a reading whose time has come would seem utterly unexceptionable. Could anyone after Orgel print "wise"? The answer, of course, is yes. As a brief bibliographic coda to this essay, I turn to the single-volume Shakespeare produced for Oxford by Gary Taylor and Stanley Wells at the same moment that Orgel was preparing his Oxford edition of *The Tempest.* In that edition, 4.1.123 of *The Tempest* reads "wise," and John Jowett provides the explanation for that decision in the 1987 textual commentary for the edition. His note is worth reprinting here:

> Roberts . . . showed that there was progressive damage to the crossbar of 'f' during printing. Error is none the less so easy that the matter does not end there. Whereas previous critics were divided as to what F actually read, almost all preferred "wise" as the more convincing reading. F's pararhyme is suspicious; *wise / paradise* is a Shakespearian rhyme. "Wife" gives trite sense and demands two grammatical licences: that "So rare a wondered" is extended to qualify "a wife", and that "Makes" has a plural subject.[33]

This is an extraordinary note. Though it starts seemingly by accepting Roberts's findings, it immediately introduces an unspecified sense of "error." One presumes that Jowett has in mind something like Kermode's note on how easily f and long s can be confused in the printing process; what is extraordinary here, then, is that Jowett appears to accept the fact that F1 originally read "wife," but he also wants to entertain the possibility that it did so in error (presumably as a compositor's error). Thus, even though what Roberts saw really did happen, that is beside the point.

I assume here that what would normally be accounted a strong bibliographical demonstration on Roberts's part is being policed precisely because of the context that Orgel adduces: that this was bibliographic work done with a feminist agenda (it hardly needs to be pointed out that the field of bibliography has been and remains heavily male dominated). Although Jowett's category of error is the closest he comes to making a bibliographic objection to Roberts, the logic of his claim leads to an undermining of any bibliographic protocols. If any reading of a text could be in error (and, of course, any can), then the textual/bibliographic evidence, even when it is uncontrovertible (as it is that F1 originally read "wife"), can only be subject to interpretation. It is, then, presumably (though this is unstated) the "bias" in Roberts's presumed interpretive stance that leads Jowett on.

Having established "wife" and "wise" as variants (rather than "wife" as the reading and "wise" as a variant produced by mechanical breakdown), Jowett appeals to "previous critics." Here, as with "error," who or what is involved goes unspecified; it is not really a matter of criticism that is being determined here; rather, it is a matter of editorial practice, and the overwhelming numbers ("almost all") mobilized on the side of "wise" represent only twentieth-century editors. Here, then, Jowett relies upon editors who have seen the Folio with their own eyes, one supposes editors with proper bibliographic training. With one hand, in his opening sentence, he has removed any support for bibliography as some kind of standard in making editorial decisions; now he relies on "proper" modern editors to give him support for "wise" as the more convincing reading. "Convincing" is, of course, a question-begging term; convincing in terms of the bibliographic evidence? Surely not, unless the fact that more copies of F1 read "wise" than "wife" (which must be true) is taken as constituting a bibliographic fact. Convincing from some critical predisposition? Presumably, but that is not where the note concludes. It concludes, rather, on questions of what is genuinely Shakespearean at the level of writing practice.[34] Yet one must suspect any claims to know what is Shakespearean, especially, as here, when the rhyme is so heavily loaded semantically. "Wise" and "paradise" presumably rhyme for Jowett because they are not trite words nor off rhymes; Jowett's "pararhyme" is a technical term that sneaks in "para"; it makes Jowett's explanation rhyme. What Jowett wants is that things alike be joined. Wives are trite. In the high masculine world of wise thoughts and enclosed gardens (the male world of the textual/bibliographic police), wives and women have no place. Let Jeanne Roberts beware. Shakespeare or the police: No grammatical licences allowed here.

The licences, however, are extraordinary; on the one hand, Jowett is probably right that "rare a wondered" does not extend to "wife." This is the only moment where Jowett's reading coincides with my own, and it points to the limits, as I have remarked, of reclaiming the line and "wife" in the name of feminism. (Indeed, here one could say that Jowett will not have "wife" because, if the word were there, it would show that Shakespeare did not have a properly modern, egalitarian view of women.) The point about "makes," I have addressed already. It is amazing that a Shakespearean editor has not noticed how often Shakespeare's subjects and verbs do not agree; has not noticed, that is, that Shakespeare had not learned eighteenth-century grammar. For, of course, what is remarkable about Jowett's note is that it goes beyond the eighteenth-century editors (who presumably do not count when he conjures up the previous critics) in demanding from the lines grammatical propriety of the kind Rowe and his followers provided by making "makes" into "make." In short, much as Jowett's reading is motivated by an animus against Roberts and the collaborative efforts that Orgel endorses in positing the time that has come, his eighteenth-century editorial procedures (he does not rely on F1 as his copytext here; he relies on the weight of tradition; he expects Shakespeare to use modern grammar) are *also* aimed at a propriety of gendered relations. Because a wife should be praised at least as much as a father-in-law and should be an independent subject (and not just grammatically), the line must read "wise." Otherwise, Shakespeare might have been a misogynist and a patriarchal poet. Jowett's reading, then, is *also* a product of the time that has come.

The question, then, of the reading whose time has come is complicated if, as I have been demonstrating, Jowett's regressive reading of "So rare a wondered father, and a wise" and Orgel's progressive reading of "So rare a wondered father, and a wife" founder on the divisions that I have been tracing. But these also suggest the resources of the present, the possibility of mobilizations that would not be available were the present a self-identical moment and were futurity therefore impossible except as some continuation of a monolithic present. That even Jowett's reading is legible as a kind of feminism is, however troubling, also an encouraging sign, for it translates the site of contention to divisions within feminism and thus to a terrain upon which a rethinking of social relations is possible. The masculinist bias in his preference for "wise" returns us, I conclude, to the complex divisions between homosocial relations that Jowett's reading affirms and to homosexual possibilities, relegated, once again, to the margins but now, I hope, not therefore to remain under the covers.

Notes

Introduction

1. Joel Fineman, *Shakespeare's Perjured Eye* (Berkeley: University of California Press, 1986); Christopher Pye, *The Regal Phantasm* (London: Routledge, 1990); Karen Newman, *Fashioning Femininity* (Chicago: University of Chicago Press, 1990).

2. Eve Kosofsky Sedgwick, *Epistemology of the Closet* (Berkeley: University of California Press, 1990).

3. Newman, *Fashioning Femininity,* 145–46.

4. Judith Butler, *Gender Trouble* (New York: Routledge, 1990).

5. Christopher Pye, *The Vanishing: Shakespeare, the Subject, and Early Modern Culture* (Durham, N.C.: Duke University Press, 2000).

6. Jeffrey Masten, "Is the Fundament a Grave?" in *The Body in Parts,* ed. David Hillman and Carla Mazzio (New York: Routledge, 1997); Leo Bersani, *Homos* (Cambridge, Mass.: Harvard University Press, 1995) and "Is the Rectum a Grave?" *October* 43 (1987): 197–222; Daniel Juan Gil, "At the Limits of the Social World: Fear and Pride in *Troilus and Cressida,*" *Shakespeare Quarterly* 52, no. 3 (Fall 2001): 336–59, esp. 336–43.

Textual Properties

1. Jerome J. McGann, "The Monks and the Giants," in *Textual Criticism and Literary Interpretation,* ed. McGann (Chicago: University of Chicago Press, 1985), 181.

2. See, for example, Randall McLeod, "UnEditing Shakespeare," *Sub-Stance* 33/34 (1982), 26–55.

3. For the term "iteration," see Jacques Derrida, "Signature Event Context," in *Margins of Philosophy,* trans. Alan Bass (Chicago: University of Chicago Press, 1982).

4. Gary Taylor, "Monopolies, Show Trials, Disaster, and Invasion: *King Lear* and Censorship," in *The Division of the Kingdoms,* ed. Gary Taylor and Michael Warren (Oxford: Clarendon Press, 1983), 109.

5. Thomas Hobbes, *Leviathan,* ed. C. B. Macpherson (Harmondsworth, Eng.: Penguin, 1968), 217.

6. Ferdinand de Saussure, *Course in General Linguistics,* trans. Wade Baskin (New York: McGraw Hill, 1966), 120.

7. Sir Philip Sidney, *A Defence of Poetry,* ed. J. A. Van Dorsten (Oxford: Oxford University Press, 1966), 25; Ben Jonson, *Discoveries* (1641), in *Ben Jonson,* ed. C. H. Herford, Evelyn Simpson, and Percy Simpson, 11 vols. (Oxford: Clarendon Press, 1925–51), vol. 8, 638.

8. All citations from *Twelfth Night* are from the Arden edition, ed. J. M. Lothian and T. W. Craik (London: Methuen, 1975).

9. Jacques Lacan, "Agency of the Letter in the Unconscious," in Lacan, *Ecrits,* trans. Alan Sheridan (New York: W. W. Norton, 1977), 151.

Shakespearean Characters

1. On the destination of the letter, see Barbara Johnson, "The Frame of Reference: Poe, Lacan, Derrida," *Yale French Studies* 55/56 (1977): 457–505; a revised version of her essay appears in Geoffrey H. Hartman, ed., *Psychoanalysis and the Question of the Text* (Baltimore: The Johns Hopkins University Press, 1978); and the texts from Derrida's *La Carte Postale* and Lacan's *Ecrits,* to which she refers. In the pages that follow, I do not address the differences between Derrida and Lacan, in part because of the persuasiveness of Johnson's arguments and in part because such texts as Derrida's *Eperons* and Lacan's *Encore* suggest some reconciliation of their positions regarding phallogocentrism.

2. All citations are from *William Shakespeare: The Complete Works,* Penguin edition, ed. Alfred Harbage (Baltimore: Penguin Books, 1969).

3. See Sir Philip Sidney, *A Defence of Poetry,* ed. J. A. Van Dorsten (Oxford: Oxford University Press, 1966), 74–75. Among the others would figure sonneteers, including Shakespeare; for a history of the trope and its uses, see J. B. Leishmen, *Themes and Variations in Shakespeare's Sonnets* (New York: Harper and Row, 1963), 25–91.

4. All citations from *Metamorphoses* are from the Loeb edition, trans. Frank Justus Miller (Cambridge, Mass.: Harvard University Press, 1960).

5. All citations from Virgil's *Eclogues* are from the Loeb edition, trans. H. Rushton Fairclough (Cambridge, Mass.: Harvard University Press, 1953).

6. On the inescapable pastoral of *The Two Gentlemen of Verona,* see Richard Cody, *The Landscape of the Mind* (Oxford: Clarendon Press, 1969), esp. 83–84, 92, and his useful reminders that Tasso's *Aminta* and Guarini's *Il Pastor Fido* figure in Silvia's name.

7. Joseph A. Porter, "Mercutio's Brother," *South Atlantic Review* 49 (1984): 31–41. The *Oxford English Dictionary* provides the literal meanings of "valentine."

8. The phrase is Paul Alpers's, from *The Singer of the* Eclogues*: A Study of Virgilian Pastoral* (Berkeley and Los Angeles: University of California Press, 1979), which I discuss in my *Voice Terminal Echo* (London: Methuen, 1986), chap. 3.

9. The Lacanian texts include the seminar on "The Purloined Letter," partially translated by Jeffrey Mehlman in *Yale French Studies* 48 (1973): 38–72, and "The Agency of the Letter in the Unconscious," in Lacan, *Ecrits: A Selection,* trans. Alan Sheridan (New York: W. W. Norton, 1977).

10. Lacan, "The Agency of the Letter," 167.

11. In *Unredeemed Rhetoric: Thomas Nashe and the Scandal of Authorship* (Baltimore: The Johns Hopkins University Press, 1982), Jonathan V. Crewe discerns a similar figure in Nashe's history of the page Jack Wilton; see, for example, 69–70.

12. This is another instance of what Derrida calls the violence of the letter and its violation of limits, propriety, boundaries, and origin; see, for example, Derrida, *Of Grammatology,* trans. Gayatri Chakravorty Spivak (Baltimore: The Johns Hopkins University Press, 1974, 1976), 101–64.

13. Jacques Lacan, "On Structure as an Inmixing of an Otherness Prerequisite to Any Subject Whatever," in *The Structuralist Controversy: The Languages of Criticism and the Sciences of Man,* ed. Richard Macksey and Eugenio Donato (Baltimore: The Johns Hopkins University Press, 1970), 193–94.

14. Lacan, "The Agency of the Letter," 147.

15. All citations are from Angel Day, *The English Secretorie* (1586, reprint, Menston, Eng.: Scolar Press, 1967).

16. For an elegant argument about character that focuses on the early plays and answers the traditional charges, see Barry Weller, "Identity and Representation in Shakespeare," *ELH* 49 (1982): 339–62. Weller argues that characters are seeking not themselves but *self-representation* (343) and that the truth of character coincides with representation. This involves refiguration within a variety of matrices: others' perceptions, social prescriptions (e.g., the dictates of love and friendship in *The Two Gentlemen of Verona*). The "being" of character, from this perspective, is its metamorphic capacity; discontinuous change is its

"essence." "The protean character of humanity may be essentially resistant to the termination of process, that is, to the translation of man from something which becomes to something which is" (350). Weller concludes his discussion by gesturing in the direction taken in this study: "[T]he most comprehensive name for the otherness through and against which the self struggles to proclaim its uniqueness is language, and discussion of identity in the early comedies requires a supplementary interrogation of the sources of language" (358). The approach I take here is also encouraged by Stephen Greenblatt's use of Lacan in the analysis of *Othello* in *Renaissance Self-Fashioning: From More to Shakespeare* (Chicago: University of Chicago Press, 1980), 244–45, and by the work of Joel Fineman, especially "Fratricide and Cuckoldry: Shakespeare's Doubles," in *Representing Shakespeare,* ed. Murray M. Schwartz and Coppélia Kahn (Baltimore: The Johns Hopkins University Press, 1980), and "Shakespeare's 'Perjur'd Eye,'" *Representations* 7 (1984): 59–86. The discussion of the sonnets that follows parallels many of Fineman's concerns, although it does not schematize the poems in his visual/linguistic dichotomy.

17. See, for example, Mary L. Fawcett, "Arms/Words/Tears: Language and the Body in *Titus Andronicus,*" *ELH* 50 (1983): 261–77, and S. Clark Hulse, "Wresting the Alphabet: Oratory and Action in *Titus Andronicus,*" *Criticism* 21 (1979): 106–18.

18. Fawcett, "Arms/Words/Tears," sees Lavinia's mouth as a *vagina dentata*; Hulse, "Wresting the Alphabet," sees fellatio in the scene.

19. Ann Thompson summarizes some points of contact in "Philomel in *Titus Andronicus* and *Cymbeline,*" *Shakespeare Survey* 31 (1978): 23–32.

20. See *Phaedrus* 259.

21. The titillating pictures in the chamber are described in act 2, scene 4.

22. All citations from Thomas Overbury are from *The Overburian Characters,* ed. W. J. Paylor (Oxford: Basil Blackwell, 1936). "What a Character Is" (92) appeared first in 1615. On the etymology, see Warren Anderson's introduction to *Theophrastus: The Character Sketches* (Kent, Ohio: Kent State University Press, 1970), xv–xvi. The most usual meaning for "character" in Greek texts is an impression stamped on a coin. On that etymology, see Marc Shell, *The Economy of Literature* (Baltimore: The Johns Hopkins University Press, 1978), 64. For some further discussion of the implications of the term for the depiction of character, see Warren Ginsberg, *The Cast of Character: The Representation of Personality in Ancient and Medieval Literature* (Toronto: University of Toronto Press, 1983), 14–19.

23. *Profitable Instructions* (1633), cited in Marion Trousdale, *Shakespeare and the Rhetoricians* (Chapel Hill: University of North Carolina Press, 1982), 8. Trousdale's demonstrations of the rhetorical placement of character in text are assumed in this discussion. Texts, as Trousdale argues, offer "a verbal structure in which possible relationships between different pieces of action are suggested

by rhetorical elaboration" (134); the locus of action is thus rhetorical *place,* copiously filled and refilled, fully and endlessly textualized: "[O]ne text is structured by another and . . . such . . . activity necessarily creates discontinuous discourses, . . . a plurality of views" (160). The speech of characters is their (re)placement within the troping of text upon text.

24. Page 25; all citations from Mulcaster's *Elementarie* are from the Scolar facsimile edition (Menston, Eng., 1970).

25. John Earle, *Micro-Cosmographie,* ed. Edward Arber (London, 1869), 21.

26. Joseph Hall, *Characters of Virtues and Vices* (1608), in *The Works of Joseph Hall,* 12 vols. (Oxford, 1837), vol. 6, 88. The standard history of the form is Benjamin Boyce, *The Theophrastian Character in England to 1642* (Cambridge, Mass.: Harvard University Press, 1947). For some connections between the character and visual epistemology, see Forrest G. Robinson, *The Shape of Things Known* (Cambridge, Mass.: Harvard University Press, 1972), 206–14. For an Ovidian character book, see *A Strange Metamorphosis of Men, Transformed in a Wilderness* (London, 1634). The Shakespearean analogue might be found in *As You Like It,* for example, "These trees shall be my books, / And in their barks my thoughts I'll character" (3.2.5–6).

27. John Donne, letter of 23 January 1614, quoted in John Carey, "Donne and Coins," in *English Renaissance Studies Presented to Dame Helen Gardner,* ed. John Carey (Oxford: Clarendon Press, 1980), 154. See also J. Eric Engstrom, *Coins in Shakespeare: A Numismatic Guide* (Hanover, N.H.: Dartmouth College Museum Publications, 1964), for an index to uses of coins in the Shakespearean text.

28. Derrida considers the relationships between phonetic alphabets and hieroglyphs in *Of Grammatology,* for example, 74–81; see also Derrida, "The Theater of Cruelty," in his *Writing and Difference,* trans. Alan Bass (Chicago: University of Chicago Press, 1978), 240–47. For a discussion of the significance of hieroglyphics for grammatology, see Gregory L. Ulmer, *Applied Grammatology: Post(e)-Pedagogy from Jacques Derrida to Joseph Beuys* (Baltimore: The Johns Hopkins University Press, 1985), 16–19.

In "George Herbert's Pattern Poems and the Materiality of Language: A New Approach to Renaissance Hieroglyphics," *ELH* 50 (1983): 245–60, Martin Elsky argues for the effect of neo-Platonic allegorizations of letters upon humanistic ideas of writing as the transcription of voice (246). The usual ascription of the origin of writing to the Egyptian hieroglyph lent symbolic and material density to the alphabet, and letters exceeded mere phonetic transcription. Elsky thinks this is to be seen in Herbert rather than in sixteenth-century English theorists like Mulcaster. The evidence presented below, however, suggests otherwise, although it does not endorse any allegorization of the materiality of the letter. Rather, its materiality is representational, as would be indicated by a passage from G. P. Lomazzo on writing as originary painting: "Characters and the use of writing were first invented to preserve the memory of the Sciences. . . . Painting is an instrument under which the treasury of memory is contained, insomuch as writing is nothing else, but a picture of *white* and *black*" (cited by Elsky, 247). The movement of the Overburian definition, from phonetic to hieroglyphic character, passes through the "shadowing" of black and white.

29. Cf. A. Bartlett Giamatti, "Proteus Unbound: Some Versions of the Sea God in the Renaissance," in *The Disciplines of Criticism*, ed. Peter Demetz, Thomas Greene, and Lowry Nelson Jr. (New Haven: Yale University Press, 1968), 437–57.

30. George Sandys, *Ovid's Metamorphosis Englished Mythologiz'd and Represented* (London, 1632), 104.

31. Booth comments on Sonnet 122 in his edition of *Shakespeare's Sonnets* (New Haven: Yale University Press, 1977), 412–15.

32. Jacques Derrida, "Freud and the Scene of Writing," in Derrida, *Writing and Difference;* cited passages appear on 226–27.

33. *Theaetetus,* trans. Francis MacDonald (Indianapolis, Ind.: Bobbs-Merrill, 1957). Derrida analyzed similar passages from the *Phaedrus* in "Plato's Pharmacy" and from the *Philebus* in "The Double Session," both in his *Dissemination,* trans. Barbara Johnson (Chicago: University of Chicago Press, 1981). *La Carte Postale de Socrate à Freud et au-delà* (Paris: Flammarion, 1980) traces the path from the representation of Socrates as writer (in a medieval illustration to a fortune-telling book) to the Freudian scene of writing.

34. Jacques Lacan, "The Subversion of the Subject and the Dialectic of Desire in the Freudian Unconscious," in Lacan, *Ecrits: A Selection,* 305.

35. Lacan, "The Agency of the Letter," 172.

36. Lacan, "The Subversion of the Subject," 304–5. Cf. Lacan's description of the subject speaking: "In this labour which he undertakes to reconstruct *for another,* he rediscovers the fundamental alienation that made him construct it *like another,* and which has always destined it to be taken from him *by another*" ("The Function and Field of Speech and Language in Psychoanalysis," in *Ecrits: A Selection,* 42).

37. See, for example, Jacques Derrida, "Force and Signification," in his *Writing and Difference,* 19–20, or *Positions,* trans. Alan Bass (Chicago: University of Chicago Press, 1981), 35–36. Derrida reviews his quarrel with Lacan in *Positions,* 111–13, n. 44; see also 113, translator's notes 47, 48.

38. Lacan's designation of the symbolic as the name of the father (e.g., in "Function and Field of Speech," 67) and his association of the symbolic with the phallus (e.g., in "The Signification of the Phallus," both in *Ecrits: A Selection,* 281–91) are not necessarily the phallogocentric endorsements that Derrida finds; see the witty exposition of Jane Gallop, *The Daughter's Seduction: Feminism and Psychoanalysis* (Ithaca, N.Y.: Cornell University Press, 1982), which

emphasizes that Lacan's is the mother's phallus. Derrida inscribes the Freudian scene in the primal scene in "Freud and the Scene of Writing," 229.

39. On the impossible sentence, see Jacques Derrida's exchange with Roland Barthes, in Macksey and Donato, *The Structuralist Controversy,* 155–56; on iterability, see Jacques Derrida, "Signature Event Context," in his *Margins of Philosophy,* trans. Alan Bass (Chicago: University of Chicago Press, 1982).

In *The Tremulous Private Body* (London: Metheun, 1984), Francis Barker takes Hamlet as a figure anticipatory of the bourgeois consciousness exemplified later in the seventeenth century; among his most provocative observations is his characterization of interiority as "a *doubling of the surface*" (28); "at the center of Hamlet, in the interior of his mystery, there is, in short, nothing. The promised essence remains beyond the scope of the text's signification: or rather, signals the limit of the signification of this world by marking out the site of an absence it cannot fill" (37).

Making Sense

1. Richard Levin, "Feminist Thematics and Shakespearean Tragedy," *PMLA* 103 (1988): 125–38. "Making Sense" responds to Levin's "Unthinkable Thoughts in the New Historicizing of English Renaissance Drama," *New Literary History* 21, no. 3 (Spring 1990): 433–37, from which all citations below are drawn.

2. See William Empson, *The Structure of Complex Words* (Ann Arbor: University of Michigan Press, 1967), 250–310, and Stanley Fish, "Normal Circumstances, Literal Language, Direct Speech Acts, the Ordinary, the Everyday, the Obvious, What Goes without Saying, and Other Special Cases," in his *Is There a Text in this Class?* (Cambridge, Mass.: Harvard University Press, 1980), 268–92.

3. Thomas Heywood, *An Apology for Actors* (1612; facsimile edition, ed. Arthur Freeman, New York: Garland Publishing, 1973), B4r.

4. William Shakespeare, *A Midsummer Night's Dream,* in *The Riverside Shakespeare,* ed. G. Blakemore Evans (Boston: Houghton Mifflin, 1974), 4.1.186–98.

5. William Shakespeare, *Romeo and Juliet,* New Arden edition, ed. Brian Gibbons (London: Methuen, 1980).

6. Jonathan Goldberg, review of *Romeo and Juliet,* New Arden, ed. Brian Gibbons, *Shakespeare Studies* 16 (1983): 343.

7. Gibbons, introduction to *Romeo and Juliet,* New Arden, 74.

Shakespearean Inscriptions

1. Rosalie Colie, *The Resources of Kind: Genre Theory in the Renaissance* (Berkeley and Los Angeles: University of California Press, 1973).

2. Stephen Orgel, "Shakespeare and the Kinds of Drama," *Critical Inquiry* 6 (1979): 107–23; Louise George Clubb, "The Arts of Genre: *Torrismondo* and *Hamlet*," *ELH* 47 (1980): 657–69.

3. All citations are from *The New Cambridge Shakespeare* (Cambridge, Mass.: Houghton Mifflin Co., Riverside Press, 1942).

4. Linda Bamber, *Comic Women, Tragic Men: A Study of Gender and Genre in Shakespeare* (Stanford: Stanford University Press, 1982).

5. Stephen Greenblatt, *Renaissance Self-Fashioning: From More to Shakespeare* (Chicago: University of Chicago Press, 1980).

6. For further arguments along these lines, see Ann Rosalind Jones, "Writing the Body: Toward an Understanding of *L'écriture Féminine*," *Feminist Studies* 7 (1981): 247–63, esp. 253–55, where Jones argues for the historic specificity of the terms "male" and "female."

7. Carolyn Heilbrun, untitled, in *Signs* 8 (1982): 182–86. For a somewhat more sophisticated argument along these lines, see Coppélia Kahn, *Man's Estate: Masculine Identity in Shakespeare* (Berkeley and Los Angeles: University of California Press, 1981); Kahn at least sees that patriarchy is problematized in Shakespeare.

8. For documentation and discussion of these remarks, see Stephen Greenblatt, "Invisible Bullets: Renaissance Authority and Its Subversion," *Glyph: Johns Hopkins Textual Studies* 8 (1981): 40–61, and Jonathan Goldberg, *James I and the Politics of Literature* (Baltimore: The Johns Hopkins University Press, 1983), chap. 3.

9. Gayatri Chakravorty Spivak, foreword to Mahasveta Devi, "Draupadi," trans. Gayatri Chakravorty Spivak, *Critical Inquiry* 8 (1981): 382–83.

10. Legally, it is true, women in Renaissance England were bound and powerless except in very special circumstances. (They were not denied the right to speak in court, however.) Yet Renaissance legal theory is full of holes, and attempts to place women in the law ran into all sorts of difficulties. These are briefly and suggestively traced in Ian Maclean's *The Renaissance Notion of Woman* (Cambridge: Cambridge University Press, 1980), 69–81, where Maclean notes that feminist arguments enter legal writing as early as Heinrich Cornelius Agrippa's *De nobilitate et praecellentia foeminei sexus* (Anvers, 1529). More broadly, Maclean's book shows that contradictions are rampant within the most conservative discourses of the Renaissance, and 1580–1630 seems to be the period in which the elaborate synthesis, which marked and limited the place of women, began to crack because of its own internal contradictions, as well as the pressures of history and alternative discourses.

11. René Girard has argued for the doubling of Antonio/Shylock and of Shylock/Portia and the problematics of difference in "'To Entrap the Wisest': A Reading of *The Merchant of Venice*," in *Literature and Society*, ed. Edward W. Said (Baltimore: The Johns Hopkins University Press, 1980); see also Leonard Tennenhouse, "The Counterfeit Order of *The Merchant of Venice*," in *Repre-*

senting Shakespeare, ed. Murray M. Schwartz and Coppélia Kahn (Baltimore: The Johns Hopkins University Press, 1980), which points to recalcitrances in the text, including the ways in which Portia replaces Shylock as the troubler of Antonio's relation to Bassanio (63, 66). For a suggestion about the ideological yoking in the trial scene, see Walter Cohen, "*The Merchant of Venice* and the Possibilities of Historical Criticism," *ELH* 49 (1982): 776.

12. Luce Irigaray, "Ce sexe qui n'en est pas un," in *Ce sexe qui n'en est pas un* (Paris: Minuit, 1977); trans. Claudia Reeder, in *New French Feminisms,* ed. Elaine Marks and Isabelle de Courtivron (New York, 1981), 103.

13. Jacques Derrida, "La Loi du genre/The Law of Genre," *Glyph: Johns Hopkins Textual Studies* 7 (1980): 176–232.

14. For a further elaboration of my argument, see my *James I and the Politics of Literature,* 230–39. I also depend upon the suggestive remarks of Orgel, "Shakespeare and the Kinds of Drama," 122–23. The best study of substitution in *Measure for Measure* is by Nancy S. Leonard, "Substitution in Shakespeare's Problem Comedies," *English Literary Renaissance* 9 (1979): 218–301.

15. Penry Williams, *The Tudor Regime* (Oxford: Clarendon Press, 1979), 234. On the development of *peine forte et dure* as a response to the notion that no one should be judged solely on the basis of others' testimony, see W. S. Holdsworth, *A History of English Law* (London: Methuen, 1926), ix, 179.

16. Summing up hundreds of commonplace books, Keith Thomas notes, woman's "chief ornament was silence, and her sole duty obedience" ("Women and the Civil War Sects," *Past and Present* 13 [1958]: 43). Yet it is precisely the work of Thomas, or of Natalie Zemon Davis, *Society and Culture in Early Modern France* (Stanford: Stanford University Press, 1975), to show the space between theory and practice. This is also the argument of Maclean, who discusses some of the equivocations with regard to the virtue of silence (*The Renaissance Notion of Women,* 15, 20–21, 23, 66). More generally, Maclean notes the contradictions between notions of sexual difference and virtues versus social differences. These matters are also debated in book 3 of Castiglione's *The Courtier,* where the prime and distinguishing virtue of the court lady is "a certain sweetnesse of language" (trans. Thomas Hoby, Everyman Library [London: J. M. Dent and Sons, 1928], 190). On the literature of female gentility, Ruth Kelso comments in *Doctrine for the Lady of the Renaissance* (Urbana: University of Illinois Press, 1956), "The purposes of these writers are too disparate and the elements too antithetic to each other; they have no central figure in common as the writers on the gentleman have" (3). Modern historians and critics, in short, must be wary of reifying Renaissance commonplaces.

17. My discussion depends throughout on Greenblatt, "Invisible Bullets."

18. "Right down to the middle of the seventeenth century, the examination of the accused is the central feature of the criminal procedure of the common law. Nor do we read anywhere that a witness could refuse to answer on

the ground that his answer might incriminate him" (Holdsworth, *A History of English Law,* ix, 199).

19. For the emblem, see Edgar Wind, *Pagan Mysteries in the Renaissance* (New York: Barnes and Noble, 1968), 12 n, 196 fig. 23.

20. Cf. Stanley Cavell, "The Avoidance of Love," in his *Must We Mean What We Say?* (New York: Scribner, 1969).

21. See, for example, descriptions of Elizabeth's behavior on progresses, in J. E. Neale, *Queen Elizabeth* (London: Harcourt, Brace, and Co., 1934), 207–10. As Maureen Quilligan notes in *Milton's Spenser: The Politics of Reading* (Ithaca, N.Y.: Cornell University Press, 1983), 215–16, Theseus's display of noblesse oblige "recalls a famous episode of Elizabeth's early career when she managed a fearful schoolmaster by telling him before he began: 'Be not afrayde' . . . and complimenting him afterward: 'It is the best that ever I heard'" (citing John Nichols, *The Progresses and Public Processions of Queen Elizabeth* [London, 1823], vol. 2, 155–59).

22. For further discussion, see my *James I and the Politics of Literature,* 28–35.

23. In a provocative essay, "'Shaping Fantasies': Figurations of Gender and Power in Elizabethan Culture," *Representations* 1 (1983): 61–94, Louis Adrian Montrose argues for the manifold ways in which *A Midsummer Night's Dream* is shaped by—and shapes—cultural fantasies; he argues that its patriarchal designs conflict with and yet crosscut the designs of the Virgin Queen. At one point, however, he admits that "in its intermittent ironies, dissonances, and contradictions . . . the text of *A Midsummer Night's Dream* discloses—perhaps, in a sense despite itself—that patriarchal norms are compensatory for the vulnerability of men to the powers of women" (75). It has been my argument here that a pursuit of such slippages within the Shakespearean text undermines apparent hegemonic discourses, that what is "despite itself" marks the limits of textual control and leads to the principal mode in which texts are cultural inscriptions.

Since this essay was written, Stephen Greenblatt, "Fiction and Friction," chap. 3 in his *Shakespearean Negotiations* (Berkeley and Los Angeles: University of California Press, 1988), and Thomas Laqueur, *Making Sex: Body and Gender from the Greeks to Freud* (Cambridge, Mass.: Harvard University Press, 1990), have initiated the historical work of recovering Renaissance discourses of sexual difference. To these might be added Lisa Jardine, *Still Harping on Daughters: Women and Drama in the Age of Shakespeare* (Brighton: Harvester Press, 1983), which offers some vigorous arguments against the ahistorical tendencies in feminist criticism explored in this essay.

Calling Out the Law

My thanks to graduate students at The Johns Hopkins University and at Duke University, with whom I discussed a number of the texts and issues raised in this paper; to Michael Moon, for helping me find the right tone; to Laurie Shannon and Kirstie McClure, for valuable brainstorming; and to Kirstie again for reminding me of the pertinence of Michel de Certeau and Jacques Rancière as well as the possibility of pleasure.

1. Michel Foucault, *The History of Sexuality: An Introduction,* trans. Robert Hurley (New York: Pantheon Books, 1978), 101. The literature on sodomy is too extensive to be summarized in a note; I depend in these opening paragraphs on work cited in and deployed in my *Sodometries: Renaissance Texts, Modern Sexualities* (Stanford: Stanford University Press, 1992), and the introduction to my *Reclaiming Sodom* (New York: Routledge, 1994). For a recent valuable addition to this literature, see Mark D. Jordan, *The Invention of Sodomy in Christian Theology* (Chicago: University of Chicago Press, 1997), which, in the service of complicating any notion of a monolithic support for the kinds of juridical apparatuses that have been mobilized against sodomy, provides telling rhetorical analyses of texts. For an essay that seeks to include women in the medieval theological categorization of sodomy and for female gender as an important aspect of male sodomy, see Karma Lochrie, "Presumptive Sodomy and Its Exclusions," *Textual Practice* 13, no. 2 (Summer 1999): 295–310.

2. The major exception to this, the Florentine Office of the Night operative from 1432–1502, is studied by Michael Rocke, *Forbidden Friendships: Homosexuality and Male Culture in Renaissance Florence* (New York: Oxford University Press, 1996). I discuss it below.

3. Although concerned with earlier materials, Bernadette Brooten's *Love between Women: Early Christian Responses to Female Homoeroticism* (Chicago: University of Chicago Press, 1996) amply demonstrates the availability of such knowledge. For an excellent comparative discussion of legal and medical "knowledge" about "tribades" in the early modern period in France and England, see Elizabeth Susan Wahl, *Invisible Relations: Representations of Female Intimacy in the Age of the Enlightenment* (Stanford: Stanford University Press, 1999), 17–42.

4. Rudolph Bell and Judith Brown, "Renaissance Sexuality and the Florentine Archives: An Exchange," *Renaissance Quarterly* 40 (1987): 485–511. The "Exchange" includes Bell, "The 'Lesbian' Nun of Judith Brown: A Different Conclusion," 485–503; "Response from Professor Judith Brown," 503–9; "From Rudolph Bell," 510–11; and "From Judith Brown," 511. Judith Brown, *Immodest Acts: The Life of a Lesbian Nun in Renaissance Italy* (New York: Oxford University Press, 1986).

5. Michel de Certeau, *The Writing of History,* trans. Tom Conley (New York: Columbia University Press, 1988), 250.

6. Michel de Certeau, "Mystic Speech," in his *Heterologies: Discourse on the Other,* trans. Brian Massumi (Minneapolis: University of Minnesota Press, 1986), 80–100, as well as de Certeau, "Language Altered: The Sorcerer's Speech," in his *The Writing of History.* De Certeau's fullest exploration of these questions occurs in *The Mystic Fable,* trans. Michael B. Smith (Chicago: University of

Chicago Press, 1992); there are also points of contact in his analysis of *The Possession at Loudon,* trans. Michael B. Smith (Chicago: University of Chicago Press, 1996, 2000).

7. De Certeau, *The Writing of History,* 262.

8. All citations are from Jacques Rancière, *The Names of History,* trans. Hassan Melehy (Minneapolis: University of Minnesota Press, 1994). I have in mind the signature essay of Stephen Greenblatt, "Invisible Bullets" (in his *Shakespearean Negotiations* [Berkeley and Los Angeles: University of California Press, 1988]), especially in its initial printing in *Glyph* 8 (1981), where the story of Carlo Ginzburg's heretic Menocchio was included.

9. For a statement of these concerns in terms of the possibilities of "impossible identification" (67) as the site of new political formations, see Rancière, "Politics, Identification, and Subjectivization," in *The Identity in Question,* ed. John Rajchman (New York: Routledge, 1995), 63–70. Rancière focuses on the worker in *The Nights of Labor,* trans. John Drury (Philadelphia: Temple University Press, 1989).

10. Valerie Traub, "The (In)Significance of 'Lesbian' Desire," first published in *Erotic Politics,* ed. Susan Zimmerman (New York: Routledge, 1992), reprinted in *Queering the Renaissance,* ed. Jonathan Goldberg (Durham, N.C.: Duke University Press, 1994), from which are taken all citations from Traub. Some materials from this essay are reworked in Traub, "The Perversion of 'Lesbian' Desire," *History Workshop Journal* 41 (1996): 24–49, which provides a broad historical frame of explanation around the question of the representation of same-gender female desire and its stigmatization; the association of the tribade in gynecological tracts with a woman with a supposedly enlarged clitoris is further developed in Traub, "The Psychomorphology of the Clitoris," *GLQ* 2 (1995): 81–113, which draws connections to colonializing narratives as well as to Freudian assumptions about lesbianism; the history of the "discovery" of the clitoris is also the subject of Katherine Park, "The Rediscovery of the Clitoris: French Medicine and the Tribade, 1570–1620," in *The Body in Parts,* ed. David Hillman and Carla Mazzio (New York: Routledge, 1997). Much revised, Traub's essays form part of her *The Renaissance of Lesbianism in Early Modern England* (Cambridge: Cambridge University Press, 2002).

11. Traub does not engage Brown's work, noting it only to suggest that its main contribution is to religious study, not to the history of sexuality ("[In]significance," 81 n. 5). In drawing this divide between theology and erotics, not only are the two domains assumed to be separate, but theology, at least, is made to appear rather monolithic. For some strong arguments against assuming that canon law represents theological thought in the formation of sodomy, see Jordan, *The Invention of Sodomy in Christian Theology.* In note 122 to the first chapter of her *Renaissance of Lesbianism* (388–89), Traub gives fuller consideration to Brown's work; emphasizing that Brown's deployment of "lesbian" imports an unwarranted modern category, she now insists that Benedetta's story

is not just to be read within the history of religion, especially since critics of Brown who have wanted to do that (Mary R. O'Neil and Caroline Walker Bynum are the critics Traub mentions) do so to deny significance of any kind to the sexual; their strategies parallel those I have noted in Bell.

12. Judith Butler, *Gender Trouble* (New York: Routledge, 1990); all citations are from this work. Butler takes this misreading to task in her *Bodies That Matter* (New York: Routledge, 1993) and has extended her arguments about a politics of the performative in *Excitable Speech* (New York: Routledge, 1997). Butler's analysis of the impossibility of securing gender or speech depends upon Derridean notions of iterability; as Richard Beardsworth argues in *Derrida and the Political* (London: Routledge, 1996), this term names "the law of law." That formulation catches the familiar Derridean move of deconstruction and conservation; what it fails to ask is why "the political" should be the same thing as the law. Many critiques, whether from a Marxist or a Foucauldian perspective, would urge caution in reinscribing the liberal fiction of the law.

13. The critique of the repressive hypothesis is the burden of the introductory volume of Foucault's *History of Sexuality,* and it is elegantly reformulated in the opening pages of *The Use of Pleasure,* trans. Robert Hurley (New York: Pantheon, 1985), 3–4. The move initiated in that volume toward technologies of the self explicitly parts from the apparatus of the licit/illicit. As Foucault comments in "The Battle for Chastity," in Foucault, *Ethics: Subjectivity and Truth,* ed. Paul Rabinow, vol. 1 of *The Essential Works of Foucault, 1954–1984* (New York: New Press, 1997), these techniques had "nothing to do with a code of permitted and forbidden actions but a whole technique for analyzing and diagnosing thought, its origins, its qualities, its dangers, its potential for temptation, and all the dark forces that can lurk behind the mask it may assume" (195). Considering Foucault's emphasis on discipline and, in his later work, on the more expansive category of governmentality—regions that are at most masked by the law but are never simply to be reduced to this particular apparatus—it is a question worth more considered treatment, why work that falls under the rubric of the "new historicism," and often labeled as Foucauldian, remains so entranced by the law. This is a question that has immediate ramifications in terms of political consequences, such as, for instance, those acutely analyzed by Wendy Brown, *States of Injury* (Princeton: Princeton University Press, 1995), where the recourse of citizens to the law as the site of the redress of social ills is shown to be an appeal that only vests more power in the state and its legal apparatuses and follows from a fundamental misrecognition of the workings of the social.

14. Alan Bray, *Homosexuality in Renaissance England* (London: Gay Men's Press, 1982); Elizabeth Pittenger, "'To Serve the Queere': Nicholas Udall, Master of Revels," in Goldberg, *Queering the Renaissance,* esp. 166–70.

15. It is around this question of non-self-recognition that Gregeory Bredbeck intervenes in "Tradition and the Individual Sodomite," chap. 4 in *Sodomy and Interpretation* (Ithaca, N.Y.: Cornell University Press, 1991), attempting to

find in literature a discursive site for sodomitical self-nomination; however, what Bredbeck in fact discovers is a set of evasions that seem assimilable to the model in Bray against which he is arguing.

16. Alan Bray, "Homosexuality and the Signs of Male Friendship in Elizabethan England," first published in *History Workshop Journal* 29 (1990): 1–19, reprinted in a slightly revised form in Goldberg, *Queering the Renaissance.*

17. Letter of 5 January 1514, cited by Rocke from *Tutte le Opera,* ed. M. Martelli (Florence: Sansoni, 1971), 1164–65. For a discussion of the political/theoretical role of sexuality in the Machiavelli-Vettori correspondence, see John M. Najemy, *Between Friends* (Princeton: Princeton University Press, 1993), esp. chaps. 7 and 9. Najemy also offers a guide to the complex textual questions; for English translations, consult James B. Atkinson and David Sices, eds., *Machiavelli and His Friends: Their Personal Correspondence* (Dekalb: Northern Illinois University Press, 1996).

18. On this point, see Alan K. Smith, "Fraudomy: Reading Sexuality and Politics in Burchiello," in *Queering the Renaissance,* ed. Goldberg, 100.

19. This point is made, for instance, by Ian Hacking, "How Should We Do the History of Statistics?" in *The Foucault Effect,* ed. Graham Burchell, Colin Gordon, and Peter Miller (Chicago: University of Chicago Press, 1991), and deployed by Mary Poovey in "Sex in America," *Critical Inquiry* 24, no. 2 (Winter 1998): 366–92.

20. The passage in Foucault's "Governmentality," in *The Foucault Effect,* ed. Burchell, Gordon, and Miller, most relevant to the discussion at hand is his consideration on page 95 of the ways in which sovereignty tied to obedience to the laws is replaced by a use of laws as tactics for the disposal of bodies, management techniques. Foucault locates the theorization of this transformation through a consideration of a late-sixteenth-century French text. See also Foucault's *Discipline and Punish,* trans. Alan Sheridan (New York: Vintage, 1979).

21. See Valerie Traub, *Desire and Anxiety: Circulations of Sexuality in Shakespearean Drama* (London: Routledge, 1992), 117–44. Traub initially argues that *Twelfth Night* "fixes the homoerotic interest onto a marginalized figure," Antonio, "whose relationship to Sebastian is finally sacrificed for the maintenance of institutionalized heterosexuality" (123), a reading that is later retracted (138) to allow for ambivalence in the closure achieved; as I will suggest below, Malvolio better fits this supposed position of stigma. Traub suggestively reads the scene of the arrest of Antonio as one in which his ravings about betrayal are symptomatic of the lack of place of his desire; "caught . . . between . . . platonic friendship and sodomy. There are literally no early modern terms by which Antonio's desire can be understood" (137). The critic most attentive to the role of Antonio has been Laurie E. Osborne; see her "The Texts of *Twelfth Night,*" *ELH* 57 (1990): 37–61, esp. 47ff., and "Antonio's Pardon," *Shakespeare Quarterly* 45 (1994): 108–14. These form the basis for chapters in Osborne's *The Trick of*

Singularity: Twelfth Night *and the Performance Texts* (Iowa City: University of Iowa Press, 1996).

22. From this, Joseph Pequigney argues in "The Two Antonios and Same-Sex Love in *Twelfth Night* and *The Merchant of Venice,*" *English Literary Renaissance* 22 (1992): 201–21, that *Twelfth Night*'s Antonio is a homosexual. Antonio and Sebastian, it should be noted, appear together again in *The Tempest,* linked conspiratorially.

23. All citations are from *Twelfth Night,* Arden edition, ed. J. M. Lothian and T. W. Craik (London: Methuen, 1975).

24. If, as the Arden gloss to 3.3.11 suggests, Illyria was known for piracy, this would also lead to thinking of Antonio as native to the place. While Antonio declares himself to be from another city than Orsino (3.3.35), Illyria, over which Orsino rules, appears to be the name of a country (2.1.1–2, 24–26), not just the city in which Antonio is apprehended.

25. This interpretation could be placed in relationship to a number of recent discussions of the play motivated by Viola's announcement that she wishes to disguise "as an eunuch" (1.3.56). Keir Elam, "The Fertile Eunuch: *Twelfth Night,* Early Modern Intercourse, and the Fruits of Castration," *Shakespeare Quarterly* 47 (1996): 1–36, connects Viola's desire for castration as "a founding trope of comedy as a dramatic genre" (10) and offers an exhaustive survey of plays that follow upon Plautus's foundational text; crucial to the argument about the potency of the castrate is both the sense of this long textual history and what is afforded to the actor playing the part; the full range of Elam's treatment on page 29. Lest the association of the leg with the penis be thought of as a dehistoricized psychoanalytic equation, it is worth recalling that one source for *Twelfth Night* cited by Elam, *Gl'ingannati,* explicitly says "leg" when "penis" is meant (23). A psychoanalytic framework, however, is not to be eschewed; Elam invokes the problematic of castration and refers to Laurie Osborne's important essay "Letters, Lovers, Lacan: Or Malvolio's Not-So-Purloined Letter," *Assays* 5 (1989): 63–89, which notes the importance of "C," "U," "T" in the reading of the letter that serves to castrate Malvolio, putting him in his place (68; a version of this essay can also be found in Osborne's *Trick of Singularity*); it might be added in this context that Toby assures Sir Andrew that if he fails to win Olivia he may call him "cut" (2.3.186). It is presumably this moment that Stephen Orgel has in mind in *Impersonations* (Cambridge: Cambridge University Press, 1986), referring to the play's "puns on 'cut' and 'cunt' (55), though he emphasizes the relationship between the part Viola plays and the theatrical *castrato,* a point also developed by Elam as a site of theatrical potency. This relationship between the boy's singing voice and castration is the subject of Dympna Callaghan, "The Castrator's Song: Female Impersonation on the Early Modern Stage," *Journal of Medieval and Early Modern Studies* 26, no. 2 (Spring 1996). Viola's assumed name, Cesario, also means "cut" (Latin *caedere,* "to cut").

26. Osborne, *The Trick of Singularity,* 90. Osborne does not connect the monetary with the sexual issues, treating the latter as what is really at stake.

27. It is probably Greenblatt's reading of nature's bias as ultimately secured by heterosexual coupling (*Shakespearean Negotiations,* 71) that has provoked the controversy; thus, Pequigney, in "The Two Antonios," attempts to reread the bias as toward same-sex couples, a point made more persuasively by Laurie Shannon in "Nature's Bias: Renaissance Homonormativity and Elizabethan Comic Likeness," *Modern Philology* 98, no. 2 (2000): 183–210. Lorna Hutson, "Not Being Deceived: Rhetoric and the Body in *Twelfth Night,*" *Texas Studies in Literature and Language* 38 (1996): 140–74, underscores the masculinist bias in Greenblatt's reading (141–43) to focus on the rhetoric through which social value is secured by those who cannot claim aristocratic privilege.

28. This reading is prompted in part by Hutson's "Not Being Deceived," but rather than simply making the social questions transcend questions of sex and gender, as she does, I seek their connections. In doing so, I follow Bray's argument in "Homosexuality and the Signs of Male Friendship" that friendship relationships are capable of being viewed as sodomitical when social hierarchies are breached.

29. As Osborne further details in "Antonio's Pardon," the question of what to do with Antonio, where to put him on stage, remained for directors, as promptbooks show. In this, Antonio's position at the end of the play coincides with that of a number of women in other Shakespearean texts—Silvia, Hermia, Helena, and Isabella, for instance—who are brought into "proper" marital position and rendered silent.

30. In the first chapter of her *Renaissance of Lesbianism* (56), Traub suggests that when Viola refers to herself as a monster (2.2.33), her allusion to her masculine attire may also conjure up hermaphroditic monstrosity (not least because she refers to herself in equivalent phrases, "as I am man" [35], "as I am woman" [37]) and, hence, tribade status.

Hamlet's Hand

1. Martin Heidegger, *Parmenides* (Frankfurt am Main: Vittorio Klostermann, 1982), 119. My commentary on Heidegger takes off from Jacques Derrida, "*Geschlecht* II: Heidegger's Hand," in *Deconstruction and Philosophy,* ed. John Sallis (Chicago: University of Chicago Press, 1987), 161–96.

2. On the difficulty of equating literacy with the ability to write, see R. S. Schofield, "The Measurement of Literacy in Pre-Industrial England," in *Literacy in Traditional Societies,* ed. Jack Goody (Cambridge: Cambridge University Press, 1968). On the problems of measuring literacy through signatures, see David Cressy, *Literacy and the Social Order* (Cambridge: Cambridge University Press, 1980). For an incisive critique of the theoretical and ideological implica-

tions of much work done by historians of literacy, see Brian V. Street, *Literacy in Theory and Practice* (Cambridge: Cambridge University Press, 1984).

3. Martin Heidegger, *What Is Called Thinking?* trans. Fred D. Wieck and J. Glenn Gray (New York: Harper and Row, 1968), 16; cf. Heidegger, *Parmenides,* 118.

4. Gregory of Nyssa, *La Création de l'homme,* trans. Jean Laplace (Paris: Editions du Cerf, 1943), 112–13, 107 (148c–149e, 144c). I am grateful to William Klein for this reference. Cf. Andre Leroi-Gourhan, *Le Geste et la parole,* 2 vols. (Paris: Albin Michel, 1964), vol. 1, 40–42, 44–56, for a modern anthropologist's endorsement of Gregory's remarks.

5. Andres Brun, *Arte muy provechosa para apprendir de escrivir perfectamente* (Saragossa, 1583), in *Scribes and Sources,* ed. A. S. Osley (Boston: David R. Godine, 1980), 180.

6. Heidegger, *What Is Called Thinking?* 17.

7. "Kein Tier hat eine Hand" (Heidegger, *Parmenides,* 118).

8. Friedrich Engels, "The Part Played by Labour in the Transition from Ape to Man," in Karl Marx and Frederick Engels, *Selected Works,* 2 vols. (Moscow: Foreign Language Publishing House, 1962), vol. 2, 80–92.

9. Elaine Scarry, *The Body in Pain* (New York: Oxford University Press, 1985), 252. I am grateful to Michael Warner for drawing this discussion to my attention.

10. All citations are from *The Complete Pelican Shakespeare,* ed. Alfred Harbage (Baltimore: Penguin Books, 1969).

11. Jacques Derrida, *Of Grammatology,* trans. Gayatri Chakravorty Spivak (Baltimore: The Johns Hopkins University Press, 1976), 92.

12. On connections between handwriting and English royalty, see Sir Edward Maunde Thompson, "Handwriting," in *Shakespeare's England,* ed. Sidney Lee and C. T. Onions, 2 vols. (Oxford: Clarendon Press, 1916), vol. 1, 284–310; Ambrose Heal, *The English Writing-Masters and Their Copy-Books, 1570–1800* (Cambridge: Cambridge University Press, 1931). There are some interesting anecdotes in Isaac D'Israeli, "The History of Writing Masters," in his *Curiosities of Literature,* 6 vols. (London: Edward Moxon, 1834), vol. 5, 284–99.

13. Roger Ascham, *The Schoolmaster,* ed. Lawrence V. Ryan (Ithaca, N.Y.: Cornell University Press, 1967), 56.

14. Newberry Library Wing Ms. ZW 639.B 382: "Recevez d'un bon oeil PRINCESSE, je vous prie, / L'ouvrage & l'ouvrier de qui le coeur n'oublie / Les tres-humbles respects qui par luy vous son deus."

15. John Hart, *A Methode or Comfortable Beginning for All Unlearned . . . to Read English* (London, 1570), fol. A6r.

16. François Furet and Jacques Ozouf, *Reading and Writing: Literacy in France from Calvin to Jules Ferry* (Cambridge: Cambridge University Press; Paris: Editions de la Maison des Sciences de l'Homme, 1982), 314.

17. I draw on my discussion in *Voice Terminal Echo* (New York: Methuen, 1986), 86–100; see also Daniel Sibony, "*Hamlet:* A Writing-Effect," *Yale French Studies* 55/56 (1977): 53–93.

18. James L. Calderwood meditates on this chain of substitute names in *To Be and Not to Be: Negation and Metadrama in Hamlet* (New York: Columbia University Press, 1983), 113ff., but he reaches conclusions about Hamlet becoming himself quite opposed to those I draw. That Hamlet's "inky cloak" invests him in writing was noted by Sibony, "*Hamlet:* A Writing-Effect," 67.

19. David Browne, *The New Invention, Intituled Calligraphia* (St. Andrews, 1622), **2r.

20. G. P. V. Akrigg, ed., *Letters of King James VI and I* (Berkeley and Los Angeles: University of California Press, 1984), 219.

21. John Brinsley, *Ludus Literarius* (London, 1612) 2v.

22. Here my discussion overlaps with that of Svetlana Alpers, *The Art of Describing* (Chicago: University of Chicago Press, 1983), 133–39 et passim.

23. Peter Bales, *The Writing Schoolmaster* (London, 1590), R1r.

24. Gerardus Mercator, *Literarum Latinarum* (Louvain, 1540).

25. Guilantonio Hercolani, *Lo scrittor utile* (Bologna, 1574).

26. Richard Gethinge, *Calligraphotechnia* (London, 1619).

27. The connection between this passage and the history of handwriting was noted by Sir Edward Maunde Thompson, "Handwriting," 287.

28. Juan Vives, *Linguae Latinae Exercitatio* (1538), in Osley, *Scribes and Sources*, 40–41.

29. Francesco Guicciardini, *Maxims and Reflections*, trans. Mario Domandi (Philadelphia: University of Pennsylvania Press, 1965), 86 (C 179).

30. See Osley, *Scribes and Sources*, 215, on Hamon (the Newberry Library owns a copy of his *Alphabet de plusieurs sortes de Lettres* [1566] that includes a page in Hamon's hand); on royal injunctions commanding secretarial imitation, see Paul Saenger, "Silent Reading: Its Impact on Late Medieval Script and Society," *Viator* 13 (1982): 367–414, esp. 406.

31. Michael Clanchy, *From Memory to Written Record: England, 1066–1307* (Cambridge, Mass.: Harvard University Press, 1979), 248.

32. Margaret Ferguson, "*Hamlet:* Letters and Spirits," in *Shakespeare and the Question of Theory*, ed. Patricia Parker and Geoffrey Hartman (New York: Methuen, 1985), 292–309, esp. 299.

33. Vives, *Linguae Latinae Exercitatio*, 41.

34. The sentence, memorably uttered by Edgar Allan Poe's M. Valdemar, appears in an epigraph to Jacques Derrida's *Speech and Phenomena*, trans. David B. Allison (Evanston, Ill.: Northwestern University Press, 1973); see 96–97 for a discussion of its significance.

35. Cited by Cressy, *Literacy and the Social Order*, 25.

36. Browne, *The New Invention, Intituled Calligraphia*, **4v.

37. William Fulwood, *The Enemy of Idleness* (London: Edward Allde, 1621), 1–2. Fulwood's book first appeared in 1568; I quote from a 1621 reprinting.

Perspectives

1. All citations are from *The Complete Pelican Shakespeare,* ed. Alfred Harbage (Baltimore: Penguin, 1969).

2. Stephen Orgel, "Shakespeare Imagines a Theater," *Poetics Today* 5 (1984): 549–61, esp. 556–57.

3. For a discussion of Shakespearean representation that shares many of the concerns of this essay, see David Marshall, "Exchanging Visions: Reading *A Midsummer Night's Dream,*" *ELH* 49 (1982): 543–75.

4. On linguistic places (topoi), see Marion Trousdale, *Shakespeare and the Rhetoricians* (Chapel Hill: University of North Carolina Press, 1982).

5. Edgar's lines have been seen in the context of perspective by Marshall McLuhan in *The Gutenberg Galaxy* (Toronto: University of Toronto Press, 1962), 15–17, and again in Marshall McLuhan and Harley Parker, *Through the Vanishing Point* (New York: Harper and Row, 1968), 14, 74–75; the emphasis in both treatments is on the fragmentation of the visual.

6. See Leon Battista Alberti, *On Painting,* trans. John R. Spencer (New Haven: Yale University Press, 1956), 45–48, 56, for the summary I offer. For a particularly stimulating discussion, see Harry Berger Jr., "L. B. Alberti: Art and Actuality in Humanist Perspective," *Centennial Review* 10 (1966): 237–77. On the subject in general, see John White, *The Birth and Rebirth of Pictorial Space* (Boston: Boston Book and Art Shop, 1967), and the review essay by Robert Klein, "Studies on Perspective in the Renaissance," in his *Form and Meaning* (New York: Viking Books, 1979). Svetlana Alpers, *The Art of Describing* (Chicago: University of Chicago Press, 1983) might point to a non-Italian tradition of representation (linking graphic representation, writing, and description), which provides an alternative to Albertian perspective within Edgar's speech.

7. For a provocative reading of these lines, see Harry Berger Jr., "The Early Scenes of *Macbeth:* Preface to a New Interpretation," *ELH* 47 (1980): 1–31, esp. 28–30.

8. On the knowledge of Italian theories in England and the terminology of sixteenth-century Englishmen, see Lucy Gent, *Picture and Poetry: 1560–1620* (Leamington Spa, Eng.: James Hall, 1981), esp. 23–25, on perspective. For a reading of Sonnet 24 that takes up many of the issues pursued here and places them within the broader context of ideas of vision in the sequence, see Joel Fineman, *Shakespeare's Perjured Eye* (Berkeley and Los Angeles: University of California Press, 1986), 135–40. See also my *Voice Terminal Echo* (New York: Methuen, 1986), 92–98.

9. On anamorphosis, especially in its literary use, see Claudio Guillén, "On the Concept and Metaphor of Perspective," in *Comparatists at Work,* ed.

Stephen G. Nichols Jr. and Richard B. Vowles (Waltham, Mass.: Blaisdell, 1968), and Ernest B. Gilman, *The Curious Frame* (New Haven: Yale University Press, 1978). For the broader cultural implications, see Stephen Greenblatt, *Renaissance Self-Fashioning: From More to Shakespeare* (Chicago: University of Chicago Press, 1980).

10. My comments depend upon Stephen Orgel and Roy Strong, *Inigo Jones: The Theatre of the Stuart Court,* 2 vols. (London: Sotheby Parke Bernet; and Berkeley and Los Angeles: University of California Press, 1973), vol. 1, 6–8, 11–12, 89.

11. Roy Strong, *The Cult of Elizabeth* (London: Thames and Hudson, 1977), 111.

12. Jacques Derrida, "The Theater of Cruelty and the Closure of Representation," in his *Writing and Difference,* trans. Alan Bass (Chicago: University of Chicago Press, 1978).

13. Aristotle, *The Poetics,* trans. W. Hamilton Fyfe (Cambridge, Mass.: Harvard University Press, 1960), 15.

14. Wallace Stevens, "The Snow Man," in *The Collected Poems of Wallace Stevens* (New York: Alfred A. Knopf, 1965), 10.

Shakespeare Writing Matter Again

1. Jonathan Goldberg, *Writing Matter: From the Hands of the English Renaissance* (Stanford: Stanford University Press, 1990).

2. Jonathan Goldberg, *Voice Terminal Echo* (New York and London: Methuen, 1986).

3. Jonathan Goldberg, "Hamlet's Hand," *Shakespeare Quarterly* 39, no. 3 (1988): 307–27; reprinted in this volume.

4. See, for example, "Textual Properties," *Shakespeare Quarterly* 37, no. 2 (1986): 213–17; "Rebel Letters: Postal Effects from *Richard II* to *Henry IV,*" *Renaissance Drama,* new series, 19 (1988): 3–28; "'What? in a names that which we call a Rose': The Desired Texts of *Romeo and Juliet,*" in *Crisis in Editing: Texts of the English Renaissance,* ed. Randall McLeod (New York: AMS Press, 1994); "*Romeo and Juliet*'s Open Rs," in *Queering the Renaissance,* ed. Jonathan Goldberg (Durham, N.C.: Duke University Press, 1994); all reprinted in this volume.

5. Richard Halpern, *The Poetics of Primitive Accumulation* (Ithaca: Cornell University Press, 1991).

6. Jonathan Goldberg, "Perspectives: Dover Cliff and the Conditions of Representation," in *Shakespeare and Deconstruction,* ed. David M. Bergeron and G. Douglas Atkins (New York: Peter Lang, 1988), excerpted in two Macmillan New Casebooks, *King Lear,* ed. Kiernan Ryan (1993); and *Shakespeare's Tragedies,* ed. Susan Zimmerman (1998). It is reprinted in this volume. The final remarks here glance at the project of my most recent book, *Desiring Women Writing: English Renaissance Examples* (Stanford: Stanford University Press, 1997).

7. For more on this, see Christopher Pye, *The Vanishing* (Durham, N.C.: Duke University Press, 2000).

Speculations

1. The assumption here overlaps Michel Foucault's argument that the author must be replaced by the "author-function," as limited and made possible by historical formations; "What Is an Author?" in Foucault, *Language, Counter-Memory, Practice,* trans. D. F. Bouchard and S. Simon (Ithaca, N.Y.: Cornell University Press, 1977). Among the signs of the dispersal of the dramatic author in Shakespeare's time are his failure to publish his plays and the evidence of ongoing revision (rather than a stabilizing of an authoritative authorial text) in at least some of the texts gathered in the 1623 Folio; in the case of *Macbeth,* as discussed below, the Folio text is not entirely Shakespearean, a condition that did not keep Heminge and Condell from publishing it. For some incisive probing of this issue, see Stephen Orgel, "What Is a Text?" *Research Opportunities in Renaissance Drama* 24 (1981): 3–6. All references are to *Macbeth,* Arden edition, ed. Kenneth Muir (London: Methuen, 1982).

2. Stephen Greenblatt, "Shakespeare and the Exorcists," in *After Strange Texts,* ed. G. S. Jay and D. L. Miller (University: University of Alabama Press, 1985), 101.

3. Greenblatt cites *John Wesley,* ed. Albert C. Outler (New York: Oxford University Press, 1964), 82.

4. Jacques Derrida, "Cogito and the History of Madness," in Derrida, *Writing and Difference,* trans. A. Bass (Chicago: University of Chicago Press, 1978).

5. Ibid., 57.

6. Greenblatt, "Shakespeare and the Exorcists," 101.

7. Jacques Derrida, *Of Grammatology,* trans. G. C. Spivak (Baltimore: The Johns Hopkins University Press, 1976), 152–57, 304; Derrida, "Qual Quelle: Valéry's Sources," in Derrida, *Margins of Philosophy,* trans. A. Bass (Chicago: University of Chicago Press, 1982): 273–306.

8. Derrida, "Cogito and the History of Madness"; Michel Foucault, "My Body, This Paper, This Fire," *Oxford Literary Review* 4 (1979): 9–28.

9. Jonathan Goldberg, "Herbert's 'Decay' and the Articulation of History," *Southern Review* 18 (1985): 5.

10. Jacques Derrida, *Positions,* trans. A. Bass (Chicago: University of Chicago Press, 1981), 57.

11. Goldberg, "Herbert's 'Decay,'" 7.

12. Derrida, *Positions,* 65.

13. Ibid., 59.

14. Andrew Parker, "'Taking Sides' (on History): Derrida Re-Marx," *Diacritics* 11, no. 3 (1981): 70.

15. Derrida, *Positions,* 49–50.

16. Andrew Parker, "Between Dialectics and Deconstruction: Derrida and the Reading of Marx," in *After Strange Texts,* ed. G. S. Jay and D. L. Miller (University: University of Alabama Press, 1985), 147.

17. Jonathan Goldberg, *James I and the Politics of Literature* (Baltimore: The Johns Hopkins University Press, 1983).

18. Frank Kermode, introduction to *Macbeth,* in *The Riverside Shakespeare* (Boston: Houghton Mifflin, 1974), 1308.

19. Geoffrey Bullough, *Narrative and Dramatic Sources of Shakespeare,* vol. 7 (London: Routledge and Kegan Paul, 1973), 444.

20. Ibid., 448. S. Booth also argues for Holinshed's "composite" composition. His thesis is that Holinshed attempts "to contain all accounts in one account" and that "the *Chronicles* are the work in English literature that most fully shares the most peculiarly Shakespearean of Shakespeare's traits: the ability constantly to shift the perception of a reader or audience from one set of principles for judgment to another" (*The Book Called Holinshed's Chronicles* [San Francisco: Book Club of California, 1968], 45, 72). There are differences between the authors, however, that Booth fails to register. Holinshed is a relentless explainer; however multiple his perspectives, he rationalizes each stage in his story; the explanations may not add up, but they are supplied. Shakespeare, on the other hand, omits such things as Holinshed's explanation of Scottish laws of succession and Lady Macbeth's ambition to be queen. Booth's description of *Macbeth*'s relationship to Holinshed echoes the commonplaces, adding to them the New Critical idea of textual complexity as the Shakespearean version of Holinshed's composite complicity: "[I]n *Macbeth* Shakespeare omits all indication that Duncan was ever a bad king or Macbeth a good one. He does, however, create a deeper and more intense conflict in his audience by causing its members to sympathize with and share the consciousness of a moral monster" (80). For a tabulation of Shakespeare's borrowings from Holinshed, see R. A. Law, "The Composition of *Macbeth* with Reference to Holinshed," *Texas Studies in English* 31 (1952): 35–41.

21. Bullough, *Narrative and Dramatic Sources of Shakespeare,* 498.

22. Ibid., 478.

23. A notable exception is Harry Berger Jr., "The Early Scenes of *Macbeth:* Preface to a New Interpretation," *English Literary History* 47 (1980): 1–31, to which I am deeply indebted in this discussion.

24. Bullough, *Narrative and Dramatic Sources of Shakespeare,* 481.

25. Ibid., 486.

26. Ibid., 488.

27. Berger, "The Early Scenes of *Macbeth.*" Without making anything of it, John Dover Wilson, in his introduction to *Macbeth* (Cambridge: Cambridge University Press, 1947), notes a version of this when he remarks that Holin-

shed's phrase for Duncan, "too much of clemencie," "came to be associated in his [Shakespeare's] mind with Macbeth himself." More exactly, Lady Macbeth transfers it to her husband. D. W. Harding notes that the source for Lady Macbeth's milk in Holinshed lies in the rebels' characterization of Duncan as a milksop; "Women's Fantasy of Manhood," *Shakespeare Quarterly* 20 (1969): 246–47.

28. Cf. Berger: "From the moment in 1.7 when Macbeth approaches the murder as a real possibility, we see his attachment to the figure of Duncan increase" ("The Early Scenes of *Macbeth*," 16). Construction continues, too, in Macduff's naming Duncan "[t]he Lord's anointed Temple" (2.3.67), "a most sainted King" (4.3.109). No one speaks about Duncan in these terms before his death, and the king is represented as rebel-besieged; as tense in his relations to them (and to those, like Macbeth, dependent upon his generosity) and as preemptory in naming his heir.

29. Such connections are noted by Kermode, introduction to *Macbeth*, and Muir, *Macbeth*. They are part of a long tradition of reading *Macbeth* in conjunction with James I fully exemplified by H. N. Paul, *The Royal Play of* Macbeth (New York: Macmillan, 1950) and A. M. Clark, *Murder under Trust; or, The Topical* Macbeth (Edinburgh: Scottish Academic Press, 1981). Such views are answered forcefully by M. Hawkins, "History, Politics, and *Macbeth*," in *Focus on* Macbeth, ed. J. R. Brown (London: Routledge and Kegan Paul, 1982), who argues against the notion of the monolithic historical background, suggesting instead that Jacobean society was an ambiguous amalgam of tense political relationships and systems; for him, Banquo, Duncan, Macduff, and Malcolm all have political and moral weaknesses, and Macbeth is not entirely a villain. The play is equivocal throughout, as was contemporary politics. Hawkins's skeptical and empirical view does not credit the power of symbolic discourse in political behavior, and the ambiguities he details are perhaps more rational than the equivocations in *Macbeth*.

The choice of reflecting James in Edward the Confessor must be set in the context of James's repeated disgust and sarcasm at the practice of touching; see D. H. Willson, *King James VI and I* (New York: Oxford University Press, 1956), 172–73. That Banquo is hardly innocent in the play has been observed by critics from A. C. Bradley (*Shakespearean Tragedy* [1904; reprint, London: Macmillan, 1956], 379–87) on.

30. Fredric Jameson, *The Political Unconscious* (Ithaca, N.Y.: Cornell University Press, 1981). At the very least, if we account for the composition of *Macbeth* in terms of the operation of Shakespeare's unconscious associations, we should recognize that the unconscious is a historical phenomenon that never operates freely and is intimately bound to social structures (e.g., the family, the state) that promote and limit autonomy.

31. Stephen Orgel, "Shakespeare Imagines a Theater," in *Shakespeare, Man*

of the Theater, ed. K. Muir, J. Halio, and D. J. Palmer (Newark: University of Delaware Press, 1983), 43.

32. Steven Mullaney, "Lying Like Truth: Riddle, Representation, and Treason in Renaissance England," *English Literary History* 47 (1980): 41. On the political significance of the witches, see the suggestive essay by P. Stallybrass, "*Macbeth* and Witchcraft," in *Focus on* Macbeth, ed. J. R. Brown (London: Routledge and Kegan Paul, 1982), which acutely situates the witches in opposition to patriarchal rule as an antistate and an antifamily. I am particularly indebted to him for suggesting that the dilemma they pose is "solved" by the attempt to form families without women (198). The "normality" of this patriarchal fantasy, and its historical refigurations, are the subject in E. K. Sedgwick, *Between Men: English Literature and Male Homosocial Desire* (New York: Columbia University Press, 1985).

33. James I, *Basilikon Doron* (1616), in *The Political Works of James I,* ed. C. H. McIlwain (Cambridge, Mass.: Harvard University Press, 1918).

34. Franco Moretti, "'A Huge Eclipse': Tragic Forms and the Deconsecration of Sovereignty," *Genre* 15 (1982): 9.

35. James I, *Basilikon Doron,* 33, 39.

36. Ben Jonson, *The Complete Masques,* ed. Stephen Orgel (New Haven: Yale University Press, 1969), 170–71. All masque citations are from this source and refer to line numbers.

37. I consider this moment in the masque from a slightly different perspective in *James I and the Politics of Literature,* 130–31. The trope of this essay and my treatment of the masque depend upon Stephen Orgel's *The Illusion of Power* (Berkeley and Los Angeles: University of California Press, 1975), which describes the form as "the mirror of the king's mind" (77).

38. Bullough, *Narrative and Dramatic Sources of Shakespeare,* 471. The relation of this entertainment to *Macbeth* was noted by E. K. Chambers, *William Shakespeare* (Oxford: Clarendon Press, 1930) and is conjectured in J. Nichols, *The Progresses of King James I,* vol. 1 (London: J. B. Nichols, 1828), 543. Bullough's text translates a page appended to Matthew Gwinne's *Vertumnus;* it may not represent the exact form of the entertainment, which is discussed by Nichols (543–45). Sir Isaac Wake, *Rex Platonicus* (Oxford, 1607) gives his account of the royal visit; his description of the entertainment explicitly mentions Macbeth, whereas Gwinne's text alludes solely to the prophecy to Banquo.

39. The subject of masculinity and femininity in the play has been discussed often; see, e.g., Harding, "Women's Fantasy of Manhood"; Berger, "The Early Scenes of *Macbeth,*" 26–28; and Berger, "Text against Performance in Shakespeare: The Example of *Macbeth,*" *Genre* 15 (1982): 64–74. M. Gohlke, "'I Wooed Thee with My Sword': Shakespeare's Tragic Paradigms," in *Representing Shakespeare,* ed. C. Kahn and M. Schwartz (Baltimore: The Johns Hopkins University Press, 1980), argues that the play centers on the eradication of the

feminine and male fantasies of self-authorship but tends to essentialize and sentimentalize the idea of the feminine, a view that can be corrected, as A. R. Jones argues in "Writing the Body: Toward an Understanding of *L'écriture Féminine,*" *Feminist Studies* 7 (1981): 255–61, only by attention to the historical particularities that would underlie psychic formations.

40. On the question of same and different in Shakespeare, see J. Fineman's acute development in "Fratricide and Cuckoldry: Shakespeare's Doubles," in *Representing Shakespeare,* ed. C. Kahn and M. Schwartz (Baltimore: The Johns Hopkins University Press, 1980), 89, 103–4, of René Girard's terms. For a rather mechanical treatment of doubling and a brief consideration of Macbeth's relationship with his wife as a son-mother pairing, see R. Rogers, *A Psychoanalytic Study of the Double in Literature* (Detroit, Mich.: Wayne State University Press, 1970), 48–51.

41. James I, *Basilikon Doron,* 24.

42. Studying the limiting aspects of masculinity, C. Asp, "'Be Bloody, Bold, and Resolute': Tragic Action and Sexual Stereotyping in *Macbeth,*" *Studies in Philology* 78 (1981), 165, suggests that Macbeth's inhuman project may be related to the sexually undifferentiated witches; the end of the play, in this view, replicates its initial stereotypes, a view also suggested by H. Felperin, *Shakespearean Representation* (Princeton: Princeton University Press, 1977). R. Horwitch, "Integrity in *Macbeth:* The Search for the 'Single State of Man,'" *Shakespeare Quarterly* 29 (1978), notes that Malcolm confesses to Macbeth's crimes in act 4, scene 3 and "may be seen as, potentially, a Macbeth in embryo" (371). It is surely to the point that his ultimate position, replicating Duncan's, as Macduff mirrors Macbeth, is offered as a success that the witches have preordained for the line of Banquo.

43. Luce Irigaray, "When the Goods Get Together," trans. Claudia Reeder, in *New French Feminisms,* ed. E. Marks and I. de Courtivron (New York: Schocken, 1981), 189; originally published as "Des marchandise entre elles," in *Ce sexe qui n'en est pas un* (Paris: Minuit, 1977). See also Irigaray, "Veiled Lips," trans. Sara Speidel, *Mississippi Review* 33 (1983): 93–131, a selection from *Amante marine: De Friedrich Nietzsche,* for an extraordinary discussion of patriarchal appropriations of the maternal. My use, like Irigaray's, is Lacanian—inflected, I hope, with the historical particularities involved in Renaissance constructions of the feminine.

44. Berger, "Text against Performance in Shakespeare," 52.

45. The question of textual autonomy can be approached from many directions. It is surely no accident that *Macbeth* was early appropriated for the New Criticism by C. Brooks, "The Naked Babe and the Cloak of Manliness," in Brooks, *The Well-Wrought Urn* (New York: Harcourt, Brace, and World, 1947), as a particularly *dense* text apt for close readings; not surprisingly, such readings have been intensely conservative. Valuable along these lines, however, is

A. Stein, "*Macbeth* and Word Magic," *Sewanee Review* 59 (1951): 271–84, with its emphasis on Macbeth's linguistic insecurity.

As Moretti, "'A Huge Eclipse,'" 32–34, argues, soliloquy (particularly in *Macbeth* and *Hamlet*) represents an excessive blockage of political process, the excrescence of ideological mystification that I have called, following him, an absolutist fantasy. Mullaney, "Lying Like Truth," 42–45, argues that the linguistic excess in *Macbeth* imbricates treason—an uncontrollable ambiguity rather than the New Critical kind. Finally, Greenblatt, in "*King Lear* and Harsnett's 'Devil Fiction,'" *Genre* 15 (1982): 239–42, and "Shakespeare and the Exorcists," seeks to describe Shakespearean autonomy as an improvisatory effect accomplished within the institutional/ideological space determined by social fictions and discourses. In their various ways, these critics move toward a demystification of autonomy and a description of the achievement of an autonomy effect. If, as I suggest, Shakespeare represents the textuality of his plays through women and allies his author function with them, Greenblatt's study of the *submission* of Desdemona (*Renaissance Self-Fashioning: From More to Shakespeare* [Chicago: University of Chicago Press, 1980])—an absorption of text and role that does not exclude her "downright violence" (1.3.249)—might prove useful in exploring the nature and representation of Shakespeare's authorial autonomy.

The Anus in *Coriolanus*

1. Cynthia Marshall, "Wound-Man: *Coriolanus,* Gender, and the Theatrical Construction of Interiority," in *Feminist Readings of Early Modern Culture,* ed. Valerie Traub, M. Lindsay Kaplan, and Dympna Callaghan (Cambridge: Cambridge University Press, 1996), 93–118; her comments on my essay occur on 118 n. 59.

2. The image, by Phoebe Gloeckner, illustrates a work of fiction, "Snake Dance," by M. I. Blue, in *Future Sex* 5 (1993): 40–41, and shows a fist emerging from a throat against an intestinal background; the gender of the hand or of the fisted figure in the image cannot be determined. It is hardly a stretch to argue that the fisted throat in Gloeckner's image is connected viscerally to a suggestion of anal fisting; her image thus makes explicit what I argue for in the reading of *Coriolanus* that follows.

3. Kenneth Burke, "Coriolanus—and the Delights of Faction," in his *Language as Symbolic Action* (Berkeley and Los Angeles: University of California Press, 1966), 96. Further citations are drawn from the same page of the essay.

4. It is worth remarking that preserving the Latin pronunciation could remind one that "ring" and "anus" are identical in that language—a point not lost in the final scene of *The Merchant of Venice.*

5. See Janet Adelman, "'Anger's My Meat': Feeding, Dependency, and Aggression in *Coriolanus,*" in *Shakespeare: Pattern of Excelling Nature,* ed. David Bevington and Jay L. Halio (Cranbury, N.J.: Associated University Presses, 1978),

reprinted in *Representing Shakespeare: New Psychoanalytic Essays,* ed. Murray Schwartz and Coppélia Kahn (Baltimore: The Johns Hopkins University Press, 1980), and the basis for sections of chapter 6 in Adelman, *Suffocating Mothers* (New York: Routledge, 1992). Cf. Jonathan Goldberg, *James I and the Politics of Literature* (Baltimore: The Johns Hopkins University Press, 1983), 186–93.

6. All citations are from Stanley Cavell, "*Coriolanus* and Interpretations of Politics," in his *Disowning Knowledge in Six Plays of Shakespeare* (Cambridge: Cambridge University Press, 1987); the *Coriolanus* essay first appeared without a postscript under the title "'Who Does the Wolf Love?': Reading *Coriolanus,*" *Representations* 3 (1983): 1–20.

7. Cavell, *Disowning Knowledge,* 169. All citations of *Coriolanus* are from the Arden edition, ed. Philip Brockbank (London: Methuen, 1976).

8. This is the relationship in the early modern period argued by Jeffrey Masten in "Is the Fundament a Grave?" in *The Body in Parts,* ed. David Hillman and Carla Mazzio (New York: Routledge, 1997), 129–45; for further thoughts about the relationship between foundational politics and modern anxieties, see Lee Edelman, "Capitol Offenses: Sodomy in the Seat of American Government," among other essays gathered in his *Homographesis* (New York: Routledge, 1994), as well as Leo Bersani, "Is the Rectum a Grave?" *October* 43 (1987): 197–222.

9. François Rabelais, *Gargantua et Pantagruel,* 1.6.

10. Gail Kern Paster, *The Body Embarrassed* (Ithaca, N.Y.: Cornell University Press, 1993), 143.

11. Paster, "Covering His Ass," in *The Body Embarrassed.* For some considerations of this topic in early modern texts, see my "*Romeo and Juliet*'s Open Rs," in *Queering the Renaissance,* ed. Jonathan Goldberg (Durham, N.C.: Duke University Press, 1994), reprinted in this volume, and "Margaret Roper's Daughterly Devotions: Unnatural Translations," in my *Desiring Women Writing: English Renaissance Examples* (Stanford: Stanford University Press, 1997), 91–113. For one example of the ways in which lesbian anal desire might overlap with gay male and heterosexual desire, see the contemporary image that I discuss in the introduction to my *Reclaiming Sodom* (New York: Routledge, 1994).

12. This is also the case in Bruce Thomas Boehrer, "Bestial Buggery in *A Midsummer Night's Dream,*" in *The Production of English Renaissance Culture,* ed. David Lee Miller, Sharon O'Dair, and Harold Weber (Ithaca, N.Y.: Cornell University Press, 1994), 123–50, whose analysis of bestiality in the play never ponders the possibility that "ass" could signify anatomically. This is worth considering, to follow a remark I make in *Sodometries* (Stanford: Stanford University Press, 1992), 275 n. 8, that Bottom and the Indian boy are in a substitutive relationship in the play.

13. See Jeffrey Masten, "Is the Fundament a Grave," in *The Body in Parts,* ed. Hillman and Mazzio, 145 n. 47.

14. Freud comments on the primordiality of fantasies of anal birth in his analysis of the Wolfman's version of the primal scene as *a tergo* ("from behind") intercourse, a point emphasized in Lee Edelman's reading of the case in "Seeing Things," *Homographesis,* 173–91. For this reason, it is suspect simply to follow the strand in Freud's thought that equates the anus with a substitute for the presumptively primordial vagina, as Paster does and as also can be seen in Avital Ronell, "*Le Sujet suppositaire:* Freud and Rat Man," in *On Puns,* ed. Jonathan Culler (Oxford: Basil Blackwell, 1988), 115–39; and in Lucinda Dixon's analysis of representations of enema procedures in early modern Dutch painting, in *Perilous Chastity* (Ithaca, N.Y.: Cornell University Press, 1995), 147–53.

15. Guy Hocquenghem, *Homosexual Desire,* trans. Daniella Dangoor, preface by Jeffrey Weeks, was recently reissued with a new introduction by Michael Moon (Durham, N.C.: Duke University Press, 1993); the original French text dates from 1972, the English translation from 1978.

16. For a crucial statement of the eroticism of friendship, see Alan Bray, "Homosexuality and the Signs of Male Friendship in Elizabethan England," *History Workshop Journal* 29 (1990): 1–19, reprinted in a slightly revised form in Goldberg, *Queering the Renaissance.*

17. These arguments are meant to counter those who see the intense male-male relations in the play as invidiously in competition with heterosexuality, that is, as the supreme instance of the supposedly typical male eroticizing of violence, inevitably at the expense of women, inevitably taking the form of male-male sexuality. See, for example, Peter Erickson, *Patriarchal Structures in Shakespeare's Drama* (Berkeley and Los Angeles: University of California Press, 1985), 5–6, for a male feminist statement of this position in a reading of the lines spoken by Aufidius to Coriolanus (Erickson's position conveniently exonerates straight men). See also Alan Sinfield, *Faultlines* (Berkeley and Los Angeles: University of California Press, 1992), 136, where the bond of Aufidius and Coriolanus is similarly treated as both stigmatizing women and aimed at effeminate men. Sinfield thus implies that male homosexual relationships should be modeled on politically progressive heterosexual lines.

Rebel Letters

1. Marjorie Garber, "Shakespeare's Ghost Writers," in *Cannibals, Witches, and Divorce: Estranging the Renaissance,* ed. Marjorie Garber (Baltimore: The Johns Hopkins University Press, 1987), 139; an expanded version of "Shakespeare's Ghost Writers" appears in Garber's *Shakespeare's Ghost Writers* (New York: Methuen, 1987). Garber performs a similar inquiry in "'Here's Nothing Writ': Scribe, Script, and Circumscription in Marlowe's Plays," *Theatre Journal* 36 (1984): 301–20. For a recent essay that further analyzes a thematics of textuality in *Richard II*—in ways akin to the exploration undertaken in this essay—see

Christopher Pye, "The Betrayal of the Gaze: Theatricality and Power in Shakespeare's *Richard II,*" *ELH* 55 (1988): 575–98.

2. Quotations from *Richard II* are from William Shakespeare, *The Complete Works,* Pelican Text Revised, Alfred Harbage, gen. ed. (Baltimore: Penguin, 1969). Quotations from the Quarto versions are from Michael J. B. Allen and Kenneth Muir, eds., *Shakespeare's Plays in Quarto* (Berkeley and Los Angeles: University of California Press, 1981).

3. Raphael Holinshed, *Holinshed's Chronicles,* ed. R. S. Wallace and Alma Hansen (Oxford: Clarendon, 1923).

4. Ibid., 38.

5. For example, James L. Calderwood, *Shakespearean Metadrama* (Minneapolis: University of Minnesota Press, 1971); Calderwood, *Metadrama in Shakespeare's Henriad:* Richard II *to* Henry V (Berkeley and Los Angeles: University of California Press, 1979); Joseph Porter, *The Drama of Speech Acts: Shakespeare's Lancastrian Tetralogy* (Berkeley and Los Angeles: University of California Press, 1979). In a number of recent essays, Harry Berger Jr. has written in opposition to such speech-centered (and stage-centered) readings of Shakespeare and in support of a version of textuality congruent with, but not identical to, the argument of this essay. For his theoretical statement, see "Bodies and Texts," *Representations* 17 (1987): 144–66; for studies of the issue in the second tetralogy, see "Psychoanalyzing the Shakespeare Text: The First Three Scenes of the *Henriad,*" in *Shakespeare and the Question of Theory,* ed. Patricia Parker and Geoffrey Hartman (New York: Methuen, 1985), 210–29; and "Sneak's Noise; or, Rumor and Detextualization in *2 Henry IV,*" *Kenyon Review,* new series, 6, no. 4 (1984): 58–78.

6. Terence Hawkes, *Shakespeare's Talking Animals: Language and Drama in Society* (London: Arnold, 1973), 51.

7. For an incisive investigation of the ideology of Shakespeare's history plays—and the ideological suppositions of the criticism on them—see Graham Holderness, *Shakespeare's History* (New York: St. Martin's, 1985).

8. Jacques Derrida, *Of Grammatology,* trans. Gayatri Chakravorty Spivak (Baltimore: The Johns Hopkins University Press, 1976), 8.

9. Ibid., 90.

10. Jacques Derrida, "Scribble (Writing-Power)," *Yale French Studies* 58 (1979): 117–47.

11. Ibid., 124.

12. Ibid., 138.

13. Hawkes, *Shakespeare's Talking Animals,* 91.

14. See Herbert Grabes, *The Mutable Glass: Mirror-Imagery in Titles and Texts in the Middle Ages and the English Renaissance,* trans. Gordon Collier (Cambridge: Cambridge University Press, 1982).

15. Jacques Derrida, *The Post Card: From Socrates to Freud and Beyond,* trans. Alan Bass (Chicago: University of Chicago Press, 1987), 29.

16. Garber, "Shakespeare's Ghost Writers," 139.

17. Angel Day, *The English Secretorie* (London, 1599), 1. William Fulwood, *The Enemy of Idleness* (London: Edward Allde, 1621), 1–2. Day's manual first appeared in 1586; I quote from the 1599 expanded printing. Fulwood's book first appeared in 1568; I quote from a 1621 reprinting. For the history of the form in England, see Katherine Gee Hornbeak, *The Complete Letter Writer in English: 1568–1800,* Smith College Studies in Modern Languages, no. 15 (Northampton, Mass.: Smith College, 1934); and Jean Robertson, *The Art of Letter Writing: An Essay on the Handbooks Published in England during the Sixteenth and Seventeenth Centuries* (Liverpool, Eng.: University Press of Liverpool, 1943). For studies of the relationship of Renaissance letter manuals to classical and medieval traditions, see A. Gerlo, "The *Opus de conscribendis epistolis* of Erasmus and the Tradition of the *Ars epistolica,*" *Classical Influences on European Culture, A.D. 500–1500,* ed. R. R. Bolgar (Cambridge: Cambridge University Press, 1971), 103–14; and Cecil H. Clough, "The Cult of Antiquity: Letters and Letter Collections," in *Cultural Aspects of the Italian Renaissance,* ed. Cecil H. Clough (Manchester, Eng.: Manchester University Press, 1976), 33–67. Day's manual often translates Francesco Sansovino's *Del secretario* (Venice, 1565).

18. Holinshed, *Holinshed's Chronicles,* 41.

19. On the economic metaphors, which I pursue here in their relationship to writing, see the classic New Critical essay by R. J. Dorius, "A Little More Than a Little," *Shakespeare Quarterly* 11 (1960): 13–26; cf. E. Rubinstein, "*1 Henry IV:* The Metaphors of Liability," *Studies in English Literature, 1500–1900* 10 (1970): 287–95.

20. Derrida, *Of Grammatology,* 35.

21. The verbal play in these lines is noted in *Henry IV, Part I,* Oxford Shakespeare, ed. David Bevington (Oxford: Clarendon, 1987), although, in usual eighteenth-century editorial terms, "engross up deeds" is described as a "quibble" on "written legal instruments of purchase" and "brave acts" (229 n. 148).

22. Stephen Greenblatt, "Invisible Bullets: Renaissance Authority and Its Subversion, *Henry IV* and *Henry V,*" in *Political Shakespeare: New Essays in Cultural Materialism,* ed. Jonathan Dollimore and Alan Sinfield (Ithaca, N.Y.: Cornell University Press, 1985), 30.

23. Compare Boethius's commentary on Aristotle, insisting that sound *(vox)* only becomes a word through an act of coinlike impression; quoted in R. A. Shoafe, *Dante, Chaucer, and the Currency of the Word: Money, Images, and Reference in Late Medieval Poetry* (Norman, Okla.: Pilgrim, 1983), 9–11.

24. Derrida, *Of Grammatology,* 91.

25. Greenblatt, "Invisible Bullets."

26. I am grateful to Jeff Rodgers for this point.

27. Derrida, *The Post Card,* 415. On the veil of heliotropic truth, see also

Derrida, "White Mythology: Metaphor in the Text of Philosophy," in Derrida, *Margins of Philosophy*, trans. Alan Bass (Chicago: University of Chicago Press, 1982). French *facteur* also means "postman," as Derrida stresses in "Le Facteur de la verité," his reading in *The Post Card* of Jacques Lacan's seminar on Edgar Allan Poe's "The Purloined Letter."

28. Abraham Fleming, *Panoplie of Epistles* (London, 1576), 5v.

29. Derrida, *Of Grammatology*, 67.

30. Derrida, *The Post Card*, 5.

31. On the relationship between Falstaff's catechism and Renaissance treatises on language, see Jane Donawerth, *Shakespeare and the Sixteenth-Century Study of Language* (Urbana: University of Illinois Press, 1984), 16.

32. See my "Textual Properties," *Shakespeare Quarterly* 37 (1986): 213–17.

33. For a study that attempts this, see John Jowett and Gary Taylor, "Sprinklings of Authority: The Folio Text of *Richard II*," *Studies in Bibliography* 38 (1985): 151–200, especially 152–55, for an argument that the "abdication episode" in the Folio may derive from a manuscript rather than from Q5, and 194–98, for an argument the F1 offers not the original scene expunged from Q1 but a later revision. Jowett and Taylor argue against the usual editorial estimation of F1 (this also extends to the text of *1 Henry IV*, as Taylor argues in "The Shrinking Compositor A of the Shakespeare First Folio," *Studies in Bibliography* 34 [1981]: 96–117), but they are so intent on proving its value against Q1 that they ignore the real editorial problem of the abdication episode; although it appears in Q1 and Q5, texts that otherwise have no authority, those first printings of the scene differ from that in F1. Those differences cannot be attributed to corruptions of the text because they are the first versions of the scene we have. Their status is problematic, to say the least; Jowett and Taylor proceed as if the only version of the abdication episode we have is the one in F1. What complicates their argument is the fact that lines that they represent as only to be found in F1 are also found in Q1. Equally problematic, and symptomatic of the treatment of the episode, is the editorial principle announced by Matthew W. Black in the Penguin edition (Baltimore, 1957): Q4 is a printing that has a "faulty copy" behind it, he claims; nevertheless "many modern editions, including the present one, prefer some thirteen fourth-quarto readings" (636).

34. Bevington, *Henry IV, Part I*, 87.

35. Ibid., 101.

36. Ibid., 206.

37. A. R. Humphreys, ed., *King Henry IV, Part I*, The Arden Shakespeare (New York: Methuen, 1974).

38. Bevington, *Henry IV, Part I*, 101.

39. Fredson Bowers, "Establishing Shakespeare's Text: Poins and Peto in *1 Henry IV*," *Studies in Bibliography*, 34 (1981): 194 n.

40. John Dover Wilson, ed., *The First Part of the History of Henry IV* (Cambridge: Cambridge University Press, 1958).

41. Quoted in ibid., 157 n.

42. Bowers, "Establishing Shakespeare's Text," 195.

43. *William Shakespeare: The Complete Works,* Oxford Shakespeare, Stanley Wells and Gary Taylor, gen. eds. (Oxford: Clarendon, 1986).

44. See the facsimile and transcription by George Walton Williams and Gwynne Blakemore Evans, eds., *The History of King Henry the Fourth, as Revised by Sir Edward Dering, Bart.* (Charlottesville: University Press of Virginia, 1974).

The Commodity of Names

The argument presented here was developed in the course of a seminar offered in the fall 1988 semester at The Johns Hopkins University. I am grateful to the participants for much stimulation and for a give-and-take that makes it difficult to claim that everything in this essay is my own (the notion is, of course, under pressure in the essay itself). In particular, I must mention Beth Pittenger and Michael Deneen, who wrote papers on this topic; although I did not have their essays before me as I wrote, they have undoubtedly influenced what I wrote (this too is implicit in the argument made in the essay).

1. See Jonathan Goldberg, "Textual Properties," *Shakespeare Quarterly* 37, no. 2 (1986): 213–17, and reprinted in this volume, which discusses the arguments for the decision to include two *King Lears* in *William Shakespeare: The Complete Works,* ed. Stanley Wells and Gary Taylor (Oxford: Clarendon Press, 1986).

2. Gary Taylor, "The Fortunes of Oldcastle," *Shakespeare Survey* 38 (1985): 100. Further page references will be cited in the text.

3. The history of the acceptance of the notion that Oldcastle became Falstaff is detailed in Rudolph Fiehler, "How Oldcastle Became Falstaff," *Modern Language Quarterly* 16 (1955): 16–28; Taylor fills out the Cobham connection in "William Shakespeare, Richard James, and the House of Cobham," *Review of English Studies,* new series, 38 (1987): 334–54.

4. William Shakespeare, *The First Part of King Henry IV,* Arden edition, A. R. Humphreys (London: Methuen, 1960); all citations are to this edition unless otherwise noted.

5. The question of verse-prose distinctions is an enormously complicated one, and nothing in my argument really depends upon the rightness of the Q1 imprint except insofar as it testifies to a much more fluid relationship between prose and verse in Elizabethan practice than in that of the eighteenth century. All sorts of evidence, including scribal and authorial manuscripts of the period, suggest that in many instances verse and prose were not always distinguished; on this, see Stephen Orgel, "Acting Scripts, Performing Texts," in *Crisis in Edit-*

ing, ed. Randall McLeod (New York: AMS Press, 1994), 251–94. Pope's decisions about versification, like those of many subsequent editors, were motivated by the desire to raise the stature of characters by having them, whenever possible, speak in verse.

6. Alexander Pope, "An Essay on Criticism," line 135, in *The Poems of Alexander Pope,* ed. John Butt (New Haven: Yale University Press, 1963), 148.

7. William Shakespeare, *King Henry V,* Arden edition, ed. J. H. Walter (London: Methuen, 1954).

8. William Shakespeare, *The Merry Wives of Windsor,* ed. H. J. Oliver, Arden edition (London: Methuen, 1971).

9. These markings of Queen Elizabeth (the allusion to her as Diana is unmistakable and is noted in John Dover Wilson's 1946 Cambridge edition of the play) and the Lord Chamberlain must give pause to anyone who thinks that Elizabethan censorship is easily comprehended. In the case of *1 Henry IV,* it is worth noting that while we think we know who caused the suppression of Oldcastle, we really do not know why—nor does the play in its present form tell us. In its present form, however, it does show that censorship could be re-marked, names could be named in the glancing of metaphoric substitution, in the replacement of the proper title with a generic one—and that these lapses could survive un-re-marked. Taylor's notion that a play presenting Oldcastle in an unfavorable light could not be endured fails to consider how the *Famous Victories,* hardly flattering in its portrait, could have made its way on stage or in print; in the very same year as *1 Henry IV* appeared, its title page announced it *"[a]s it was plaide by the Queens Majesties Players."* The pertinence of the *Famous Victories* to the composite character of Falstaff—derived not only from that play's Oldcastle but also from several other characters (a point about origins that also disturbs the notion of the propriety and proper naming of characters)—has often been documented; see, for example, James Monaghan, "Falstaff and His Forebears," *Studies in Philology* 18 (1921): 353–61; D. B. Landt, "The Ancestry of Sir John Falstaff," *Shakespeare Quarterly* 27 (1976): 199–200; Norman Davis, "Falstaff's Name," *Shakespeare Quarterly* 28 (1977): 513–15; G. Walton Williams, "Some Thoughts on Falstaff's Name," *Shakespeare Quarterly* 29 (1979): 82–84.

10. As the title of his essay suggests, Taylor depends upon John Dover Wilson, *The Fortunes of Falstaff* (Cambridge: Cambridge University Press, 1943) for his historic reconstruction. It is, of course, the case, that what Dover Wilson offers is not the real character but an interpretation of it, one marked by a high moral tone, one that can find little to say on behalf of Falstaff. (On the ideological ramifications of Dover Wilson's work, see Graham Holderness, *Shakespeare's History* [Dublin: Gill and Macmillan, 1985], 90–95 passim.) This is by no means the only version of the character possible, nor is it the one prevailing in criticism, which, on the whole, has found itself more attracted to the old reprobate than not. Moreover, it is worth noting that the very title of Taylor's essay enacts

the argument I am presenting here; it simply replaces a name and restores the true reading. But it also therefore loses its name in the allusion, and the true reading it would substitute is not the only one. Against Dover Wilson, one could marshal not only previous "sentimental" defenders of Falstaff like A. C. Bradley but also his contemporary New Critical opponent William Empson or, finally, various new historicists (notably Stephen Greenblatt) who read *1 Henry IV* as a more contestatory historical site. Above all, one would have to reckon with the sheer popularity of Falstaff and even, as Walter Cohen has argued in *Drama of a Nation* (Ithaca, N.Y.: Cornell University Press, 1985), 225–26, with his mobilization for revolutionary politics: These would not disappear if he were given another name, much as Taylor might wish that to be the case.

11. That phantasmatic is, of course, explored in much theoretical work, especially that of Jacques Derrida and Jacques Lacan, and it is upon that work that this critique relies. But even within a philosophical approach that is in many respects closer to Taylor's suppositions, these fantasies about the self-identity and absolute guarantee of the proper name come into question. Saul Kripke, in *Naming and Necessity* (Cambridge, Mass.: Harvard University Press, 1980), imagines an originary moment in the baptismal scene of naming; but what the name means thereafter is confirmed by chains of transmission that can never be returned to that originary moment. Kripke stops the chain only by assuming that the discourses of science offer an objective real against and through which the identity of the proper can be secured, but this is an intensely problematic gesture once the historicity of scientific truth is introduced—as problematic as the theological guarantees that Taylor assumes. It is nonetheless notable that Kripke does not for a moment assume that a proper name, as transmitted, as used, as cited, and so on, ever can correspond to its originary ground: "What is true is that it's in virtue of our connection with other speakers in the community, going back to the referent himself, that we refer to a certain man" (94). That going back, I argue, is an infinite regress, and even when we look at a particular person at a particular time—call him Shakespeare—it is impossible to say that his "integrity" assures some unbreached interiority. The conditions of writing are never absolutely free, nor is it possible to separate external censorship from internally imposed censorship, nor is it necessary to see the historic and its transmissions as solely a field of error that could somehow be restored to a truth (claimed to be historical) without error. That phantasm haunts all rationales of copytext and their intense dehistoricization. For a recent exploration—and explosion—of the construct of foul papers (the author's hand) as the guarantee of texts, see Paul Werstine, "Narratives about Printed Shakespearean Texts: 'Foul Papers' and 'Bad Quartos,'" *Shakespeare Quarterly* 41 (1990): 65–86.

12. John Milton, "On the New Forcers of Conscience," line 20 in *John Milton*, ed. Stephen Orgel and Jonathan Goldberg (Oxford: Oxford University Press, 1990), 84.

13. See, for example, A. R. Humphreys, introduction to Shakespeare, *The First Part of King Henry IV,* lxviff. Like many editors, Humphreys wishes he could claim that authorial foul papers stand behind the earliest printings of *1 Henry IV,* but he marshals the evidence for "signs of fair copy" (lxvii), including reasonably standardized speech prefixes and an attention to "minute details" (lxviii) of pointing and elision that suggest scribal intervention. Similarly, David Bevington (in his volume edited for the Oxford Shakespeare [Oxford: Oxford University Press, 1987]), finds "Shakespeare's corrected papers" or "a scribal copy" behind the remarkably "clean" Q0 and Q1 (90). (Not the least-remarkable feature of the editing of this play is that the derivative quality of the so-called Q1 has been ignored.) Bevington also takes up the questions of Oldcastle and defends the retention of "Falstaff." It should be clear that he and I are not making the same argument; he would have the name secure a final intentionality represented by Shakespeare continuing to write with the name "Falstaff," and while I agree that that retroactivity bears upon the original re-marking in *1 Henry IV,* I part company with the assumptions made about what the name secures. Bevington avers that with the name "Falstaff" the author makes a "fictional . . . contract" (108) with the audience. That, however, is Bevington's fiction, and it, as much as Taylor's, is tied to the phantasmatic properties believed inherent in the proper name. If Falstaff's name, especially as explicit substitute, secures anything, it is the impossibility of such stabilization through the proper name.

14. John Jowett, "The Thieves in *1 Henry IV,*" *Review of English Studies,* new series, 38 (1987): 325–33. Jowett's essay is capable of being read otherwise, against its grain (as I have been reading Taylor). By itself, it reads almost as a parody of Taylor's method, rifling the pages of history to try to discover some proper names—of real historical figures—who would have found themselves offended by the play's Harvey and Russell. When it turns to the marks of those names in the text of *1 Henry IV,* the essay tries, desperately, not to see revision taking place after the original performance; it wishes, that is, to make the revision merely nominal. Nonetheless, Jowett also finds evidence that a new character emerges in revision, as the original Russell splits to become sometimes Bardolph, sometimes Gadshill. Although it would take more than a note to work this out, in my reading of the evidence presented by Jowett, a compelling case can be made that this revision postdates the original performance. And in terms of the argument made above—about the pertinence of the name of Gadshill, the "setter" of the robbery (and perhaps of the robbery of the original names as well)—it is worth emphasizing the impropriety of Gadshill's name, a proper name and a place-name as well, for it intimates what is true of all proper names, in whatever version of the play we have or might have had: that the proper name is always subject to dispersal.

15. If so, then another of Taylor's scenarios is called into question, the

desire he projects upon Heminge and Condell, staying the printing of *1 Henry IV* so that they might reprint the original text. If all that would have taken was the substitution of names, why would they have needed another text? By Taylor's own account, they had the text in hand already.

16. A further sign of this embarrassment can be seen in Jowett's untitled commentary in Stanley Wells and Gary Taylor, with John Jowett and William Montgomery, eds., *William Shakespeare: A Textual Companion* (Oxford: Clarendon Press, 1987): "The prefix *'Old'* for Falstaff at 1.2.122/374 probably stands for Oldcastle (a conceivable alternative is 'Old man')" (351). What leads Jowett to conceive this alternative? Presumably, Taylor's thesis that Shakespeare was done with Oldcastle when he moved on to subsequent plays (the prefix should not be there if Taylor's chronology is correct, or if *1 Henry IV* is to be preserved in its "integrity" as an "individual work of art"; this is a fine instance of how historic fixing is allied to suppressive singularity). And why the substitute? By what logic is it generated? By logic of the generic by which Shakespeare's foul papers preserve such names, which always come to be individualized, but also, and powerfully opposing this ideology of the proper, because the name "Oldcastle" (that cant term) triggers the generic and its destabilization of the proper name. The text of *2 Henry IV* keeps putting into Falstaff's mouth the lines "I am old, I am old," insisting on a relationship to Oldcastle through the generic suggestion that exceeds his name. "I am old" does not name Oldcastle properly, but neither does his proper name.

Hal's Desire, Shakespeare's Idaho

This essay includes materials (mainly drawn from a chapter entitled "Desiring Hal") reworked from my *Sodometries* (Stanford: Stanford University Press, 1992). The earliest drafts of this essay profited from the advice and enthusiasm of Michael Moon and Eve Kosofsky Sedgwick, while its current state would not have been possible without Jonathan Brody Kramnick.

1. For the purposes at hand, the most notable exception would be Heather Findlay's "Renaissance Pederasty and Pedagogy: The 'Case' of Shakespeare's Falstaff," *Yale Journal of Criticism* 3 (1989): 229–38. Findlay reads Hal as the locus of a homophobia inflicted upon the more or less sodomitical Falstaff, an argument that mine seeks to further by marking ways the play fails to deliver the exemplary Hal that Findlay's reading assumes. By so doing, I hope to move sodomy from the archaic and marginal position that it occupies in Findlay's essay and to allow it the space of a recognition that would trouble the play's received readings of various critical stripes.

2. Phyllis Rackin, *Stages of History* (Ithaca, N.Y.: Cornell University Press, 1990).

3. See, for example, Jeffrey Weeks, *Coming Out: Homosexual Politics in Britain from the Nineteenth Century to the Present* (London: Quartet Books,

1977, revised 1990), as well as his *Sex, Politics, and Society* (London: Longman, 1981).

4. Michel Foucault, *The History of Sexuality: An Introduction,* trans. Robert Hurley (New York: Random House, 1978).

5. Eve Kosofsky Sedgwick, *Epistemology of the Closet* (Berkeley and Los Angeles: University of California Press, 1990).

6. Joseph Pequigney, *Such Is My Love* (Chicago: University of Chicago Press, 1985).

7. Alan Bray, *Homosexuality in Renaissance England* (London: Gay Men's Press, 1982).

8. Eve Kosofsky Sedgwick, *Between Men: English Literature and Male Homosocial Desire* (New York: Columbia University Press, 1985).

9. Alan Bray, "Homosexuality and the Signs of Male Friendship in Elizabethan England," *History Workshop Journal* 29 (1990): 1–19.

10. "For the respectes aforesaid in all former ages and in the most civill countreys and commons wealthes, good Poets and Poesie were highly esteemed and much favoured of the greatest Princes. . . . king *Henry* the 8, her *Majesties* father, for a few Psalmes of *David* turned into English meetre by Sternhold, made him groome of his privy chamber & gave him many other good gifts' (George Puttenham, *The Arte of English Poesie* [1589], in *Elizabethan Critical Essays,* ed. G. Gregory Smith, 2 vols. [Oxford: Oxford University Press, 1904], vol. 2, 16–17).

11. See Arthur Marotti, "'Love Is Not Love': Elizabethan Sonnet Sequences and the Social Order," *ELH* 49 (1982): 396–428.

12. Stephen Greenblatt, "Fiction and Friction," in his *Shakespearean Negotiations* (Berkeley and Los Angeles: University of California Press, 1988), 66–93; the final pages are especially pertinent to the critique offered above.

13. Lisa Jardine, *Still Harping on Daughters,* rev. ed. (New York: Columbia University Press, 1989).

14. Michael Warner, "Homo-Narcissism; or, Heterosexuality," in *Engendering Men,* ed. Joseph A. Boone and Michael Cadden (New York: Routledge, 1990), 190–206.

15. Marjorie Garber, *Vested Interests* (New York: Routledge, 1992).

16. Sedgwick, *Between Men,* 44.

17. Ann Rosalind Jones and Peter Stallybrass, in "Fetishizing Gender: Constructing the Hermaphrodite in Renaissance Europe," in *Body Guards,* ed. Julia Epstein and Kristina Straub (New York: Routledge, 1991), 80–111, have suggested that the biologistic bias in gender definition (the assumption that genitals are the physical bedrock upon which gender is founded) is questionable not only theoretically, as has often been argued, but also historically; they claim the assumption is a modern one and not to be found in Renaissance texts about the body, which posit sociolegal definitions of gender as the bedrock of difference.

18. All citations are from *1 Henry IV* and *2 Henry IV,* Arden editions, ed. A. R. Humphreys (London: Methuen, 1960 and 1966, respectively).

19. These patriarchal phantasmatics are traced by Louis Adrian Montrose in "'Shaping Fantasies': Figurations of Gender and Power in Elizabethan Culture," *Representations* 2 (1983): 70–71. Although Montrose connects the lines that Theseus speaks in 1.1.47–51 to the fight over the Indian boy, he is silent about the sexual connection the child represents; for that point, one can turn to Jonathan Crewe, *Hidden Designs* (New York: Methuen, 1986), 148–51, for a somewhat pathologizing view of Oberon's desire for the boy as, in Crewe's terms, his "pathic." Nevertheless, Crewe sees that the boy is written much as the young man is in the sonnets, and that as changeling he is the very locus for a series of crossings in the play.

20. Hal's imagery answers his initial accusation that Falstaff is "fat-witted with drinking of old sack" (*1 Henry IV,* 1.2.2); the connection between "vapors" and flatulence is made over and again in Ben Jonson's *Bartholomew Fair* (1614, pub. 1631), in *The Complete Plays of Ben Jonson,* ed. G. A. Wilkes, 4 vols. (Oxford: Oxford University Press, 1981–82).

21. William Empson, *Some Versions of Pastoral* (London: Chatto and Windus, 1935; reprint, London: New Impression, 1950), 102–9, in the essay on Shakespeare's Sonnet 94.

22. *King Richard II,* ed. Peter Ure (London: Methuen, 1956).

23. These are not unlike the terms of patriarchy described by Luce Irigaray in *This Sex Which Is Not One,* trans. Catherine Porter (Ithaca, N.Y.: Cornell University Press, 1985), 192–93. Where this critique parts company with Irigaray is in her supposition that such male-male relations (for example, the pederasty that lurks in father-son relations) mask homosexuality *tout court* as the secret of homosociality (this is the argument that her nonce word "hom[m]osexuality" conveys), since it leaves no room for the recognition that the policing of homosexuality is complicit with the policing of women and that there is a world of difference between homosexuality and homophobia. This is a point argued against Irigaray by Craig Owens in "Outlaws: Gay Men in Feminism," in *Men in Feminism,* ed. Alice Jardine and Paul Smith (New York: Methuen, 1987), 223–24, which draws upon the exemplary discussions of Eve Kosofsky Sedgwick, such as the one in her introduction to *Between Men,* 19–20.

24. I am grateful to Jonathan Brody Kramnick for suggesting to me this crucial overlap.

25. Judith Butler, "The Lesbian Phallus and the Morphological Imaginary," *Differences: A Journal of Feminist Cultural Studies* 4, no. 1 (1992): 164.

26. This is much less true for women, given their position under patriarchy and their definitional status acquired through marriage. But it is not entirely untrue, as Valerie Traub begins to suggest in "Desire and the Difference It Makes," in *The Matter of Difference,* ed. Valerie Wayne (Ithaca, N.Y.: Cornell

University Press, 1991), 81–114, an essay included in Traub's *Desire and Anxiety: Circulations of Sexuality in Shakespearean Drama* (London: Routledge, 1992).

27. See W. H. Auden, "The Prince's Dog," in his *The Dyer's Hand* (New York: Random House, 1948), which does make some valuable connections between the sonnets and the relationship in the play but which also insists on the fat knight's narcissism, infantilism, feminization, and alcoholism.

28. Patricia Parker, *Literary Fat Ladies* (London: Methuen, 1987) declares Falstaff an "obvious Shakespearean 'fat lady'" (20) on the basis of his girth and his tongue; it is difficult to see in whose interest such an identification is made.

29. Michael Moon and Eve Kosofsky Sedgwick's "Divinity: A Dossier/A Performance Piece/A Little-Understood Emotion," *Discourse* 13 (1990–91): 12–39, offers a sustained meditation on these questions. For the relationships between body size and social organization in the transition to capitalist social organization—toward the modernity incipient in Shakespeare's plays—see Stephen Mennell, "On the Civilizing of Appetite," *Theory, Culture, and Society* 4 (1987): 373–403, especially his discussion on page 397 of the ways in which an older aristocratic corpulence becomes the body of the poor as the new regimes of civilization preach restraint. Falstaff's body is, in these terms, legible under both the old and new regimes.

30. This is Valerie Traub's argument in "Prince Hal's Falstaff: Positioning Psychoanalysis and the Female Reproductive Body," *Shakespeare Quarterly* 40 (1989): 456–74. "The homoerotics of the Henriad deserve fuller treatment," Traub notes, only immediately to figure that sexuality as Hal's masculinity played in relation to Falstaff's femininity (465).

31. *Henry IV, Part I,* the Oxford Shakespeare, ed. David Bevington (Oxford: Clarendon, 1987).

32. I owe this connection to Jonathan Brody Kramnick.

33. For example:

> A woman's face, with Nature's own hand painted,
> Hast thou, the master-mistress of my passion;
> A woman's gentle heart, but not acquainted
> With shifting change, as is false women's fashion.
> (lines 1–4)

Citations of the sonnets are from William Shakespeare, *The Sonnets and Love's Complaint,* ed. John Kerrigan (Harmondsworth: Penguin, 1986).

34. All citations from the Arden edition, *Henry V,* ed. J. H. Walter (London: Methuen, 1954).

35. Phantasmatic because the mechanisms of repression are, as Foucault argued, productive, but phantasmatic, too, because the private is continually policed and regulated to this day, and the sanctioned forms of sexuality that are secured are the ones that ensure the perpetuation of procreative sex within a

compulsory heterosexuality. The 1986 U.S. Supreme Court decision in *Bowers v. Hardwick,* denying any constitutional right to private consensual acts of what the court termed "homosexual sodomy," makes this all too clear.

36. The man "who'd given him the poison, . . . pinched his foot hard, and asked him if he could feel it, and Socrates said not. After that he felt his shins once more; and moving upwards in this way, he showed us that he was becoming cold and numb" (Plato, *Phaeto,* trans. David Gallop [Oxford: Oxford University Press, 1975], 72). I am aware of the caveat offered by Gary Taylor in his note to the Oxford *Henry V,* 2.3.22–24, but the resemblance seems too striking to ignore.

37. Joseph A. Porter, *Shakespeare's Mercutio* (Chapel Hill: University of North Carolina Press, 1988), reads Mercutio as a figure for Marlowe, and his relationship with Romeo in counterpoint to Romeo's relationship with Juliet.

38. Elizabeth Pittenger, "Dispatch Quickly: The Mechanical Reproduction of Pages," *Shakespeare Quarterly* 42 (1991): 389–408.

"What? in a names that which we call a Rose"

1. Fredson Bowers, "What Shakespeare Wrote," in his *On Editing Shakespeare* (Charlottesville: University Press of Virginia, 1966), 120. Pope (*The Works of Mr. William Shakespear* [London: Jacob Tonson, 1723], vol. 6, 271) essentially follows Q1 at this point:

> 'Tis but thy name that is my enemy:
> What's *Mountague*? it is not hand, nor foot,
> Nor arm, nor face—nor any other part.
> What's in a name? that which we call a rose,
> By any other name would smell as sweet.

2. Random Cloud, "The Marriage of Good and Bad Quartos," *Shakespeare Quarterly,* 33 (1982): 421–31. This essay develops the notion of the "infinitive text," referred to below, which has been highly influential on the argument presented here; I also develop points first essayed in my review of the New Arden *Romeo and Juliet* in *Shakespeare Studies* 16 (1983): 343–48. My chief indebtedness in this essay is to Stephen Orgel, "What Is a Text?" *Research Opportunities in Renaissance Drama* 24 (1981): 3–6; Orgel, "Shakespeare Imagines a Theater," in *Shakespeare, Man of the Theater,* ed. K. Muir, J. Halio, and D. J. Palmer (Newark: University of Delaware Press, 1983); Orgel, "The Authentic Shakespeare," *Representations* 21 (1988): 1–26; and his edition of *The Tempest* (Oxford: Oxford University Press, 1987).

3. Quarto texts cited from *Shakespeare's Plays in Quarto,* ed. Michael J. B. Allen and Kenneth Muir (Berkeley and Los Angeles: University of California Press, 1981).

4. *Romeo and Juliet,* New Arden edition, ed. Brian Gibbons (London and New York: Methuen, 1980).

5. Stanley Wells, "The Bettering of Burby," *Times Literary Supplement* 4030 (20 June 1980): 710; further citations from Wells are all from this page.

6. In Stanley Wells and Gary Taylor, with John Jowett and William Montgomery, eds., *William Shakespeare: A Textual Companion* (Oxford: Clarendon Press, 1987): 294. Further citations from Jowett are all from this page. Wells was the secondary editor of *Romeo and Juliet* and cosigned the notes on the text.

7. *Romeo and Juliet,* ed. J. Dover Wilson and G. I. Duthie (Cambridge: Cambridge University Press, 1955, 1961).

8. The exact limits of this relationship have been the subject of much debate; for one example, see Richard Hosley, "Quarto Copy for Q2 *Romeo and Juliet,*" *Studies in Bibliography* 9 (1957): 129–41. One feature shared by Q1 and Q2 at this point is the use of italics for the Nurse's lines. This is an especially baffling fact, and one that has not been considered sufficiently. If one supposes, as seems arguable, that the typeface here replicates the hand in which the lines were written, then the script behind the text must have been written in an italic hand. It is difficult to imagine what kind of copy would so be written; theatrical scripts were normally written in secretarial hand. Italic was reserved for presentation copies and would have been produced by a professional scribe. All accounts of Q1 assume rushed work by the actors; it seems to me very unlikely that they would have written an italic hand. Moreover, if the typography is to be trusted, italic was used only for the Nurse's part; it is doubtful that what is reproduced in Q1 is the actor's part, however, for it is hard to imagine why that part would have been written out in that hand. I have no solution to this dilemma; but it troubles the notion of memorial reconstruction.

9. See John Dover Wilson, "The New Way with Shakespeare's Texts II. Recent Work on the Text of *Romeo and Juliet,*" *Shakespeare Survey* 8 (1955): 81–99.

10. G. I. Duthie, "The Text of Shakespeare's *Romeo and Juliet,*" *Studies in Bibliography* 4 (1951–52): 3–29.

11. This is the theory advanced by Hardin Craig, *A New Look at Shakespeare's Quartos* (Stanford: Stanford University Press, 1961), 54–65.

12. Fredson Bowers, "The Method for a Critical Edition," in his *On Editing Shakespeare,* 87.

13. The best case is made by Paul L. Cantrell and George Walton Williams, "The Printing of the Second Quarto of *Romeo and Juliet* (1599)," *Studies in Bibliography* 9 (1957): 107–28. They argue that since Q2 is so close to Q1 in shared accidentals for the stretch where Q1 stands demonstrably behind Q2, other moments, which are textually close but which lack shared accidentals, cannot show Q1 influence on Q2. The major evidence for them is the speech prefixes used in Q1 and Q2 and the assumption that the Q2 compositors were

particularly faithful in reproducing Q1 speech prefixes only in the limited portion of act 1 where Q1 served as copytext for Q2.

14. P. A. Daniel, *Romeo and Juliet, Parallel Texts of the First Two Quartos* (London: New Shakespeare Society, 1874), v.

15. Harry R. Hoppe, *The Bad Quarto of Romeo and Juliet* (Ithaca, N.Y.: Cornell University Press, 1948). Hoppe builds upon the suppositions of E. K. Chambers in *William Shakespeare,* 2 vols. (Oxford: Clarendon Press, 1930), vol. 1, 341–45, and of W. W. Greg, who endorses Hoppe's work in *The Editorial Problem in Shakespeare,* 2nd ed. (Oxford: Clarendon Press, 1951), 61–64, and in *The Shakespeare First Folio* (Oxford: Clarendon Press, 1955), 225–35.

16. *The Tragedy of Romeo and Juliet,* ed. Richard Hosley (New Haven: Yale University Press, 1954), 141.

17. The F1 line that serves as the title to this essay is not repeated, for example, by Nicholas Rowe, who returns to the Q2 reading of the passage (*The Works of Mr. William Shakespear,* 7 vols. [London: Jacob Tonson, 1709], vol. 5, 2096). This line is the same in both 1709 editions.

18. Richard Hosley, "The Corrupting Influence of the Bad Quarto on the Received Text of *Romeo and Juliet,*" *Shakespeare Quarterly* 4(1953): 11–34.

19. A comparison between Q1 and Q2 at these points will reveal both situations that I have been suggesting. Q2 offers two versions of the "grey eyed morn" lines, first for Romeo, then for Friar Laurence. The version of the speech in Q1 (D4r) is assigned to the friar—and it is very close to the version in Q2 that is also given to him (D4v). If Q2 represents first and second shots at the lines, Q1 has chosen the second shot; however, Q2 could also represent an alternative ending to the scene, and Romeo's version could be the second shot. The fact that it comes first in Q2 does not mean that it was written first. There is no way of knowing at what point the possibility that Romeo would speak the lines was introduced. If Hoppe is to be believed, the actor playing Romeo was one of the reporters of Q1; thus, in the performance represented by that text, the lines were not spoken by Romeo.

Romeo's final soliloquy as represented in Q2 is clearly an anthology of possibilities; there are at least two ways of ending the soliloquy. One starts twice, "I will beleeue, / Shall I beleeue" (L3r). Q1's "O I beleeue" (K1v) seems closer to that first alternative, and closer to the shorter ending that is offered immediately. Still, it ends with lines that have their parallel in the longer ending provided by Q2. The situation here is manifestly complex: Either Q1 chose from the longer versions represented in Q2—chose and rearranged—or Q2 represents various additions and relocations to Q1 or a manuscript. Again, there is no way of deciding which was the case, or in what order they occurred. The supposition that this speech is faultily reported depends upon hypotheses that will not stand scrutiny: Lines said to be cut may never have existed; to claim that differences must be actors' transpositions and anticipations assumes that an author cannot make exactly the same kinds of revisions; to deny the authorial origin of lines said to be weak assumes that Shakespeare never wrote bad verse.

20. Two major instances of rewriting—act 2, scene 6 and Paris's final soliloquy in act 5, scene 3—especially embarrass Hoppe's notion of a reported text, since he believes that the actors playing Romeo and Paris were the reporters. Hoppe argues that the fatigued actors mangled the final scenes of the play and that act 2, scene 6 never was in the play as performed and thus was entirely made up from bits and pieces of the play (185). Yet it is equally possible that the end of the play was different and that Romeo's reporting in act 2, scene 6 is as "accurate" as elsewhere (i.e., that the "accurate" parts of Q1 are unrevised parts). The kind of melange that Hoppe finds could also be an argument in favor of Shakespeare's authorship: He too would have bits and scraps of the play in his memory. Even if, as some have supposed, this alternative scene and soliloquy are by another hand—Henry Chettle is proposed by Sidney Thomas in "Henry Chettle and the First Quarto of *Romeo and Juliet*," *Review of English Studies*, new series, 1 (1950): 8–16—that does not damage the possibility of recognizing the scenes as Shakespearean, once one admits that collaboration was a normal procedure in the theater (the notion that a Shakespeare play must be entirely Shakespeare's relies on a concept of authorship that is not confirmed by Elizabethan theatrical procedures, nor by other plays, such as *Macbeth*, that are usually treated as "by Shakespeare"). Furthermore, the desire to deny Shakespearean authorship for these alternatives involves the usual circular arguments about unchanging authorial style as well as the belief in the unique entity *Romeo and Juliet*.

21. One such text is Michael Warren's edition, *The Complete King Lear, 1608–1623* (Berkeley and Los Angeles: University of California Press, 1989), which offers all the substantive texts in a box; unsewn, the pages are ready for dissemination. The truly utopian text would be even more radically unstitched.

22. Jacques Derrida, "L'Aphorisme à contretemps," in his *Psyché: Inventions de l'autre* (Paris: Galilee, 1987), 528. There is a complex wordplay in French that has no English equivalent: "Roméo est Roméo, et Roméo n'est pas Roméo. Il n'est lui-même qu'à se départir de son nom, il n'est lui-même que dans son nom. Roméo ne peut s'appeler lui-même que s'il se départit de son nom, il ne s'appelle qu'*à partir de* son nom."

23. In both Q1 and Q2, the Friar asks that rosemary be stuck on the "corpse"; the stage direction is found only in Q1 (I2v).

24. The variability of words—or flowers—is suggested in the lexicon provided by Jacques Bellot's French-English phrasebook, *Le Maistre d'ecole Anglois / The Englishe Scholemaister* (London, 1580), in its "Posye or Nosegay of Loue," an anthology of poetic flowers, including rosemary: "Rosemary cleapte, signifieth, Hope of grace, or Good will. Rosemarye vncleapte, is taken for Refuse,

Reiection of Disdayne. Rosemarye blowne cleapte, sheweth, Full loue, Assured comfort, or Ioyfull loue. Rosemary blowne, vncleapte, signifieth Dissembling" (G2v–3r).

25. The 1609 text is cited from *Shakespeare's Sonnets,* ed. Stephen Booth, second printing, with "Additional Notes" (New Haven: Yale University Press, 1978).

26. Cf. Joel Fineman, "Shakespeare's *Will:* The Temporality of Rape," *Representations* 20 (1987): 25–76; "As we know from *Romeo and Juliet,* where a 'purloined' (i.e., post-poned) letter is what causes the lovers' tragedy, literary letters *always* arrive at their destination precisely because they *always* go astray" (75 n. 35). In the play, it remains to be added, the Friar's potion—connected to poison and to the apothecary's potion—figures the possibility of a literalism evident when Romeo reads Juliet's simulated corpse as an actual one. He is caught within the play of the letter "R" that has moved him from Rosaline to Juliet as Rosemary, the flower of the corpse. The poisoned letter is the dead letter. This textual effect is that of the open "Rs" of the play, to recall another textual crux and to suggest a further sexual route that might be pursued. One guide to these questions would be Joseph A. Porter, *Shakespeare's Mercutio* (Chapel Hill: University of North Carolina Press, 1988), 160–63.

27. One intersects the work "banished," in 3.3.54–56 (Gibbons; there are versions of the lines in both Q1 and Q2), where, if Rolf Soellner's argument in "Shakespeare and the 'Consolatio,'" *Notes and Queries* 199 (1954): 108–9, is to be believed, the Friar's consolation is derived from Erasmus's *De conscribendis epistolis.*

28. If Q1's "part thy name" (D1v), for example, is regarded as a memorially or compositorially corrupt line, what is to be made of Q2's "Came more and more, and fought on part and part, / Till the Prince came, who parted either part" (A4v) or of its "Your part in her, you could not keepe from death. / But heauen keepes his part in eternall life" (K3r). (If those lines were in Q1, someone would no doubt suspect their repetitions as signs of corruption.) Those who believe in memorial corruption might argue here that Q1 remembers lines that Q2 lacks, and it has misplaced them in Juliet's added "part." But what about the possibility that Q2's additional lines occasioned the cut in Q1? Or the possibility that Q1 suggested the lines in Q2?

29. Reproduced with permission from the copy of the 1623 folio in the Thomas Fisher Rare Book Library, University of Toronto.

30. See S. W. Reid, "The Editing of Folio *Romeo and Juliet,*" *Studies in Bibliography* 35 (1982): 43–66, esp. 57. Reid's explanation assumes that Q2 was marked up to tell the compositor to insert a question mark and to delete the apostrophe in Q3 "What's." The argument seems to be a bit strained, since it has the compositor not only reverse what was asked but remove both the apostrophe and the "s." An alternative hypothesis, which would traffic even more spectacularly, could imagine an uncorrected state of F1 (which is not known to

exist) that read, "What in a name" and in which the two additions marked were inserted at the wrong places.

Romeo and Juliet's Open Rs

1. Brian Gibbons, introduction to *Romeo and Juliet,* New Arden edition, ed. Gibbons (London: Metheun, 1980), 70. For further evaluations of this edition, see my review of it in *Shakespeare Studies* 16 (1983): 343–48, and Stanley Wells's review in *Times Literary Supplement* 4030 (20 June 1980): 710. G. Blakemore Evans in his New Cambridge edition of the play (Cambridge: Cambridge University Press, 1984) devotes pages 16–20 to "language, style and imagery" in familiar formalist terms.

2. I take the term from its usage by Eve Kosofsky Sedgwick, *Between Men: English Literature and Male Homosocial Desire* (New York: Columbia University Press, 1985), and in the pages that follow I depend upon her arguments throughout the book as well as their particular application to Shakespeare in the chapter "Swan in Love."

3. Coppélia Kahn, "Coming of Age in Verona," first published in *Modern Language Studies* 8 (1977–78): 5–22, reprinted in *The Woman's Part,* ed. Carolyn Ruth Swift Lenz, Gayle Greene, and Carol Thomas Neely (Urbana: University of Illinois Press, 1980), 171–93.

4. The 1609 text is quoted from *Shakespeare's Sonnets,* ed. Stephen Booth (New Haven: Yale University Press, 1978), Sonnet 9, lines 9–12.

5. Joel Fineman's account in *Shakespeare's Perjured Eye* (Berkeley and Los Angeles: University of California Press, 1986) compulsively reproduces this distinction, even claiming for Shakespeare nothing less than the invention of "the poetics of heterosexuality" (18), yet as he moves to take up the issue of cross-coupling, and with it the phenomena of the pricked prick and the cut cunt (see, e.g., 275ff.), as he terms them, the difference between hetero- and homosexuality is breached. Nonetheless, the mode of breaching is by the route of castration and thus operates under the aegis of the Oedipal and thereby within the heterosexualizing argument that allows for difference only under that rubric.

6. Work on the historicity of gender that lends support to these suppositions include Stephen Greenblatt's "Fiction and Friction," in his *Shakesperean Negotiations: The Circulation of Social Energy in Renaissance England* (Oxford: Clarendon Press, 1988), esp. 73–86; Thomas Laqueur's *Making Sex* (Cambridge, Mass.: Harvard University Press, 1990); and Ann Rosalind Jones and Peter Stallybrass's "Fetishizing Gender: Constructing the Hermaphrodite in Renaissance Europe," in *Body Guards,* ed. Julia Epstein and Kristina Straub (New York: Routledge, 1991).

7. See Janet Adelman, "Male Bonding in Shakespeare's Comedies," in *Shakespeare's Rough Magic,* ed. Peter Erickson and Coppélia Kahn (Newark: University of Delaware Press, 1985); 80–81 are on *Romeo and Juliet.*

8. G. Blakemore Evans also cites Williams at this point in his New Cambridge edition, but he then misunderstands the implications of the Nurse's speech: "Obviously she can't read or spell, and because of its rude associations she decides that 'Romeo' and 'rosemary' must begin with some other letter" (115). The Nurse, however, registers that she stops herself from saying a word that sounds like it begins with an "R" but does not; Evans's swipe at the Nurse's illiteracy displaces, one suspects, his discomfort at the associations implicated in the Nurse's assonance.

9. I am grateful to Natasha Korda not only for pointing this out to me but also for a set of notes she prepared on the crux in Mercutio's lines that have helped me think through the points argued here.

10. For a glance at this "retention" (anal?) and its supposed restoration of an original unavailable in any text that might claim to be close to a Shakespearean original, see Random Cloud, "The Marriage of Good and Bad Quartos," *Shakespeare Quarterly* 33 (1982): 430–31. For a defense of the properness of this scandalous reading by the modern editor who first printed it in his 1954 Yale edition of the play, see Richard Hosley, "The Corrupting Influence of the Bad Quarto on the Received Text of *Romeo and Juliet*," *Shakespeare Quarterly* 4 (1953): 21. Hosley would rather have "open-arse" than allow his text to be "contaminated" by the "bad quarto," Q1, which reads "open *Et caetera*" (D1r) at this spot.

11. For pursuit of the crux about the name of the rose, up to the point engaged in this essay, I refer the reader to my "'What? in a names that which we call a Rose': The Desired Texts of *Romeo and Juliet*," written for and delivered at the 1988 session of an annual conference at the University of Toronto on editorial and textual matters, reprinted in the volume of papers from that meeting, *Crisis in Editing: Texts of the English Renaissance*, ed. Randall McLeod (New York: AMS Press, 1994), and reprinted in this volume. In that essay I call into question the usual supposition that of the two quarto editions of the play, Q1 (1597) is simply a "bad quarto" (shaped by the memories of actors and the imposition of nonauthorial materials), while Q2 (1599) is authoritative and derived from Shakespeare's hand; rather, I suggest, both texts arise from a theatrical milieu of continual revision and rewriting, and no modern text of the play can fail to consult both or can easily adjudicate differences between the two texts—differences that often include Q2's offering of more than one version of the same set of lines—in the hope of arriving at final or original authorial intention. I argue that intentionality was never so limited.

The crux involved in 2.1.38 will be unraveled in the discussion that follows; in Q1 the line alludes to an "open *Et caetera*" (D1r), which, were one to take that script as depending solely on stage performance, would mean that this reports the line as spoken (i.e., as speaking and possibly evading speaking more forthrightly), though it is also possible to regard the *"Et caetera"* either as a way of naming otherwise what need not be named any more forthrightly or as an evasion of more direct naming supplied by the printer and not following what the actor actually said.

At this point, Q2 reads "open, or," (D1v), and, it is assumed, as I discuss below, that "or" represents a misreading by the compositor of Shakespeare's hand ("ers" is assumed to have been in the manuscript); the notion that "arse" was once really in the text or spoken on stage is not quite so easily made, however, since the comma in Q2 might indicate that a pause, and not a word, was offered at this spot. Again, one faces the dilemma of whether an unsaying said more than the more forthright reading offered by Gibbons; whether the lines in each earlier text have been censored, and if so, by whom; what, if anything, was actually spoken by the actor at this point, or indeed, whether there was one way in which this line ever was delivered; or, finally, whether this massive textual problem does not also correspond to the very nexus of the utterly unspeakable/absolutely commonplace nature of anal sex, in this instance dictated by all the proprieties surrounded by the supposed unbreachable difference between the allowable spheres of male-male intimacy and the excoriated one called sodomy, or between the supposition that the only "good" sex performed by male-female couples is procreative and conducted under the auspices of marriage, everything else being capable of being called, once again, sodomy.

12. I follow Joseph A. Porter here, who argues in *Shakespeare's Mercutio* (Chapel Hill: University of North Carolina Press, 1988) that the lines "involve the idea of Mercutio's taking Rosaline's place not only as conjurer but also as container of Romeo's phallus," though I do not follow him in wishing to make this the "fleeting apparently subliminal trace of sexual desire on Mercutio's part" (157), since that assumption implies that homoerotic desire must operate within the regimes of a closet that, I think, might more appropriately be seen as part of the modern apparatus of sexuality, with its markers of homo- and heterosexuality. Since these desires are not distinguished and their boundaries are more fluid in Shakespeare's time, there is no need to make them unavailable, which locating homoeroticism as subliminal does. On pages 160–62, Porter ably dismantles the heterosexualizing readings of this moment, in which even an open-arse is read as a figure for female genitalia, the most extraordinary of such instances perhaps being that of Eric Partridge, *Shakespeare's Bawdy* (1947; reprint, London: Routledge, 1990): "'An open *et-caetera*' must here mean 'an open arse'. Yet my interpretation of Shakespeare's 'open *et-caetera*' as 'pudend' is correct, for the opening clearly refers to the female cleft, not the human anus. With the human bottom regarded as involving and connoting the primary sexual area, compare the slangy use of *tail* for the human bottom in general and for the female pudend in particular" (101–2). While Porter valuably insists that Mercutio's lines are about sodomy, his concession that "of course the sodomy is heterosexual" (161) could be seen as complicit with the heterosexualizing of Partridge and other commentators on the line precisely because it differentiates homo- and heterosexual sodomy. The acts are not so distinguishable; moreover,

the conceptual range of the term "sodomy" in the period does not heed the hetero-homo distinction, as Alan Bray makes clear as a starting point in his discussion in *Homosexuality in Renaissance England* (London: Gay Men's Press, 1982), 14. My arguments above about a transgressive sodomy, and its link to cross-gender relations, seek to void this diacritical marker, and the move seems to me important both because it takes account of the history of sexuality and also because it opposes the ways in which the distinction of homo- and heterosexual sodomy was mobilized in the U.S. Supreme Court decision in *Bowers v. Hardwick,* which denied any fundamental constitutional right for acts of so-called homosexual sodomy while guaranteeing the legality of the act for heterosexuals.

13. See Joseph A. Porter, "Mercutio's Brother," *South Atlantic Review* 49 (1984): 31–41, and the fuller development of the argument in his *Shakespeare's Mercutio,* 1–10, 145–63.

Under the Covers with Caliban

1. See Eve Kosofsky Sedgwick, *Epistemology of the Closet* (Berkeley and Los Angeles: University of California Press, 1990), chap. 1, 75–76.

2. Alden T. Vaughan and Virginia Mason Vaughan, *Shakespeare's Caliban: A Cultural History* (Cambridge: Cambridge University Press, 1991), 10, quoting Folio page 2. Rowe's edition of Shakespeare appeared in 1709.

3. Yet as Peter Hulme points out in *Colonial Encounters* (London: Routledge, 1986), the lines admit Caliban's humanity by way of "an eminently misreadable double negative" (114); as Hulme notes, in addition to Caliban's bestial/demonic/human forms in various descriptions of him, he figures as "a man and not a man according to Miranda's calculations" (107).

4. Matthew W. Black and Matthias A. Shaaber, *Shakespeare's Seventeenth-Century Editors, 1632–1685* (New York: Modern Language Association, 1937), 95.

5. Frank Kermode, ed., *The Tempest,* New Arden edition (London: Methuen, 1954); I cite the lemma to 1.2.282. The original Arden edition, ed. Morton Luce (London: Methuen, 1901), fails to record the "he/she" emendation.

6. Here are the texts in question:

> Then was this island
> (Save for the Sunne that he did littour heere,
> A frekelld whelpe, hag-borne) not honour'd with
> A humane shape.
>
> (F2, 1632)

> Then was this Island
> (Save for the Sun that he did littour here.

A frekelld whelp, hag-born) not honour'd with
A humane shape.

(F3, 1664)

Then was this Island
(Save for the Sun that he did littour here.
A frekel'd whelp, hag-born) not honour'd with
A human shape.

(F4, 1685)

7. See Stephen Orgel, introduction to *The Tempest,* ed. Orgel (Oxford: Clarendon Press, 1987), 18–19; as well as his essay "Prospero's Wife," in *Rewriting the Renaissance,* ed. Margaret Ferguson, Maureen Quilligan, and Nancy Vickers (Chicago: University of Chicago Press, 1985), 54.

8. James I, *Basilikon Doron* (1616), as discussed in Jonathan Goldberg, *James I and the Politics of Literature* (Baltimore: The Johns Hopkins University Press, 1983), 141–43.

9. For a pertinent critique, within the context of historical/critical accounts of witchcraft in the Renaissance, of a dehistoricizing reduction of questions of femininity to questions of the mother in psychoanalytically inflected feminist criticism, see Karen Newman, *Fashioning Femininity and English Renaissance Drama* (Chicago: University of Chicago Press, 1991), chap. 4.

10. It is just such a fantasy of male genius that governs Peter Greenaway's *Prospero's Books* (1991), in which John Gielgud (as Prospero) recites everyone's lines.

11. For an argument congruent with this one, see Ann Rosalind Jones and Peter Stallybrass, "Fetishizing Gender: Constructing the Hermaphrodite in Renaissance Europe," in *Body Guards,* ed. Julia Epstein and Kristina Straub (New York: Routledge, 1991), which concludes that fixing gender on genitals is an eighteenth-century development and that, in the Renaissance, gender could be located elsewhere. Their final examples include other body parts, such as the mouth (which will be important for the argument that follows below), or clothing as sites of gender identification.

12. See Thomas Laqueur, *Making Sex* (Cambridge, Mass.: Harvard University Press, 1990); and the use of Laqueur's model in Stephen Greenblatt, *Shakespearean Negotiations: The Circulation of Social Energy in Renaissance England* (Berkeley and Los Angeles: University of California Press, 1988), chap. 3; and in Stephen Orgel, "Nobody's Perfect; or, Why Did the English Stage Take Boys for Women?" *South Atlantic Quarterly* 88 (1989): 7–29.

13. *The Tempest,* ed. J. Dover Wilson and Arthur Quiller-Couch (Cambridge: Cambridge University Press, 1921).

14. Arthur Evans, *Witchcraft and the Gay Counterculture* (Boston: Fag Rag Books, 1978).

15. Evans depends here on Henry Charles Lea, *Materials toward a History of Witchcraft,* ed. A. C. Howland, 3 vols. (Philadelphia: University of Pennsylvania Press, 1939), vol. 2, 485: "[V]os viri cum succubis and *[sic]* vos mulieres cum incubis fornicati estis, Sodomiam veram et nefandissium crimen misere cum illis tactu frigidissimo exercuistis."

16. Jeffrey Richards, *Sex, Dissidence, and Damnation* (London: Routledge, 1991), 143.

17. E. William Monter, *Witchcraft in France and Switzerland: The Borderlands during the Reformation* (Ithaca, N.Y.: Cornell University Press, 1976), 136, 198. A similar view of the relationship between sodomy and witchcraft accusations is offered by Guido Ruggiero, *The Boundaries of Eros: Sex Crime and Sexuality in Renaissance Venice* (New York: Oxford University Press, 1985), 140, who regards the two crimes as parallel instances of the policing of "the normal and the abnormal"; in a note, he further speculates on the relationship and distribution of these accusations (196 n. 135).

18. Cited in E. William Monter, *Frontiers of Heresy: The Spanish Inquisition from the Basque Lands to Sicily* (Cambridge: Cambridge University Press, 1990), 280. Monter details executions for sodomy and for witchcraft in separate chapters of this study but does not draw connections between them.

19. Paul Brown, "'This Thing of Darkness I Acknowledge Mine': *The Tempest* and the Discourse of Colonialism," in *Political Shakespeare,* ed. Jonathan Dollimore and Alan Sinfield (Ithaca, N.Y.: Cornell University Press, 1985); G. R. Quaife, *Godly Zeal and Furious Rage: The Witch in Early Modern Europe* (London: Croom Helm, 1987), 99. Quaife continues by referring to one claim that the devil had a three-pronged penis, thus "permitting him to engage in coitus, sodomy and fellatio simultaneously." In his reviews of previous scholarship, he notes those who have thought of witchcraft prosecutions as policing nonheterosexual relations, whether among women or among men. For further documentation of witchcraft involving anal sex with the devil, see Jeffrey Russell, *Witchcraft in the Middle Ages* (Ithaca, N.Y.: Cornell University Press, 1960), 391. John Boswell, *Christianity, Social Tolerance, and Homosexuality* (Chicago: University of Chicago Press, 1980), 235, has a passing consideration of the witchcraft/sodomy/heresy nexus.

20. Retha M. Warnicke, *The Rise and Fall of Anne Boleyn* (Cambridge: Cambridge University Press, 1989), 194.

21. Alan Bray, *Homosexuality in Renaissance England* (London: Gay Mens Press, 1982), 21; Bray turns to Drayton on the following page.

22. Michael Drayton, "The Moone-Calfe," in *The Works of Michael Drayton,* ed. J. William Hebel, 5 vols. (Oxford: Basil Blackwell, 1932), vol. 3, lines 178, 190.

23. Heinrich Kramer and James Sprenger, *Malleus Maleficarum,* trans. Montague Summers (1928; reprint, New York: Dover, 1971), 30.

24. Thomas Weld, a minister, cited by Carol F. Karlsen, *The Devil in the Shape of a Woman* (New York: Vintage Books, 1989), 17–18. As Karlsen comments, going on to cite Weld further to this point, the monstrous births were seen as the analogues to the monstrous beliefs of Hutchison and her followers. Such accusations against witches are a particular instance of the phenomenon that Marie-Helene Huet studies in *Monstrous Imagination* (Cambridge, Mass.: Harvard University Press, 1993), in which the monstrous imagination of the mother is said to be responsible for deformed offspring. This phenomenon is also discussed in Audrey Eccles, *Obstetrics and Gynaecology in Tudor and Stuart England* (Kent, Ohio: Kent State University Press, 1982), who also notes that sodomy and bestiality were among the supposed causes of deformed offspring (65).

25. David Sundelson does so in "So Rare a Wonder'd Father: Prospero's *Tempest*," in *Representing Shakespeare*, ed. Murray M. Schwartz and Coppélia Kahn (Baltimore: The Johns Hopkins University Press, 1980), although the lines are adduced in the context of Prospero's "impotence" in Milan (35); Sundelson does note that once on the island, Prospero assumes paternal and maternal powers.

26. Sundelson, "So Rare a Wonder'd Father," 41. As Sundelson continues to explicate this scene, he reads the greedy mouth as making a female demand, and the scene of venting as a parody of childbirth and an expression of female loathing; while the latter point is not to be denied, I do not think one can simply collapse this scene onto a female body.

27. On the former point, see Hulme, *Colonial Encounters;* for the latter, see Jonathan Goldberg, *Sodometries* (Stanford: Stanford University Press, 1992), part 3.

28. *The Tempest,* ed. George Steevens (London: 1778).

29. See Jeanne Addison Roberts, "'Wife' or 'Wise': *The Tempest* 1.1786," *Studies in Bibliography* 31 (1978): 203–8.

30. Frye notes at 4.1.123 that "some copies of F read 'wife'"; *The Tempest,* The Penguin edition, ed. Northrop Frye (Baltimore: Penguin Books, 1959).

31. Howard Horace Furness, ed., *The Tempest,* a new variorum edition (Philadelphia, 1892).

32. Andrew Marvell, "The Garden," lines 63–64, in *The Poems and Letters of Andrew Marvell,* ed. H. M. Margoliouth, 2 vols. (Oxford: Clarendon Press, 1952), vol. 1, 49.

33. Stanley Wells and Gary Taylor, with John Jowett and William Montgomery, *William Shakespeare: A Textual Companion* (Oxford: Clarendon Press, 1987), 616.

34. One could compare here the note in Luce's 1901 Arden edition, which, as ambivalent as Kermode's, prints "wise" and yet seems in the note to prefer "wife"; one of the arguments in the note is that "the rhyme of Paradise with wise is a blemish, and it could hardly have been intentional."

Permissions

Most of the chapters in this book were published previously, in different versions, in the following articles and chapters. I am grateful to the original publishers for permission to reprint.

"Textual Properties" originally appeared in *Shakespeare Quarterly* 37, no. 2 (1986): 213–17.

"Shakespearean Characters: The Generation of Silvia" originally appeared in Jonathan Goldberg, *Voice Terminal Echo* (London: Methuen, 1986), 68–100, 175–79.

"Making Sense" originally appeared in *New Literary History* 21 (1990): 457–62.

"Shakespearean Inscriptions: The Voicing of Power" originally appeared in *Shakespeare and the Question of Theory*, ed. Patricia Parker and Geoffrey Hartman (London: Methuen, 1985), 116–37.

"Calling Out the Law" will appear in *Solon and Thespis: Law and Theater in the English Renaissance,* ed. Dennis Kezar (forthcoming).

"Hamlet's Hand" originally appeared in *Shakespeare Quarterly* 39, no. 3 (1988): 307–27.

"Perspectives: Dover Cliff and the Conditions of Representation" originally appeared in *Shakespeare and Deconstruction,* ed. David M. Bergeron and G. Douglas Atkins (New York: Peter Lang, 1988), 245–65.

"Shakespeare Writing Matter Again: Objects and Their Detachments" originally appeared in *Shakespeare Studies* 28 (2000): 240–43.

"Speculations: *Macbeth* and Source" originally appeared in *Shakespeare Reproduced,* ed. Jean E. Howard and Marion F. O'Connor (London: Methuen, 1987), 242–64.

"The Anus in *Coriolanus*" originally appeared in *Psychoanalysis, Historicism, and Early Modern Culture,* ed. Carla Mazzio and Doug Trevor (New York: Routledge, 2000), 260–71.

"Rebel Letters: Postal Effects from *Richard II* to *Henry IV*" originally appeared in *Renaissance Drama,* new series, 19 (1989): 3–28.

"The Commodity of Names: 'Falstaff' and 'Oldcastle' in *1 Henry IV*" originally appeared in *Reconfiguring the Renaissance,* ed. Jonathan Crewe, special issue of *Bucknell Review* 35 (1992): 76–88.

"Hal's Desire, Shakespeare's Idaho" originally appeared in *Henry IV,* ed. Nigel Wood (London: Open University, 1995), 37–64.

"'What? in a names that which we call a Rose': The Desired Texts of *Romeo and Juliet*" originally appeared in *Crisis in Editing: Texts of the English Renaissance,* ed. Randall McLeod (New York: AMS Press, 1994), 173–202.

"*Romeo and Juliet*'s Open Rs" originally appeared in *Queering the Renaissance,* ed. Jonathan Goldberg (Durham, N.C.: Duke University Press, 1994), 218–35.

"Under the Covers with Caliban" originally appeared in *The Margins of the Text,* ed. D. C. Greetham (Ann Arbor: University of Michigan Press, 1997), 105–28.

Index

Jonathan Goldberg is Sir William Osler Professor of English Literature at The Johns Hopkins University, where he has taught for the past fifteen years; he has also taught at Temple, Brown, and Duke universities. He is the author of six previous books in the field of Renaissance studies, including *James I and the Politics of Literature, Sodometries,* and *Desiring Women Writing,* as well as a recent book on Willa Cather. He is the editor of *Reclaiming Sodom* and *Queering the Renaissance.*